THOMAS MANN

Henry Adams
Edward Albee
A. R. Ammons
Matthew Arnold
John Ashbery
W. H. Auden
Jane Austen
James Baldwin
Charles Baudelaire
Samuel Beckett
Saul Bellow
The Bible
Elizabeth Bishop
William Blake
Jorge Luis Borges
Elizabeth Bowen
Bertolt Brecht
The Brontës
Robert Browning
Anthony Burgess
George Gordon, Lord
  Byron
Thomas Carlyle
Lewis Carroll
Willa Cather
Cervantes
Geoffrey Chaucer
Kate Chopin
Samuel Taylor Coleridge
Joseph Conrad
Contemporary Poets
Hart Crane
Stephen Crane
Dante
Charles Dickens
Emily Dickinson
John Donne & the Seven-
  teenth-Century Meta-
  physical Poets
Elizabethan Dramatists
Theodore Dreiser
John Dryden
George Eliot
T. S. Eliot
Ralph Ellison
Ralph Waldo Emerson
William Faulkner
Henry Fielding
F. Scott Fitzgerald
Gustave Flaubert
E. M. Forster
Sigmund Freud
Robert Frost

Robert Graves
Graham Greene
Thomas Hardy
Nathaniel Hawthorne
William Hazlitt
Seamus Heaney
Ernest Hemingway
Geoffrey Hill
Friedrich Hölderlin
Homer
Gerard Manley Hopkins
William Dean Howells
Zora Neale Hurston
Henry James
Samuel Johnson and
  James Boswell
Ben Jonson
James Joyce
Franz Kafka
John Keats
Rudyard Kipling
D. H. Lawrence
John Le Carré
Ursula K. Le Guin
Doris Lessing
Sinclair Lewis
Robert Lowell
Norman Mailer
Bernard Malamud
Thomas Mann
Christopher Marlowe
Carson McCullers
Herman Melville
James Merrill
Arthur Miller
John Milton
Eugenio Montale
Marianne Moore
Iris Murdoch
Vladimir Nabokov
Joyce Carol Oates
Sean O'Casey
Flannery O'Connor
Eugene O'Neill
George Orwell
Cynthia Ozick
Walter Pater
Walker Percy
Harold Pinter
Plato
Edgar Allan Poe
Poets of Sensibility & the
  Sublime

Alexander Pope
Katherine Ann Porter
Ezra Pound
Pre-Raphaelite Poets
Marcel Proust
Thomas Pynchon
Arthur Rimbaud
Theodore Roethke
Philip Roth
John Ruskin
J. D. Salinger
Gershom Scholem
William Shakespeare
  (3 vols.)
  Histories & Poems
  Comedies
  Tragedies
George Bernard Shaw
Mary Wollstonecraft
  Shelley
Percy Bysshe Shelley
Edmund Spenser
Gertrude Stein
John Steinbeck
Laurence Sterne
Wallace Stevens
Tom Stoppard
Jonathan Swift
Alfred, Lord Tennyson
William Makepeace
  Thackeray
Henry David Thoreau
Leo Tolstoi
Anthony Trollope
Mark Twain
John Updike
Gore Vidal
Virgil
Robert Penn Warren
Evelyn Waugh
Eudora Welty
Nathanael West
Edith Wharton
Walt Whitman
Oscar Wilde
Tennessee Williams
William Carlos Williams
Thomas Wolfe
Virginia Woolf
William Wordsworth
Richard Wright
William Butler Yeats

These and other titles in preparation

Modern Critical Views

THOMAS MANN

Edited and with an introduction by
Harold Bloom
Sterling Professor of the Humanities
Yale University

CHELSEA HOUSE PUBLISHERS ◊ 1986
New York ◊ New Haven ◊ Philadelphia

© 1986 by Chelsea House Publishers, a division of Chelsea
House Educational Communications, Inc.
  133 Christopher Street, New York, NY 10014
  345 Whitney Avenue, New Haven, CT 06511
  5014 West Chester Pike, Edgemont, PA 19028

Introduction © 1986 by Harold Bloom

Printed and bound in the United States of America

∞ The paper used in this publication meets the minimum
requirements of the American National Standard for Permanence
of Paper for Printed Library Materials, Z39.48–1984.

Library of Congress Cataloging-in-Publication Data
Thomas Mann.
  (Modern critical views)
  Bibliography: p.
  Includes index.
  1. Mann, Thomas, 1875–1955—Criticism and
interpretation. I. Bloom, Harold. II. Series.
PT2625.A44Z8916 1986   833'.912   86–6806
ISBN 0–87754–725–4 (alk. paper)

Contents

Editor's Note

This volume gathers together a very full representation of the most useful literary criticism devoted to the enormous range of Thomas Mann's fiction. The essays, which span more than half a century, are arranged here in the order of their original publication. I am grateful to Marijke Rijsberman for her erudition and judgment in helping to locate and choose them.

The book begins with the editor's introduction, which centers upon Mann's novel *The Beloved Returns* (*Lotte in Weimar*) and its relation to Mann's essays on Goethe and Freud, so as to sketch something of the problematical aspects of the novelist's ambivalence towards the greatest German writer, his prime precursor. Since all of Mann's fiction is a kind of symbolic autobiography, the chronological sequence starts appropriately with Hermann J. Weigand's reading of Mann's first novel, *Royal Highness*, with its shrewd suggestion that the book is an early reflection of the lifelong agon between Thomas and Heinrich Mann, his older brother and fellow novelist.

Vernon Venable's account of structural elements in *Death in Venice* brings a modified Marxist perspective to the analysis of Mann's most famous short novel. His most celebrated longer fiction, *The Magic Mountain*, is the subject of Erich Heller's ironic dialogue, which mirrors the abyss of endless ironies in the book itself. A very different mode, the high decadence of the Aesthetic movement, is invoked in George C. Schoolfield's adroit exegesis of *The Black Swan*, with its dark sense of the quintessentially German quality of the novel. The same sense is necessarily present in Gunilla Bergsten's study of *Doctor Faustus* as an authentically historical depiction of the Nazi era. An emphasis upon timeless myth is the very different center of Isadore Traschen's investigation of *Death in Venice*, which provides also a useful contrast to Venable's more socially oriented analysis of the same work. Still another contrast with the historical exegesis of *Doctor Faustus* comes in Eva Schaper's study of irony in that formidable novel. These contrasts, and others, are subsumed in the remarkable essay by Peter Heller, which finds in

Mann's marginal and deliberately limited ambivalences a kind of dialectic that almost governs the alternation between ironic skepticism (verging upon nihilism) and mythic quasi-belief throughout *The Magic Mountain, Joseph and His Brothers,* and other works.

A more specific, indeed quite personal level of commentary pervades Erich Kahler's remarks upon *The Holy Sinner* and *Felix Krull* as rambunctious performances in which Mann relaxed after his strenuous labors upon *Doctor Faustus.* Much more sober, as befits its craftsmanlike subject, is the solid analysis of the early *Buddenbrooks* by Larry David Nachman and Albert S. Braverman. Their emphasis upon Mann's control of the alternation between societal conformity and the aesthetic inner life is a familiar one in studies of Mann, but its relevance to *Buddenbrooks* is substantial and clear.

Another fine contrast enters with Oskar Seidlin's agile exegesis of Mann's weird number symbolism in his representation of the Dionysian vitalist, Mynheer Peeperkorn, in *The Magic Mountain.* This instance of virtuosity is a prelude to Hilary Heltay's subject in her essay on the subtler virtuosities of Mann's later narrative technique, with particular reference to the Joseph novels. A particular virtuoso technique, that of the parodistic narrator in *Doctor Faustus,* is the concern of William M. Honsa, Jr., in his contribution, a concern reflected also in Benjamin Bennett's view of the parodistic structure of myth in *Tonio Kröger.*

Myth, an obsessive technique in Mann, is again the center in Elaine Murdaugh's reading of *Joseph and His Brothers,* where the development of consciousness and an emergent theology are seen as Mann's ways of returning to the aesthetic strength of the archaic. The famous if rather overvalued novella, *Mario and the Magician,* is analyzed by Allan J. McIntyre as another example of ironized myth in Mann, overdetermined but partly redeemed by aesthetic artifice. Michael Mann, the novelist's youngest son, in a moving lecture on his father's work, turns aside critics of Mann's ironic stance by coming to rest upon the readiness to accept fate, or one's own character, as Mann's truest legacy. Character, and its inevitable relationship to destiny, is again the subject in Daniel Albright's overview of the earlier work and in Lawrence L. Langer's meditation upon the *topos* of death in *The Magic Mountain.*

The two most recent essays in this volume are distinguished examples of Mann criticism at its most sophisticated and mature. Norman Rabkin skillfully employs the context of Shakespeare's late romances to illuminate Mann's late romance, *The Holy Sinner.* In a fitting conclusion to this book, Martin Price renders an exegesis of *Felix Krull* worthy both of that delightful fiction and of the comic muse whom Price brilliantly invokes.

Introduction

I

The greatest of modern German literary scholars, Ernst Robert Curtius, observed that European literature was a continuous tradition from Homer through Goethe, and became something else afterwards. Thomas Mann is part of that something else, which begins with Wordsworth and has not yet ended. Mann, too ironic to study the nostalgias, nevertheless was highly conscious of his lifelong agon with his true precursor, Goethe. It was a loving agon, though necessarily not lacking in dialectical and indeed ambivalent elements. From his essay on "Goethe and Tolstoy" (1922) through his remarkable triad of Goethe essays in the 1930s (on the man of letters, the "representative of the Bourgeois Age," and *Faust*) on to the "Fantasy on Goethe" of the 1950s, Mann never wearied of reimagining his great original. The finest of these reimaginings, the novel, *Lotte in Weimar*, was published in Stockholm in 1939. We know it in English as *The Beloved Returns*, and it is surely the most neglected of Mann's major fictions. Mann is renowned as the author of *The Magic Mountain*, the tetralogy *Joseph and His Brothers*, *Doctor Faustus*, *Death in Venice*, and *Felix Krull*, while even the early *Buddenbrooks* remains widely read. But *Lotte in Weimar*, after some initial success, seems to have become a story for specialists, at least in English-speaking countries. Perhaps this is because Goethe, who exported splendidly to Britain and America in the time of Carlyle and Emerson, now seems an untranslatable author. Or it may be that Goethe's spirit has not survived what happened in and through Germany from 1933 until 1945.

In his essay on *Faust*, Mann remarks that the poem depicts love as a devil's holiday. The meditation upon Goethe's career as a man of letters centers itself in a remarkable paragraph that is as much on Mann as on Goethe:

But this business of reproducing the outer world through the inner, which it re-creates after its own form and in its own way, never does, however much charm and fascination may emanate from it, quite satisfy or please the outer world. The reason is that the author's real attitude always has something of opposition in it, which is quite inseparable from his character. It is the attitude of the man of intellect towards the ponderous, stubborn, evil-minded human race, which always places the poet and writer in this particular position, moulding his character and temperament and so conditioning his destiny. "Viewed from the heights of reason," Goethe wrote, "all life looks like some malignant disease and the world like a madhouse." This is a characteristic utterance of the kind of man who writes: the expression of his smarting impatience with mankind. More of the same thing than one would suppose is to be found in Goethe's works: phrases about the "human pack" in general and his "dear Germans" in particular, typical of the specific irritability and aloofness I mean. For what are the factors that condition the life of the writer? They are twofold: perception and a feeling for form; both of these simultaneously. The strange thing is that for the poet they are one organic unity, in which the one implies, challenges, and draws out the other. This unity is, for him, mind, beauty, freedom—everything. Where it is not, there is vulgar human stupidity, expressing itself in lack of perception and imperviousness to beauty of form—nor can he tell you which of the two he finds the more irritating.

We would hardly know that this aesthetic stance is that of Goethe rather than Flaubert, of Mann rather than T. S. Eliot. It seems Mann's shrewd warning to us is that the true man or woman of letters always exists in opposition to the formlessness of daily life, even when the writer is as socially amiable and spiritually healthy as Goethe and his disciple, Thomas Mann. That spiritual health is the subject of the grand essay by Mann on "Goethe as Representative of the Bourgeois Age," which nevertheless makes clear how heroically Goethe (and Mann) had to struggle in order to achieve and maintain such health:

As for Goethe, I may make an observation here having to do with certain human and personal effects and symptoms of the anti-ideal constitution; an observation which, indeed, leads me so far into intimate and individual psychology that only indications are possible. There can be no doubt that ideal faith, although it must be prepared for martyrdom, makes one happier in spirit than belief in a lofty and completely ironic sense of poetic achievement without values and opinions, entirely objective, mirroring everything with the same love and the same indifference. There are in Goethe, on closer examination, as soon as the innocence of the youthful period is past, signs of profound maladjustment and ill humour, a hampering depression, which must certainly have a deep-lying uncanny connection with his mistrust of ideas, his child-of-nature dilettantism. There is a peculiar coldness, ill will, *médisance,* a devil-may-care mood, an inhuman, elfish irresponsibility—which one cannot indulge enough, but must love along with him if one loves him. If one peers into this region of his character one understands that happiness and harmony are much more the affair of the children of spirit than of the children of nature. Clarity, harmony within oneself, strength of purpose, a positive believing and decided aim—in short, peace in the soul— all this is much more easily achieved by these than by the children of nature. Nature does not confer peace of mind, simplicity, single-mindedness; she is a questionable element, she is a contradiction, denial, thorough-going doubt. She endows with no benevolence, not being benevolent herself. She permits no decided judgments, for she is neutral. She endows her children with indifference; with a complex of problems, which have more to do with torment and ill will than with joy and mirth.

Goethe, Mann, and nature are everywhere the same; their happiness and harmony are aesthetic constructs, and never part of the given. Contradictory, skeptical, and full of the spirit that denies, Goethe and Mann triumph by transferring "liberal economic principles to the intellectual life"; they practice what Goethe called a "free trade of conceptions and feelings." The late "Fantasy on Goethe" has a delicious paragraph on the matter of Goethe's free trade in feelings:

Goethe's love life is a strange chapter. The list of his love affairs has become a requirement of education; in respectable German society one has to be able to rattle off the ladies like the loves of Zeus. Those Friederikes, Lottes, Minnas, and Mariannes have become statues installed in niches in the cathedral of humanity; and perhaps this makes amends to them for their disappointments. For the fickle genius who for short whiles lay at their feet was never prepared to take the consequences, to bear the restriction upon his life and liberty that these charming adventures might have involved. Perhaps the fame of the ladies is compensation to them for his recurrent flights, for the aimlessness of his wooing, the faithlessness of his sincerity, and the fact that his loving was a means to an end, a means to further his work. Where work and life are one, as was the case with him, those who know only how to take life seriously are left with all the sorrows in their laps. But he always reproved them for taking life seriously. "Werther must—must be?" he wrote to Lotte Buff and her fiancé."You two do not feel *him*, you feel only *me* and *yourselves*. . . . If only you could feel the thousandth part of what Werther means to a thousand hearts, you would not reckon the cost to you." All his women bore the cost, whether they liked it or not.

It is to this aspect of Goethe as "fickle genius" that Mann returned in *The Beloved Returns,* which can serve here as representative both of the strength and limitation of Mann's art of irony.

II

After forty-four years, the model for the heroine of Goethe's notorious *The Sorrows of Young Werther* goes to Weimar on pilgrimage, not to be reunited with her lover, now sixty-seven to her sixty-one, but rather in the hopeless quest to be made one both with their mutual past, and with his immortal idea of what she once had been, or could have been. For four hundred pages, Mann plays out the all but endless ironies of poor Lotte's fame, as the widowed and respectable lady, who has her limitations but is nobody's fool, both enjoys and endures her status and function as a living mythology. Mann's supreme irony, grotesque in its excruciating banalities, is the account of the dinner that the stiff, old Goethe gives in honor of the object of his passion, some forty-four years after the event. Poor Lotte, after being treated as a kind of amalgam of cultural relic and youthful indiscretion shrived by temporal decay, is dismissed by the great man with a palpably insincere: "Life has held us sundered far too long a time for me not to ask of it that we may meet often during your sojourn."

But Mann was too cunning to conclude his book there. A marvelous final meeting is arranged by Goethe himself, who hears Lotte's gentle question, "So meeting again is a short chapter, a fragment?" and replies in the same high aesthetic mode:

"Dear soul, let me answer you from my heart, in expiation and farewell. You speak of sacrifice. But it is a mystery, indivisible, like all else in the world and one's person, one's life, and one's work. Conversion, transformation, is all. They sacrificed to the god, and in the end the sacrifice was God. You used a figure dear and familiar to me; long since, it took possession of my soul. I mean the parable of the moth and the fatal, luring flame. Say, if you will, that I am the flame, and into me the poor moth flings itself. Yet in the chance and change of things I am the candle too, giving my body that the light may burn. And finally, I am the drunken butterfly that falls to the flame—figure of the eternal sacrifice, body transmuted into soul, and life to spirit. Dear soul, dear child, dear childlike old soul, I, first and last, am the sacrifice, and he that offers it. Once I burned you, ever I burn you, into spirit and light. Know that metamorphosis is the dearest and most inward of thy friend, his great hope, his deepest craving: the play of transformation, changing face, greybeard to youth, to youth the boy, yet ever the human countenance with traits of its proper stage, youth like a miracle shining out in age, age out of youth. Thus mayst thou rest content, beloved, as I am, with having thought it out and come to me, decking thine ancient form with signs of youth. Unity in change and flux, conversion constant out of and into oneself, transmutation of all things, life showing now its natural, now its cultural face, past turning to present, present pointing back to past, both preluding future and with her dim foreshadowings already full. Past feeling, future feeling—feeling is all. Let us open wide eyes upon the unity of the world—eyes wide, serene, and wise. Wouldst thou ask of me repentance? Only wait. I see her ride towards me, in a mantle grey. Then once more the hour of Werther and Tasso will strike, as at midnight already midday strikes, and God give me to say what I suffer—only this first and last will then remain to me. Then forsaking will be only leave-taking, leave-taking for ever, death-struggle of feeling and the hour full of frightful pangs, pangs such as probably for some time precede the hour of death, pangs which are dying if not yet death. Death, final flight into the flame—the All-in-one—why should it too be aught but transformation? In my quiet heart, dear visions, may you rest—and what a pleasant moment that will be, when we anon awake together!"

In some complex sense, part of the irony here is Mann's revenge upon his precursor, since it is Mann who burns Goethe into spirit and light, into the metamorphosis of hope and craving that is *The Beloved Returns*. Mann and Goethe die each other's life, live each other's death, in the pre-Socratic formulation that so obsessed W. B. Yeats. But for Mann, unlike the occult Yeats, the movement through death into transformation is a complex metaphor for the influence relationship between Goethe and his twentieth-century descendant. What Mann, in his "Fantasy on Goethe," delineated in his precursor is charmingly accurate when applied to Mann himself:

> We have here a kind of splendid narcissism, a contentment with self far too serious and far too concerned to the very end with self-perfection, heightening, and distillation of personal endowment, for a petty-minded word like "vanity" to be applicable. Here is that profound delight in that self and its growth to which we owe *Poetry and Truth,* the best, at any rate the most charming autobiography the world has seen—essentially a novel in the first person which informs us, in the most wonderfully winning tone, how a genius is formed, how luck and merit are indissolubly linked by an unknown decree of grace and how a personality grows and flourishes under the sun of a higher dispensation. Personality! Goethe called it "the supreme bliss of mortal man"— but what it really is, in what its inner nature consists, wherein its mystery lies—for there is a mystery about it—not even he ever explained. For that matter, for all his love for the telling word, for the word that strikes to the heart of life, he never thought that everything must be explained. Certainly this phenomenon known as "personality" takes us beyond the sphere of purely intellectual, rational, analyzable matters into the realm of nature, where dwell those elemental and daemonic things which "astound the world" without being amenable to further elucidation.

The splendid narcissism of Mann, at his strongest, is precisely daemonic, is that profound delight in the self without which works as various as *The Magic Mountain* and *Doctor Faustus* would collapse into the weariness of the irony of irony.

III

In his remarkable essay, "Freud and the Future" (1936), Mann wrote the pattern for his own imitation of Goethe:

The ego of antiquity and its consciousness of itself were different from our own, less exclusive, less sharply defined. It was, as it were, open behind; it received much from the past and by repeating it gave it presentness again. The Spanish scholar Ortega y Gasset puts it that the man of antiquity, before he did anything, took a step backwards, like the bull-fighter who leaps back to deliver the mortal thrust. He searched the past for a pattern into which he might slip as into a diving-bell, and being thus at once disguised and protected might rush upon his present problem. Thus his life was in a sense a reanimation, an archaizing attitude. But it is just this life as reanimation that is the life as myth. Alexander walked in the footsteps of Miltiades; the ancient biographers of Caesar were convinced, rightly or wrongly, that he took Alexander as his prototype. But such "imitation" meant far more than we mean by the word today. It was mythical identification, peculiarly familiar to antiquity; but it is operative far into modern times, and at all times is psychically possible. How often have we not been told that the figure of Napoleon was cast in the antique mould! He regretted that the mentality of the time forbade him to give himself out for the son of Jupiter Ammon, in imitation of Alexander. But we need not doubt that—at least at the period of his Eastern exploits—he mythically confounded himself with Alexander; while after he turned his face westwards he is said to have declared: "I am Charlemagne." Note that: not "I am like Charlemagne" or "My situation is like Charlemagne's," but quite simply "I am he." That is the formulation of the myth. Life, then—at any rate, significant life—was in ancient times the reconstitution of the myth in flesh and blood; it referred to and appealed to the myth; only through it, through reference to the past, could it approve itself as genuine and significant. The myth is the legitimization of life; only through and in it does life find self-awareness, sanction, consecration. Cleopatra fulfilled her Aphrodite character even unto death—and can one live and die more significantly or worthily than in the celebration of the myth? We have only to think of Jesus and His life, which was lived in order that that which was written might be fulfilled. It is not easy to distinguish between His own consciousness and the conventionalizations of the Evangelists. But His word on the Cross, about the ninth hour, that "*Eli, Eli, lama sabachthani?*" was evidently not in the least an outburst of despair and disillusionment; but on the contrary a lofty messianic sense of self. For the phrase is not original, not a spontaneous outcry. It stands at the beginning of the Twenty-second Psalm, which from one end to the other is an announcement of the Messiah. Jesus was quoting, and the quotation meant: "Yes, it is I!" Precisely thus did Cleopatra quote when she took the asp to her breast to die; and again the quotation meant: "Yes, it is I!"

In effect, Mann quotes Goethe, and thus proclaims "Yes, it is I." The ego of antiquity is simply the artist's ego, appropriating the precursor in order to overcome the belatedness of the influence process. Mann reveals the true subject of his essay on Freud just two paragraphs further on:

Infantilism—in other words, regression to childhood—what a role this genuinely psychoanalytic element plays in all our lives! What a large share it has in shaping the life of a human being; operating, indeed, in just the way I have described: as mythical identification, as survival, as a treading in footprints already made! The bond with the father, and the transference to father-substitute pictures of a higher and more developed type—how these infantile traits work upon the life of the individual to mark and shape it! I use the word "shape," for to me in all seriousness the happiest, most pleasurable element of what we call education (*Bildung*), the shaping of the human being, is just this powerful influence of admiration and love, this childish identification with a father-image elected out of profound affinity. The artist in particular, a passionately childlike and play-possessed being, can tell us of the mysterious yet after all obvious effect of such infantile imitation upon his own life, his productive conduct of a career which after all is often nothing but a reanimation of the hero under very different temporal and personal conditions and with very different, shall we say childish means. The *imitatio* Goethe, with its Werther and Wilhelm Meister stages, its old-age period of *Faust* and *Diwan*, can still shape and mythically mould the life of an artist—rising out of his unconscious, yet playing over—as is the artist way—into a smiling, childlike, and profound awareness.

The profound awareness is Mann's own, and concerns his own enactment of the *imitatio* Goethe. Subtly echoed and reversed here is Goethe's observation in his *Theory of Color* to the effect that "even perfect models have a disturbing effect in that they lead us to skip necessary stages in our *Bildung,* with the result, for the most part, that we are carried wide of the mark into limitless error." This is also the Goethe who celebrated his own originality as well as his power of appropriating from others. Thus he could say that: "Only by making the riches of the others our own do we bring anything great into being," but also insist: "What can we in fact call our own except the energy, the force, the will!" Mann, acutely sensing his own belatedness, liked to quote the old Goethe's question: "Does a man live when others also live?"

The Goethe of *The Beloved Returns* is not Goethe, but Mann himself, the world parodist prophesied and celebrated by Nietzsche as the artist of the future. E. R. Curtius doubtless was accurate in seeing Goethe as an ending and not as a fresh beginning of the cultural tradition. Mann too now seems archaic, not a modernist or post-Romantic, but a belated Goethe, a humanist triumphing through the mystery of his own personality and the ironic playfulness of his art. Like his vision of Goethe, Mann too now seems a child of nature rather than of the spirit, but laboring eloquently to burn through nature into the transformation that converts deathliness into a superb dialectical art.

HERMANN J. WEIGAND

Thomas Mann's Royal Highness *as Symbolic Autobiography*

In his brief essay "On *Royal Highness*" (1910) Thomas Mann wrote:

> The ruler whom I really had in mind is the one of whom Schiller's
> Charles the Seventh says: "Thus the minstrel should be at the
> king's side. Both of them dwell on the pinnacle of humanity."
> The allusive analysis of the existence of the sovereign as a formal,
> unreal, superreal one and the salvation of "highness" through
> love: that is the theme of my novel. Full of understanding sym-
> pathy for every sort of "special case," it preaches humaneness
> (*Menschlichkeit*).

Here Thomas Mann states with complete clarity that it was the parallel
between the life of the ruler and his own mode of life as an artist which
attracted him to this particular subject. Thus he portrays a human type with
the autobiographer's intimate, expert knowledge. Near the end of the same
essay he writes that the professional critics had racked their brains to discover
how in the world he might have hit upon this remote and resistant subject—

> just as if I had ever been concerned with any "subject" other than
> my own life. Who is a poet? He whose life is symbolic. In me

From *Thomas Mann: A Collection of Critical Essays,* edited by Henry Hatfield.
English translation by Henry Hatfield, © 1964 by Prentice-Hall, Inc. The German
version of this essay appeared in *PMLA* 46 (1931), © 1931 by the Modern Language
Association of America.

11

lives the belief that I only have to tell tales about myself in order to speak for the age, the generality of men; and unless I cherished this belief I could rid myself of the toil of production.

The life of the sovereign—to reverse the parallel—is also symbolic. Indeed, this is one of the most significant axiomatic truths which Dr. Überbein imparts to the young prince Klaus Heinrich:

> What am I? An assistant teacher. Not a completely ordinary one—all right—but still nothing more. A very definable individual. But you? What are you? That is harder to say . . . Let's say an essence, a sort of ideal. A vessel. A symbolic existence, Karl Heinrich, and therefore a formal existence.

The "very definable individual" stands for himself; the "symbolic existence" on the other hand is representative, and Überbein says:

> To be representative, to stand for many, while playing one's own role, to be the heightened and disciplined expression of a multitude—representing, of course, is more and higher than simply being.

With these words the creative writer proudly and openly declared his faith in his high rank in the scale of human types and in his dignity. Although representative, formal existence is really "of course" larger and higher than the simple way of life, he elsewhere justifies its pre-eminence by his express indication that the demands of formal accomplishment are much more searching than those of a solid, practical (*inhaltlich*) sort. Klaus Heinrich experiences this himself when he plunges into the study of the elements of government and economics, and when Thomas Mann informs us of this incident, the symbolic reference is obvious:

> Moreover, he found that it was not difficult to comprehend all that, if one really applied oneself. No, this whole earnest reality in which he now participated; this simple-minded, coarse structure of interests, this system of obvious if logically arranged needs and necessities, which innumerable young people of ordinary birth had to get into their cheerful heads, so that they could pass their examinations in the field—it was far less difficult to control than he, on his heights, had believed. Representing, he found, was more difficult.

In this passage then, the symbolic and autobiographical nature of the work is clearly established by the author himself; in broad outline it is shown in the work itself. Since, however, the "professional" critics at the time of publication (1909) showed not the slightest inkling of what the work was really about, and since the novel was also monstrously misinterpreted when it appeared in an American translation, it is a rewarding task to investigate this "allusive" work further, with reference to the relations which connect the life-style of the poet and artist with that of the sovereign. Needless to say, in this discussion, that part of Thomas Mann's life work which must be consulted as a basis of comparison is that which had already been published when *Royal Highness* appeared; I shall refrain from mentioning the further formulations and variations of the artist's style of life which Mann's last two decades have presented to us.

Anyone who has absorbed, with alert mind and senses, *Tonio Kröger,* Mann's first extensive work of fiction to treat the nature and the problems of the modern artist, would probably understand the few direct hints in which the author of *Royal Highness* indicates that the existence of the sovereign, in our novel, possesses a symbolic meaning along with a literal one. In the first conversation between Grand Duke Johann Albrecht and the Jewish physician Dr. Sammet, the existence of the sovereign, so sharply segregated from the norm of ordinary life, is contained in an extensive frame of reference which includes the exceptions and special cases in a sublime as well as a disreputable sense. "Sublime-disreputable"—does not this double predicate circumscribe the artist's hybrid nature, as it appears and becomes aware of itself in the personality of Tonio Kröger? Yet one must read between the lines, I suppose, to take Dr. Sammet's words as a reminder of this theme. We are given a second, quite casual but more direct hint when we, along with Klaus Heinrich, see his photograph in a shop window, "next to those of artists and great men, whose eyes gazed out from the loneliness of renown." For the initiate, Thomas Mann speaks more clearly when he has the assistant declare to his princely pupil that the latter "walked on humanity's heights"; for everyone who remembers Schiller's *Maid of Orleans* from his school days supplies the missing line about the minstrel. When finally Klaus Heinrich and a real poet meet, face to face, the prince gains insight into a strictly ascetic existence, wholly focused on form, which he himself feels to be related to his own. "He doesn't have a comfortable or easy time of it," Klaus Heinrich tells his sister the princess, after the audience. "And that's what matters, Albrecht, that one doesn't have a comfortable time of it"— those were the words with which he had vindicated the dignity of his own purely formal profession against his brother's disdainful attitude.

In the person of Axel Martini, to be sure, the disreputable aspect of the poetic calling is strongly emphasized. This somewhat veils the fact of the intrinsic affinity, for the prince's utterly naïve ignorance about matters of poetry provokes the writer (who had been summoned to the audience) to self-revelation of a comical, ironic hue. The ethos of his disclosures, after all, differs markedly from the type of questionableness which is inherent in the Prince's empty, unsubstantial style of life. Evidently Thomas Mann was concerned, in contrast to the carefully benevolent irony and delicate consideration with which he treated the very questionable strain in the nature of his allegorical twin, to draw the actual poet with all the more bold and vigorous strokes, so to speak as a figure of disenchantment.

Once one has noticed the equation of the formal, representative existence of the ruler with that of the poet, the parallels become completely clear. The individual points may be conveniently grouped around four problems, which, in their totality, express the essential presuppositions of Thomas Mann as artist and creative writer. These are 1: the heroic-ascetic ethic of an existence focused on the achievement of exemplary form; 2: the questionable nature of a human type in which all content is volatilized into form; 3: the path of development to a full humanity, to synthesis of the values of form and content—redemption; 4: the tie to the community; popularity and representation as a calling.

I. THE HEROIC-ASCETIC ETHIC

The effect of a folk tale on Klaus Heinrich's psyche, when he was a child, is symbolic of the renunciation of the "raptures of ordinary life"—to quote *Tonio Kröger*—as the correlative of a lofty, exceptional position. When listening to the adventures of fairy princes and princesses, other children feel a heightening, an elevation of their natures above actuality and ordinary life, whereas Klaus Heinrich and his little sister regarded "those figures as their own sort, with a relaxed sense of being equally highborn." Carried over to the sphere of art, this means: the person who belongs to this sphere and has his home in its high regions is denied the easy heightening and elevation above the everyday level which the average person feels when occasionally, for moments or hours, he abandons himself to the magic spell of art. Also symbolic is the vivid experience of terrible loneliness, which swept over the thirteen-year-old Klaus Heinrich in the midst of the bleak magnificence of the "silver hall," of which Mann states: "And it was cold in the silver Hall of Candles, as in the hall of the Snow Queen, where children's hearts freeze stiff." That art is a sphere of coldness Tonio Kröger had learned quite well enough. Indeed he too characterizes the act of artistic creation not so much as a liberation and redemption as, rather, a "chilling of emotion and placing it on ice." The whole atmosphere of the Hall of State, a concentrated emblem of severely formal existence, is a symbol of the artist and his passionate and exclusive endeavor to create form: "Severe and empty splendor prevailed here and a formal symmetry of arrangement which presented itself, self-contained, unconcerned with purpose or comfort—a high and zealous service no doubt, which seemed far removed from relaxed lightheartedness, which obliged you to decorum and discipline and controlled self-abnegation." "Loneliness and being shut off from happiness, from a happy-go-lucky life" as one's destiny; "an exclusive and severe focusing on creative achievement"—an achievement which must give the appearance of easy mastery and spontaneity though it is the product of the most disciplined exertion of one's energies; giving up "spontaneity" and the "joys of intimate confession": these are indeed the principles which put their stamp both on the pedagogy of the Prince's tutor and on the self-education of the artist. After all, part of the artist's manner of working, as Thomas Mann relates from his own experience, is "a sort of patience—no, far more! a doggedness, an obstinacy, a discipline and enslavement of one's own will which are hard to conceive of; and which often strain the nerves, believe me, to the breaking point." And if he ever succumbs to the temptation to let himself go and, with the cover of a punch bowl on his head, perhaps, to share in the delights of ordinary life, he must pay a bitter penalty.

The poet Axel Martini, too, who praises the full enjoyment of life in such fiery words, has a tale to tell about that: "Renunciation is our pact with the Muse; our strength and dignity is based upon it, and life is our forbidden garden, our great temptation, to which we yield at times, but never to our own good." And later: "For living hygienically—that is our whole ethic." We are reminded of Tonio Kröger's bitter question whether the artist is a man at all: "Ask 'woman' about that!" Related in its severe, ascetic fulfilment of duty to the ethic of the categorical imperative, and owing much both in ascetic severity and in the lofty, confident sense of being chosen to Nietzsche's inspiration, the existence of the sovereign and of the artist is of markedly aristocratic nature; with proud contempt it puts the merely human in its place. For the merely human means good nature, relaxation, lack of dignity, putting up with mere attempts instead of severe achievement; in a word, it is the human-all-too-human. Therefore Dr. Überbein reverses the eighteenth-century paradox: "He is a prince! . . . He is more than that; he is a human being!" By now the paradox has degenerated to a flabby untruth, and he states emphatically: "That is mere humanity, but at heart I'm not very much for humanity; I take the greatest pleasure in speaking disparagingly about it!" And Thomas Mann has the same pedagogue utter, in its most extreme form, the credo of the artist, creating, in full awareness, on the lonely heights: "Spirit (or intellect-*Geist*) is the tutor who insists implacably on dignity, yes, who actually creates dignity; he is the archenemy and aristocratic antagonist of all humane and humanitarian good nature (*Gemütlichkeit*)."

II. QUESTIONABLENESS

But now the seamy side of this severe self-discipline intent on form alone. Even as a small child, Klaus Heinrich has the experience that his mother— she too achieves virtuosity in her own specialty—saves up all her tenderness and motherliness for public occasions. Within the intimacy of the family, on the other hand, she displays very little of this warmth; and the "proud" insight dawns on the little, pitiably docile prince: "that in accordance with the nature of things it was not fitting for us to feel simply and thus to be happy, but rather that it was our lot to make our affection vividly clear and to display it at court functions, so that the hearts of the guests might swell." When every energy is expended on "making clear" and display, what is left for emotion per se? Is not this whole cult of form calculated to volatilize all sense of essential substance and make an expression which has no corresponding content become rigid, empty form? How frighteningly empty an education during whose course the pupil grasps the fact that every objective element of instruction is basically a sheer pretext, that the dignified and courteous gesture of shaking hands with the teacher was really "more important and essential than all the lessons that came between handshakes." How systematically mendacious is a type of coaching which encourages the student, after he has reached a perfidious secret understanding with his teacher, to simulate, by raising his hand, a knowledge which he does not possess! Thus bluffing is an axiom of life! And all his development is shaped in accordance with this principle: his year at the preparatory school, his year at the university, his year in the army and his so-called grand tour (*Bildungsreise*). His sphere of activity is similarly constructed when his destiny involves taking over his brother's "representative" duties, the journeys and official speeches and layings of cornerstones, the open audiences in the castle, which, with their emphasis on meticulous observation of etiquette, are primarily devoted to the purpose of diverting the petitioner from the real point of his request. One thinks also of the questions apparently inspired by the most pertinent interest—words of praise, of encouragement, which make a fool of the unsuspecting burgher—except for cases when an artful fellow, a man whose nature is related to the ruler's, a sovereign of the spirit, is summoned to one of these audiences and gives vent to his irony—which leads to a priceless situation.

Let us confirm, by quoting a confession of Tonio Kröger, that in this semblance of an existence, in this systematically cultivated falsity of feeling, the whole problematic nature of the artist is symbolically reflected. Tonio's language is clear:

> One works poorly in the spring, surely; and why? Because one feels. And because whoever believes that a creator is allowed to feel is a bungler. Every genuine and honest artist smiles at the naïveté of such blunders—perhaps sadly, but he smiles. For what one says must never be the main thing; it is rather raw material, neutral in and of itself. From it the artist must put together the aesthetic structure, with easy, calm superiority. . . . Emotion, warm, heartfelt emotion is always banal and unusable; worthy of art are only the irritations and cold ecstasies of our corrupted, our artistic, nervous system.

In Tonio Kröger's case the problematic nature of an existence entirely focused on semblance reaches its height in the remark that in the realm of art "it is perhaps a matter of a gift with extremely evil preconditions, extremely questionable in itself"; and in his personal confession that he felt— "transferred into the intellectual sphere—all the suspicions about the artist-type" with which his honest ancestors had confronted jugglers and roaming acrobats. In Klaus Heinrich's case the analogous state of affairs is formulated as a question, decisive in his relations to Imma, which he himself expresses as a humbly hesitant supplication: "Couldn't you put a little trust in me?" Trust, that is the essential point. A personality whose every fiber is in the grip of the service of form; which habitually "works up" everything substantial and essential, treating it as mere neutral raw material; which—to use Tonio Kröger's words again—is subservient to artistic aims even "when hands clasp each other, lips meet, when man's gaze is blinded by feeling,"— is it at all possible, in human terms, to feel trust in such a personality? At first Imma's answer—though she does regard the Prince with some warmth—must be: "It is quite impossible to have any trust in you." "To be a poet means to sit in judgment on oneself"—Thomas Mann is one of those artists whose conscience subscribes to this motto of Ibsen's.

III. REDEMPTION

And yet the antinomy between formal and essential existence is not Thomas Mann's last word. That the opposition of form and essence is not an absolute but a dialectic one, which can and must be reconciled in a higher synthesis—Thomas Mann professes this conviction at the end of *Tonio Kröger*, by letting the hero of his *novella* find his way back from emotional torpor to humanity. Chilling and slaying emotion with the purpose of refining it into sheer form is a process of artistic development which must inevitably be undergone, so that artistry may grow into full humanity. If the artist has attained mastery of form through the passionate yet ascetic sacrifice of all his humanity, he must then find again the road to ingenuous emotion, to being a human simply and unpretentiously. Otherwise artistry cannot mean a general heightening of innate human talents but only the variation of a special endowment—subtly interesting to be sure, but incapable of really living. Of the "artist," love for the human, the living, the ordinary, makes the "poet."

Tonio Kröger finds the way back to humanity; Klaus Heinrich first has to find that there *is* a way. For from the cradle his life has lacked any true content, and his education has systematically frustrated all his capacities of becoming substantial. Surely these were latent in him, for he had the urge to "rummage about." Thus an extraordinary, fortunate chance must intervene in his life, so that the vessel of his life, having been shaped as sheer form, may be filled with substance. Love for a woman who is equally marked, remote from life, and lonely, builds a bridge for him. A kindly providence arranges that the fulfilment of his longing for his own happiness is made to depend on his learning to devote a real, sympathetic interest to the cares of his own people and of the individual. He took his first step on his new path when he began to subject Dr. Überbein's ascetic, "antihappiness" ethic, his provocative insistence on achievement, to muted criticism. He calls this ethic decent but profoundly unfortunate, and sinful into the bargain, "for it is a sin against something more splendid than his severe decency, this I now realize, and he tried to educate me to this sin too, for all his fatherliness. But now I've outgrown his guidance—in this point I really have." Here it is a matter of the concept of humility, of accepting fate, whether it bring us pleasant or harsh experiences, of redemption from the stiff, obstinate pride of individualism. When he becomes aware of the actual state of his country's finances, he starts zealously to study economics; and his personality is gradually freed, during his common studies with Imma, of its chilling air, its insistence on decorum. The eccentric countess may let herself go in his presence, and Klaus Heinrich, with kindly indulgence, agrees to call her "Frau Meier" for the time being. Thus, symbolically speaking, Klaus Heinrich is gradually redeemed from the state of being merely an artist and becomes a poet; thus he vividly experiences the synthesis of form and essence. Both "perceptively observing and playing his role," he will henceforth live at Imma's side, uniting humaneness with decorum. Mann's final formula is: "Highness and love—a severe happiness."

IV. POPULARITY AND REPRESENTATION AS A CALLING

The form of life and the development of the protagonist have appeared, in all their basic aspects, as a metaphor, in which Thomas Mann is actually telling of his own nature as artist and poet, with all its problems. The metaphor, however, has a further range: it concerns not only the sovereign, but also the complementary concept, the people, and the mutual relationships which tie the people and the sovereign together. If we pursue the interpretation of this side of the metaphor, we arrive at insights which are important and in part downright surprising.

A political scientist who happened to read *Royal Highness* in a leisure hour might well reach the conclusion that this work was devoted to an ingenious philosophical justification of monarchy as the form of government which most appropriately expresses the essence and will of a people. In fact, Thomas Mann does not tire of pointing out that basically the people glorifies itself at festivals when apparently it is celebrating its sovereign, that it cries "Long live the king!" and really means itself, that in the sovereign it is searching for the "heightening" wish-picture of its own being. Granted that the author's actual liking for the monarchical form of government—in the abstract—plays its part, it is still important to note that the people's demonstrations of affection towards other, quasi-public personages is based on the same suppositions. Why does it wildly cheer the soubrette Mizzi Meyer, who is not beautiful, barely pretty, and sings with a shrill voice? Because as long as this blond, thickset person with her blue eyes, her broad cheek bones set a bit too high, her healthy, gay, but also often sentimental air, stands bejeweled, rouged, illuminated from all sides, on the stage before the crowd, it finds its own type, glorified, in her. "Yes, the people applauded itself when it applauded her."

But what else is the poet's significance but a similar glorification of the people, higher to be sure? "The people wishes to see its best, its higher nature, its dream, yes, something like its soul represented in its sovereign," we read in the very first chapter. If we substitute the word "poet" for "sovereign" in this passage, the statement clearly contains the formula for the representative calling and the lofty task of the creative writer. It is this calling, this task of which Mann gives an accounting here.

The poet's acknowledgment of his representative character and his fitness for this task imply two presuppositions. The first is the abandonment of a purely individualistic attitude. The concept of autonomous genius à la Nietzsche, which is responsible only to itself and knows no law but the heightening of its own personality and cares only for itself, is replaced by the idea of obligation to the whole and responsibility towards the cultural community. The poet feels that he is the highest member of that community. What the poet expresses is not only his own subjective feeling but the urge to higher things which slumbers even in the dull crowd and appears, transmuted to clear self-awareness, only in him, the most refined distillation of the "popular soul," as it were. Wherever Klaus Heinrich went, colorless life was transfigured and became poetry: "the dull burgher, in frock-coat and top hat, became aware of his own worth and was moved." That is the poet's effect: he redeems the longing of the "popular soul" from its dullness by helping it to become conscious.

The second point: so that the poet may actually have this elevating, redeeming effect of bringing happiness, there must be a living sense of intimate kinship and reciprocal affinity between the people and the poet. When it is absent, this fortunate effect does not exist. In Albrecht II, the sickly, neurasthenic, overbred aristocrat, whose body and instincts do not reflect the nature of the people in any way, it does not find its "heightened" wish-picture. It cannot shout "Long live Albrecht" and mean itself, and for his part, he finds representation a ridiculous calling. He describes it with the revealing term "monkey business." On the other hand, Klaus Heinrich with his broad cheek bones, characteristic of the nation, and his broad hand— and his correspondingly simpler psychological make-up—rejoices in his "representative" calling and enjoys the happiness of popularity. That is not a very profound but splendid and inclusive sort of intimacy, which to some extent compensates both the sovereign and the poet for the fact that their private lives are exposed to all the world.

The reference to Thomas Mann's own situation is obvious. He has himself so often and so clearly stressed his love for the burgher's way of life, his psychological affinity to the class from which he sprang, that it would be redundant to discuss the point at length. He achieved the happiness of popularity early in life, as the tremendous success of *Buddenbrooks* bears witness. That, on the other hand, he does not fail to recognize the danger which popularity implies for the man of exceptional talent is made clear in

Klaus Heinrich's youthful experience when he behaves in all too ordinary a fashion at the "citizen's ball" and thus unleashes drives which find satisfaction in dragging down the high, the elite, to the level of vulgarity. Further evidence is his elder brother's serious admonition, contained in his congratulations when Imma becomes Klaus Heinrich's fiancée: "I wish you happiness, but not too much, and hope that you will not bask too much in the love of the people."

I shall leave it to Thomas Mann's biographers to comment on the well-known fact that his wooing of the lady who became his wife and the happiness of his young marriage are reflected in *Royal Highness*. But we cannot ignore another personal relationship here, one which has nothing to do with the general public's habit—which Mann has sharply criticized—"of sniffing about in the author's personal affairs when confronted by his absolute achievement." For me there is no doubt that Klaus Heinrich's relation to Albrecht corresponds essentially to Thomas Mann's relation to his elder brother Heinrich. Heinrich Mann, the over-refined, neurasthenic individualist, is related to Albrecht's type. Far removed from any sense of solidarity with the burgher sphere, he has coined this formula to express the idea of the burgher: "So I call all those who have ugly feelings and moreover lie when they express their ugly feelings." There is a further affinity in the fact that Heinrich Mann's coldly controlled, sophisticated art of the grotesque has not made contact with the general public. It is Heinrich who turns over to his brother Thomas the dignified task of representative achievement; Heinrich who warns his brother of the dangers of popularity and admonishes him not to take things in too relaxed a way. Presumably the remark which follows Albrecht's congratulations, spoken when he raises his lids from his blue eyes with their lonely expression, refers to Heinrich: "And in this moment it became clear that he loved Klaus Heinrich." And we hear Thomas Mann paying ungrudging tribute to his brother's aristocratic genius in Klaus Heinrich's words to Albrecht: "I have always looked up to you, because I have always felt and known that you are the more aristocratic, the higher of us two, and I am only a plebeian compared to you." It is amazing, by the way, that such an abundance of parallels in problems, matter, and motifs joins the creative work of the two brothers, despite the most distinct difference in their temperaments. It is reasonable to expect that this complex of intellectual relationships will be subjected before long to the most thorough investigation.

In this essay the symbolic and autobiographical elements of *Royal Highness* have not indeed been exhaustively treated, but their basic features have been elucidated. Everywhere this novel has turned out to be a variation of the same theme which Thomas Mann had already treated very searchingly in *Tonio Kröger*. A variation, not a repetition, for the intellectual features of *Tonio Kröger* and of the work devoted to Klaus Heinrich differ as do those of the youth from the man's. Thus Tonio is a person torn apart, not really at home in either of the two worlds to which his service and his love are devoted, and only at the end does he dimly sense the resolution of the antinomy of his nature. In Klaus Heinrich's case, on the other hand, the ethical character of formal achievement is much more strongly emphasized from the very beginning; and the concept of the poet's tie to the community, which gives his calling its representative value, is the foundation which supports the whole structure of the work. A decisive difference in mood and tone corresponds; while a painfully emotional pathos colors the style of *Tonio Kröger,* this "didactic fairy tale" is recounted in the mood of benevolently smiling, warily kind irony.

It is impossible to end this essay without referring to a third dialectic variation of the theme of the problematic nature of the vocation of artist and poet, with which Thomas Mann surprised the public only two years later. Symbolically, *Death in Venice* is also autobiographical, even though Mann was only thirty-six years old when he conceived of the figure of Gustave Aschenbach, who is at the height of his fame and already over fifty. For the figure of Aschenbach, the hero of creative work, who creates the illusion of strength and health (though he is laboring on the brink of exhaustion) until he suddenly and completely collapses, implies an anticipation of tragic possibilities which are inherent in the artist of his own type. Aschenbach's fate signifies a projection summoned up by the author as a warning to himself, like the aging Ibsen's Solness, Allmers, Borkmann, and Rubek. And thus the classically severe "master style" of this *novella* harmonizes with the process of dissolution which it describes. Its uncanny, horrible tragic nature is of a precipitous sublimity which excludes any expression of banal compassion.

VERNON VENABLE

Structural Elements
in Death in Venice

In a literary epoch that has produced such figures as Gertrude Stein, James Joyce, Paul Valéry, and T. S. Eliot, it is not surprising that little should have been said about Thomas Mann as an innovator. Orderly interest in contemporary spiritual and social problems and respect for the orthodoxies of syntax are virtues that have not been at an artistic premium. Any new ways Mann has of saying things occasion so little cognitive discomfort that they have been generally assumed to be old, familiar ways, and the things he says are so clearly to the contemporary point that his chief fame has been as a kind of mentor, like André Gide and D. H. Lawrence.

To be esteemed as a mentor, however, is doubtless quite as embarrassing to Mann as to have his artistry taken for granted. Although he makes frequent use of ethical subject-matter, the inspiration of his fiction differs fundamentally from the messianic muse of Lawrence and Gide and acts neither from prophetic ardor nor towards doctrinal conclusions. (I speak only of his fiction, of course, not of his essays or of his recent public letters and addresses.) And while he misbehaves with his medium no more than they do with theirs, he manages, nevertheless, to make it serve a new technique.

The clue to this new technique lies in the dualism or polarity which always characterizes Mann's subject-matter. Such large antitheses as life and death, time and individuality, fertility and decay, flesh and spirit, invariably constitute the themes of his novels. Mann never allows this dualism to be-

From *The Structure of Thomas Mann,* edited by Charles Neider. © 1947 by New Directions Publishing Co. Originally entitled *"Death in Venice."*

come vitiated, for it is the formal and operative principle of his aesthetic. He never prefers one term of his antithesis to the other, for his interest is not in arguing theses but in developing themes. Hence we misunderstand his fiction if we isolate individual symbols from their dualistic context in order to lend the weight of Mann's authority to questions of conduct.

The life-death theme, which has been more often the focus of his attention than any other, is a good case in point. Not once in any of his novels, so far as I have been able to discover, does this theme assert the simple, unequivocal proposition that all men are mortal. People sometimes die, to be sure; death often negates life in a kind of dialectical way, but quite as often we find life spoken of in such terms as "inorganic matter become sick," or "the existence of the actually-impossible-to-exist." In Mann's scheme death and life, life and death both unremittingly affirm and unremittingly negate each other in a paradox worthy of Zeno. Actually, Mann's interest in paradox is even more final than was Zeno's, for Zeno saw in his paradoxes only a convenient means of refuting those philosophers who held that the world was plural; while Mann sees, in his, the very core and heart of his world:

> Beautiful is resolution. But the really fruitful, the productive, and hence the artistic principle is that which we call reserve. In the sphere of music we love it as the prolonged note, the teasing melancholy of the not-yet, the inward hesitation of the soul, which bears within itself fulfilment, resolution, and harmony, but denies it for a space, withholds and delays, scruples exquisitely yet a little longer to make the final surrender. In the intellectual sphere we love it as irony: that irony which glances at both sides, which plays slyly and irresponsibly—yet not without benevolence—among opposites, and is in no great haste to take sides and come to decisions; guided as it is by the surmise that in great matters, in matters of humanity, every decision may prove premature, that the real goal to reach is not decision, but harmony accord. And harmony, in a matter of eternal contraries, may lie at infinity; yet that playful reserve called irony carries it within itself as the sustained note carries the resolution.

Mann, then, is first and foremost an ironist, but this is scarcely a novelty for a writer. Secondly, he is a symbolist, and in one respect his symbolism is not even modern. His cemeteries mean death, his jungles stand for life, his Peeperkorns mean spontaneous vitality, and his Naphtas mean overrefined intellectuality in the conventional way in which Dante's *selva oscura* stands for spiritual darkness, or the flag for the country—not in the *symboliste* manner in which "patience amiable, amiably" signifies Gertrude Stein's idea of Bernard Faÿ, or "the hyacinth girl" a very personal aspect of Eliot's *Weltschmerz* [world-weariness].

Now Mann could doubtless have accomplished many of his ironic purposes within the bounds of conventional symbolism. Every typical death symbol, for example, could have been given its counterpart in a typical life symbol, every jungle could have its adjacent cemetery, every Peeperkorn his Naphta. But so deepseated, so radical is Mann's irony that it will not allow him an unambiguous feeling even about an individual symbol: in the jungle, which represents life at its most lush, he sees the breeding place of the plague; the "little O" which Peeperkorn is forever shaping "with forefinger and thumb ... the other fingers standing stiffly erect beside it," is clearly a phallus, but to Mann it is just as clearly a cipher; the "lying-down position" of the body is the posture of repose, healing, and love-making, but it is also the posture of sickness, dying, and the grave; the bark of the quinine tree is medicinal but poisonous, that of the deadly upas tree both aphrodisiacal and lethal; the ancient burial urn is covered with fertility symbols.

It is to this insatiable ironic temper, I believe, that we may ascribe chief responsibility for the newness of Mann's symbolism. In the process of trying to achieve the symbolic identifications which his irony demands, he has created a new technique for the exploitation of poetic meaning, a technique in which no symbol is allowed univocal connotation or independent status, but refers to all the others and is bound rigorously to them by means of a highly intricate system of subtly developed associations. Such a system constitutes the structure of each of his major novels. Its function is always synthetic: one by one the various antithetical symbols are identified with each other and finally fused into the single, nuclear, paradoxical meaning which Mann wishes to emphasize. There is no escape from this meaning; at every point the reader's characteristic tendency to stray off into realms of private association is checked by the rigid poetic logic of the story, and he is led ineluctably to the specific response which Mann intends that he shall experience. This represents, I believe, a singularly successful solution to what Stevenson thought the most difficult of all poetic problems: not that of getting the reader to feel, but of making him feel in precisely the way in which the poet thinks he ought to feel. Poets who work within the bounds of rigidly controlled symbolic references sometimes achieve results more like mathematical demonstrations or bank statements than poems. Mann, however, consistently manages to produce effects that are genuinely poetic. I should like to examine the short novel, *Death in Venice,* which is perhaps the finest expression of his genius in this respect, in order to discover how his system of structural symbolic associations operates.

II

Death in Venice is a powerful, strangely haunting, and tragic story about a middle-aged artist who takes a holiday from his work, and finds himself held in Venice by the charms of a twelve-year-old boy until he goes to seed in a most shocking way, and at last succumbs to the plague which he might otherwise have fled. There is no more of a plot than that. There are other people, however, who wander in and out of the story apparently at random, but who leave their mark both on the artist, Aschenbach, and on the reader: a red-haired, snub-nosed traveler, whose vitality and air of distant climes first suggest to Aschenbach that he himself go off on a trip; a painted and primped old scapegrace from Pola who gets on Aschenbach's Venice-bound steamer with a coterie of young men; a gondolier, of sinister aspect, who rows Aschenbach from Venice to the Lido and vanishes without collecting his money; a mendicant singer who, shortly before Aschenbach's death, goes through his comic turns on the porch of the hotel, smelling all the while of the carbolic acid which has become associated with the plague.

These people seem to serve only as atmosphere, to be quite unrelated both to one another and to the development of the story, but in truth they constitute the very structure of its elaboration. One is reminded of the musical form known as the passacaglia, where a ground bass, repeating the same theme over and over again for progressive variations in the upper register, occasionally emerges into the treble itself, with the effect of affirming emphatically the singleness of the thematic material in both registers.

In *Death in Venice,* the treble is the simple narrative sequence of Aschenbach's voyage, his life on the Lido, his love for the boy Tadzio, and his death. The ground bass is the "life and death" theme repeated as a sort of undertone to the story by those characters who seem to have no very obvious connection with the proper narrative content.

Before attempting to understand how the symbols of the bass are related to those of the treble, it should be remarked that despite the almost mathematical precision with which the intricate associations are accomplished, they are not meant to be understood. To be free from artificiality, from the appearance of tour de force, such a highly complicated formal pattern must gain its effectiveness immediately; that is, not through rational processes. This is a comparatively easy accomplishment for the musician, whose medium does not involve meaning, but it demands rare subtlety from a writer.

Mann's deftness is, of course, prodigious, and he contrives to keep his for-malized meanings from the explicit attention of the reader largely by the simple technical expedient of hiding them from Aschenbach himself.

For example, Aschenbach never notices—and hence the reader seldom does—that the vital stranger who aroused in him the desire to stop working and to try merely living for a while is the same man as the sinister gondolier who later ferries him to the Lido and his eventual death, and that the clown-ing beggar of the hotel porch is none other than the gondolier still further down at the heel. Nor is he ever aware that this ubiquitous person bears a shocking resemblance to the loathsome old fop from Pola. Least of all does it occur to him that all of these questionable people, as morbid caricatures of the heroes of his own novels, are really merely images of himself and his loved-one Tadzio, though it is this final identification which constitutes the meaning and effect of the entire story.

If, as readers, we are not supposed to be consciously aware of these relationships, we may, as critics, proceed to seek them out. The life and death theme is announced at the very beginning of the story: Aschenbach is waiting by the North Cemetery when he sees a wandering stranger. His reveries proper to the funereal setting, sober, necroscopic, are changed by this man's striking vitality into extravagant fancies of the jungle, lush with phallic imagery. Death and life, entering the scene thus hand-in-hand, induce their characteristic emotions, and Aschenbach's heart knocks "with fear and with puzzling desires."

At this point, a retrospect of Aschenbach's life as man and artist breaks the narrative, and we are introduced to the second important symbol. This time, it is not a person of the story, but a *type* of person found in Aschen-bach's own stories—a kind of character that proclaims much the same virtues as does the figure of Saint Sebastian in painting, and that represents to Aschenbach's readers a new ideal for spiritual and moral heroism. This figure is really Aschenbach's artistic projection of his own personality, an apothe-osis of his own "distinguishing moral trait," and though it is not yet at this place associated with the first symbol, the stranger of the cemetery, it already begins, obviously, to reflect its symbolism on Aschenbach. Equally impor-tant, it reintroduces the life-death theme of the ground bass, for this para-doxical "hero-type" combines "a crude and vicious sensuality capable of fanning its rising passions into pure flame" with "a delicate self-mastery by which any inner deterioration, any biological decay was kept concealed from the eyes of the world."

These are the grounds for a gruesome association which soon follows; the shameless old fraud from Pola—Aschenbach's fellow-traveler to the southland where he has been drawn by his "puzzling desires"—this revolting old man, weazened and rouged, decayed and feeble, but more waggish and gay than any of his young companions, is none other than a loathsome travesty of the Sebastian-like hero-type: in him, the hero's "crude and vicious sensuality" burns no "pure flame" but reeks of perversion; the "delicate self-mastery" which distinguishes Aschenbach's characters and is the controlling principle of his own art, appears here as ugly artifice, and "biological decay" shows doubly horrible through the old man's paint.

But Aschenbach fails to see the image of himself; indeed, even when, towards the end of the story, he himself resorts to cosmetics in his wooing of Tadzio, the kinship does not occur to him. And though he is now "fascinated with loathing" at the old man on the boat, he does not remember his "fear and desire" of the cemetery, or even the vital stranger, whose insolence and habit of grimacing were not unlike the old dandy's. Neither does the reader make this association consciously, but the ground is nonetheless well prepared for the reappearance of the stranger when the ship docks at Venice.

This time the stranger is not framed in the portico of a funeral hall, to be sure, but he *is* riding a gondola: "strange craft . . . with that peculiar blackness which is found elsewhere only in coffins—it suggests silent, criminal adventures in the rippling night, it suggests even more strongly death itself, the bier and the mournful funeral, and the last silent journey." And as Aschenbach transfers from the ship to be rowed by this modern Charon on his own last journey, he observes guilelessly "that the seat of such a barque, this armchair of coffin-black veneer and dull black upholstery, is the softest, most luxurious, most lulling seat in the world." This time the "desire" has taken the form of a "poisonous but delectable inertia." But "fear" is there also, deriving from the illicit aspect of the gondolier, whose present dilapidation hides his identity both from us and from Aschenbach and renders his vitality and pugnacious insolence distinctly menacing. The red hair, however, the snub nose, the long, white savage teeth and the frail build are those of the vital stranger; there are even certain frayed remnants of his former costume if we were but to observe them, and his second disappearance is quite as uncanny as his first.

The life-death theme, firmly established by these devices, is now taken up for development by the story proper, the details of which I need not enter into here. Rumors of the plague run an increasingly sinister counterpoint to Aschenbach's growing love for Tadzio, his young fellow-guest at a hotel on the Lido. An ominous odor of death thus conditions but intensifies the seductiveness of this new life-symbol until the climax of the story when the stranger, entering for the third and last time, performs his antics for the hotel audience.

He is a beggar now, and smells of disinfectant. Even his arrogance has become tainted with obsequiousness. In the repulsively suggestive movements of his mouth, in "his gestures, the movements of his body, his way of blinking significantly, and letting his tongue play across his lips," our symbol of organic life reveals himself to be as rotten at the core as the sleazy old cheat of Pola. The latter, we may remember, "showed a deplorable insolence . . . winked and tittered, lifted his wrinkled, ornamented index finger in a stupid attempt at bantering, while he licked the corners of his mouth with his tongue in the most abominably suggestive manner." And the vital stranger's smell is the smell that has become associated with the constant rumors of death. Aschenbach goes, the next day, to the tourist office to inquire about these rumors. He learns that they are true: there is death in Venice, death that was hatched as pestilence in jungle swamps. And the jungle had meant *life* to Aschenbach, had lured him away from the stern and desiccating discipline of his existence to seek "an element of freshness" for his blood, to live!

That night he has a dream in which he joins a fertility dance in the heart of the jungle—an orgiastic nightmare, compounded of fear and desire, which completes the annihilation of his "substance . . . the culture of his lifetime." "His repugnance" at the awful carousal, "his fear, were keen—he was honorably set on defending himself to the very last against the barbarian, the foe to intellectual poise and dignity. But . . . his heart fluttered, his head was spinning, he was caught in a frenzy, in a blinding, deafening lewdness— and he yearned to join the ranks of the god." When the obscene symbol was raised at last, he could resist no longer; he abandoned himself to the hideous debauchery and "his soul tasted the unchastity and fury of decay."

A short coda-like section completes the development of the symbol of imposture; then, in a concluding synthesis, the hero-type symbol is resolved. The symbol of fraud is no longer the old fop, but Aschenbach himself. Harassed by chronic apprehensiveness, ravaged by his illicit passion, undone by the anguish of his dream, Aschenbach begins to show the marks of death. But "like any lover, he wanted to please."

And when, after a scandalous pursuit of his loved one through the infected alleys of Venice, he sits by the cistern in the deserted square with his mouth hanging open, panting for breath, sticky with sweat, trembling, lugubrious and old, but with blossoming youth painted on his lips and cheeks, dyed into his hair, sketched about his eyes—as he sprawls thus in ghastly caricature of his own spiritual and moral ideal, we not only do not loathe him, but we temper with a new access of sympathy the loathing we originally felt for the old cheat of Pola. For when the magnificent stranger showed his frailty, we felt how it must be with everyone.

The synthesis which brings the story to an end reveals the full meaning of the hero-type symbol, and effects at the same time a final merger of all the other meanings. At the sacrifice of his art, of his ideals, of his very life itself, Aschenbach found Tadzio; now Tadzio, the object of his sacrifice, the goal of his desire, the instrument of his death, reveals that he *is* Aschenbach's art, his own ideal creation, and thus is Aschenbach himself no less than are the stranger and the cheat.

The scene which accomplishes this dénouement was prepared for in Aschenbach's first meeting with Tadzio. After days of worshiping the god-like beauty of the boy at a distance, but of giving no outward sign of his feelings, indeed scarcely admitting them even to himself, Aschenbach chanced to come face-to-face with him so suddenly one evening that "he had no time to entrench himself behind an expression of repose and dignity," but smiled at him in infatuated and undisguised admiration. And the exquisite smile which Tadzio gave back to his smitten admirer was "*the smile of Narcissus* (the italics throughout are mine) bent over the reflecting water, that deep, fascinated, magnetic smile with which he stretches out his arms *to the image of his own beauty* . . . coquettish, inquisitive and slightly tortured . . . infatuated and infatuating." Quite broken up by the episode, Aschenbach sought solitude in the darkness of the park, and as he whispered fervently the "fixed formula of desire . . . 'I love you!'" his voice was for none but his own ears. That the "*night-smell of vegetation*" pointed up the frenzy of his passion in his scene, is typical of the faithfulness and subtlety with which Mann introduces fragments of his bass theme into the details of the treble.

Unknowing, Aschenbach was confronted with the image of his own beauty. What was the image but the Sebastian-like hero-type, his own apotheosis, his spiritual essence—parodied in the old cheat, revealed in its uncompromising duplicity in the stranger, and displayed in its pathos in the painted Aschenbach?

Now, in the final scene, that ideal is at last glorified again by the frail, the exquisite Tadzio. Tadzio is out on a sand-bar in the ocean. His playmates of the beach have brutalized and humiliated him, but he stands haughty and graceful, "separated from the mainland by the expanse of water, separated from his companions by a proud moodiness . . . a strongly isolated and unrelated figure . . . placed out there in the sea, the wind, against the vague mists." Here he is the true Sebastian, the living hero-type—that figure which by a power of "more than simple endurance," by "an act of aggression, a positive triumph . . . (is) poised against fatality . . . (meets) adverse conditions gracefully . . . stands motionless, haughty, ashamed, with jaw set, while swords and spear-points beset the body." He is Aschenbach's ideal incarnated.

And he is outlined against the sea. Once before he was outlined thus—long ago, when for the first time Aschenbach learned the full poignancy of his beauty. Aschenbach then, too, was seated in his beach chair, but he had been watching the sea, pondering its power over him, feeling himself drawn to it

> because of that yearning for rest, when the hard-pressed artist hungers to shut out the exacting multiplicities of experience and hide himself on the breast of the simple, the vast; and because of a forbidden hankering—seductive, by virtue of its being directly opposed to his obligations—after the incommunicable, the incommensurate, the eternal, the non-existent. To be at rest in the face of perfection is the hunger of everyone who is aiming at excellence; and what is the non-existent but a form of perfection?

And then, suddenly, "just as his dreams were so far out in vacancy . . . the horizontal fringe of the sea was broken by a human figure; and as he brought his eyes back from the unbounded, and focused them, it was the lovely boy who was there."

Now, at the last, Tadzio is standing out there again, beyond the shore this time, out in the vast expanse itself. Slowly he turns from the hips, looks over his shoulder with twilight-grey eyes toward the artist seated on the shore, and seems to beckon to Aschenbach to come. Once more arousing himself to the call of his own spiritual form—out from the incommensurate, the incommunicable, the non-existent—the stricken artist stands up to follow, then collapses in his chair.

III

This is an outline, by no means exhaustive, of the symbol structure of *Death in Venice*. The clearest view of Mann's synthetic technique, and of the nature of the change that occurs in an individual symbol during the process of synthesis, is furnished by the episodes which involve the vital stranger, first in the cemetery, second in the gondola, and third on the hotel porch.

To connote the life-death antithesis in the episode of the cemetery, three pairs of symbols are used: the stranger versus the funeral hall, Aschenbach's jungle fancies versus his necroscopic reveries, his desire versus his fear. These fall roughly into the three realms of physical things, of ideas, and of emotions.

In the gondola episode, the same three realms are preserved, each with two symbols: in the world of things the gondola opposes the stranger; ideally, Aschenbach's attention is divided between the gondola's luxurious comfort and the illicit aspect of the stranger; and feelings of fear still mingle with his desire.

Some interesting things follow from this rather dull arithmetic. In the first episode, the symbols were for the most part unambiguous: the stranger meant life and life only; the cemetery, death and death only. Further, they were mutually exclusive in their functions: the stranger supplanted the cemetery as a focus of attention, the jungle images disposed entirely of thoughts of the grave. Finally, the causal progression between Aschenbach's physical impressions and his emotional reactions seemed also to be without ambiguity: the stranger was solely responsible for his jungle fancies and these fancies alone aroused his desire, just as the funeral hall alone inspired his morbid reveries and these, presumably, his fear. But let it be noted that even in this first episode, fear and desire held the emotional stage together! Ambiguity had already begun.

In the gondola episode the situation is very different. Synthetic activity is well under way, and the ambiguity which marked the emotional realm in the first instance extends here to the other two realms. The stranger still seems to be the physical symbol of life and the gondola of death, but in the realm of Aschenbach's ideas the whole thing is confused; the vital stranger looks "illicit" and "perverse" to him, capable, indeed, of those very "criminal adventures in the rippling night" which were originally brought to mind by the death-symbol, the gondola. And the gondola, "coffin-like barque" though it be, is by this time, in Aschenbach's dream fancy, naught but the "most luxurious seat in the world." Thus his desire—that "poisonous but delectable inertia"—issues from the death-symbol, "from the seat of the gondola itself," while his fear is of the vital stranger!

The merging of the life and death symbols, initiated in the emotional realm during the scene in the cemetery, now absorbs the symbols in the realm of Aschenbach's ideas, and, because one is never sure which of his ideas is caused by the gondola and which by its conductor, even the symbols of the physical realm begin to be drawn in.

It remains for the third episode to complete the synthesis. Here the same three realms are preserved: the stranger goes through his physical antics on the hotel porch: Aschenbach indulges in some new reflections about the jungle, and his dream is an orgy of emotion. But in each realm there is now only one symbol, no longer two: the fuzzy boundaries distinguishing life from death have disappeared entirely and these antitheses have become functions of single symbols: decay is seen in the vital stranger himself; the lush jungle is known as the source of the plague; the fertility-dance is felt as a carousal of death. Even the causal chain which, in the other episodes, connected the three realms, is missing here; indeed, the three realms are quite separate in time. The stranger, with no necroscopical setting now but smelling of death itself, makes his final awful bow, and departs from the story. *The next day,* in no connection with the stranger, Aschenbach learns from someone at the tourist office that the plague was hatched in the jungle and thinks his morbid thoughts. The anguish of fear and desire, which he experiences in his dream many hours later, constitutes still a separate event.

What has happened to the symbols in these transmutations? In the episode of the cemetery, and even in that of the gondola, each symbol in each realm contributed its own small part to the construction of the total life-death meaning. In the last episode, however, the entire connotation is contained in each symbol, and the others are not needed to complete it. The symbols have lost their discursive character and taken on, each for itself, a sort of synoptic one; so their function in the climax is not, as in the other instances, to build up to the meaning in three separate times. The intensifying effect of such synoptic repetition needs no comment.

The same general principles govern the resolution of the fraud and the hero-type symbols, though these, of course, are more inclusive in their synthetic function, embracing Aschenbach and Tadzio as well as the stranger. A single, total meaning is slowly built up out of separate elements—the vital stranger, Aschenbach, the hero-type, the old cheat, and Tadzio, each contributing his small share. The meaning is summarized first in the climax by the stranger alone; then it is given again in its entirety by Aschenbach in the episode of the cosmetics; finally it is repeated a third time, in still a different way, by Tadzio on the sand bar.

The most interesting product of the complicated structural relations which this analysis has brought to light is, to me at least, the poetic simplicity of mood which distinguishes one's response to *Death in Venice.* The type of control which makes it possible has been rejected by most contemporary poets, probably under the influence of the tradition of *symbolisme.* Two points are usually raised against it: first, that the rational or logical element in it tends to falsify poetry's true object—indeterminate, fluctuating, concrete reality as presented to immediate experience; and, secondly, that it leaves no room for that exquisite quality of response which, under the name *sens du mystère,* is often identified with what Poe referred to as the "vague and therefore spiritual effect" of "suggestive indefiniteness." How Mann provides for what Poe was talking about we have already remarked. His control operates entirely below the reader's conscious attention; meanings are never forced, they are intimated and suggested rather than stated, and the reader is allowed the illusion, at least, of a good deal of imaginative freedom.

But the feeling of mystery which characterizes authentic poetic response is not, I believe, merely this feeling of freedom of reference. The problem is less simple; it is probably not a technical one at all. Poor poets fail to conjure up mystery even with methodical mystification, yet it often flourishes in classical poetry in the full light of logical reference from symbol to meaning. I suspect that *mystère* is to be sought rather in the aspect of experience comprehended in a poem than in the form of its elaboration. At this level there is essential, not artificial, mystery, deriving, perhaps, from the nature of experience itself. Both the nuance of private feeling, the "immediate experience" of the *symbolistes,* and Mann's "infinity" where, "in a matter of eternal contraries," harmony lies—both of these are, in the last analysis, quite un-understandable, and hence, unsusceptible of totally adequate communication. At the level of *mystère,* the mediated experience is no less valid a poetic object than the immediate one.

These, however, are properly questions for aesthetics rather than for literary criticism. Here I have been concerned less with the latent content of poetry, with its mystery, than with that other quality which is often forgotten today but which Mann has so richly remembered—the quality of lucidness, of intelligibility, by whose virtue the incommunicable *seems,* at least, to be communicated.

ERICH HELLER

Conversation on The Magic Mountain

I have decided to break the monotony of a monologue which has all the time, and no doubt noticeably, been a disguised conversation—a conversation with myself, with fellow critics, and not least with Thomas Mann. In a letter written exactly one year before his death he said that "Thou com'st in such a questionable shape" had been "only too familiar to me as a manner of addressing myself." It seems appropriate, then, that questions should be asked.

Q: And music. There is the celebrated chapter about Hans Castorp's favorite gramophone records. Are they not all, although only one piece is German, about our great romantic fascinations, above all about death?

A: Yes, romantically played, as if by arrangement with Friedrich Schlegel, on a most advanced electro-technical contraption. The chapter is yet another instance of the extraordinary organization of the novel. Again, it seems to retell the whole story, this time in the guise of meditations on pieces by Verdi, Bizet, Debussy, Gounod, and Schubert.

Q: A strange assortment. The selection not of a musician—

A: —but of a novelist who calls Hans Castorp's great love by the abiding name of Hippe.

Q: Abiding? The love story Thomas Mann tells is about Hans and Clavdia. Hippe is merely a memory. But what's in the name?

A: Death. Pribislav Hippe. Pribislav is a Polish name—like Tadzio in *Death*

From *Thomas Mann: The Ironic German.* © 1958 by Erich Heller. Regency/Gateway, Inc., 1979.

in Venice; and Hippe is the German for scythe, an instrument which belongs to the medieval image of Death. Clavdia Chauchat, to whom Hans Castorp finally "returns the pencil," which in a first boyish feat of passionate daring he borrowed from the admired schoolmate, is Pribislav Hippe's feminine incarnation. She has his "Kirghiz" eyes and husky voice, and her profound identity with him is sealed by Hans Castorp's blood.

Q: Blood? I can remember no such drama.

A: Can't you? Hans Castorp has been a visitor in the sanatorium for only a few days. One morning he ventures on a first lonely walk into the mountains. As he is lying on a bench by a stream, trying to stop an ominous bleeding at the nose (soon he will be a patient himself), his mind is suddenly invaded by the schoolyard scene with Hippe. The memory of it has the articulate presence of a vision. And only after this experience does Hans Castorp know that he is in love with Clavdia Chauchat. But what is more: it *remains* the same love. The sex does not matter. Think of Hans Castorp's sleepy thoughts when, in extreme danger of falling asleep in the snow, he meditates, without any apparent motivation, upon pencils and genders in French: "*Son crayon!* That means her pencil, not his pencil, in this case; you only say *son* because *crayon* is masculine. The rest is just a silly play on words."

Q: Do you mean to suggest that Hippe is to Clavdia as Proust's Albert is to Marcel's Albertine?

A: There is not need for suggestion. I merely mean what Thomas Mann not only meant but made abundantly clear: that Clavdia is to the young Hans Castorp what Hippe was to the boy Hans Castorp. In neither case is it a passion from which marriages are made. On the contrary, it is the "unreasonable love" which Hans himself, in a conversation with Clavdia, equates with death and calls by the names of *res bina* and *lapis philosophorum,* names he has learned from Naphta, who, however, added to them "the double-sexed *prima materia.*" And of Hans's passion for Clavdia Thomas Mann says that it was "a risky and homeless variety of the lovesick folly, mingled frost and fire, like a dangerous fever, or the October air in these altitudes. What it lacked was those emotions which could have bridged the two extremes."

Q: Which two extremes?

A: The two extremes between which romantic love enacts its comedies and tragedies: a definable desire and an indefinably tenuous hope.

Q: That she will yield?

A: That life will yield.

Q: Oh, I remember: yield a meaning rather than a hollow silence. The kind of thing the Flying Dutchman expects of Senta when he sings of the "sinister glow" of which he is not sure whether it is love. No, no, he sings, "it is the longing for salvation." If only he could have it "through such an angel." I daresay you are right, and the sex of the angel makes little difference if it is salvation one wants by it, not children.

A: That is why I said the name of Hans Castorp's abiding love was Hippe. Death. Life is always in danger of obliteration when those two extremes touch each other and the yearning for salvation becomes fused with the desire of the senses. Listen: "The term he had set for his holiday had long since passed. He no longer cared. The thought of returning home did not even occur to him." Why can't he ask her to return with him? Because of external obstacles? These are merely the feeble external symptoms of the inward state of affairs: Hans Castorp does not want a wife; he wants the adventure in permanence, he wants ecstasy as the daily level of living, he wants the bliss which transcends life and lasts forever. It is the romantic variation on death and salvation. Hence he does not even wish to know Clavdia—except biblically. He seeks to preserve that yearning of which Thomas Mann says that it is "the product of defective knowledge," and the exciting tension which exists "between two beings who know each other only with their eyes," and "the hysteria of suppressed communications and undeliverable messages." You remember these passages?

Q: I do.

A: You are quite wrong. Forgive the didactic trick. They do not come from *The Magic Mountain*. Of course, they might; but they come from *Death in Venice*. Tadzio or Clavdia—the nature of the passion is the same. You remember how it ends: after Hans Castorp's long and patient waiting—for on the morning following the night of the *mardi gras* Clavdia departed—she comes back to the mountain in the company of Mynheer Peeperkorn.

Q: Senta with the Flying Dutchman.

A: I doubt it. He needs no angel of salvation. She is his mistress, woman to a man. And Hans Castorp's passion all but dissolves. Only now has he outgrown the Hippe love the other name of which is Death. To the slight annoyance of Clavdia he makes friends with Peeperkorn, the big, inarticulate, tottering mystery.

Q: Yet another representative. He represents Life.

A: Without the slightest detriment to his own. Representative or not, admit that as a literary creation he is a surpassing success. Admit—grudgingly,

if you like, but admit—that your outburst of a while ago did grave
injustice to Thomas Mann on at least one point: you implied that he
divests his creatures of their individual existence for the sake of their
typicality. It is untrue. Thomas Mann time and again succeeds in achieving the apparently impossible—namely, in squaring Schlegel's literary
circle and giving life to seemingly preconceived ideas as if they were
naturally conceived children of the imagination; which is only another
way of saying that you are wrong in thinking of his ideas as literally
"preconceived." They belong to an imaginative order, not an excogi-
tated scheme. Think of Thomas Buddenbrook, or Tony, or Christian!
Think of Mynheer Peeperkorn!

Q: Who is a representative of Life.

A: If so, then not without irony. True, he is Dionysus, almost as painted by
Reubens, and a colonial Dutch coffee-planter, as unforgettably described
by Thomas Mann. But his model is not Life but Art: a poet—Gerhart
Hauptmann. Also, he kills himself.

Q: Yes, he kills himself. I remember an extraordinary weapon.

A: Specially constructed for suicide. It is a mechanical imitation of the fangs
of a poisonous tropical snake, the engineered semblance of a demon
from such a jungle as Gustav Aschenbach saw in his Dionysian nightmare.

Q: An engineered demon—your Friedrich Schlegel would have loved it. But
before you draw your representative conclusions from the fact that Life
kills itself with a most intelligently and scientifically constructed monster, don't forget that Naphta, unmistakably representative of Mind,
also commits suicide—in an act of sheer supererogation. He had never
been alive.

A: And is, like Settembrini, dwarfed by the advent of Peeperkorn. They cease
to exist in his presence.

Q: Mind dwarfed by Life.

A: Whereas Peeperkorn, in his Dionysian inarticulateness, cuts an excellent
figure in the company of his true peers, the mighty mountain cataract
and the eagle in the sky. He acknowledges, almost applauds, their great
performances like someone who intimately knows what an achievement
it is to be a good mountain cataract or a good eagle—a force of nature.
Not to be one is to him the deepest humiliation. This is why he must
kill himself at the approach of impotence. He fears that the tropical
fever from which he suffers will destroy, or has already destroyed his
power of answering, as he calls it, the demands of feeling.

Q: Life without Mind.

A: Your prompting is better than your intention. Life without Mind. Then you also know why Naphta never comes to life: Mind without Life. Peeperkorn's and Naphta's suicides may be Thomas Mann's way of killing his oldest pair of irreconcilable opposites. Neither Life nor Mind can exist the one without the other. "It is impossible to separate Nature from Mind without destroying both Life and Art." Goethe knew that. Thomas Mann comes to know it again after much "*Weltentzweiung*," much "sowing of categorical discord," as Hans Castorp calls the intellectual activities of Naphta and Settembrini—or perhaps of the author of *Meditations of a Nonpolitical Man*.

Q: So it is for the sake of overcoming a "categorical discord" that Dionysus has to be made sick and Priapus impotent? Irony with a vengeance. *Placet experiri.* Yes, it pleases Thomas Mann to experiment. With what? With all the aspects of—did you say, truth? Or did you say that all the aspects together constitute the "hollow silence" of the age? You did speak of "that lucidly handled chaos" of *The Magic Mountain*, where "hardly anything remains itself," and spoke of it with a puzzling undertone of romantic hope.

A: Which reminds me of Novalis's saying that "true anarchy will beget religion, and religion will rise from the chaos of destructions as the glorious founder of a new world." You are wrong in suspecting that I find it easy to share such cataclysmic hopes.

Q: But you do seem to see something positive in that chaos where everything is not itself but something else. Laziness is learning. Living is dying. Love is disease. Music is death. Clavdia is Pribislav. No amount of debate will clarify matters so hopelessly tangled.

A: No amount of debate. As Hans Castorp watches Settembrini's and Naphta's dialectical battles, this is how Thomas Mann describes his feelings: "The principles and points of view constantly trespassed upon one another's domains, there was no end of inner contradictions; and as it became more and more difficult for Hans Castorp's civilian sense of responsibility to make a choice between opposed positions, or even to keep them neatly apart in his mind, so the temptation grew to plunge headforemost into Naphta's 'morally untidy universe.'"—Even in your most biased mood you must at least concede that Thomas Mann is far from being an uncritical supporter of this state of affairs. The passage continues: "It was the universal topsy-turvydom, the world at cross-purposes with itself, the great confusion, which, more than the 'wrongheadedness' of the partner, oppressed the soul of each disputant. And Hans Castorp sensed that this was the true cause of their exasperation." These are not the words of a champion of chaos.

Q: The true cause of my exasperation is the virtuoso literary manner with which Thomas Mann self-consciously creates a "significant" work of art out of the apparently desperate uncertainty concerning the significance of anything. I understand that it is the vaguely sensed meaninglessness of his life which, in the novel, sends Hans Castorp to the Magic Mountain and keeps him there for seven years. This meaninglessness colors every one of his experiences, even his love. But where everything is colored by meaninglessness, of what can anything be truly significant? If I let you go on, you will say in a minute what every single interpreter of *The Magic Mountain* has said: that, among other things, it is a "symbolic novel." And as the book—how did Friedrich Schlegel put it?—"judges itself," *The Magic Mountain* probably says so itself.

A: It does. You may be thinking of Naphta's description of the initiation rites to which a novice is subjected if he wishes fully to enter the community of Freemasons. "Magic pedagogy," "alchemist levitation," "transsubstantiation," "hermetics," and finally the tomb, "the place of corruption" which is also "the receptacle wherein the material is prepared for its final transformation and purification"—these are the terms Naphta uses when he tells Hans Castorp of the mysteries of the mystery religion. It is clear, I think, that they stand at the same time for the education young Castorp receives as the hero of the *Bildungsroman*. And then again: "The way of the mysteries and of the purification . . . leads through the fear of death and the sphere of corruption; and the apprentice, the neophyte, is the spirit of youth in person, guided by shrouded figures who are nothing but the shadows of the mystery." All this, I am sure, is meant to reflect upon the novel itself.

Q: And the most shadowy of the shadows is no doubt Herr Naphta himself, the Nietzschean Jesuit and full-time mouthpiece. Yet I expect that what is meant is the whole shrouded party of Hans Castorp's educators: Settembrini, Behrens, Madame Chauchat, Mynheer Peeperkorn. If these are the shadows of the mystery, pray you, what precisely is the mystery?

A: You don't mean "precisely," do you? Anything may be precise except a mystery. May I remind you of Thomas Mann's very Goethean definition of "symbolic significance"? The occasion is Hans Castorp's growing enchantment with Schubert's song of the linden-tree, and his ever clearer realization of its "meaning." The song acquires great significance for him, and Thomas Mann asks: "In what does the significance of a significant subject lie? In the fact that it points beyond itself, that it is the expression and representation of something general, something universal, of a whole world of thought and feeling. . . ." There is only one "precise" way of describing a mystery, or suggesting a "whole world of thought and feeling": to find their concrete symbols. The passages I have just read out to you are, I think, disguised declarations by the novelist concerning the intention of his novel. Yes, he meant to write a symbolic novel.

Q: You see! I am asking you how anybody can arrive at anything significant in a meaningless world, and you answer: by writing a symbolic novel. Symbolic of what?

A: And what if I said: symbolic of the difficulty of writing a novel, significant of the vital irony of an artist who produces works of art against, and almost from, the ubiquitous suggestion that it is meaningless to produce works of art?

Q: It would not be an answer. It would be a joke.

A: You were polite enough not to laugh when a little while ago I spoke of the *ne plus ultra* of irony in Thomas Mann's literary art from *The Magic Mountain* onward. I really meant the same thing. However, it would be a joke if I meant anything less than a work of art. As I mean a work of art, it is serious. For a work of art is the vindication of meaning.

Q: Even if it is symbolic of meaninglessness?

A: If it is a work of art, it will be in some sense symbolic. If it is symbolic, it can only be symbolic of meaning—although it may say: "The world is meaningless."

Q: We are ourselves approaching the grand confusion, the *quazzabuglio* of Messrs. Naphta and Settembrini. I shall soon be as speechless as young Castorp is on those occasions.

A: And you will *tell* me that you are. "I am speechless," your speech will say. And it will not be unlike a work of art saying: "Everything is meaningless. If it were quite true, it could not be said—not be a work of art. The worst is not, so long as we can say, "This is the worst." There is reason for rejoicing as long as tragedies can be written. The preserved form of a piece of literature gives the marginal lie to the expressed conviction that everything is in a state of dissolution. It is an exceedingly ironical situation—a situation which has found in *The Magic Mountain* its appropriately ironical literary shape. Never before has the falling apart of all things been treated with so intensely conscious an artistic determination to hold them together.

Q: By the arrangement of words on a page?

A: Yes. And therefore as facts of the mind. And therefore as a human reality. If this were not the case, literature would not be worth the paper it is written on. The story of *The Magic Mountain* is, as it were, told twice: once as a series of incidents and experiences, and then again as a series of imitations conveyed through the very shape of the work. The arrangement between the two is not smoothly harmonious, but ironical and contrapuntal, like the two parts, the one Apolline, the other Dionysian, of a dream Hans Castorp has in the snow, the "dream poem of humanity" he composes on the verge of death, which teaches him the true state and status of *Homo Dei,* the lord of all contradictions, "between mystic community and windy individualism." It would be a bad and unconvincing dream had it to rely for its authenticity only on the story told. Its proof is in the telling.

Q: You mean in the form, not in the content? I understand. The form, you mean, tells a story of its own, a story which stands in a contrapuntal relationship to the series of incidents?

A: Yes; and as a *Bildungsroman* it stands in the same ironical relationship to the rules of the genre. Wilhelm Meister, the model hero of such a novel, begins as an *Originalgenie* and ends as a useful member of society. Hans Castorp begins as a useful member of society and ends approaching the state of being an *Originalgenie.*

Q: Yet he eventually leaves the Magic Mountain to do his duty by his country.

A: Which happens to be about to destroy itself in war; and most probably will destroy its citizen Castorp. We catch a last glimpse of him amid the shrapnel of a battlefield in Flanders.

Q: And if he survives?

A: If you insist on playing this literary parlor game, my guess is that he would write a novel.

Q: I agree. With all that hermetic education in him, he cannot possibly go back to being a shipbuilding engineer in Hamburg. So he will be a writer and write a novel—most probably *The Magic Mountain.* The Eternal Recurrence—

A: —will not take place. For here we end our conversation.

Q: It is an unsatisfactory ending—a little *too* ironical. You appear to be saying two things. Firstly, that it is the aim of an education for life to produce writers of fiction; and secondly, that to acquire true identity means to lose one's identity. For you have previously told us that, according to Thomas Mann, the loss of identity is the professional hazard of literary men.

A: "Literature" and "nonidentity" are, in this case, the aesthetic incognito which a man, incapable of accepting a meaningless existence, chooses in a world which insists upon living as if life were meaningless. Kierkegaard meant something similar when he defined irony as the incognito of the moralist.

Q: Why has Kierkegaard's moralist got to use an incognito?

A: "Because he knows that his manner of existing inwardly cannot be expressed in terms of the world." Such is our world that sense and meaning have to be disguised—as irony, or as literature, or as both come together: for instance in *The Magic Mountain*.

GEORGE C. SCHOOLFIELD

Thomas Mann's The Black Swan

In 1953, Thomas Mann published *Die Betrogene* [*The Black Swan*], in which a fifty-year-old Rhenish widow feels an erotic attraction to her young son's American tutor, suffers the pangs of unrequited love (and the embarrassed glances of her children), confesses her passion to the American, and arranges a rendezvous with him, which she never keeps; instead, a hemorrhage forces her to enter the hospital, where the physicians, in the course of their exploratory operation, find her uterus consumed by cancer. One fears that the literary fortunes of the middle-aged woman may have begun to sink again. [The woman whose appetites were at variance with her age and, presumably, her charms, was a figure of obscene fun—and worse—for the tellers of medieval legend.] While Mann does not indulge in classical abuse of his Rosalie von Tümmler, he does bring her to a nasty end. There is a trace of the callous obscenity of the past in the pranks which Mann has nature play upon her trusting worshipper; Rosalie is "deceived" because she believes that the bleeding which heralds her fatal illness is really the return of menstruation—that nature, heeding her wish for rejuvenation, has once more called her womanhood to life. . . .

Thomas Mann's Ken Keaton is still another of those terrifying innocents abroad [the clean-cut young American who, without evil intent, wrecks the

From *The Germanic Review* 30, no. 1 (January 1963). © 1963 by Columbia University Press. Originally entitled "Thomas Mann's *Die Betrogene*."

delicate balance of an older and subtler culture]. Apart from Imma Spoel-
mann in *Königliche Hoheit* [*Royal Highness*] (whose presence—in accordance with an earlier European literary tradition of the rich savior from
America—is anything but ruinous for Klaus Heinrich's grand duchy) and
Wendell Kretzschmar in *Doktor Faustus* (less a living being than a mouthpiece of musical theories), Ken Keaton is Mann's only extended portrait of
an American—indeed, he is the author's only "Stockamerikaner [typical
American]." (Mann's pureblooded American men of science, Dr. Water-
cloose in *Königliche Hoheit* and Adrian Leverkühn's imaginary Mr. Capercailzie, are the hastiest of caricatures.) Mann's treatment of Ken Keaton is
not unfriendly; but it does contain some elements of that European condescension against which the author inveighed in "Comprendre." One source
of Keaton, with his good-looking guilelessness, may have been the Princeton
"boys" to whom Mann lectured on *Faust*; another model was probably a
chance acquaintance who made a deep impression on the ill and aging author.
While Mann was a patient at Chicago's Billings Hospital in the spring of
1946, his attention was caught by a twenty-four-year-old intern, Dr. Carlson.
In his handsome healthiness and his narrowness of interests, Carlson must
have seemed the apotheosis of American youth:

> Der hübsche Carlson . . . war von der High School, deren Bil-
> dungsziele nichts Überspanntes haben, ohne Collegebesuch so-
> gleich auf die Medical School gekommen . . . und wußte
> offenkundig in aller Welt von nichts etwas als von der Chirurgie,
> für die er ebenso offenkundig geboren und in der er glücklich
> war. Noch sehe ich ihn in Gummihemd und Schürze eine Schub-
> bahre auf Gummirädern mit einer lakenverhüllten Gestalt darauf
> in jungenhaftem Trab durch die Korridore . . . vor sich her trei-
> ben,—ein vergnügt einseitiges, gut anzuschauendes und tüchtiges
> Stück Leben.
>
> (*Die Entstehung des Doktor Faustus*)

[Good-looking young Carlson . . . had moved from high school—
the cultural aims of American high schools are not particularly
ambitious—directly to medical school without attending college.
. . . Obviously, he knew nothing about anything except surgery,
for which he had just as obviously been born and in which he
was happy. I still see him in his rubber apron, pushing a stretcher
on rubber wheels, with a sheet-swathed figure on it, at a youthful

trot down the halls. . . .—a cheerfully one-sided, capable, and simple soul, good to look at.

(*The Story of a Novel: The Genesis of Dr. Faustus*, trans. Richard and Clara Winston. New York: Knopf, 1961)]

Ken Keaton is happily one-sided; his best subjects in college were "history and athletics." He is pleasant to look at: his arms (like those of Clawdia Chauchat, Felix Krull, Zaza, and Zouzou) are particularly attractive, and his T-shirt (compare Carlson's rubber shirt) calls attention to them. He is able: in his relaxed way, he is a splendid tutor in American English for Eduard, Rosalie von Tümmler's son. Yet he is poorly trained; like Carlson's high school, the "college in Detroit, Michigan" through which Ken has worked his way does not appear to have had the highest "Bildungsziele [cultural aims]." (Luckily for Mann and other patients, Carlson *had* enjoyed a superior medical training.) In the tale, of course, Mann adds a good many details to the outline provided by Carlson. Keaton's most winning quality is perhaps that he is "childlike," a virtue which, although Carlson doubtless possessed it, was not expressly mentioned in his case. Ken's pronunciation exercises for Eduard are delightfully naive (and tell a good deal about the American's non-pedagogical interests and ideals): "'Scrr-ew the top on!' sagte er [he said]. 'I sllept like a top.' 'Alfred is a tennis play-err. His shoulders are thirty inches brr-oaoadd'" [*The Black Swan*, trans. Willard R. Trask. New York: Knopf, 1954. Further references are from this translation]. His German conversation charms the Düsseldorfers with its "kindlichen Wendungen [childlike turns of phrase]," his American way of eating—cutting up his meat and then putting his knife hors-de-combat while he takes his fork in his right hand—fascinates Teutonic eyes. (Professor Kuckuck in *Felix Krull* says of the same American eating habit: "'Hat etwas Kindliches, nicht wahr?' ['There's something childlike about it, isn't there?']" Ken has been wounded in the war; as Rosalie pathetically says: "'[Er] hat . . . eine seiner Nieren auf dem Altar des Vaterlandes geopfert' ['He sacrificed one of his kidneys on the altar of his fatherland']." Even this wound has made him no more mature; for some reason or other, Mann associated the loss of a kidney with the figure of the boyish seducer, and Rudi Schwerdtfeger, an earlier German version of Ken Keaton in *Doktor Faustus*, has likewise undergone an operation, "die ihn eine seiner Nieren gekostet hatte [which had cost him one of his kidneys]." In the scenes at Holterhof, near the end of *Die Betrogene*, the high-spirited American is placed in contrast to the one-armed veteran who serves as a guide at the rococo palace. The guide, wooden in manner and soured on life, is infinitely less attractive than Ken; yet he has a rough maturity which our American hero neither possesses nor wants to possess. In doing the most menial tasks "to work his way through college," Ken has worn gloves to protect his "weißen . . . herrschaftlichen Hände [white, . . . aristocratic hands]."

In "Aus einem Brief über 'Die Betrogene' an Thomas Mann" ["From a Letter to Thomas Mann about *The Black Swan*"], Theodor Adorno has acutely observed that there is something picture-askew about Ken Keaton's place in time: "Die Figur des Ken trägt, wenn ich mich nicht irre, alle Zeichen eines Amerikaners aus dem späten vierziger oder aus den fünfziger Jahren und nicht aus dem Dezennium nach dem *ersten* Weltkrieg [The figure of Ken bears, if I am not mistaken, all the signs of an American of the late forties or fifties and not the decade after the First World War]." One can discover plenty of evidence to support Adorno's observation. Ken's father, demonstrating the lability of American social conditions, had been active in various lines of work, "einmal als broker, einmal als Leiter einer Tankstelle, und im realestate business hatte er zeitweise auch etwas Geld gemacht [broker, manager of a gas-station—from time to time, too, he had made some money in the real-estate business]." The restlessness of the American in his occupational life is perennial, of course; but the sequence of jobs held by Keaton senior smacks more of the late twenties or the thirties than of the age of the automobile's infancy. Ken's eternal T-shirt, which exposes his arms so effectively, is an article of dress popular among ex-G.I.'s, not among ex-doughboys; his freedom of manner—his calling Rosalie by her first name, "nach seinen heimischen Begriffen nicht einmal eine besondere Kühnheit [in his American view, not even a particular liberty]," and his extremely casual dress—seems an unlikely phenomenon in an American reared in "a small Eastern city" during the years before 1917. Finally, for his wound, received in the late fighting at Compiègne, Ken has been given "das Purple Heart," a medal he could not have possessed at the time of the story's action; the Purple Heart was created by George Washington in 1782 as a decoration for bravery, but only three were actually awarded. The new Purple Heart, bestowed on those wounded or killed in the service of the United States, was established on the bicentennial of Washington's birth, in 1932; it was widely given only during the Second World War and after. Ken does not belong to the American generation whose members had a brief taste of occupation duty at Koblenz; instead, he is an occupier, a most charming one, of Germany after 1945.

Adorno surmises that Mann placed the story in the twenties on Rosalie's account, because "eine Existenz wie die der Frau von Tümmler heute wohl nicht vorgestellt werden könnte [an existence such as that of Frau von

Tümmler could hardly be depicted today]," and because Mann wished to put recent happenings at a distance, "gerade das Nächste zu distanzieren, in Vorwelt zu verzaubern, jene Vorwelt, mit deren besonderen Patina auch der Krull es zu tun hat [to put the near at a distance, transformed into an earlier world, the same, with its special patina, as that which Krull inhabited]." Elaborating upon Adorno's conjectures, one might say the following: Rosalie has been placed in the past to make her all the more charming, to make her connection with—and her representation of—an older and better Germany, with "das Volk der Dichter und Denker [the people of poets and thinkers]," all the clearer, all the more direct. Conversely, Ken has been "borrowed" from the present (i.e. the years after 1945)—and traces of the loan have not been very carefully covered—because he is a contemporary threat to Europe, to the place which, as Thomas Mann says in "Comprendre," was once "Herz und Hirn der Welt [heart and mind of the world]." At the same time, Ken, like the Americans whom Mann castigates in "Comprendre," deeply respectful of the European past and frivolously indifferent to its future, is made by Mann to attack the younger culture which has borne him: "'He didn't care for America,' er machte sich nichts daraus, ja fand es mit seiner Dollarjagd und Kirchengängerei, seiner Erfolgsbigotterie und kolossalen Durchschnittlichkeit, vor allem aber mit seinem Mangel an historischer Atmosphäre, eigentlich greulich [He 'didn't care for America'; indeed, with its pursuit of the dollar and insensate church-going, its worship of success and its colossal mediocrity, but, above all, its lack of historical atmosphere, he found it really appalling]." It is, in a sense, Ken's passion for the historical that awakens his interest in Rosalie; she of course has not been able to conceal her own *faible* for him. Ken is in Europe looking for the old, the richly textured, the "un-American"; significantly, he has no affairs in Germany with girls of his own age or younger, but only with older women. "Deutschland! Das war sein Lieblingsland [Germany! That was the country he loved]." Ken loves the mellow culture that he is going to kill.

Rosalie von Tümmler is as much a type, in her own way, as Ken is in his. She comes from the Rhineland, the home of the full-blown Romanticism of Brentano's lyrics and Schumann's Third Symphony, the home of German liberalism, of Schurz and the Kinkels, of that Rhenish "Lebensfreude [joy of living]" which Mann found so attractive: Felix Krull, like Rosalie von Tümmler, regards the world as "eine große und unendlich verlockende Erscheinung . . . , welche die süßesten Seligkeiten zu vergeben hat [a great and infinitely enticing phenomenon, offering priceless satisfactions]" (*Bekenntnisse des Hochstaplers Felix Krull [Confessions of Felix Krull: Confidence Man,* trans. Denver Lindley. New York: Knopf, 1955]). In his enthusiasm

for the Rhine, the German patriot Mann attempts, as it were, to make up
for his portrait of Kaisersaschern, the fearfully gloomy Central German town
where Adrian Leverkühn was born. Resident in industrial Duisburg during
the twenty years of her marriage, Rosalie—living up to the vitality of her
married name (tümen, "sich drehen [to rotate oneself]")—has moved to
Düsseldorf upon her husband's death in an automobile accident at the beginning of the war. Immermann, recently arrived in Düsseldorf, wrote "Die
Rheinlande sind das heitere Blut, die Phantasie, der fröhliche Sinn Preußens
[The Rhineland is the bright blood, inventive imagination, and merry character of Prussia]," and these qualities no doubt helped Frau von Tümmler
decide on her move. The specific reasons given for the choice of a new home
are the city's splendid parks (Rosalie is a great nature-lover) and the opportunities the Kunstakademie [academy of arts] would afford Anna, Rosalie's
artist daughter; but the whole ambiance of Düsseldorf was of a kind to appeal
to, and to foster, Rosalie's smiling and liberal Romanticism. In literature,
Düsseldorf was the home of Heine and Das Buch Le Grand, and the scene
of Freiligrath's trial (and acquittal) for having written the "revolutionary"
poem, "Die Toten an die Lebenden" ["The Dead to the Living"]; in the
theater, it had sheltered the great innovators, Immermann and Grabbe; in
music, it had provided a temporary and happy home for Mendelssohn and—
despite whatever hopes the composer may have had concerning the salutary
Rhenish mood—a mortally dangerous post for Schumann; Cornelius and
Schadow gave it paintings, the former's of the Christian-Romantic persua-
sion, the latter's illuminated by a heartier moonshine. One cannot know
whether Rosalie is aware that she lives against such a suitable background;
but one can ascertain that she is familiar, in literature, with a forefather of
German liberalism and of German Romanticism, in particular with those of
his plays most closely associated with the Rhineland, with the Mannheim
theater. The bits of Schiller with which she shines belong to works from the
master's Rhenish days, to Kabale und Liebe and Hofmarschall von Kalb
(coming across a peculiar odor in the forest, Rosalie remembers the notorious
"Bisamgeruch [odor of music]" the courtier spreads, and to Fiesco (refusing
to dismiss Ken, Rosalie quotes the second half of "Der Mohr hat seine Arbeit
getan, der Mohr kann gehen [The Moor has done his work, the Moor can
go]").

However, Rosalie is more than a happy matron who fits nicely into
Düsseldorf's atmosphere, has a charmingly ruddy nose, and uses, to her
daughter's horror, a Ripuarian dialect (a habit she shares with another German friend of America, Konrad Adenauer). In his "Phantasie über Goethe,"
Thomas Mann quotes Goethe's remark that "'man muß von Natur richtig

sein, so daß die guten Einfälle immer wie freie Kinder Gottes vor uns da-
stehen und uns zurufen: Da sind wir!' [one must be good by nature, so that
good ideas stand before us always and like free children of God call out to
us, 'Here we are!'] To these words of Goethe, Mann subjoins the observation:
"An [der Natur] hängt er, sie glaubt er, ihr dankt er [To (nature) he clings,
he trusts in her, he is thankful to her]." The same may be said of Rosalie;
for she is a woman who, prevented for a while from following her heart's
urge toward Ken, never distrusts that heart's dictates, any more than she
would distrust nature's other signals. "'Mir geht das Herz über alles' ['To
me the heart is supreme']" is the climactic phrase of her long dispute with
her daughter Anna as to the correctness of her passion. And it should not
be assumed that Rosalie, at the sight of Ken's handsome arms, has redis-
covered a heart long forgotten. Her passion for the young man does not have
the perverse quality of that of Madame Houpflé for Felix Krull, or of Tennessee Williams's Mrs. Stone for her Italian lover. These ladies, fashioning
their existences in the "Hotel Saint James and Albany" or in American Express offices, need their admirers in order to find some content for otherwise
empty lives; Rosalie's love for Ken is simply an extension, or an intensification, of a fullness she has known from the beginning. She has always lived
by her heart's wisdom, following its commands in such matters as the care
of her children, her choice of a home, and her love of roses, so that, meeting
Ken, she has every right to do what her heart tells her.

This "ausgepichte Romantikerin [incorrigible romanticist]," as she calls
herself, is surrounded by several Germans of a distinctly less Romantic ilk:
her daughter Anna, her son Eduard, her friends the Rollwagens, and her
daughter's erstwhile suitor, Dr. Brünner. By means of these subsidiary figures—especially Anna—Mann is able to provide Rosalie's character with a
relief, and, at the same time, to indulge in a little *Zeitkritik* [criticism of the
times]. Anna is an artist; but, although she has come to the home of that
school of painting defined by Goethe as possessing "eine gewisse heitere
Sinnlichkeit [a certain cheerful sensuality]" and familiar to Americans as the
breeding ground of Emanuel Leutze's *Washington Crossing the Delaware,*
she has not chosen a style of graphic art which has anything to do with
nature. Anna's "sternly intellectual, abstractly symbolic art" does not at all
please her mother, who chose a dwelling for her little brood in, appropriately
enough, the Cornelius-Strasse; Rosalie begs her daughter to paint "'etwas
fürs Herz. . . . etwas Herzerquickendes' [something for the heart . . . something to refresh the heart']." As close a friendship as mother and daughter
are able to maintain, Rosalie is painfully (and sometimes a little patroniz-
ingly) aware that her elder child is out of harmony with nature. In her frank

way, she remarks upon the fact that Anna suffers violent pain during menstruation, whereas she, Rosalie, never did; and, while she does not say so, it
is plain enough that she thinks Anna's pains are somehow connected with
her "refusal" to admit the reality of nature and nature's ways. Yet Rosalie
is full of sympathy for her daughter; she knows that the nascent spinster has
had her detestation of nature forced upon her, and by nature itself. Anna
has a clubfoot. Such bodily affliction may bring wisdom (as it does in Fon-
tane's apothecary Gieshübler in *Effi Briest*), but it scares away love; and poor
Anna's heart has been broken, her mother knows, by the young chemist,
Dr. Brünner. When Anna, parodying Schiller's "Es ist der Geist, der sich den
Körper baut [It is the spirit that builds the body]," says: "'Es ist der Körper,
der sich die Seele schon bildet nach seinem Stande [For it is the body that
molds the soul, in accordance with its own condition],'" she speaks from
observation of herself: her soul has been permeated with cold mistrust because of her body's flaw. Rosalie, however, cannot agree with her, for in her
own case she has seen how the soul does not accompany the body into the
mild and dignified matron's estate; when, later on, she believes that her own
menstruation has begun again, she gives the soul credit for a victory over
the body: "'Die Seele [erweist] sich als Meisterin über den Körper [the soul
proving herself mistress over the body].'" Anna is impressed, she confesses,
by this miraculous work the enamored soul of her mother has evidently
wrought upon the flesh; but still she hesitates to give the soul—which she,
following her mother's usage, identifies with Rosalie's beloved "nature"—
the credit which Rosalie thinks is its due. In these conversations around the
Schillerian theme of "Geist [spirit]" and "Körper [body]," Mann's famous
irony is constantly at work: both partners use a vocabulary in which "Seele
[soul]," and "Körper [body]," is nature's ally; Rosalie, nature's trusting
child, argues for the power of the spirit; Anna, intellect's champion, must
fight for a cause she detests, the cumbersome flesh. The conversations are
ended only with the tale itself: nature kills her loving child, and
Dr. Muthesius, the attending physician, hints that the passion for Keaton,
this final heeding of nature's suggestion, may have started the process of
Rosalie's death: "'doch rate ich Ihnen, meine Vermutung zu übernehmen,
dass die Geschichte vom Eierstock ausging,—von unbenützten granulösen
Zellen nämlich, die seit der Geburt da manchmal ruhen und nach dem Ein-
setzen der Wechseljahre *durch Gott weiss welchen Reizvorgang* [italics added]
zu maligner Entwicklung kommen' ['Yet I advise you to adopt my opinion,
which is that the whole story started from the ovary—that is, from immature
ovarian cells which often remain there from birth and which, after the men-

opause, *through heaven knows what process of stimulation*, begin to develop malignantly']."

Anna opposes Rosalie's love of the natural on a level of noble debate; Eduard, the Rollwagens, and Dr. Brünner stand in semi-inarticulate opposition to Rosalie's naturalness. Eduard is the budding technician, whose chief ambition is to escape "dem langweiligen Humanismus [those boring humanities]" of the classical gymnasium for the technical academy, whence he hopes to go on to England, "oder auch gleich ins Eldorado der Technik, nach den Vereinigten Staaten [or perhaps straight to the El Dorado of technology, the United States]." One sees little of Eduard, but one can guess that he has not been pleased at his mother's decision to leave Duisburg's fascinating industries for the parks and academies of Düsseldorf. Eduard's relationship to his mother is, for all its appropriate affection, a flimsy one: nature simply does not exist for him; Anna, knowing it exists, rejects it. Nonetheless, Eduard, by virtue of his youthful enthusiasm, would seem to have more of the traditional "deutsche Innerlichkeit [German inwardness]" than do the Rollwagens or Dr. Brünner, whose portraits Mann sketches with a few master strokes. It is instructive to compare Mann's skill in depicting German men of industry with Hans Scholz's or Gerd Gaiser's efforts in the same direction; Scholz, in Dr. Gutzka of *Am grünen Strand der Spree* [*On the Green Shore of the Spree*], and Gaiser, in Herr Förckh of *Schlußball* [*The Final Ball*], need pages to accomplish what Mann can do with the briefest of inferences. Of the Rollwagens, "dem Maschinenrollwagen und seiner Frau [the machine factory Rollwagen and his wife]," one knows but that they give expensive parties and that Rollwagen makes bad punch by pouring "zweifelhaften Apfelsinenschabau [questionable orange cordial]" (a distinctly second-rate ingredient) and "deutschen Sekt [domestic champagne]" (probably second-rate, too, but intended to impress guests) into Mosel wine. (The Rollwagens, incidentally, have turned up in Thomas Mann before, in *Doktor Faustus,* where Ines Institutoris fears that one of the "rassige Töchter [racy daughters]" of the Rollwagen family will steal her lover, Rudi Schwerdtfeger, away.)

As for Dr. Brünner, who abandons poor Anna to marry well, he is the least attractive of the figures around Rosalie; for he is a "praktischer Streber [a practical and ambitious man]," a chemist, "nach dessen Sinn es gewesen war, die Wissenschaft möglichst bald zu Geld zu machen [considering it to be wise to turn science into money as soon as possible]." However, as unambiguous as Brünner may seem, he is a reflector designed by Mann to catch light from several sides. As a technician, he is far less appealing than young

Eduard, for he has no essential love of his work; likewise, he comes off worse than Rollwagen, who makes no bones about his financial passion. Brünner is an arch traitor to the idealistic and Romantic Germany of which Rosalie is a perhaps anachronistic representative; one cannot believe that, if Anna had been lucky enough to land Brünner, her mother would have been satisfied with her new son-in-law. As a matter of fact, Rosalie seems unmoved by the "bräunliche Mannespracht [swarthy, masculine handsomeness]" of Brünner, as unmoved by him as she is excited by Ken Keaton. The reason for her indifference is not difficult to find. Brünner, the "Gegenstand der Schwärmerei aller Mädchen und Frauen der Gesellschaft [(one who) aroused the enthusiasm of all the girls and matrons in Düsseldorf society]," even as Ken later would be, is false; he uses his good looks and his conversational talents to capture "eine reiche Fabrikantentochter aus Bochum [the wealthy daughter of a manufacturer . . . of Bochum]." Ken, however, is true; he acquires culture and collects admiring women not because he thinks they will bring him ultimate financial reward, but merely because he likes them.

It should not be forgotten that Ken Keaton, the American, offers Rosalie's Romanticism a complement she cannot find in her children or her friends; "namentlich seine große Natürlichkeit nahm sie für ihn ein [his great naturalness in particular prepossessed her in his favour]." Defending her passion before Anna, Rosalie returns again and again to Ken's simple naturalness, which is, despite the difference in real and cultural age, so much like her own. Using words that offer a typically indissoluble Mannian mixture of irony and seriousness, she tells Anna: "'Immer spielst du auf seine Durchschnittlichkeit an, und willst ihn mir damit ausreden, daß du ihn, wenn nicht direkt, so doch andeutungsweise als simpel, als einen einfältigen Jungen hinstellst. Aber du vergißt, daß Einfalt etwas Erhabenes und Siegreiches sein kann, und dass seine Einfalt den großen demokratischen Geist seines weiten Heimatlandes zum Hintergrunde hat' [You keep harping on his averageness, and, in doing so, by calling him, if not directly, then by implication, a simpleminded, ingenuous youngster, you mean to talk me out of him. But you forget that ingenuousness can be something noble and victorious, and that the background of his ingenuousness is the great democratic spirit of his immense country']." The irony which peeks through these words is, of course, Mann's; his creation believes what she says, and lays herself open to the charge (as she does with each of her enthusiasms) of being a credulous Romantic. Anna, who *does* regard Ken as an uncultured simpleton from beyond the western seas, warns her mother about her credulity with a sharpness reminiscent of the section of the "Comprendre" essay where Mann warns Europe against too great a trust in American selflessness. But Anna's words have no effect other than briefly to repress Rosalie's passion for her partner in naturalness. "Deutsche Innerlichkeit [German inwardness]" has long been wont to throw itself into the noble simplicity of America's embrace, sometimes with sad results, as in the cases of Lenau in Ohio and Hauptmann in Connecticut or, in literary creation, in the figures of Ferdinand Kürnberger's *Der Amerikamüde* [*The Man Tired of America*]. Yet sometimes the union has turned out well, too, as in the historical examples of Carl Schurz and Theodor Thomas; and Kafka's Karl Roßmann, on his way to the nature-theater of Oklahoma, has not been destroyed by America.

It will not do, in an age when literature draws ever more heavily on mythic sources, to dispose of Rosalie and her circle with a discussion of their proximity to, or distance from, the spirit of German Romanticism. Nature, and its worship, are older phenomena than Romanticism; the main stuff of primitive religions, nature had such strength that she could not even be excluded from Christianity. Even though *Commonweal*'s critic, John Sullivan, found the very names in *Die Betrogene* "funny sounding," Mann had chosen them carefully; Anna and Rosalie both bear names which lead the reader backward in time to the Christian past and prepare him to discover the roots of mother and daughter in an even earlier religious tradition. Although Anna is Rosalie's daughter, her name has the aura of greater age: Luke 2:36 tells of "Anna, a prophetess . . . of great age, who departed not from the temple, worshipping with fastings and supplications day and night," and thus Anna von Tümmler is provided with a name suitable both to her oldish ways and her devotion to her chastely abstract art. Christian tradition has, however, another Anna whose story adds still another aspect to Mann's artistic spinster: Anna, the wife of Joachim, is said to have given birth to Mary despite her great age. Thus Anna's name serves still another end: it not only makes Rosalie's daughter seem older than her years, but hints that Rosalie has predicted something of her own imagined good fortune—the late "return" of feminine functions—as she gave her little girl her name. On the other hand, Rosalie's name is a "young" one; it is borne in Christian legend by Saint Rosalia, the patron saint of Sicily, the eternal maiden who is said to have lived from her fourteenth year as a hermitess on Monte Pellegrino behind Palermo. Of her damp green grotto, Goethe wrote: "vielleicht hat die ganze Christenheit . . . keinen heiligen Ort aufzuweisen, der auf eine so unschuldige und gefühlvolle Art verziert und verehrt wäre [perhaps all of Christendom boasts . . . of no holy place which could have been adorned and honored in a way so innocent and full of feeling]" (Palermo, April 6, 1787). The Sicilians, sensitive to the vernal attributes of Rosalia and dissatisfied with the late summer day (September 4) allotted her in the church calendar, very appropriately discovered her relics on June 15 (1625), and so brought her close, in the popular imagination, to the role of a springtime goddess. Even that poet of the night, E. T. A. Hoffmann, was attracted to the Sicilian saint; in the blood-and-thunder finale to *Die Elixiere des Teufels* [*The Devil's Elixirs*], Aurelie, her hair decked with myrtle and roses (the latter the favorite flower of Rosalie von Tümmler) advances to Saint Rosalia's altar, likewise rose-bedecked; after her murder, she is carried to her grave on a rose-trimmed bier. Saint Rosalia's spiritual presence casts a redeeming shimmer over these ghastly scenes, very much as Rosalie von Tümmler's devotion to natural beauty makes her dreadful fate—if it is a dreadful fate— more endurable, albeit more ironic.

The Düsseldorf Rosalie is no more a purely Christian figure than Palermo's Rosalia is; they both grow out of the pagan world. Sending *Die Betrogene* to his friend and correspondent, the Hungarian mythologist Karl Kerényi, Thomas Mann provided the little book with a dedication, "diese kleine Mythe von der Mutter Natur [this little myth about Mother Nature]," and the word "Mythe" was not a simple attempt to flatter the recipient. In 1940, Mann had read *Das göttliche Mädchen* [*The Divine Maiden*] of Kerényi, one of several writings of the mythologist to indicate the identity of mother and daughter, of Demeter and Kore or Ceres and Persephone. Kerényi demonstrated how Demeter, ravaged by Zeus, rages at her "loveless" fate and gives birth to Kore, who in her own turn is raped by Hades. Demeter is placated, however, for her double rape (for, as Kerényi repeatedly emphasizes, Demeter and Kore are essentially identical figures) by the return of Kore to earth: spring comes, and Demeter allows the world to bear fruit once again. The theme has been used by Hermann Broch in *Der Versucher* [*The Bewitchment*] (in which Broch extends the goddess-pair into a goddess-trinity), and Mann employs it in *Die Betrogene*; working quite independently of each other, Broch and Mann both chose to emphasize not Demeter-Erinys, the angry and scolding Demeter, but the Demeter kindly and reconciled. In *Der Versucher,* Broch's Mother Gisson, married young to an experienced man, has been widowed early, after bearing two children, a son and a daughter, the latter of whom, Martha, is patently discontent with her lot. At a similarly tender age, Rosalie has also married an experienced man (even after his marriage, Major von Tümmler persisted in keeping up his erotic adventures); she has borne a son and a daughter, of whom the latter is a discontent Kore, too, although Anna's reasons are different from Martha's. The mothers are different on the surface, the one a Tyrolean peasant woman and the other a Rhenish lady; but in essence they are the same: two Demeters who love nature dearly, and who, by the nature of their marriages and their husbands' early deaths, have been "raped"—cheated of some of nature's pleasures. They chide their respective daughters for their lack of rapport with nature: Martha does not love her husband and so has fallen out of nature's magic circle. Anna is kept from love by nature and so detests nature's power. The two younger women are discontent Kores, the one "raped" in a loveless union, the other forced into loveless virginity, and neither having her mother's consolation of a mystical (and here, unerotic) contact with nature.

Mother Gisson, however, is an aged woman whose life-substance is serene wisdom, a wisdom she uses as a weapon against the seducer from afar, the foreigner who would lead her village into quasi-Nazistic practices; Rosalie is ready to enter the lists of love once more—to succumb to the foreigner, and to experience in herself a second springtide. She resolves this time not to be "raped," as she was once by von Tümmler's will: she herself will be, she thinks, the taker: "'Diesmal bin ich's, die begehrt, von mir aus, auf eigene Hand und habe mein Auge auf ihn geworfen wie ein Mann auf das junge Weib seiner Wahl' ['This time it is I who desire, of my own will and motion, and I have cast my eyes on him as a man casts his eyes on the young woman of his choice']." Yet, as she perceives almost immediately, this "manly" attitude of hers cannot be maintained: she must return to the painful role of the woman, of which she nonetheless is proud, "stolz auf den Schmerzensfrühling meiner Seele [filled with pride in the flowering spring of pain in my soul]." Ken also, boyish as he is, turns out to have a pronouncedly "manly" role at the tale's mythic level. Mann persuades his readers—Ken's knowledge in the difficult field of mythology is somewhat less believable than his skill in history—that the American is an adept at folklore. A Rhenish custom particularly attractive to Ken is that of the "Lebensrute [rod of life]," which he describes for an amused Eduard, a disgusted Anna, and an enchanted Rosalie: "daß nämlich die Burschen in der Weihnachts- und der Osterzeit die Mädchen und auch wohl Vieh und Bäume mit frischen Birken- und Weidengerten schlügen, oder 'pfefferten' oder 'fitzten,' wie sie es nannten, wobei es auf Gesundheit und Fruchtbarkeit abgesehen sei,—ja, das sei ein Brauch, ein urtümlicher, und das gefalle ihm. 'Schmackostern' heiße das Pfeffern oder Fitzen im Frühjahr [village lads gathering fresh birch and willow rods at Christmas or Easter and striking ('peppering' or 'slashing,' they called it) the girls, and sometimes cattle and trees, with them to bring health and fertility—that was a 'custom,' an age-old one, and it delighted him. When the peppering or slashing took place in spring, it was called 'Smack Easter']." Rosalie cannot get Ken's description of these fertility rites out of her mind. During the erotic phantasies prompted by the sight of Ken in his T-shirt, Rosalie returns to the image of the "wand": "Ich aber bin mit der

Lebensrute geschlagen, er selbst, der Nichtsahnende, hat mich damit gefitzt und gepfeffert, Schmackostern hat er mir angetan [But it is I who have been struck by the rod of life, he himself, all unknowing, has slashed me and peppered me with it, he has given me my Smack Easter]"—note that Rosalie has been especially impressed by "Schmackostern [Smack Easter]," the vernal form of the rites. Later on, Rosalie almost forgets Ken in her delight at the "Lebensrute" itself, which "hat nicht nur die Seele, hat auch den Körper getroffen und ihn wieder zum fliessenden Brunnen gemacht [has reached not my soul alone but my body too and has made it a flowing fountain again]." It is no wonder that Rosalie makes such easy acquaintance with the "life-switch": the "Rute [rod]" is a somewhat refined descendant of the phalli which Demeter's initiates employed during the celebration of the Eleusinian mysteries. "Der invalide Sprachlehrer [the invalid language-teacher]," as Anna calls Ken in an effort to cancel out his magic power with an epithet implying ineffectuality and impotence, is in reality Triptolemus, the simple cowherd from a wild land (Eleusis), who became Demeter's favorite—he is the main male figure of the Eleusinian rites.

In Broch's *Der Versucher* the retelling of the Demeter-Kore story gets out of hand: Broch at times becomes so interested in working out its variations that the novel's political and sociological implications are ignored. Mann, however—who did not have Broch's horror of being "ein bloßer Geschichtelerzähler [a simple storyteller]"—is able to join the myth at the core of his tale to the story's broadly human import in an unobtrusive but wholly effective way. Demeter is a goddess who snatches victory out of defeat, or, more specifically, beauty and life out of ugliness and death. Hades abducts Kore as she is picking flowers on a meadow, and carries her to Hell in a chariot drawn by black horses; Demeter, by her obstinacy—one thinks of Rosalie's obstinate devotion to nature—compels Kore's return. Her triumph is not a complete one; Hades' gardener, Ascalaphus, mockingly remarks that Kore has eaten seven seeds from a pomegranate in Hell's garden, and thus she is condemned to spend a part of each year in the realm of death; but each year she can also return, bringing spring with her. Mann's Demeter-Kore (using Kerényi's theory of the identity of the two figures), Rosalie, is put up against Demeter's dilemma not by the rape of her daughter, but by her own confrontation with a tormenting paradox, the paradox to which Yeats gave a partial expression in his poem about an old woman's passion, "Crazy Jane Talks with the Bishop":

> Love has pitched his mansion in
> The place of excrement.

The paradox is that love, the best and the continuing force of life, has its dwelling in the midst of filth, and, finally, in rottenness and decay. The keystone of Rosalie's nature-cult, when she first appears, is the belief that nature is beautiful, and thus worthy of boundless trust; her dogma must be tested, just as Demeter must be tested when Kore is taken from her to nature's darkest and most cloacine corner. Early in *Die Betrogene*, Rosalie and Anna go for a walk, during which something happens "das an Spott gemahnte [something that had a suggestion of mockery]." (One wonders if the scene was not prompted by Baudelaire's "Une charogne," where the poet and his love, out strolling one fine summer morning, come across "une charogne infâme.") The ladies smell musk, and, upon investigation, discover that the perfume arises from some putrescent material: "Es war, am Wegesrand, ein in der Sonne kochendes, mit Schmeißfliegen dicht besetztes und von ihnen umflogenes Unrathäufchen ... Auf kleinem Raum waren da Tierexkremente, oder auch menschliche, mit faulig Pflanzlichem zusammengekommen, und der weit schon verweste Kadaver irgendeines kleinen Waldgeschöpfes war auch wohl dabei [It was there by the roadside, seething in the sun, with blowflies covering it and flying all around it—a little mound of excrement. ... The small area represented [*sic*] a meeting-ground of animal, or perhaps human, faeces with some sort of putrid vegetation, and the greatly decomposed body of some small woodland creature seemed to be present too]." Rosalie, nature's best friend, has been betrayed by nature; the betrayal, taking the form of graveolence, has caught her at her tenderest spot, for Rosalie, the lover of roses, cannot endure "fabrizierte Riechstoffe [manufactured scents]" and has begged her daughter to try to express natural "Düfte in Farben [odors in color]." Here, in the woods whose Romantic "Atem der Natur [breath of Nature]" and "süßer Lebenshauch [sweet, living breath]" Rosalie has just apostrophized, nature has produced a mockery of beauty, a sham aroma which disgusts the strollers. The "Unrathäufchen [little mound of excrement]" puts a question that Rosalie will have to answer before her death: is her faith in nature justified? Can Demeter save Kore from Hades? Or is nature the great trickster, who in the end will destroy us all, having seduced us into loving her? Does Felix Schimmelpreester's play on his name (*Felix Krull*) contain a final joke and a final truth: "'Die Natur ... ist nichts als Fäulnis und Schimmel, und ich bin zu ihrem Priester bestellt, darum heiße ich Schimmelpreester' ['Nature ... is nothing but mould and corruption, and I am her high priest. The high priest of mould, that's the real meaning of Schimmelpreester' (*Confessions of Felix Krull: Confidence Man*, trans. Denver Lindley. New York: Knopf, 1955)]"?

The final pages of *Die Betrogene*, in which the fifty-year-old "May-child" is brought toward her answer and her death, are as excellent, in their compact allusiveness, as anything in Mann's oeuvre. From *Der Zauberberg* [*The Magic Mountain*] on, Mann employed an increasingly discursive manner, at once fascinating and wearying, as if he were a literary Richard Strauss—the Strauss of the tone poems. In *Der Erwählte* [*The Holy Sinner*] and *Die Betrogene,* he turned to a trimmer neoclassical style, a reverse not unlike that made by Strauss in his late works, such as *Capriccio.* His sentences are still as filled with reference and inference as ever, but now he has abandoned the augmented symphony for the chamber group; every note is audible, and every note counts. In 1910, Thomas Mann wrote to his brother that he was reading Kleist's prose, "um mich so recht in die Hand zu bekommen [in order to make myself sure-handed]," and *Königliche Hoheit,* on which he was at work at the time, is an early and not completely successful product of his urge to simplification. The Holterhof episode of *Die Betrogene* is a happy accomplishment of the aims of forty-three years before.

Rummaging through the architectural monuments of the old Duchy of Berg, Ken Keaton discovers that he has not seen the palace of Holterhof, on the Rhine south of Düsseldorf. It is early spring, and Rosalie suggests an excursion, by motorboat, to the rococo mansion and gardens which Count Goltstein, the stadtholder of Karl Theodor of the Palatinate, had commissioned for his master long ago. Ken charters the launch, and on a Sunday morning the little company, mother, daughter, son, and tutor, sets out on its Rhine journey. The skipper's appearance seems vaguely sinister: "ein Mann mit Ringen in den Ohrläppchen, rasierter Oberlippe, und einem rötlichen Schifferbart unterm Kinn [a man with rings in his ear-lobes, clean-shaven upper lips, and a reddish mariner's beard under his chin]"—the earrings suggest a wild way of life quite out of keeping with the solid Cornelius-Straße, and the beard makes one think of Charon, the bearded boatman. The beard's very color will put the student of German literature on his guard, since he knows how many villains have had red hair: Ruodlieb's *rufus,* Schiller's Wurm, Freytag's Veitel Itzig, and Hofmannsthal's "der Rothaarige [redhead]," the false friend of Andreas. Little more is seen of the boatman; having accomplished his task, having suggested betrayal and death, he stands quietly at the wheel.

The central actor on the launch is Rosalie, who "schien den elementaren Reiz der Wasserfahrt von Herzen zu genießen [seemed to be heartily enjoying the elemental charm of the journey by water]." Entranced, she makes up a "Singsang [singsong]" to the great river and to nature itself: "O Wasserwind, ich liebe dich; liebst du auch mich, du Wasserwind . . . Du Wasserwind, wie lieb' ich dich! [O water-wind, I love thee; lovest thou me, O waterwind? . . .

How I love thee, O water-wind!]" The wind has a special meaning for Rosalie, as Mann has pointed out at the beginning of the tale: "sie sprach auch gern von Windbestäubung, will sagen: vom Liebesdienste des Zephirs an den Kindern der Flur . . .—eine Art der Befruchtung, die ihr besonders anmutig schien [She discoursed happily on wind pollination—or, rather, on Zephyrus' loving service to the children of Flora . . .—a method of fertilization which she considered particularly charming]." Sailing up the Rhine with the object of her desires, Rosalie finds her maidenly enthusiasm for this chastest kind of intercourse kindled again; and one remembers that the "May-child," despite her years and her children, is still virginal in spirit. (After she has sung her song, Rosalie notices that Ken's handkerchief is hanging "lang aus der Brusttasche [way out of his breast pocket]"; turning suddenly, her eyes opened wide, she stuffs it back into his pocket, with the admonition: "'Sittsam, sittsam, junger Mann!' ['Propriety, propriety, young man!'].") Coming to the story's end, the reader realizes that Rosalie, like "die Kinder der Flur [the children of Flora]," has been impregnated from afar—with death; Dr. Muthesius hints that a "Reizvorgang [process of stimulation]" has caused her cancer, but, if it has, it is like the wind, for Rosalie has never had intimate relations with Ken. Maidenhood, chaste intercourse, and death are thus the strains of Rosalie's song. Her repetitive, vague, and musical words seem an echo of the greatest of the Rhine's poets, who, with "Auf dem Rhein," "Die Loreley," and "Der Schiffer im Kahne," created a kind of Rhenish thanatopsis, showing how enchantment with love (and with nature's power, embodied in the river) led the enamored to their deaths. Brentano's "Der Schiffer im Kahne" ends:

> So sang zu einem schönen Kind
> Ein Schiffer auf dem Rhein,
> Da trieb ihn schnell der Wispelwind
> Zum Binger Loch hinein.

> [So sang to a beautiful child
> A boatman on the Rhine,
> Then quickly the Wispelwind drove him
> Into Binger Loch]

The "Wasserwind [Water-wind]," Mann's "Wispelwind," drives Rosalie to her "Binger Loch," Holterhof, where in a dark and hidden chamber she will fall for a second into Ken's arms.

The voyagers have a picnic on the boat, and the signal is given for the transformation of Rhenish Romanticism into Rhenish rococo: the voyage to a Cytherean isle, the water-borne picnic, and its companion flirtations are standard apparatus of the rococo lyric and rococo art. At ten-thirty the company lands near Holterhof, and Rosalie, not Ken, gives the skipper his obolus. The visitors wander along a damp meadow path, and then enter the palace park. The park has not merely the traditional "altherrschaftliche Natur ... wohlgepflegt und gestutzt [venerable, seignorial landscape, well cared for and well clipped]" but also exotic and "prehistoric" plants, "fremdartige Koniferen, farnblättrige Buchen, und Keaton erkannte den kalifornischen Mammutbaum, die Sumpfzypresse mit weichen Atemwurzeln [strange conifers, fern-leafed beeches, and Keaton recognized the California sequoia and the swamp cypress with its supplementary breathing-roots]." The botanical disquisitions of the aged Mann, which grow tedious in the Lisbon chapters of *Felix Krull,* are much briefer and more tellingly used here: before entering the rococo gardens proper, one is reminded, through natural symbols, the sequoia and the swamp cypress (with its soft breathing roots), of Ken's monolithic American simplicity and the manifoldness of Rosalie's perceptivities, as well as the fragility of her hold on life. But the sudden dive into the prehistoric world has still another function. Mann has given his palace not its actual name—for "Holterhof" is in fact Schloß Benrath, the famous late rococo creation of Nicolas de Pigage—but the name of some prehistoric fortifications lying at the town of Hilden, about five kilometers to the east. One does not, of course, need to know the implication of Holterhof's name to be made suddenly aware of prehistoric formlessness, of the swampy and ancient world of pteridophyta and taxodiaceae. It is a world which frightens Rosalie, a cruel nature, the world of the "Unratschäufchen [little pile of excrement]." "Rosalie nahm an diesen Sehenswürdigkeiten kein Interesse. Natur, meinte sie, müsse vertraut sein, sonst spräche sie nicht zum Gemüt. Aber die Parkherrlichkeit schien es ihrem Natursinn überhaupt nicht sehr anzutun [Rosalie took no interest in these curiosities. Nature, she considered, must be familiar, or it did not speak to the heart. But the beauty of the park did not seem to hold much charm for her]." It is not until she sees the black swans on the castle pond that she livens up again.

Indeed, the mansion of Holterhof-Benrath itself seems an unlikely sort of place to appeal to Rosalie. She is, to be sure, not a declared enemy of the rococo, or at least of certain of its aspects. She has suggested to Anna that, when painting a still life "fürs Herz [for the heart]," she might choose as her subject "'einen frischen Blumenstrauß, so anschaulich, daß man seinen entzückenden Duft zu spüren meinte, bei der Vase aber stünden ein paar zierliche Meißener Porzellanfiguren, ein Herr, der einer Dame eine Kusshand zuwirft, und alles müßte sich in der glänzend polierten Tischplatte spiegeln' [a fresh spray of lilac, so true to life that one would think one smelt its ravishing perfume, and a pair of delicate Meissen porcelain figures beside the vase, a gentleman blowing kisses to a lady, and with everything reflected in the gleaming, polished table-top']"; and those favorite subjects of rococo art, Amor and Psyche, are her favorites, too, all the more because Psyche, bending over the sleeping Amor, smelled the "Himmelsarom [heavenly aroma]" of roses. For her, as for her fellow Rhinelander Krull, who admires the gracefully vigorous eighteenth century art of Lisbon, the rococo must be connected with the "Blumenstrauß [spray of lilac]," it must be aromatic and alive. About Holterhof, however, there is an air of rotten age, which the place may have had from the beginning. The master under whom the castle was built was not the vigorous Jan Wellem, the founder of Düsseldorf's gallery, whose equestrian statue graces the square before the town hall; but the weak Karl Theodor, the puppet of priests and actresses, who, although he gave the city its art academy, ignored Düsseldorf more and more, and finally moved his capital away from the Rhineland altogether, from Mannheim to Munich. Karl Theodor had helped Düsseldorf to decay, and his summer residence, Holterhof-Benrath, is itself gnawed around the edges: a lonely poplar stands on an islet in the castle pond, the rose-colored facade is crumbling, the clock, held aloft by an angel, is forgetful of time, the guide has but one arm; but worst, perhaps, are the signs of the rococo's decayed erotic energy: "Mythologisch leichtgeschürzte Figuren, Pan und seine Nymphen, standen auf Sockeln zu seiten der tiefreichenden Fenster, verwitternd wie die vier Sandsteinlöwen, die, grämlich von Miene, die Pranken gekreuzt, Freitreppe und Auffahrt flankierten [Figures clad with mythological scantness, Pan and his nymphs, stood on pedestals beside the long windows, flaking away like the four sandstone lions which, with sullen expressions, their paws crossed, flanked the steps and the ramp]."

The sightseers are led into the palace—after an embarrassing episode, in which Ken, giving way to his American high spirits, and his passion for Europe, mounts one of the sandstone lions—by the one-armed castellan. The air inside Holterhof's rosy facade, like the "Moderduft [odor of mould]" surprisingly emitted by the rosebush of the "Altes Schloß [Old Castle]" in *Königliche Hoheit* [*Royal Highness*], is redolent of "vermuffte Kälte [musty chill]," and the musty coolness is juxtaposed to the "rechenschaftsfreie Üppigkeit, unbedingter Wille zum Vergnügen [unbridled luxuriousness, unqualified insistence on gratification]" that the palace's unambiguous decorations bespeak. Ken leads his lady through the chambers of past life and present death, holding her by the elbow (a practice which, like putting the fork in the right hand, Mann evidently finds either childlike or childish:

"Jeder Amerikaner führt so seine Dame über den Fahrdamm [Every American takes his lady across the street in this fashion]." The guide, routinely
indecent, demonstrates one of the mechanical tricks by which the rococo
spiced its eroticism; he opens a false mirror, exposing a stairway beside
which a Pan-figure stands; "geschürzt mit einem nicht authentischen Blatt-
gewinde, etwas zurückgelehnten Oberleibes [kirtled with a spurious festoon
of leaves; leaning back a little]," the Pan smiles "über seinem Bocksbart
priapisch bewillkommnend ins Leere [down into the space over his goat's
beard, priapic and welcoming]." Hot sensuality and cold death are combined
in the statue's artificial yet suggestive pose; and the same macabre intimation
is made to the party by the hidden passageway the guide shows them, "einen
ins Ungewisse führenden Gang . . . aus dem Moderduft drang [a passageway
leading into darkness and exhaling an odor of mold]." Rosalie, who has let
the party outdistance her and Ken by losing one of her sightseer's slippers,
finds her way into the passage with Ken's help; once inside, in the corridor
and then in a causeuse filled with dead air, she makes a voluble confession
of her love to Ken. The American, not offered the chance to make a verbal
reply, gives mute indications of his own interest. Long ago, in Heinrich
Mann's *Der Untertan* [The Patrioteer], one of Diederich Hessling's flames,
Käthchen Zillich, had been horrified by the grave-like causeuse of Netzig's
Stadttheater: seeing herself in the chamber's mirror, she cried out: "'In dem
Spiegel seh' ich aus wie meine tote Großmutter' ['In the mirror I look like
my dead grandmother']." Now, in the "totes Lustgemach [dead pleasure
chamber]" of Holterhof, Rosalie has a similar—and perhaps more justified—
sensation. "'Hu, Totenluft' . . . 'Wie traurig, Ken, mein Liebling, dass wir
uns finden müssen hier bei den Abgestorbenen. In Schloß der guten Natur,
umfächelt von ihrem Duft, im süßen Gedünst von Jasmin und Faulbaum,
hab ich geträumt, da hätte es sein, da hätt' ich dich küssen sollen zum
erstenmal und nicht in diesem Grabe!' ['Ugh, it smells like death' . . . 'How
sad, Ken my darling, that we have to be here amid this decay. It was in kind
Nature's lap, fanned by her airs, in the sweet breath of jasmines and alders,
that I dreamed it should be, it was there that I should have kissed you for
the first time, and not in this grave!']." Having arranged a rendezvous, they
find their way back to the park and to Rosalie's children; they return to
Düsseldorf by trolley "durch Fabrikbezirke und vorbei an Kolonien von
Arbeiterhäusern [through industrial districts and past colonies of workmen's
houses]," a contrast-backdrop to the myth-filled Rhine of the trip south,
and a final repetition of the theme—a time-honored one in the German
novel: one thinks of Raabe's *Pfisters Mühle*—of the surrender of Germany to the Eduards and the Rollwagens and the Brünners. During the night,

Frau von Tümmler becomes violently ill: "Sie hatte die Kraft gehabt, zu klingeln, aber ohnmächtig fanden die Herbeieilenden, Tochter und Magd, sie in ihrem Blut [She had had the strength to ring, but when her daughter and the maid came hurrying in, they found her lying in a faint in her blood]." She is taken to the hospital, from which she does not return.

Of the excursion's many events, one has made a particularly deep impression on Rosalie, deeper even, it would seem than her moments with Ken. She mentions it as she stands briefly in Ken's embrace ("'der Schwan war böse' ['the swan was angry']"), and as she lies on her deathbed. Preparing for the Rhine journey, Rosalie has recalled the black swans which swim on Holterhof's pond—the birds, it is inferred, arouse quite mixed feelings in her. On the one hand, she likes the crowds one usually meets at such public monuments as Holterhof, but Anna prefers "'die vornehme Traurigkeit des schwarzen Schwanenpaars auf dem Wassergraben' ['the aristocratic sadness of the pair of black swans in the moat']." Perhaps they, as well as her love for Ken and for nature, have drawn her southward along the Rhine. It may be that lines from Brentano's "Der Schiffer im Kahne" are at work in her subconscious here, too:

> O wähnend Lieben, Liebeswahn,
> > Allmächtiger Magnet.
> Spann einen Schwan an meinen Kahn
> > Der stets nach Süden geht
>
> [O maddening love, love's madness
> All-powerful magnet,
> Harnessed a swan to my boat
> That always goes to the south]

Seeing the swans on their "rather slimy" pond, Rosalie calls: "'Da sind sie! ... Wie schön sie sind!' ['There they are! ... How beautiful they are!']," and starts to give them the dry bread which Ken has been carrying just for this purpose. Since it is warm from his body, she nibbles on it herself, at the same time slyly calling attention to her "restored womanhood" by her reply to Ken's objection ("'But it is old and hard!'"); "'Ich habe gute Zähne!' ['I have good teeth']," she answers. One of the swans, giving way to the notorious bad temper of his kind, spreads his dark wings and hisses; the company is at once amused and a little frightened, and Rosalie tosses the birds their food. Gloomy Anna remarks "'Ich fürchte ... daß der Böse dir den Raub an seinem Futter nicht leicht vergessen wird' ['Yet I fear ... that the old devil won't soon forget your robbing him of his food']"; but Rosalie, optimistic as ever, takes her words as a jest. Later on, awakening from her post-narcotic sleep in the hospital, Rosalie recalls Anna's fear, which has become a part of her dreams: "'Anna, mein Kind, er hat mich angezischt.' 'Wer, liebste Mama? 'Der schwarze Schwan' ['Anna, my child, he hissed at me.' 'Who, dearest Mama?' 'The black swan']." As she drifts into death, she mentions—or simply remembers: Mann leaves the point in intentional obscurity—the swan again and again: "Des Schwans aber gedachte sie noch öfter in den folgenden paar Wochen, seines blutroten Schnabels, des schwarzen Schlags seiner Schwingen [But she often remembered the swan during the next few weeks, his blood-red bill, the black beating of his wings]."

The swan is one of the most ambiguous of mythological birds, even as its own nature is ambiguous: it is dignified, yet irascible, ugly in the fledgling state and beautiful as an adult, pure of color yet at home on the slimy pond. In classical literature, it is the bird of Apollo and so of poets (from which comes the practice of calling literary and musical artists "swans": one recalls those of Dirce and Mantua, of Boberfeld and Pesaro); but Mann can scarcely be concerned with this attribute of the bird: *Die Betrogene* has less to say about the problem of the artist than any of Mann's other works—another respect, by the way, in which it is unlike *Der Tod in Venedig* [*Death in Venice*]. According to a more complicated tradition, the swan is the bird of love: Ovid's Venus is pulled through the air by swans (*Metamorphoses*, X, 708) and swans, "duxerunt collo qui iuga nostra suo [whose necks have drawn our vessel]," signal an end to Ovid's instruction in love (*Ars amatoria*, III, 810). Propertius tells how Venus lends her swans to the poet of love (III,3,39) and Horace has the erotic poet simply turned into a swan (*Carmina*, IV,2,25); however, the swan's best-known erotic appearance in antiquity is that in which Zeus, as the *Venus-Gärtlein* [*Venus-garden*] has it, "muß, aus Liebes-pein, / in ein'm Schwan verwandelt sein [must, from pain of love, / be changed into a swan]." In the most famous of his rapes, Zeus found a swan's shape suitable for approaching Leda; this tale is merely, as Kerényi and Jung have shown, a late version of a tale of Kore's rape, a tale told in the Cyclian epic, *Cypria*: "Here, the bride—the original Kore—was called Nemesis, the bridegroom and the seducer, Zeus. Pursued by the god's desire, the goddess transforms herself into various beasts of the earth, sea, and air. In this last mutation, as wild birds of the primeval swamp—she as a goose, he as a swan—the two divinities celebrate their marriage as a rape." Mann has given a sign of his intentions by planting two primeval trees, the "Mammutbaum [sequoia]" and the "Sumpfzypresse [swamp cypress]," at the entrance to Holterhof; he has completed the mythological groundstream in his novel by showing that Ken Keaton is not just the good shepherd Triptolemus of the Demeter-Kore tale, but also a kind of Zeus, who "rapes" his Demeter-Kore—or, in Mann's ironic retelling, causes her false bloom and death by his mere presence. Zeus, in another of his lustful transformations, raped Europa; Ken, in his Zeus-role, does the same. The sad difference in these rapes is that, while Kore-Leda gives birth to Helen, and Kore-Europa to Minos, Rhadamanthos, and Sarpedon, Rosalie-Kore and Leda and Europa grown old—apparently gives birth to nothing but death. Thus, if Rosalie as Demeter, the faithful goddess of and believer in nature, may not be betrayed in her faith, Rosalie as Kore surely is betrayed: she dies.

Which partner is to blame for Rosalie's destruction, the aging Kore herself or the young American Zeus? The color of the swan would indicate that Mann puts the blame at Ken's feet. The black swan is traditionally a "rara avis" (see Juvenal, *Satires*, VI, 165), and so is the American in the Düsseldorf of the 1920s; the black swan is also a bird of seduction and death, something that Rosalie, with her passion for Romanticism, may have known. In Tchaikovsky's *Swan Lake*, the magician's daughter, Odile, is dressed in black as she tries to lure Siegfried to destruction (to the strains of the familiar "Black Swan" music); in Sibelius's *Swan of Tuonela*, the swan, on a black river, is at once the bird of desire and death. The *Kalevala*'s hero, Lemminkäinen, must kill the swan of Tuona, before he can win his bride; he—not the swan—dies bloodily in the attempt. Rosalie too has ascended the dark river to find the swan and her death; if the black swan (and Ken) are not directly to blame for Rosalie's death, if she—who has felt herself to be a young man, going out after the bride of her choice—has merely been lured into destruction by the swan or by the American, the swan's very presence—and Ken's—still has caused her destruction. In antiquity, the learned reader of Artemidorus's *Oneirocritica* (*Interpretation of Dreams*) would literally have been frightened to death if he dreamt of a swan that made noises at him, for he knew such behavior meant his demise. Rosalie hears the swan's angry hissing at Holterhof, she hears it again in the dreams before her passing. Has she, or has the reader of Artemidorus, the right to blame the black swan for its noisy appearance? Or does death have a source beyond the American's sudden coming to Düsseldorf, the swan's sudden anger?

Ken Keaton, after all, is not any more the cause of Rosalie's age than young Dr. Carlson of Billings Hospital was the cause of Thomas Mann's illness. In Celtic mythology the black animal stands for death, and especially death by age, a symbolization Yeats used for the concluding lines of *The Countess Cathleen*:

> The years like great black oxen tread the world,
> And God the herdsman goads them on behind,
> And I am broken by their passing feet.

From Yeats's line the American novelist Gertrude Atherton took the title of her *Black Oxen* (1923), a book which became a best-seller, in America and in Europe. Its popularity, it must be admitted, derived less from its artistic qualities than from its peculiar message; "women from all over the English-speaking world wrote to me wanting to know if my book were a fairy-tale or if it were really true that they might hope to renew their youthful energies." (One cannot help wondering if Mann's American publishers did not choose the title of the English version of *Die Betrogene*, *The Black Swan*, because of some memory of Atherton's old success.) The plot of *Black Oxen* will not seem totally unfamiliar to the reader of *Die Betrogene*. Lee Clavering, a handsome young American journalist and veteran of the First World War, falls in love with a 58-year-old countess, Mary Zattiany, a native American who, however, has become completely Europeanized. And she has undergone another change, too: she has fallen in with a Viennese physician, who has rejuvenated her flesh if not her spirit. A friend, Hohenbauer, finally persuades her that she must not allow her new "possession of sexual magnetism in a superlative degree" to blind her to the fact that, spiritually, she is old. It is possible, although no conclusive proof is presently available, that Mann's fable may have derived from Atherton's celebrated novel, or that, having heard the anecdote which is said to be the heart of *Die Betrogene*, he then remembered the American novel and took some details from it. Another reason for Mann's vaguely inappropriate placing of the novel in the 1920s rather than the 1940s might be found here; rejuvenation was a leading fad of the earlier decade. The Viennese physician who worked the wonder on Mary Zattiany is patterned after Eugen Steinach (1862–1944), the teacher of Miss Atherton's own American rejuvenator and the author of *Verjüngung durch experimentelle Neubelebung der alternden Pubertätsdrüsen* [*Rejuvenation through experimental revitalization of the aging puberty glands*]; Steinach's respectable scientific work and that of the Russo-French physician, Sergei Voronoff, prepared the way for the rejuvenative physicians (and quacks) who set up shop during a decade which, even in its fashions, set such special store on youth. The two stories of rejuvenation—however related in material they may or may not be—come to quite different ends. Mary Zattiany is dissuaded from marrying Clavering by Hohenbauer's words: "'as young as you may appear, you have no more illusion in your soul than when you were a withered old woman in Vienna.'" Abandoning her passion, Mary decides to become a leading force in European diplomacy. Rosalie has remained young in spirit her whole life through; she persists in the physical illusions to which her youthfulness of soul helped give birth, and dies, as it were, of these illusions. The spirit fails Mary, whose menopause has been cancelled out by what, to Rosalie, would be repugnantly unnatural means; the flesh fails Rosalie. The words exchanged between Rosalie and Ken at the swan's pool get a new meaning, when the reader, looking back, realizes how Rosalie's flesh has betrayed her. The bread is Rosalie's body, "old and hard" but warmed to brief life by the contact with Ken; Rosalie tries to snatch her body from the black swan of old age, but to no avail. She is a Demeter who has not saved Kore. The flight of the black swan, or the tread of the black oxen, cannot be stopped.

Now, returning to the political inferences of *Die Betrogene,* one may conclude that Mann has absolved Ken of at least part of the guilt for Rosalie's destruction: if he has helped bring it about, he has been an unwitting accomplice. Rosalie abandons herself to foolish and mortal phantasies (part of the "Reizvorgang [process of stimulation]" which Dr. Muthesius mentions), just as old Europe, with its "schwächliche und selbstvergessene Verfallenheit . . . an Amerika [weak and self-forgetful decline . . . with regards to America]" (*Nachlese*) has put itself into a position both dangerous to itself and incompatible with its venerable culture. Rosalie is seduced by Ken because she wants to be seduced, because she expects a new youth; Ken is a seducer essentially uninterested in—and unworthy of?—his prey: he cries "'Hi!'" and "'On, old chap'" as he rides Holterhof's weatherbeaten sandstone lion. Seen politically, Mann's conclusion is not flattering to either partner in the affair; and the affair is fatal for one of them. The ancient literary pattern, mockery of the amorous old woman, has been used to drive a cruel point home. Seen from a nobler standpoint, that of the human character, the two partners come off considerably better, and Thomas Mann proves himself a fit holder of the title Erika Mann invented for him, a patriot of humanity (*Das letzte Jahr* [The Last Year]). Ken, for all his lacks, for all the American "Nervenlosigkeit" [nervelessness]" of which Mann seems to accuse him, has lived in accord with nature as best he could; Rosalie has done the same, and, because she belongs to an older culture, with a great deal more awareness of what she is doing. The last lines of the tale show how boundless, and yet how perceptive, her devotion to nature is: "'Anna, sprich nicht von Betrug und höhnischer Grausamkeit der Natur. Schmäle nicht mit ihr, wie ich es nicht tue. Ungern gehe ich dahin—von euch, vom Leben mit seinem Frühling. Aber wie wäre denn Frühling ohne den Tod? Ist ja doch der Tod ein großes Mittel des Lebens, und wenn er für mich die Gestalt lieh von

Auferstehung und Liebeslust, so war das nicht Lug, sondern Güte und Gnade'
['Anna, never say that Nature deceived me, that she is sardonic and cruel.
Do not rail at her, as I do not. I am loth to go away—from you all, from
life with its spring. But how should there be spring without death? Indeed,
death is a great instrument of life, and if for me it borrowed the guise of
resurrection, of the joy of love, that was not a lie, but goodness and mercy'].''
It would seem impossible, then, to call the story "parody of the cruellest
sort.'' Rosalie, to use a truism, has realized that one cannot live forever; and,
to use a constant in German literature from "Selige Sehnsucht" ["Blessed
Yearning"] to the end of the Tenth Duino Elegy, she has perceived that death
deepens life, and that life does—both in a physical and ideal sense—grow
out of death. Or, returning to her mythic center: she has refused to be
Demeter Erinys, scolding and disappointed. Instead, she is Demeter the boun-
tiful, because she has seen that Kore *must* go down to hell in order to return.
And Rosalie can be grateful to nature on a more personal score: what has
been cruel in nature's trick on her? The last months of her active life were
spent in happy desire; her suffering was brief. And it may be that Rosalie,
ready, like Mann's Goethe, to accept a world, "die von End-Ursachen und
End-Zwecken frei ist und in der das Böse wie das Gute sein Recht hat [that
is free of final causes and final results, in which evil has its rightful place
along with the good]," would not have complained had nature given her
neither a closing dream of love nor a mild death. Like the Rhine boatman
in Brentano's poem, she would say:

> Du blauer Liebeskelch, in dich
> Sank all mein Frühling hin,
> Umdüfte mich, vergifte mich,
> Weil ich dein eigen bin.

> [O blue love's cup, in you
> Sank down all my spring,
> Perfume me, poison me,
> For I am your own.]

She is, perhaps, the most German of all Mann's creations.

GUNILLA BERGSTEN

Doctor Faustus
as a "Historical" Novel

PHILOSOPHIES OF HISTORY

If *Doctor Faustus* is a "historical novel," Mann seems as a historian less interested in "how things actually were" than in the hidden meaning of events. The description of Jonathan Leverkühn's "visible music" indicates symbolically what Mann intended with his novel:

> To the small amount of physical apparatus which Adrian's father had at his command belonged a round glass plate, resting only on a peg in the center and revolving freely. On this glass plate the miracle took place. It was strewn with fine sand, and Jonathan, by means of an old cello bow which he drew up and down the edge from top to bottom made it vibrate, and according to its motion the excited sand grouped and arranged itself in astonishingly precise and varied figures and arabesques. This visible acoustic, wherein the simple and the mysterious, law and miracle, so charmingly mingled, pleased us lads exceedingly; we often asked to see it, and not least to give the experimenter pleasure.

Another natural phenomenon captures Jonathan Leverkühn's imagination: the mysterious hieroglyph-like traceries on certain New Caledonian shells. Here again a pattern of great artistry awakens Jonathan's Faustian urge to

From *Thomas Mann's "Doctor Faustus."* English translation by Krishna Winston. © 1969 by The University of Chicago. The University of Chicago Press, 1969. German version © 1963 by Gunilla Bergsten.

break nature's code. For he has no doubt that these patterns mean something, even if it cannot be formulated: "that Nature painted these ciphers, to which we lack the key, merely for ornament on the shell of her creature, nobody can persuade me."

What is extraordinary and mysterious about these phenomena is that lifeless materials seemingly arrange themselves into sophisticated patterns. The existence of these patterns suggests some higher power; it encourages human beings to seek a deeper meaning in nature. The fate of Adrian Leverkühn, that is, the historical fate of the German nation, likewise forms a complicated but consistent pattern. But does this consistency result from chance; or do hidden forces and principles direct the course of history? There can be no doubt that Mann gave very serious consideration to this question when writing *Doctor Faustus,* but it is difficult to determine how he pictured these forces or principles to himself. For Mann seems to work with several theories at once; for one and the same event or phenomenon in the novel or in historical reality Mann furnishes various explanations. Both in the discussion of historical questions and in the portrayal of Adrian's personal evolution we find elements of a philosophy of history. Since Adrian symbolizes Germany, it is safe to assume that factors affecting his development apply *mutatis mutandis* to the development of the nation.

Mann takes extraordinary care to indicate the background of every event connected with Adrian. In some respects *Doctor Faustus* is an exemplary naturalistic novel, not only because of the scientific exactitude of external detail and the wealth of precise description, but also because of the emphasis on determinism. Heredity and milieu determine Adrian's life as much as the lives of the French naturalists' heroes. His bluish-greyish-greenish eyes are explained as a mixture of his parents' blue and black eyes; Mann obviously intended an allusion to the mixture of blond Nordic stock and dark Alpine stock that forms the German national physiognomy. Adrian's migraine headaches and his penchant for speculation are inherited from his father; since the romantics, melancholy pondering has been designated a Nordic trait. Adrian's musical talent comes from his mother; Mann thus portrays musicality as the South's contribution to the German soul.

Determinism manifests itself most clearly in the course of the illness that leads to Adrian's collapse. Following the visit to Hetaera, the physiological aspect of Adrian's life is determined—precise medical explanations establish this beyond a doubt—but the predisposition to disease has been present from the beginning. Adrian seeks out the kind of love that Hetaera can offer because he is basically cold and thus excluded from normal human relationships. Yet this coldness tends to produce its opposite; Adrian is disgusted by sensuality but cannot escape its lure. The two poles in Adrian's nature, sensuality and abstract idealism, are characteristic of German romanticism, and romanticism, according to "Germany and the Germans," anticipated much of National Socialism. Because the German spirit lacked equilibrium it was susceptible to seduction, to the Wagnerian infection.

Adrian's inner development likewise follows rigidly deterministic lines. Here Mann seems to have made almost exclusive use of Freudian categories. Freud particularly emphasizes that psychological development can be explained in strictly causal terms. Adrian displays several neurotic symptoms: excessive unsociability, the belief that he brings death to those around him, and so forth. A psychoanalytical search for childhood causes of his neurosis uncovers ample material. Thus Adrian's attachment to a certain kind of milieu can be seen as a bond with his mother; Adrian in fact always finds his way to typical mother-figures. His two favorite spots in Buchel and Pfeiffering are the hill and the pond, both Freudian symbols for the mother. The psychoanalyst would explain Adrian's attempt to drown himself in the pond as regression or infantilism. In this episode Adrian's symbolic function is unmistakable: German life in the period Mann is treating was characterized by regression to the primitive and archaic in the cult of Wotan and the mysteries of "Blood and Soil."

Mann offers what seems to be a psychoanalytical interpretation of yet another factor in Adrian's life. Many of Adrian's neurotic symptoms can be traced back to a psychic trauma destined to determine his whole further development: to the meeting with Hetaera. We can find considerable evidence that this was how Mann wished the borrowed Nietzsche episode understood. In his essay on Nietzsche (1947), Mann gives the following analysis of Nietzsche's reaction to his experience in the brothel: "But it had been nothing more nor less than what psychologists call a 'trauma,' a shock whose steadily accumulating after-effects—from which his imagination never recovered—testify to the saint's receptivity to sin." If Adrian's life symbolizes Germany's historical development, the deterministic explanation of his life represents a deterministic explanation of German history. Mann unquestionably regards the German catastrophe as the last link in an iron chain of causal factors. Yet purely causal explanations are incapable of evoking by themselves that strange pattern, "wherein the simple and the mysterious, law and miracle, so charmingly" mingle.

Mann's very first writings give substantial proof that he is anchored in the German dialectical tradition; two constants in his work are the antitheses between the burgher and the artist, between nature and the spirit. With this foundation Mann might be expected to lean toward a dialectical interpre-

tation of history. We have already seen that Mann sets up a dialectical structure for the history of theology and music; periods of "subjectivity" and
license alternate with periods of orthodoxy, classicism or "objectivity."
Adrian articulates this principle for art and music, but his words hold true
for intellectual development as a whole: "But freedom is of course another
word for subjectivity, and some fine day she does not hold out any longer,
some time or other she despairs of the possibility of being creative out of
herself and seeks shelter and security in the objective. Freedom always in-
clines to dialectical reversals. She realizes herself very soon in constraint,
fulfils herself in the subordination to law, rule, coercion, system—but to
fulfil herself therein does not mean she therefore ceases to be freedom."
Brahms's treatment of Beethoven's sonata form is cited as an illustration,
but even earlier Zeitblom uses similar categories to describe the transformation of the original Reformation into Lutheran orthodoxy.

Although history in *Doctor Faustus* moves in pendulum swings, one
can hardly speak of a dialectical interpretation of history in the Hegelian
sense, for it is doubtful whether the antitheses in the novel ever come to rest
in a synthesis. Marxist critics tend to overlook this fact and interpret *Doctor
Faustus* in terms of the class struggle, as a novel of the decay and decline of
the bourgeoisie. Such an interpretation distorts Mann's central concerns.
Doctor Faustus nowhere offers anything like a synthesis; certainly we find
no suggestion of a potential communist paradise; the novel suggests instead
that any *rapprochement* between the two poles of "subjectivity" and "objectivity" invokes the demonic. Music again serves as a symbol in the following response by Zeitblom to the contrasts in Adrian's work: "the
espressivo takes hold of the strict counterpoint, the objective blushes with
feeling. One gets the impression of a glowing mould; this, like nothing else,
has brought home to me the idea of the daemonic" Can such a mechanism
be observed in history? We shall indeed see later that Mann considers Germany's evolution a sort of "demonization" process. But first we must discuss
another interpretation that Thomas Mann offers for the historical events that
play into *Doctor Faustus*.

Mann perceives a tendency to repetition in the structure of Germany's
intellectual development. The pattern of rebellion against objective form by
subjective feeling fits several periods in musical and theological history, and
since Mann uses these periods as the basis of his version of history, one may
justifiably speak of a sort of cyclical interpretation of history. The novel
suggests in several ways that the intellectual and political upheavals in twentieth-century Germany simply recapitulate what occurred in the time of Luther. The section on Adrian's fellow theologians in Halle illustrates this

theme: in their life style and their opinions the students and professors participate in modern conditions and tendencies, while their names link them to Reformation times.

But repetition manifests itself even more concretely. Adrian's life falls into three periods all spent in very similar surroundings. The farm at Buchel scarcely differs from the Pfeiffering estate near Munich where he lives during most of his adult creative life, and after his collapse he returns to spend his last ten years at home. Before settling in Pfeiffering he passes more than a year in the Italian village of Palestrina, which in several respects bears a striking resemblance to Pfeiffering.

The similarities between the Buchel and Pfeiffering farms and their occupants are as great as would be compatible with the novel's claim to realism. Zeitblom himself draws attention to the curious parallelism; when describing Adrian's home he points out correspondences between Buchel and Pfeiffering as "an extraordinary likeness and reproduction." Buchel's layout, with the hill and the cold pond, is repeated in Pfeiffering's Rohmbühel and Klammerweiher, and the Leverkühns' great linden becomes the Schweigestills' elm. Adrian's brother resembles Gereon Schweigestill, and Ursula resembles Clementine Schweigestill. The Pfeiffering family does not have a second son, "which rather strengthened the case than otherwise, for who would this second son have been." The watchdog Suso reappears as Pfeiffering's Kaschperl, and the milk maid Hanne's place is taken by Waltpurgis in Pfeiffering. Father Leverkühn has much in common with Max Schweigestill, including the tendency to brood and a disposition to migraine. Both are reflective smokers who exude a pleasant smell of pipe tobacco.

The correspondences between the mother figures are even more striking. Of Elsbeth Leverkühn Zeitblom says: "The hair half covered the ears . . . it was drawn tightly back, as smooth as glass, and the parting above the brow laid bare the whiteness of the skin beneath," and he particularly mentions "the capable brown hands with the wedding ring on the right one . . . neither coarse nor fastidiously cared for." He singles out the same features in Else Schweigestill: "her brown hair, only touched with grey, drawn smoothly away from the parting, so that you saw the white skin," "her well-shaped capable little hands with the plain wedding ring." And he says of Peronella Manardi, "hair . . . with at most a faint silver network on the smooth head," "small, work-hardened hands, the double widow's ring on the right one."

Palestrina is not strictly speaking an "imitation" of Adrian's other milieus, but certain features clearly suggest Buchel and Pfeiffering. Zeitblom describes the top of the mountain above Palestrina as a spot dear to himself and his wife, and the cloisterlike atmosphere of Pfeiffering is recreated in

Palestrina by the monastery garden Adrian frequents. Zeitblom confirms that these features form part of a pattern in Adrian's life when he says of Adrian's winter headquarters in Rome, "The role of the cloister garden of Palestrina was played in Rome by the Villa Doria Pamfili."

Although we thus have sufficient evidence for a principle of repetition in the structure of the novel, Mann's habit of operating with parallel explanations for one and the same phenomenon prevents us from ascertaining whether he subscribes to one unqualified philosophy of history. We are, however, entitled to recall that the *Joseph* novels and *The Beloved Returns* are permeated with the idea of recurrence, which forms the core of the "mythic method" as used in the twentieth century. Joyce's *Ulysses,* the prime example of the contemporary mythic novel and considered by Mann to be related to his *Doctor Faustus,* is deeply indebted to Vico's cyclical concept of history.

Mann's portrayal of history in the *Joseph* novels plays on mythic man's conception of time as an eternal cycle. The mythic pattern constantly repeats itself, reincarnated in different human beings, who play their parts according to timeless rules. Thus Joseph calmly and proudly accepts the three-day torture in the spring, aware that it is part of his role as a chosen one; for Joseph is an incarnation of the god Tammuz-Adonis who is buried and passes to the Underworld to wait for resurrection. This myth can be linked to history, the symbol of the grave foreshadowing the historical Christ. Joseph can likewise be seen as a reincarnation or repetition of earlier figures, some of them legendary. In *Doctor Faustus* we find this very form of recurrence; the concept of "Faustian" man plays the same part as the myth of Tammuz-Adonis in *Joseph and his Brothers.* Beethoven, Nietzsche, and Adrian all reincarnate or reenact the Faust myth as Mann interprets it.

Mann's interest in the recurrence theory dates back to before his systematic studies of mythology. An interesting comment of 1926 tells us:

> German heads, and not only professorial heads, harbor a strong belief in historical recurrence, and especially recurrence in the history of ideas. Thus historical interest at present centers on the German romantic revolution of the early nineteenth century against the Enlightenment, idealism, and classicism of the eighteenth century, that is, on the antithesis between belief in humanity and belief in nationality.

Mann avoids mentioning his own stand on the matter, but one may assume from his long admiration for Nietzsche and Schopenhauer and profound knowledge of their works that he largely shares the romantics' view.

Nietzsche's concept of "eternal recurrence" stems from Schopenhauer, who rejects causality as a regulative principle in historical and individual affairs. Schopenhauer treats the problem in his essay *On the Four-Fold Foot of the Principle of Sufficient Reason,* in which he draws a parallel between causality and temporality, regarding them both as functions of the human intellect, as Kantian categories. As a disciple of the Indian philosophers, Schopenhauer contends that the veil of Maya prevents us from seeing reality without illusion. In his Schopenhauer essay, written in 1938, only five years before he started work on his *Doctor Faustus,* Mann chooses for discussion precisely this idea of Schopenhauer's.

Following in Schopenhauer's footsteps, Nietzsche cannot consider time, space, and causality anything but illusions. In the section "Against Causality" of his *Will to Power,* Nietzsche develops this theme: time and space do not exist "for themselves." Changes are nothing but phenomena of our own representation. Seeing causal links in a succession of events is a mistake: *"There is no such thing as a cause or an effect."* The fact that we can predict the course of an event with fair accuracy is based not on the law of cause and effect but on *"the recurrence of 'identical cases.'"*

In his Nietzsche essay of 1947 Mann echoes this criticism of overemphasis of causal connections. The example he chooses is significant for our discussion of *Doctor Faustus:* he attacks those who would see Fascism as a direct result of Nietzsche's pronouncements. According to Mann, more is at issue than a simple causal reaction. Fascism seized upon and put into practice ideas that were in the air; Nietzsche had simply acted as an extremely sensitive instrument, registering the spirit of a new age before it became patent. Mann further remarks that the modern skepticism of science toward all laws of causality corroborates Nietzsche's claims. And when in his novels Mann uses the concept of "recurrence of identical cases," he is at once holding faith with his philosophical mentor Nietzsche and concurring in a belief that influenced many of his contemporaries.

Another philosopher of history who must be mentioned is Oswald Spengler, whose famous *Decline of the West* (1918) has many external features in common with Mann's historical thinking. Spengler sees cultures as organisms that undergo a recurrent cycle of birth, flowering and death. Such concept pairs as culture-civilization and soul-intellect remind one of the *Betrachtungen eines Unpolitischen,* which appeared the same year as Spengler's work. In view of these similarities, it may seem strange that Mann expresses open hostility to Spengler. In his short essay "On the Theory of Spengler" (1924), he speaks of Spengler's "hyena-like gift of prophecy." Bitter polemics alternate with biting irony. Of his more objective arguments, the following deserves our interest:

> Intellectualism, rationalism, relativism, cult of causality, of the "natural law"—with all that his theory is saturated; and against that leaden historical materialism the materialism of a Marx is sheer blue-sky idealism.

One of Mann's reasons for rejecting Spengler's philosophy of history is that it overemphasizes causality; Mann thus takes his place beside Nietzsche in the battle against the materialistic view of history. Many of his contemporaries share this attitude, particularly the expressionists. In 1925 Albert Soergel's monumental survey of modern German literature summarized the expressionists' program as follows: "Down with the tyranny of the law of causality in literature!"

Among the modern researchers who directly or indirectly influenced Mann's speculations on mythology is C. G. Jung. Jung, to be sure, does not hold a cyclical view of history, but his doctrine of archetypes, "lived vita" as Mann calls them in an essay of 1936, is a clear reaction against causal determinism. It is symptomatic that one of the fundamental points of difference between Freud and Jung was precisely the concept of causality. We have already pointed out that the naturalistic and deterministic features of *Doctor Faustus* contain echoes of Freud, and we suggested that Adrian's psychic abnormality might be interpreted as a traumatic neurosis. In Jung's terminology, Adrian's life becomes a role played in imitation of an archetypal model. Here we have a striking example of the manifold structure of meaning in the novel; as one can analyze it using the categories of causal determinism on the one hand and of myth and type on the other, one can adopt the terminology of either Freud or Jung. As a matter of fact, several years before *Doctor Faustus* Mann had already linked the two systems in a manner that proves of interest for our discussion of *Doctor Faustus*. In "Freud and the Future" he writes:

> Infantilism—in other words, regression to childhood—what a role this genuinely psychoanalytic element plays in all our lives! What a large share it has in shaping the life of a human being; operating, indeed, in just the way I have described: as mythical identification, as survival, as a treading in footprints already made!

Here neurotic bonds are identified with mythic recurrence, and both explanations are relevant for Adrian's fate.

Wherever we find the idea of recurrence in Mann's works, it is associated with evolution. This combination is present to some extent in *Tonio Kröger* and becomes a major theme in the *Joseph* novels and *The Beloved Returns*. One critic uses the fitting simile of spiral motion for this modified version of recurrence. Joseph's life repeats the lives of earlier mythic figures, but within the repetition he is allowed a certain amount of freedom and thus given the possibility of becoming a responsible "provider." In his Goethe novel Mann sums up this idea in the formula "recurrence enhanced by awareness."

In *Doctor Faustus,* too, the idea of recurrence appears in alliance with the idea of evolution, but a decisive change has occurred. In Mann's earlier works the spiral moved upward into higher realms of the spirit; in *Doctor Faustus* it moves downward into the realm of darkness and the demonic.

HISTORY MADE "DEMONIC"

We have already seen that "Germany and the Germans" tries to trace Germany's downward path to the demonic and destruction. Mann seeks to explain the nation's plunge into a catastrophic war by its intellectual history; he sets himself the riddle to solve of "why their good, in particular, so often turns to evil, becomes evil in their hands." For one of Mann's fundamental contentions is that Germany's originally good and praiseworthy qualities have become corrupted. "Inwardness," the source of German metaphysics, music, the Reformation, and romanticism, produces, according to Mann, "melancholy"—rather than tragic—results: "Wicked Germany is merely good Germany gone astray, good Germany in misfortune, in guilt, and ruin."

How does Mann portray this "demonization" in *Doctor Faustus?* Instances of inwardness make their appearance early in the novel, bearing the characteristics that Mann designates as the root of the evil: intimacy with the irrational and demonic forces of life, an inclination toward profundity and mysticism. The evolution of some of the names that figure in Adrian's childhood environment points unmistakably to demonization. The hill near the farm is called Mount Zion, and the watchdog is named after the medieval mystic Heinrich Suso. When these childhood surroundings recur in Pfeiffering, significant changes have taken place in the names: the hill is now called the Rohmbühel, a name taken from the Faust chapbook. The milkmaid's name, Waltpurgis, suggests witchery and magic. The pious mystic has been replaced by Kaschperl, the devil himself. Elsewhere in the novel we encounter the name Kaspar in connection with Weber's *Freischütz*, and Adrian uses the name for the devil. Zeitblom dwells on the fact that Adrian and the dog have a mystical bond. Suso is said to be "by no means good-natured to strangers." But he is really dangerous when "let free to roam the court at night." This description seems to suggest that the German soul's greatest peril arises from what the romantics called "the nocturnal side of Nature," those aspects that lie outside the control of light and reason.

The deterioration of German inwardness symbolized by the changing names corresponds to the line from romanticism to Hitler plotted in "Germany and the Germans." There we noted that Mann often employs words like "diabolical" and "hell" in connection with Hitler. The word "dog" also occurs frequently. The expression "go to the dogs" is a common one, but Mann's predilection for it is striking. In a radio talk of 1941 he says, for example:

> I admit that what is called National Socialism has long roots in German life. It is the virulent perversion of ideas which always harbored the germ of corruption, but which were by no means foreign to the good old Germans of culture and education. There these ideas lived in grand style; they were called "romanticism" and held much fascination for the world. One may well say that they have gone to the dogs and were destined to go to the dogs, as they were destined to go to Hitler.

In a speech given the same year he compares Hitler's voice to the "voice of a raging dog"; one thinks immediately of the "yapping of the yard dog" Kasperl in *Doctor Faustus*.

Apart from the symbolism of names, Mann has various other ways of presenting the demonic potentialities of German inwardness. At the beginning of the novel Zeitblom asks "whether a clear and certain line can be drawn between the noble pedagogic world of the mind and the world of the spirit which one approaches only at one's peril," a question which "is very pertinent to my theme." Shortly thereafter Zeitblom illustrates the difficulty of making a clear distinction. He stresses Jonathan Leverkühn's contemplativeness and mysticism, as well as his Faustian "speculation" and experimentation. Jonathan's innocent and engaging thirst for knowledge and his interest in research both contain a questionable element, and Zeitblom approves of the interpretation "that all this had quite close relations with witchcraft, yes, belonged in that realm and was itself a work of the 'Tempter.'" The Faustian urge to probe the universe and coax forth nature's secrets can easily degenerate into diabolical presumption and arrogance.

Adrian's explorations of the ocean depths and the universe occupy a much later stage in this development—or degeneration. He recounts his adventures to Zeitblom in the evening—"when Suso, the yard dog, in other words Kaschperl was loosed from his chain and allowed to range the courtyard." Adrian's companion, Professor Capercailzie, is an unmistakably demonic figure. Adrian's urge "to fling himself in the ocean of the worlds" terrifies the good humanist Zeitblom, who sees in it an unholy desire for knowledge. It exceeds the limits of the human and the humane; the proper label for such undertakings is "devil's juggling."

Adrian's descent into the "virginal night" perhaps symbolizes a special form of "inwardness," that is, the exploration of the abysses of the human soul. The sense of shame mentioned in the following quotation would be as much justified in the case of the nether regions of the soul as of the sea:

> Adrian spoke of the itch one felt to expose the unexposed, to look at the unlooked-at, the not-to-be, and not-expecting-to-be-looked-at. There was a feeling of indiscretion, even of guilt, bound up with it, not quite allayed by the feeling that science must be allowed to press just as far forwards as it is given the intelligence of scientists to go. The incredible eccentricities, some grisly, some comic, which nature here achieved, forms and features which seemed to have scarcely any connection with the upper world but rather to belong to another planet: these were the product of seclusion, sequestration, of reliance on being wrapped in eternal darkness.

If one assumes that Mann means here the shocking revelation of hidden aggressions—predatory mouths . . . obscene jaws"—by depth psychology, one must also realize that Mann did not consider depth psychology a product of moral degeneration; its function in this context is to discover certain human inclinations that were later to be unleashed by National Socialism.

The symbolism of Adrian's fantasies about outer space carries much the same significance. Adrian is fascinated by the theory of a constantly exploding and expanding universe; we are reminded first of the twentieth-century scientific triumphs in which Germany played an important part. But symbolically the theory suggests Germany's dreams of national expansion and world domination. When Zeitblom protests with "religiously tinged humanism" against Adrian's astronomical fantasies, his terminology echoes the speeches with which Mann bombarded Germany in the early 1940s when it was trampling all human values under foot:

What reverence and what civilizing process born of reverence can come from the picture of a vast impropriety like this of the exploding universe? Absolutely none. Piety, reverence, intellectual decency, religious feeling, are only possible about men and through men, and by limitation to the earthly and human. Their fruit should, can, and will be a religiously tinged humanism, conditioned by feeling for the transcendental mystery of man, by the proud consciousness that he is no mere biological being, but with a decisive part of him belongs to an intellectual and spiritual world, that to him the Absolute is given, the ideas of truth, of freedom, of justice; that upon him the duty is laid to approach the consummate.

In "Germany and the Germans" Mann calls the drive for national expansion the expression of another "highly valuable, positive trait," the "inner boundlessness," "universalism and cosmopolitanism" of the Germans. Mann observes that this trait has been perverted into the drive for hegemony in Europe and the world. According to Mann, cosmopolitanism is in fact characteristic of some of the most highly "representative" Germans, among them Goethe and Nietzsche; Adrian Leverkühn, in accordance with his symbolic role, shares this trait. In the student discussions Adrian meets his friends' patriotic arguments with light irony; his principal opponent in the discussions bears the descriptive name of Deutschlin. Adrian's attention is directed outward toward Europe, an orientation that comes out in his esteem for foreign literatures. He often takes the texts for his compositions from the works of English, French and Italian poets.

Adrian's cosmopolitanism emerges most clearly in the chapter on the impresario Fitelberg, who attempts in vain to lure Adrian and his music into the world. Fitelberg praises the curious combination of Germanness and cosmopolitanism in Adrian's work. Zeitblom remarks earlier that Adrian's music is very German, "music of Kaisersaschern," and Fitelberg agrees: "C'est 'boche' dans un degré fascinant." At the same time he praises Adrian's "broadmindedness in the choice of his texts, ce cosmopolitism généreux et versatile." But this admirable attitude of Adrian's is obstructed by his typically German unwillingness to commit himself to the rest of the world. Fitelberg understands and respects this feeling, but he cautions Adrian about it, and appropriately he slips into reflections that apply to the German nation as a whole.

Fitelberg sees Adrian's withdrawal to Pfeiffering, "ce refuge étrange et érémitique," as an expression of the typically German inclination toward isolation that grows out of a sense of being somehow unique: "You do not want to hear about other destinées, only your own, as something quite unique—I know, I understand. . . . You pay tribute to an arrogant personal uniqueness—maybe you have to do that." This tendency seems to Mann one of the sure sources of the German catastrophe. Later Fitelberg continues in the same vein: "You probably do not realize, cher Maître, how German is your répugnance, which, if you will permit me to speak en psychologue, I find characteristically made up of arrogance and a sense of inferiority, of scorn and fear. I might call it the ressentiment of the serious-minded against the salon world." "Arrogance and a sense of inferiority"—that is the dangerous combination of characteristics that Thomas Mann designates in his 1933–34 diaries as the fertile soil in which Nazi ideology rooted; in "A Brother" he assigns them to Hitler himself. As Fitelberg comes to the end of his remarks, he is no longer talking about Adrian and his music. He openly discusses German nationalism, drawing a parallel to Jewish nationalism; any other form of nationalism is "child's play" by comparison. In parting he issues a clear warning, the very same warning that Mann had been giving since the beginning of the 1930s: "With their nationalism, their pride, their foible of 'differentness,' their hatred of being put in order and equalized, they will get into trouble."

Mann considers the Germans' theological bent another of the basically admirable traits that can become corrupted, with catastrophic results. Interest in religion and theology is closely related to the German love for speculation and brooding that we see in Jonathan Leverkühn, who pores over both the sacred texts and Luther's commentaries in the old family Bible. Adrian displays the same combination of Faustian tendencies and Lutheran Protestantism as his father. Adrian's devout parents are pleased that he begins his academic career as a student of theology in Halle. But at the first mention of Adrian's choice of a profession, we are given to suspect that he is not motivated by his father's seemingly innocent piety. Zeitblom is shocked at his friend's choice; he says: "I divined very clearly—that he had made his choice out of arrogance."

The theological instruction offered at the University of Halle proves highly dubious. The demonic features of Professor Kumpf (Luther reincarnated) shrink to insignificance in comparison with the diabolical doctrines of Schleppfuss. When Mann summarizes the bold dialectics of Schleppfuss's lectures, he almost uncannily undermines the entire philosophical and theological thought of the renowned nineteenth century, built on the irresponsible manipulation of abstractions. Mann shows how the dialectical method works to dissolve fixed oppositions, thereby paving the way for the collapse of morality and the destruction of traditional values that took place under Nazism. The following quotation from Schleppfuss illustrates this effect: "For he received, if I may so express myself, dialectically speaking, the blasphemous and offensive into the divine and hell into the empyrean; declared the vicious to be a necessary and inseparable concomitant of the holy, and the holy a constant satanic temptation, an almost irresistible challenge to violation." What makes theology suspect, however, is less its potential historical implications than its affinity for the demonic. Schleppfuss exemplifies for Zeitblom the idea "that theology by its very nature tends and under given circumstances always will tend to become daemonology." In his farewell address Adrian describes his study of theology as a step toward his pact with the devil: "So did I feed my arrogance with sugar, studying divinity at Halla Academie, yet not for the service of God but the other, and my study of divinity was secretly already the beginning of the bond and the disguised move not Biblewards, but to him, the great religiosus." His theology study is also only a preliminary step toward his real career: "For who can hold that will away, and 'twas but a short step from the divinity school over to Leipzig and to music, that I solely and entirely then busied myself with figuris, characteribus, formis conjurationum, and what other so ever are the names of invocations and magic." "Germany and the Germans" likewise maintains that music and theology are connected and originate in German inwardness. Mann there calls music "Christian art with a negative prefix"; the two disciplines share the disposition toward abstract speculation and mysticism that Adrian inherits from his father and expresses emphatically in his compositions. As we have seen, Adrian is fascinated by abstract or magical number relationships and constellations.

It is these features that Mann stresses when, in "Germany and the Germans," he relates the dangerous elements in the German soul to musicality. He proceeds to describe music as the typically German art form:

> Music is calculated order and chaos-breeding irrationality at once, rich in conjuring, incantatory gestures, in magic of numbers, the most unrealistic and yet the most impassioned of arts, mystical and abstract. If Faust is to be the representative of the German soul, he would have to be musical, for the relation of the German to the world is abstract and mystical, that is, musical,— the relation of a professor with a touch of demonism, awkward and at the same time filled with arrogant knowledge that he surpasses the world in "depth."

What constitutes this depth? Simply the musicality of the German soul, that which we call its inwardness, its subjectivity, the divorce of the speculative from the socio-political element of human energy, and the complete predominance of the former over the latter. Europe always felt it and understood its monstrous and unfortunate aspects.

Thus even the gift whereby Germany so greatly enriched Western culture, musicality, proves to contain seeds of the German catastrophe. On this point we see how uncompromisingly Mann settles his accounts with the tradition of German culture. We can also guess what it must have cost Mann to cast suspicion on the cultural and intellectual values that underlay his entire life and work. *Doctor Faustus* is not merely an indictment of Germany's destiny. It is the artist's indictment of himself.

Doctor Faustus and Mann's political and historical writings of the 1930s and 1940s represent Germany's development in the preceding five centuries as a process of decay, in the course of which admirable qualities succumb to exaggeration and unfortunate combinations and acquire a demonic character that smoothes the way for Nazism. Mann distinguishes several facets in the nation's catastrophic situation: politico-historical, psychological, moral, and religious or metaphysical, and he tries to track down the specific source of evil in each of these fields.

Having cited a few examples to show how Mann traces the course of the degeneration process, we must still face up to a question touched on earlier: What forces control history? Do events have a meaning and a goal, or is everything pure chance? As we saw, Mann uses at least two explanatory principles, that of causal determinism and that of the "recurrence of identical cases." Those principals run parallel; Thomas Mann does not commit himself one way or the other. Yet neither of these explanatory principles answers our question. Merely describing the laws or mechanisms that seem to rule events will never reveal their meaning. Meaning can only be determined within a religious or metaphysical context. It seems undeniable that in *Doctor Faustus* Mann tries to interpret history from a religious and metaphysical point of view. To support this intuition, we must seek the key to the symbolism of music and especially of Adrian's last composition, *The Lamentation of Dr. Faustus*.

ISADORE TRASCHEN

The Uses of Myth
in Death in Venice

In reviewing Joyce's *Ulysses* in 1923 T. S. Eliot observed that

> In using the myth [of the *Odyssey*], in manipulating a continuous
> parallel between contemporaneity and antiquity, Mr. Joyce is pur-
> suing a method which others must pursue after him. ... It is
> simply a way of controlling, of ordering, of giving shape and a
> significance to the immense panorama of futility and anarchy
> which is contemporary history. It is a method already adumbrated
> by Mr. Yeats, and of the need for which I believe Mr. Yeats to
> have been the first contemporary to be conscious. ... Instead of
> the narrative method, we may now use the mythical method.

Eliot was, of course, affirming his own practice as well, his recreation the
year before of the "long narrative poem" in *The Wasteland*. Yet, as we know,
back in 1911 Thomas Mann had already employed the mythical method in
giving shape to *Death in Venice* by drawing upon Nietzsche's concept of the
Apollonian-Dionysian mythology in *The Birth of Tragedy*. But Mann anticipated Joyce and Eliot by drawing upon still another area of myth, one
apparently disguised so well that it has gone unnoticed. This area of myth
has been established by Joseph Campbell in his exhaustive and brilliant study,
The Hero with a Thousand Faces [Joseph Campbell, *The Hero with a Thousand Faces* (New York: Pantheon Books, 1949). All further references will

From *Modern Fiction Studies* 11, no. 2 (Summer 1965). © 1965 by Purdue Research
Foundation.

be to Campbell]. This study reveals that the heroes of mythology undergo a common pattern of experience; Campbell calls this pattern the monomyth. The monomythic pattern is that of the Adventure of the Hero, divided into the phases of Departure, Initiation, and Return. Gustave von Aschenbach, Mann's hero, does not return. Thus the last phase of the monomyth points to the difference between the divine comedy—the reunion with the Deity— which actually or figuratively shapes the old myths, and the tragedy which shapes *Death in Venice*. The mythic hero's adventure takes place in a world which, even if haunted by unfriendly spirits, is nonetheless made for him; Aschenbach's adventure takes place in a world he does not belong to, a formless, polyglot, perverse, cosmopolitan society. This difference in the last phase suggests that Mann will use the mythic pattern ironically, parodistically, again anticipating Joyce and Eliot.

Death in Venice, then, embodies two primary myths, the Apollonian-Dionysian and the monomyth. But what I have said about the corresponding patterns of Mann's tale and the monomyth is hardly sufficient evidence that Mann was drawing upon this mythic type; *Bildungsroman* and picaresque novels can be shown to have the same pattern, with a "happy" ending. That Mann would have turned to myth is likely from his own earlier work, stimulated as it was by the strong disposition toward myth in the nineteenth century, particularly in Germany. Further, that myths had common patterns was a familiar notion by 1911—*The Golden Bough* had already been an influence for some twenty years. But that *Death in Venice* is the first to use the mythic method as a way of giving shape and significance to contemporary history by manipulating a continuous parallel between contemporaneity and antiquity still needs to be demonstrated. This I will now do, and at the same time show how Mann integrated the monomyth into the Apollonian-Dionysian mythology.

In the first phase, that of departure, the monomythic hero is one who is exceptionally gifted and frequently honored by society; so with Aschenbach, the master of official, Apollonian art, and so officially von Aschenbach since his fiftieth birthday. But Mann is at once ambiguous about his hero, for the name means both life and death. *Bach* is a brook or stream, a life symbol; but also the root of Bacchus, or Dionysus, a death symbol here, as is *Asch*, ashes. The condition in myth which gives rise to the adventure is an underlying uneasiness in the hero and society. In our story the social uneasiness is owing to the plague which has been menacing Europe for some months, the personal uneasiness *apparently* to overwork. In myths this condition is presented openly as disastrous: "In apocalyptic vision the physical and spiritual life of the whole earth can be represented as fallen or on the point of falling into ruin" [Campbell]. Mann, though, beguiles the reader through understatement: with Europe and Aschenbach menaced, his hero responds with a short stroll. We are beguiled further by the casual account of the chance meeting, as often in myths, with a stranger, here standing in the portico of the mortuary chapel. But Mann is pointing to an apocalyptic moment, for the stranger is standing above "two apocalyptic beasts"— plague and death in our story. Now Mann unleashes the full apocalyptic vision; stimulated by something unpleasant in the stranger, Aschenbach suddenly feels a "widening of inward barriers," and this brings on "a seizure, almost an hallucination." "Desire projected itself visually," and it takes the form of a tropical marshland, a jungle rampant with male and female symbols of sexuality. The jungle is the source of the plague; and it is in India, where the cult of Dionysus presumably originated; thus the plague symbolizes the apocalyptic, destructive force of Dionysus. Now with the mythic hero, an apocalyptic event signalizes the beginning of a moral rebirth; the summons of a stranger usually marks "the dawn of religious illumination and 'the awakening of the self,'" followed by the "mystery of transfiguration." In *Death in Venice* all this is realized with tragic irony in Aschenbach's religious debauch, the awakening of his self to sensual lawlessness, and his mock transfiguration.

The hallucination points to a modern refinement of the mythic material. Mann said he came late to Freud, yet the phrase, "Desire projected itself visually," and the "Freudian" symbols throughout suggest a familiarity with Freud's work; *The Interpretation of Dreams* had come out some twelve years before *Death in Venice*. Thus the landscape of the monomyth, filled with sinister figures, is in this sense the naïve, external equivalent of the terrain of Aschenbach's inner self. He journeys to the darkest recesses of the self, to the unconscious. From this point of view the action of the story is the gradual unveiling of Aschenbach's unconscious, fully revealed in the Dionysian orgy through the appropriately Freudian dream mechanism.

Who is the stranger? He is "the herald" of the myth who summons the hero to the adventure, the "carrier of the power of destiny," often loathsome and underestimated; he calls up feared, unconscious forces. So Aschenbach feels an unpleasant twinge, but in a minute forgets the stranger, pushing him out of his consciousness. But Aschenbach's unconscious has been sounded, and the hallucination follows. In the myths, as Campbell observes, "The regions of the unknown (desert, jungle, deep sea, alien land, etc.) are free fields for the projection of unconscious content." Jungle, sea and alien land all figure crucially in *Death in Venice,* and if we stretch a point about the sandy beach, the desert too. Now why does the stranger resemble the others

Aschenbach meets, all of whom share many features with Aschenbach and, to a lesser extent, Tadzio? Vernon Venable has pointed out that "as morbid caricatures of the heroes of his [Aschenbach's] own novels [they] are really images of himself and his loved-one Tadzio"; in other words, projections of Aschenbach's unconscious. The stranger's features make it clear that the latent forces are an ambiguous mixture of refinement and coarseness, which will be manifest later in Aschenbach as homosexuality and bestiality. The ambiguities in his appearance reflect the Apollonian-Dionysian polarity. The man is beardless, with milky freckled skin; this suggests youthful innocence, yet with homosexual implications—all pointing to Tadzio. His red hair, though, indicates sensuality, as does his snub-nose, a notable aspect of the mask of the satyrs in Greek tragedy. The snub-nose also suggests the human skull, or death, the consequence of sensuality in our story; the stranger resembles Dürer's "Death." Mann's use of the snub-nose as a Dionysian symbol becomes positively brilliant when we remember it was a feature of Socrates, at first Aschenbach's rationalizing Apollonian spokesman. In the *Symposium* Socrates is further described as having a face "like that of a satyr"; and he is also called a "bully," the term Mann uses for the Dionysian guitarist at the hotel—Dionysus had an epiphany in the form of a bull. All this points to the Dionysian underlife in what this supreme rationalist says to Phaedrus-Tadzio. Further ambiguities in the stranger are indicated by his indigenous rucksack and yellowish woolen suit which are oddly coupled with a straw hat suggesting the South. The stranger is also bold, domineering, ruthless, and possibly deformed, all Dionysian elements. Like many of the others, he has long, white, glistening teeth, suggesting the threatening Dionysian animal; the threat is brought to the surface in the unhealthy teeth of Tadzio which carry out the motif of the Dionysian plague.

These exotic qualities, aspects of the theme of dislocation, stimulate a longing for travel in Aschenbach which leads to a loss of control, a farewell to disciplined work. So in the adventure of the monomythic hero that which is "somehow profoundly familiar to the unconscious—though unknown, surprising, and even frightening to the conscious personality—makes itself known." And the consequence is that "what formerly was meaningful may become strangely emptied of value." For Aschenbach, too, the old occupations are no longer attractive, and though terrified, he feels an inexplicable longing for the new. "The familiar life horizon has been outgrown; the old concepts, ideals, and emotional patterns no longer fit; the time for the passing of the threshold is at hand" [Campbell]. He whimsically decides he will go on a journey, but not—and here the whimsy is overtaken by his unconscious—all the way to the Dionysian tigers of his hallucination. A night in a *wagon-lit*—a phrase which sounds the motifs of the Dionysian night, sleep, and death; three or four weeks of lotus eating—the familiar Apollonian temptation of Odysseus, with an undertone of the "lethargic element" [Friedrich Nietzsche, *The Birth of Tragedy* (in the *Philosophy of Nietzsche,* Modern Library, New York, n.d.) All further references will be to Nietzsche] of the Dionysian—this beguiles Aschenbach, all he believes he will allow himself.

As the monomythic hero sets out on his journey he sometimes has a guide; so Aschenbach parodistically studies "railway guides." Supernatural aids are frequent. "The first encounter of the hero-journey is with a protective figure (often a little old crone or old man) who provides the adventurer with amulets against the dragon forces he is about to pass"; and "ageless guardians will appear." The figure is parodied in the ageless young-old man encountered on the boat. And though repellent, he suggests to Aschenbach the "amulets" he will eventually use in his pursuit of Tadzio: carmine cheeks, strawberry lips, etc. In the more sophisticated myths supernatural guides often take the form of "the ferryman, the conductor of souls to the afterworld" [Campbell]. This is parodied in the gondolier, Charon with his incoherent muttering which foreshadows Tadzio's blurry tongue—the inarticulate, the bestial which overcomes Aschenbach. The gondolier forces Aschenbach to submit to his will, even if, as Aschenbach says in his first overt surrender, this means sending him "down to the kingdom of Hades," that is, the unconscious, the demonic. The sinister aspect of the man is further indicated by the casually realistic fact that he has no license to ferry people, so that he cannot stay for Charon's usual fee. The passage of the hero is often made in the belly of a whale, which functions as the womb in which he is reborn. In parodistic contrast the coffin-gondola is the tomb foreshadowing the death of Aschenbach; in both cases the passage is over water, here the ambiguous symbol of life and death.

In crossing the first threshold the hero feels a strong urge to venture beyond the protection of his own society; so Aschenbach is dissatisfied with the island off the Adriatic because the people are mostly Germanic, Austrian; also because the cliff formations do not provide easy access to the sea, the death-wish object. He rejoices in cosmopolitan Venice—in strange places the unconscious is freed. Campbell points out that "incestuous *libido* and patricidal *destrudo* are thence reflected back against the individual and his society in forms suggesting threats of violence and fancied dangerous delight." There is incest in the implied son-father relationship of Tadzio and Aschenbach, who never had a son and so was presumably untutored in his potential homosexuality. The implication of incest is reinforced by the fact that it is the leitmotif in the Greek mysteries of the initiatory second birth.

Thus in the *Bacchae* Zeus's cry to his son Dionysus is what Aschenbach is really saying to Tadzio: "Dithyrambus, come / Enter my male womb." Aschenbach's surrender to his homosexual and incestuous feelings is a blow at his respectable father, his fatherland, and the entire bourgeois structure—passion is like crime, Mann points out.

The monomythic hero encounters threatening as well as protective figures. Some are "adroit shapeshifters." They try to seduce him by appearing as attractive young men. Aschenbach meets the same person, not merely in different shapes, but in different stages of youth—parodied in the case of the young-old man. These figures are the shifting shapes of his unconscious. Again, the hero often meets wild women; these would be the maenads in the Dionysian dream. But where the hero overcomes the dangers, in Mann's ironic treatment Aschenbach surrenders to their degenerate sexuality. The most familiar of these figures is the disarming Pan, who appears in a passage of unusual symbolic density. Its tempo, gentle then increasingly violent, is analogous to that of the entire story. It opens in Apollonian innocence: "At the world's edge began a strewing of roses [Homer's "rosy-fingered dawn"], a shining and a blooming ineffably pure; baby cloudlets hung illuminated, like attendant amoretti, in the blue and blushful haze." This is love without sex, the "pure" thing. But after this disarming correspondence between nature and Aschenbach's first sense of his feelings for Tadzio, Mann works in overt male and female sex symbols which fuse with images of a pronounced Dionysian kind:

> purple effulgence fell upon the sea, that seemed to heave it forward on its welling waves; from horizon to zenith went great quivering thrusts like golden lances, the gleam became a glare; . . . with godlike violence . . . the steeds of the sun-god mounted the sky . . . like prancing goats the waves on the farther strand leaped among the craggy rocks. It was a world *possessed*, peopled by Pan, that closed round the spellbound man . . . [my italics].

The movement from innocence to sensuality illustrates the bondage of the Apollonian to the Dionysian. In the passage quoted even the innocent opening is implicit with depravity when we consider another aspect of Mann's technique that Venable has pointed out, the poetic structure of associated images. For example, the innocent red of the roses and the "blushful" haze are linked to the sensual red of the hair and lashes of the strangers, the cheeks and lips of the young-old man and the later Aschenbach, the ripe and dead-ripe strawberries, etc.; the "blushful" haze itself contains a first awareness of sex. The innocent blue is linked with Tadzio's bluish teeth (physical decay), the bluish sand (decay and sterility) of the ticket seller, the various sailor blouses (homosexuality), the ocean (formlessness), etc. The purple suggests the Dionysian wine, and the gold reminds us of Dionysus-Tadzio's curls. Similarly, the four golden steeds of Apollo are also the four horses of the Christian-Dionysian apocalypse. Perhaps the finest irony in the paragraph is the first of several parodies of the transformation and rebirth of the monomythic hero. As Aschenbach is assaulted by this Apollonian-Dionysian vision, he feels "strangely [suggesting the strangers and the stranger god] metamorphosed" by "forgotten feelings, precious pangs of his youth, quenched long since by the stern service that had been his life and now returned." This feeling of rebirth is of course illusory, one of the many forms his temptations take.

Among the dangers encountered in crossing the threshold to the unknown are "the clashing rocks (Symplegades) that crush the traveler, but between which the old heroes always pass," for example, Jason and his Argonauts, and Odysseus. The rocks stand for "pairs of opposites (being and not being, life and death, beauty and ugliness, good and evil, and all the other polarities that bind the faculties to hope and fear)." But where the heroes of myth succeeded in passing through, Aschenbach is crushed by them, the face of innocence turning out to be evil. For a while, though, there is the possibility that he may escape. The faintly rotten scent of swamp and sea which he breathes in ambiguously "deep, tender, almost painful draughts" forces him to flee for his life. His escape, his salvation, is a passage through the very valley of regrets, a parodistic reversal of values. But his luggage has been shipped in the wrong direction, and this provides Aschenbach with an excuse to return to his hotel. On the return trip a wind comes up from the sea and the waves are now "crisping," that is, curling (in the original, *gekrauselten*, with the same meaning)—Aschenbach is being driven by the ambiguously lively sea to his death, to curly-haired Tadzio-Dionysus, who, it should be noted, resembles the god. The death symbolism in the apparently life-giving "crisping" is made clear at the end: as Aschenbach sits on the beach for the last time, "little crisping [*krauselnde*] shivers" run across the wide stretch of shallow water. The idea of death is reinforced by the cold and shallow water, the deserted beach, and the out-of-season (another frequent kind of dislocation) autumnal look; but most interestingly by a camera on a tripod, at the edge of the water, apparently abandoned, its black cloth snapping in the freshening wind. The tripod, a prize in the funeral games for Patroclus, carries with it overtones of the Apollonian Homer; it is also the seat of the priestess of Apollo at Delphi, secured when Apollo slew the python. Linked with the black cloth and the camera, it suggests the death of plastic, Apollonian art, and the birth of the pseudo-Apollonian, mechanical art of the camera. The death symbolism in this scene is consummated in the figure of Tadzio as the youthful Hermes Psychopompos (translated as Summoner), conductor of souls to the dead, fused with the sea. Yet the sea, the "misty inane," is still for Aschenbach "an immensity of richest expectation" just as Tadzio is still "pale and lovely."

The figure of Hermes concludes the sequence of mythological persons who make up one kind of temptation on the Road of Trials. They are all attractive, and they all remind us of Tadzio. They appear innocent at first, as with Apollo and Amor; become somewhat suspect, as with Narcissus; then openly fatal like Dionysus. Along the way we meet others too; pairs like Apollo and Hyacinth, and Zeus and Ganymede, suggesting homosexuality. These two pairs, incidentally, may be seen together with Narcissus in a room in the Bargello Palace in Florence; they are the creations of the unmarried Cellini.

The second phase of the adventure of the monomythic hero is that of Initiation, and it begins with the Road of Trials we have just noted. "Once having traversed the threshold, the hero moves in a dream landscape of curiously fluid, ambiguous forms, where he must survive a succession of trials." Aschenbach's trials develop on the boat to Venice. The trip is a kind of dream-passage. His "time-sense falters and grows dim" under the impact of the vast sea; and in his dreams the "strange, shadowy figures" of the elderly coxcomb and the goat-bearded man pass and repass through his mind. In the gondola a "spell [Dionysian term] of indolence [lotus motif] overtakes him; the "thought passed dreamily" through him that he had fallen into the clutches of a criminal. He fails this trial, too, for the thought "had not power to rouse him to action." The voyage to the underworld is another typical trial, as with Odysseus, Theseus, and Hercules, but where the mythical hero wills it, Aschenbach surrenders to it; he allows Charon to impose his will on him, and accepts Hades as his destiny; that is, he surrenders to the forces of his unconscious.

Symbolically, the Road of Trials is the hero's descent into "the crooked lanes of his own spiritual labyrinth," a precise formulation of Aschenbach's adventure. Now the image of Venice as a labyrinth—an exact translation— is used twice, both times when Aschenbach is pursuing Tadzio. This should not be taken as a conventional, dead metaphor, for its mythic content bears directly on our analysis. There is, first, an ironic analogy to Theseus as Aschenbach loses his bearings in the labyrinth—not merely geographically, but also morally and spiritually. The primary significance of the image lies elsewhere, though; according to Robert Graves, the labyrinth served in Crete and Egypt as "a maze pattern used to guide performers of an erotic spring dance." Thus Aschenbach's sterile pursuit of Tadzio parodies the fertility rite of the earlier cultures.

In the initiation phase the "ultimate adventure, when all the barriers and ogres have been overcome, is commonly represented as a mystical marriage . . . of the triumphant hero-soul with the Queen Goddess of the World. This is the crisis at the nadir, the zenith, or . . . within the darkness of the deepest chamber of the heart." This triumphant marriage is presented with savage irony in the first climax, the dream of the Dionysian rites. In the myth, the soul marries the Queen Goddess; in the dream, body copulates with body. This apocalyptic fall is the ironic counterpart of the heroic apotheosis in the monomyth. The apocalyptic climax, further, is set in the center of Greek irrationalism, showing its destructiveness; the second, philosophic climax—between Socrates-Aschenbach and Phaedrus-Tadzio—is set in the center of Greek rationalism, showing its inadequacy. Aschenbach's fall is in tragic contrast to the salvation of the mythic hero who, after his trials, can now concentrate "upon transcendental things"; the lesson of the second address to Phaedrus is that man can not endure transcendence, that poets in particular "can not walk the way of beauty without Eros as our companion and guide." We should note Mann's pacing, from the violent tempo of the apocalyptic vision to the calm, yet moving detachment of the philosophic discourse.

After the trials the monomythic hero is reborn or undergoes a metamorphosis. Mann presents a parody of both possibilities in the interlude between the two climaxes, the scene with the hotel barber. He is clearly no ordinary one. His garrulousness is a realistic echo of actual barbers, but his verbal flourishes—as elegant as his manual—indicate that this "oily one" is a parody of the magician or shaman performing the fertility rites of death and rebirth. He "restores" Aschenbach by washing his hair "in two waters," ambiguously clear and dark; "and lo," magically, Aschenbach's hair is black—he is young again, reborn. This parody of the fertility ritual is pursued further. The "delicate carmine" on Aschenbach's cheeks corresponds to the red dye, extracted from the Dionysian ivy, used to color the faces of male fertility images; and his lips are the color of the ironically ripe strawberries (*Erdbeere*), hence a mock-fertility symbol. Aschenbach is both "transformed" and "reborn." "Young again," he goes off "in a dream" to "fall in love as soon as he likes"—a shattering line. Aschenbach is in effect wearing the mask of Dionysus, like the young-old man he was repelled by earlier. In the *Symposium* Socrates' "outer mask is the carved head of the Silenus; but . . . what temperance there is residing within!" With Aschenbach there is no Socratic transcendence of sensuality; the outer mask reflects his inner self. And with our modern sense of the perpetual tensions of the inner life, we can either marvel at Socrates' equilibrium, or we can question the Platonic psychology. Mann questioned it in the entire story, and specifically in the second Platonic discourse by showing that spiritual heights and sensual abyss are the same. Plato himself seems to be aware of this elsewhere when he has the drunken Alcibiades charge that Socrates "clothes himself in language [Platonic] that is like the skin of the wanton satyr."

Aschenbach is "metamorphosed into the satyr" [Nietzsche], a parody of Nietzsche's glorification of this creature as "truth and nature in their most potent form." As with the hero in myth, he "assimilates his opposite (his own unsuspected self)." But for the [mythic] hero this action means that he must put aside his "pride, his virtue, beauty, and life, and bow or submit to the absolutely intolerable." Aschenbach puts aside his pride and virtue, and he does submit, but out of depravity, not humility.

The last phase of the adventure is The Return of the Hero—but Aschenbach does not return. It is true that in the myths the hero occasionally refused to return, taking up "residence forever in the blessed isle of the unaging Goddess of Immortal Being." Odysseus's seven years with Calypso may be an echo of this. Midway in his adventure, in his Apollonian phase, Aschenbach does feel "transported to Elysium . . . to a spot most carefree for the sons of men . . . entirely dedicated to the sun and the feasts of the sun." But the sun-Apollo-Tadzio is destructive Dionysus. Aschenbach makes one effort to leave, then surrenders to his blissful fall. His death is his ultimate refusal of society. When the mythic hero does will to return, he brings a transcendental message, one which will put an end to passing joys, sorrows, and passions. This transcendentalism is parodied in Aschenbach's ravaging sensuality. At the end the hero of myth achieves a "world-historical triumph"; Aschenbach's tragedy symbolizes the decline of European civilization.

From this demonstration of Mann's use of myth it is fair to conclude that *Death in Venice* is the first novel of our time to apply the symbolic mode with all the complexity and multiplicity of theme of *Ulysses* or *The Wasteland*, and the first to use myth to control and order what Eliot called the futility and anarchy of the modern world. Why then did Mann's innovation go unremarked? In part, no doubt, because of the way he disguised his use of myth; in part, too, because of the fact that he subdued his material to the conventional narrative form. Mann never abandoned the old form, though he took more and more liberties with it. Since the novel is a bourgeois form, the strain Mann put on it while leaving it apparently intact constituted a formal analogy of the substantive strain he put on bourgeois values and mores. In *Death in Venice* and elsewhere the orderly, bourgeois surface worked as a formal understatement of and an ironic container for Mann's radical themes. It beguiled the bourgeois reader with its apparent conventionality while at the same time disturbing him with anti-bourgeois matter in the anti-bourgeois symbolic mode. And one principal matter was myth; more precisely, modern man's relation to it.

We can explore Mann's views on this subject further by inquiring into the connection between the two areas of myth that Mann used. How do they work together? From the modern point of view we can say that the ancient sense of life as realized in the monomyth was both "naïve" and profound. It was profound in its images of the underlife; it was "naïve" in its confidence in an orderly resolution, usually through the union of the human and divine. But Mann saw that our modern sense has been even more naïve, as in our Apollonian, dreamlike illusion of a rational, myth-denying civilization; or our cult of art as a substitute religion, with the esthetic attitude superseding the ethical. Mann saw the analogy between the monomyth and the modern experience; but he also saw that where the "naïve" past took cognizance of the underlife, we did not. And so he set his Apollonian hero on a modern road of trials, a journey not through but *into* life, into the deep well of the unconscious where the Dionysian passions thrive. *Death in Venice* is a warning that art is not life nor a substitute for it; and a prophecy—fulfilled all too well—of the fate of our naïve, European civilization, its fall into barbarism.

Nor did Mann naïvely embrace Nietzsche's clamor for myth. In the closing pages of *The Birth of Tragedy* Nietzsche declares,

> Without myth every culture loses its healthy creative natural power: it is only a horizon encompassed with myths that rounds off to unity a social movement. It is only myth that frees all the powers of the imagination and of the Apollonian dream from their aimless wanderings . . . the mythless man remains eternally hungering amid the past, and digs for grubs and roots.

Yeats and Lawrence responded passionately and naively to this kind of call; and Eliot only somewhat less so—the metaphor of "roots" as well as others suggests he was conscious of Nietzsche at the time of *The Wasteland*. Mann did not respond so simply, and I would guess that it was just that humanism which Eliot and others deplored which made him more critical. Consider Mann's use of Nietzsche's conception of the Apollonian-Dionysian polarity. At times, certainly, *Death in Venice* seems to be a direct, though creative

transcription of Nietzsche's work. For example, Tadzio as "the noblest moment of Greek sculpture" symbolizes Nietzsche's idea of the highest reaches
of Apollonian art; or Nietzsche's observations that "the dithyrambic chorus
is a chorus of transformed beings, whose civic past and social position are
totally forgotten" is undoubtedly the inspiration of Aschenbach possessed
by the satyrs and the stranger god in the dream orgy; and Mann's imaginary
Platonic discourses seem to be a re-creation of Nietzsche's attack on Socratic
rationalism. But Mann was too sane to go all the way to the tiger, to champion Nietzsche's romantic, Blakean doctrine that "excess revealed itself as
truth"—wisdom for Blake. What Mann did was to take the concept of the
union of the Apollonian and the Dionysian, show their coexistence within
the individual and the tragic consequences which might follow. But he went
further. Steadfast in his conviction of the ambiguity in all ideas, he proceeded
to parody Nietzsche's as he had the modern myths of civilization and art.
For example, Nietzsche approvingly cites Lucretius as saying that in dreams
"the glorious divine figures first appeared to the souls of men; in dreams
the great shaper beheld the splendid corporeal structure of superhuman
beings"; this is parodied in the animal-like men in the dream orgy. And
Aschenbach's frequent dream state, we remember, is filled with sinister rather
than glorious figures—perhaps a Freudian parody, further, of Nietzsche's
notion of dream as a metaphor of Apollonian art. Again, Nietzsche is lyrical
about the prospect that "under the charm of the Dionysian . . . the union
between man and man [is] reaffirmed"; this is mocked everywhere, in all
the suggestions of homosexual degeneracy and in the last dream. Indeed, the
dominant homosexuality undoubtedly parodies Nietzsche's often-repeated
phrase that the genius of Greek tragedy lies in the "fraternal union" of the
Apollonian and Dionysian. Again, Nietzsche says that the Dionysian drunken
reality "seeks to destroy the individual and redeem him by a mystic feeling
of Oneness," a phrase parodied in Aschenbach's fallen state of oneness with
the stranger god. Further, for Nietzsche individuation is "the prime cause of
evil"; but Aschenbach's surrender to the Dionysian mass is evil, a consequence of his loss of individuality. For Nietzsche the Dionysian orgies signify
"festivals of world-redemption and days of transfiguration"; in *Death in
Venice* they signify world decline and disfiguration. A sketch of the evolution
of the story in terms of the Nietzschean mythology rather than the monomyth
is the clearest indication of Mann's ironic use of *The Birth of Tragedy*. From
this point of view—and with the reservation that the Apollonian and Dionysian are ambiguously present from the beginning—the story may be divided
into three esthetic phases: (1) Christian, as symbolized by Aschenbach's fictional hero, St. Sebastian; (2) pagan-Apollonian, as in the sun motif and the

sculptural metaphors of Tadzio; and (3) pagan-Dionysian, as symbolized by the plague, which now comes to the foreground, and the dream orgy. But the third phase also marks the ascent of vulgar art, that of the guitarist, the barber, and the camera. Hence it is the *un*esthetic phase—another way of marking Aschenbach's decline.

Mann made full use of the insights of the Apollonian-Dionysian polarity, expanding it beyond the fatal passion of an old man for a young boy into a symbolic tale about—among other things—the relation between art and life, the artist and society, the aristocratic past and the bourgeois present, the North and South, Platonic idealism and bodily eroticism, the conscious and the unconscious . . . about, we might say, civilization and its discontents. But Mann was not swept up by Nietzsche's romantic glorification of the polarity. In fact, just as Mann's ironic treatment of the monomyth points up the rootless existence of modern man, so his parodistic treatment of *The Birth of Tragedy* points to a disagreement with Nietzsche's optimistic prophecy of a rebirth of tragedy, with its traditional regenerative function. Nietzsche's view is reflected in a summary observation of the significance of the Apollonian-Dionysian polarity. He says that the Apollonian illusion is "the assiduous veiling during the performance of the tragedy of the intrinsically Dionysian effect: which, however, is so powerful, that it ends by forcing the Apollonian drama itself into a sphere where it begins to talk with Dionysian wisdom, and even denies itself and its Apollonian conspicuousness." What we have in this passage is an elegant phrasing of the familiar archetypal pattern of death (the denial of the Apollonian self) and transcendence-rebirth (the discovery of Dionysian wisdom). And exactly here is where Mann is most critical in his parody. Is transcendence possible for a modern tragic hero? It is in the bleakest Greek and Shakespearean tragedies where the hero believes that the cosmos, no matter how irrational and unjust, is significant for him. But with the breakdown of this belief in the last century or so, any final affirmation now is more like an empty gesture, made in an empty theatre, with no gods on the stage or in the audience. It is this which shapes our conception of the modern tragic hero. Where once his recognition of himself as a poor, naked, forked animal led to his eventual transcendence of that fact, in *Death in Venice* each recognition by Aschenbach of his capture by Tadzio-Dionysus leads only to the acceptance of his further spiritual decline. His collapse symbolizes the breakdown of the European will, of European civilization confronted by the forces of darkness. And yet, we must add, this is not Mann's last word. Some thirty-five years later in *Doctor Faustus,* in the context of the barbarous underworld of Nazism, Adrian Leverkühn confronts the diabolic in himself and realizes the "transcendence of despair . . . in which the voice of mourning . . . changes its meaning; it abides as a light in the night." Leverkühn convinces us of his transcendence by his unceasing creativity, realized by selling his soul to the devil; transcendence is possible only through despair, through the diseased "hellish yelling" in his masterwork, *The Lamentation of Dr. Faustus*. But surrender to disease destroys Aschenbach's creativity; he abdicates his creative powers. Thus Kenneth Burke is surely wrong in reading the Socratic doctrine of transcendence whereby corruption is transformed into a saving of souls as applicable to Aschenbach. It is precisely Socrates' idea of transcendence which Mann repudiates in the second imaginary conversation with Phaedrus-Tadzio.

But if Mann has in good measure parodied Nietzsche in *Death in Venice,* the fate of the mythless and rootless Aschenbach would nonetheless indicate a sympathy with Nietzsche's views on the necessity of myth, both psychologically and as a mode of knowledge. If modern rationalistic man denies myth as folk nonsense, the primal forces which myths embody will take their revenge on him. And yet, how perilous a literary, fashionable turn to myth might be is fully indicated in *Doctor Faustus* in the figures of the proto-Nazi intellectuals. Campbell summarizes the adventure of the mono-mythic hero with the observation that it is fundamentally inward—"into depths where obscure resistances are overcome, and long lost, forgotten powers are revivified, to be made available for the transfiguration of the world." Mann's point is that the revivification of these powers is not necessarily an occasion for celebration, and indeed may well be a death spasm, as with Germany under the Nazis. Once or twice Nietzsche seems to be aware of the destructive alternative to the glorious fusion and interdependence of the Apollonian and Dionysian. "Indeed, it seems as if the myth [of Oedipus] were trying to whisper into our ears the fact that wisdom, especially Dionysian wisdom, is an unnatural abomination; that whoever, through his own knowledge, plunges nature into an abyss of annihilation, must also expect to experience the dissolution of nature in himself." But this is rare, and it hardly qualifies his rapture. It may be that such passage, with its ambiguous regard of the Apollonian-Dionysian polarity, was the final touch to Mann's inspiration. For inspiration is generated in Mann by the ambiguity which paralyzes most of us.

Mann was among those who pointed to the absence of a vital myth as a fatal quality of modern existence. In doing so he gave us a marvellously complex expression of what is probably the central concern of our time—or was before the thermo-nuclear bomb made all questions but that of survival irrelevant—the problem of realizing our irrational drives within the framework of a rational society. In the modern polar view of existence developed by the romantics, reason, common sense, and civilization dry us up and emotion, unreason, and nature revitalize us. This polarity takes on varied expression: abstract-concrete, essence-existence, science-art, objective-subjective, thought-feeling, mind-body, reason-passion, classicism-romanticism, society-individual, conventional-authentic, bourgeois-artist, god-devil. We may be sympathetic with this romantic existentialist revolt, with its attempt to return men to themselves; still, *Death in Venice*—foreshadowing *Doctor Faustus*—is a reminder that one-sided excess may bring not only Dionysian wisdom but destruction as well, that if the virtues of science, reason, and civilization are of ambiguous value, so are those of myth, passion, and the so-called natural life. It is a reminder, too, that those of us who have only an external, literary relation to myth are peculiarly ripe for debauchery—intellectual as well as sensual.

EVA SCHAPER

A Modern Faust:
The Novel in the Ironical Key

The novel with [Thomas Mann] has become its own critique—which is to say that the novel in his hands becomes fully ironical. What makes *Doctor Faustus* a twentieth century document of wider than literary significance is what I would call the pathos of the *inadaequatio rei:* the awareness of the partial or total inadequacy of the current and traditional modes of description and expression for the presentation of the modern situation of anguish and dissolution. The modern imagination finds itself defeated in the attempt to explain that which is being both constructed and distorted in the very act of explanation, and the writer who confesses the creed of silence has become a familiar figure of our time. Wittgenstein's "kicking away the ladder" as something worth doing despite the apparent futility was a heroically ironical gesture *vis-à-vis* total silence. And Thomas Mann's *Doctor Faustus,* which he himself referred to as this *"Monstrum aller Romane,"* is a sustained effort to speak on the brink of silence. The result is often almost ludicrous talkativeness.

Irony, with the Romantics, had been the mode in which full self-consciousness of the spirit was alone bearable. Irony, for modern man since Kierkegaard, has become the last valid attitude in the face of the absurd, born out of full recognition of the impossibility of saying things directly. Irony is left as the only alternative to despair—although the latter can lead to other literary modes familiar to us through the existentialist experiment in fiction. Thomas Mann's novels, from *Buddenbrooks* and *Tonio Kröger* to

From *Orbis Litterarum* 20, no. 3 (1965). © 1965 by Munksgaard, Copenhagen.

Felix Krull, never abandon the outward appearance of the traditional novel, that is to say, they are never experimental in their purely formal aspect. All the old devices are there—the storyteller, the hero, the rounded life-span or span of action, the richness of epic material; yet the ironical orientation achieves in the end a transformation of this traditional edifice from within, a complete recasting of all traditional roles as re-enacted in the ironical key. For the irony discernible in Thomas Mann's novels, and in particular that which makes *Doctor Faustus* so remarkable, is not just another aspect of the novel: it is the mode in which the whole work in all its complexity is played out.

It would be futile to attempt a discussion of irony as such, since the ironical mode can only be pointed to as the way in which the novel's material is handled. To speak about irony in the abstract would lead to itself a highly ironical situation. I shall instead discuss what *Doctor Faustus* is about, from a number of different viewpoints, hoping that the ironical key of the thematic variations thus presented will become audible. The perspectives employed are still very selective and dictated by personal preference for certain strands of interpretation. They do not claim to add up, even in conjunction, to the scandalous profusion of the whole novel—that has to be read and assimilated in detail, like every other work of the creative imagination.

DOCTOR FAUSTUS AS A FICTITIOUS BIOGRAPHY

For a work of the creative imagination it *is,* despite the deliberate appearance to the contrary. The book, by a perfectly legitimate literary device, pretends to be a biography. The full title is *Doctor Faustus: The Life of the German Composer Adrian Leverkühn as Told by a Friend.* This is an old and respectable device of fiction, here used by Thomas Mann with what can only be described as an ironical slant. For the device dates back to an age when the novel had to fight for its place by pretending to be fact. Once the freedom of fiction was triumphantly established, the device either receded in importance or lost its device character and became part of the fictional framework, accepted as such. But with Thomas Mann it once more is a deliberate gesture, designed to draw attention to itself, not with the intention to deceive, for we no longer need be deceived in order to accept, but in order to put into question the complete creative freedom which the novel of the twentieth century claims as its belated birth-right. This use of the device is ironical, because it inverts the original function and expresses Thomas Mann's scepticism with regard to the possibility of pure invention. His readers are warned.

The title as given in the English translation does not quite correspond to the original; in fact, it cannot, for *Tonsetzer*—"he who puts tones together"—has no exact English equivalent. "Composer" lacks the element of humble craftsmanship and homely familiarity with the old-fashioned. This intentionally archaic suggestion of a quiet, regulated, orderly world at a creatively low temperature highlights all the more the tempestuous suggestion evoked by the main title—*Doctor Faustus*. The title states in miniature Thomas Mann's ironical attempt to provide reassuring crutches and a strict, hyper-traditional framework for what he himself called his "wildest novel." It is a foretaste of what is to happen in the novel, on many different levels, most strikingly perhaps with regard to the development of modern music, where the return to strict polyphony, to closely knit and completely bound music, is to establish an ironical framework for the musical presentation of the wildest agony of the spirit.

Deliberate archaism in musical terms is reinforced throughout the novel by the deliberate archaism of the language in which much of the story is told, especially in those scenes which explore the borderlands of sanity or rationality. The extreme instances of openly archaic language, clearly imitating sixteenth-century German usage, occur in the contexts in which the demonic in any form or disguise is at stake. Here again the irony is obvious, for such topics cannot be approached directly, since nobody seriously believes in them—not even in the novel of which they form such an important part. The highly artificial linguistic devices mitigate the embarrassment that would result from a more direct treatment. These excursions into sixteenth-century German are remarkably well motivated within the novel. The archaic form is used as a kind of private language between the biographer and his friend Adrian Leverkühn, the subject of his biography, in order to parody a university teacher to whom they had both been exposed in their student days. This teacher, whose subject was demonology as a fringe topic in Protestant theology, treated his fascinating and openly scandalous subject-matter with the ironical linguistic slant parodied later by his pupils for a more serious purpose, namely the discussion of the unleashing of hidden forces in music and general awareness, and for the reports of the encounter with the devil in the phantasies of an overheated brain. The linguistic archaism used in Leverkühn's letters to the biographer have the uncanny effect of homely reassurance, whilst we feel the foundations of the hero's mental balance shaking. The incongruity thus achieved is often superbly funny.

But apart from these parodies of linguistic usage of the past, which form only a small part of the book, the novel as a whole has a faintly archaic ring, an old-maidenish, and in all its articulateness, slightly stilted manner. Again, this is fully deliberate. The language is excessively involved, complicated to the point of self-defeating intricacy, ridiculously German in its pedantic attempt to give the fully qualified, fully accurate statement. Trying to include everything, it often manages to say next to nothing, or to entangle itself in all the snares of linguistic excess. Thomas Mann delights in using with great skill the language, even the jargon, of the German intellectual, and he portrays with frightening exactness the many tortured ways in which it can break down. Thus the first sentence is a masterpiece of deliberate failure. It breaks down half-way through the elaborate string of intricate clauses and sub-clauses, the narrator struggling to recover the thread (which is never lost in substance, only in grammar) with his "I beg to begin again." This, incidentally, is one of the few complaints to be made against the excellent English translation: it breaks up the monstrous first sentence, and substitutes a tame "to resume" for the more exasperating "I beg to begin again." As Erich Heller has remarked *à propos* Thomas Mann in translation, "any other language lacks the native training in sustained breathlessness."

Thomas Mann uses throughout the book the cumbersome language of his narrator with consistent and systematic ambiguity, thus in the long run ironically achieving complete success through the cumulative effect of linguistic half-failures and near-misses of communication. The tiresome mode of expression wears the reader at first, but oddly grows on him as the narrator plods on, creating a mood of indulgent protectiveness for the pedantic but lovable, exasperating but innocent Serenus Zeitblom. The narrator is aptly named to conjure up the image of a balanced, learned, well-meaning, if somewhat mediocre personality. "I am by nature wholly moderate, of a temper, I may say, both healthy and humane, addressed to reason and harmony; a scholar and *conjuratus* of the 'Latin host' not lacking all contact with the arts (I play the viola d'amore) but a son of the Muses in the academic sense which by preference regards itself as descended from the German humanists of the time of the 'Poets.'" Adrian Leverkühn's extraordinary story is told by this ordinary person, the well-educated and slightly pompous schoolmaster-friend of the great and turbulent composer. This oddly complex and yet simple-minded biographer is a master-stroke of the novelistic imagination. The life story of a genius, a sick but great man, recorded in a hesitant, dry, pedantic, old-fashioned manner, incorporates perhaps Thomas Mann's greatest achievement in irony: the demonic dissolution described in utterly undemonic language. The novel does not even try to find an adequate form for its violent subject matter; rather, through the deliberate juxtaposition of manner and substance, Thomas Mann states the important insight that there comes a point when violence and terror can no longer receive adequate representation. The irony of the timid biographer makes it frighteningly clear that the really demonic becomes truly horrifying when seen through the eyes and the mind of the sober and commonplace, even the bureaucratic and scientific. Through the device of a narrator who is at first glance hopelessly ill-equipped by temperament for the task of telling the story which he then so miraculously well conveys by means of his very shortcomings, Thomas Mann finds an ironical way of escape from the traditional artistic necessity to achieve adequacy of literary substance and literary manner: their very contrast and incompatibility reveal more than perfect adequacy ever could.

Serenus Zeitblom, the humanist, is a "good German"; this appears to be almost a contradiction in terms, even for the narrator himself, who realizes and discusses his own problem together with countless others which the act of relating his friend's story, under the conditions of the approaching German catastrophe, raises for an open-minded and unbiased intelligence such as he hopes to bring to his task. Thus Zeitblom forges ahead, at times nearly despairing of ever attaining his end, at others with genuine if occasionally pompous humility applying himself doggedly to his purpose.

The biography of a friend, whom he believes to have known better than anybody else, grows into a document which makes amply clear how little in fact he understands, despite the frantic accurateness of the amassed detail. The saga of Adrian Leverkühn, whom the biographer confesses to love more than his own humble self, emerges as the story of an essentially unlovable person, far removed from tenderness and sympathy into a region which even the infinite compassion of the friend only manages to indicate—through the unconscious irony of loving nevertheless. Further, this biography is not just the story of an extraordinary person, but at the same time the story of a great musician, and the account of a major revolution in musical history. As such it is told by a man who does not understand music very deeply, at least not as a musician, and who yet succeeds in conveying to us that Adrian Leverkühn was a musician of genius. This is done not only in accurate reminiscences of Adrian's own theoretical reflections, but also in laborious analyses of the difficult and intricate music here involved. The musical chapters are so adequate in their sober and repetitive grappling with structural and musicological problems that one begins to wonder whether it is perhaps the case that only the safe, the sound and unproductive can explain to us the creations of a genius. Again, I take it, this is one of Thomas Mann's ironical intentions.

Seeing the elaborate tapestry of Adrian Leverkühn's life, of the development of modern music, and of the downfall of Germany emerge before our eyes becomes an exciting adventure, undertaken all the time against the plodding and interminably qualifying procedure of Zeitblom. The tantalising pedantry turns out to be a perfect safeguard against either empathy or premature moral involvement, since we are doubly distanced from the happenings in the novel by virtue of Serenus Zeitblom's pen, and by virtue of our seeing past and through the good friend and humanist into that which he does not even claim to understand fully himself.

DOCTOR FAUSTUS AS AN AUTOBIOGRAPHY

Doctor Faustus is not in any straight sense part of Thomas Mann's autobiography, but the author has made no secret of having incorporated, in plain reportage, much of his own experience, to the extent of freely using real events and real people as events and characters in the novel. Further, he makes his narrator begin writing down Adrian Leverkühn's biography on the day he himself began to write the novel, thus achieving in the coincidence of his own and the narrator's time perspective of telling the story a singularly fruitful way on intertwining "telling time" and "time told," that is to say, time of fictional writing and the time of Adrian's life as told by Zeitblom (this makes use of Günther Müller's distinction of *Erzählzeit* and *erzählte Zeit*). The "time told," the time span of the actual biography, coincides with the time span of Thomas Mann's own first-hand experience of living in the Europe and the culture from the *fin de siècle* into the thirties; and the "telling time" covers the catastrophic end of the war and the German dissolution both from Zeitblom's perspective inside the novel and inside the "Fortress Europe," and from Thomas Mann's Californian perspective of a passionately involved but coldly reasoning observer. Ample use is made of the various possibilities of introducing autobiographical material on these several levels. Thus real events and people are sometimes introduced in subtle disguises, sometimes in such complete undisguise that the reader is not even given a choice between straight and transposed reading but remains in the curious state of tension which true *montage* imposes. It is impossible to decide from case to case whether the real elements incorporated are too important to be transformed into fiction or just too trivial, or, alternatively, whether the transposed characters and events are too significant to remain undisguised or too insignificant to become part of the fiction. Games of detection can certainly be played with this novel at great length, and critics have been eager to accept the invitation offered so generously—and they have often come to grief over it. Thomas Mann himself confessed to the principle of *montage*, thus making this novel, if an autobiography at all, a very disturbing kind of autobiography. For in *montage* the artist, whilst still adhering to the primacy of creativity in arrangement, demonstrates a radically sceptical attitude to the value of total creative invention. The *montage* artist, in whatever medium, proclaims in his work that the traditional conventions of complete homogeneity of all elements on the artistic level from which a coherently integrated illusion is built up, are exhausted and worn out. The creative imagination of the modern artist feeds ruthlessly on anything other than itself, and often deliberately refuses to mitigate the shock of direct, not distanced or disguised recognition. Thomas Mann in embracing *montage* so openly, shows an indulgent contempt for the novel as traditionally understood. He replaces the principle of thoroughgoing fiction, in which all extraneous elements have to be transformed before they can become integrated fictitious events and persons, by the principle not simply of *montage,* but of ironical *montage.* It will become clearer in a moment what I mean by this.

Thomas Mann himself in the *Genesis* speaks with extraordinary clear-sightedness of his resemblance to James Joyce in this respect. "I had held the prejudice that alongside Joyce's eccentric avantgardism my work was bound to seem like lukewarm traditionalism. To be sure, this much is true: a link with tradition, no matter how parodistic that link is, makes for easier accessibility, opens the way for a degree of popularity. But this is more a matter of attitude than of essence." He quotes with approval from Harry Levin's study of James Joyce: "Neither *A Portrait of the Artist* nor *Finnegan's Wake* is a novel, strictly speaking, and *Ulysses* is a novel to end all novels," and then continues himself thus—"this probably applies to the *Magic Mountain* and *Joseph* story, and equally well to *Doctor Faustus.*" T. S. Eliot's question "whether the novel has not outlived its function since Flaubert and James, and whether *Ulysses* should not be considered an epic" paralleled my own question whether in the field of the novel nowadays the only thing that counted was what was no longer a novel. There are sentences in Levin's book which touched me with a strange intensity. "The best writing of our contemporaries is not an act of creation, but an act of evocation, peculiarly saturated with reminiscences." And this other one: "He [Joyce] has enormously increased the difficulty of being a novelist."

Thomas Mann here acknowledges what so many modern writers know and practise: that the modern mind can no longer fully escape into fiction. This is a highly ironical situation, for the modern artist had to become, in the field of creative literature, fully self-conscious in order to achieve the unbridled freedom of fiction. Yet once achieved, it has obviously led to its own negation. The greatest novels of our time are not "novels" in the sense of fully imagined realities, thoroughly shaped by the creative imagination.

This might be a summary of the overall dialectic ironically presented in *Doctor Faustus*. The time we live in, a true transition period in every sense of the word, is witness to the exhaustion from within of most accustomed modes of living and thinking—and also of most accustomed modes of writing. That this exhaustion is the product of reaching the highest point in a development which was to free the imagination from the fetters of fact, is the irony of the dialectical process: once the point of no return is reached, there remains only the road to excess which breeds its own negation.

The author's own observations on his becoming involved in the *montage* technique form a fascinating document, showing this oddly mixed form as creating its own conventions.

> That Professor Zeitblom begins his narrative on the same day that I myself put the first lines on paper is characteristic of the entire book, of the curious brand of reality that clings to it, which seen from one aspect is total artifice. It is part of the playful effort to achieve precise—precise to the point of being infuriating— realization of something fictional: the biography and the character of Leverkühn. This work, moreover, took a curiously ruthless form, and I was constantly amazed by the way its fantastic mechanism drew upon factual, historical, personal, and even literary data. As in the "panoramas" shown in my childhood, palpable reality was for ever indistinguishably merged into painted perspectives and illusions. This montage technique was continually startling, even to me, and gave me cause to worry. Yet it rightly belongs to the conception, to the "idea" of the book; it has to do with the strange and licentious spiritual relaxation from which it emerged, with its figurative and then again literal directness, its character as arcanum and confession, so that, as long as I was working on the book, the concept of its public existence did not enter my mind.

And again at a later stage: "Besides, I was still far too greatly under the spell of a work that was confession and sacrifice through and through and hence would not be bound to considerations of mere discretion, a work that took the form of the most disciplined art and at the same time stepped out of art and became reality. And yet this reality in its turn referred back to the work itself, it was responsible in certain cases more to form than to truth, was metaphorical and phantasmal."

Thomas Mann does not use the word "irony" here, yet it is strangely present in what he says. And he states quite clearly that the autobiographical

centre of the novel is presented in an ironical inversion of the traditional
habit of lending the hidden "I" of the novel all the richness of specification
and characterization a novelist can muster, since here at least there should
be no lack of imagined and projected reality by which to model the central
character. It is the reverse in *Doctor Faustus*: the hidden "I" is split into two
not even complementary figures, and both of them, Leverkühn and Zeitblom,
remain in the full novelistic sense only shadow figures, devoid of outward
appearance—and that within a novel which abounds in fully sensuous, entirely realised fictional characters. Thomas Mann himself remarked: "Only
the characters more remote from the centre of the book could be novelistic
figures in the picturesque sense—all the Schildknapps, Schwerdtfegers,
Roddes, Schlaginhaufens, etc. But not the two protagonists, who had too
much to conceal, namely, the secret of being identical with each other."
Identical, that is to say, in the author himself, who achieved in *Doctor Faustus* a new and startling fictional autobiography.

DOCTOR FAUSTUS AS A HISTORICAL NOVEL AND AS A NOVEL ABOUT THE GERMAN FATE

This novel does not fall easily into the genre of the historical novel,
although it can be read as a fascinating document for the time span from
the turn of the century to the end of the Second World War. Thomas Mann's
own historical awareness is faithfully reflected in the elaborately prepared
backcloth to the life history of his hero and that of his narrator, and the
Genesis facilitates a straight historical reading in the most rewarding manner.
For a reader who was often too deeply involved in the cataclysmic events up
to the end of the war to remember in each case exactly how contemporary
strands of events interwove, Thomas Mann's novel together with the *Genesis*
provides more exciting and certainly more deeply moving historical reading
than many a documentary account of the same period. For it is the shock of
recognition which counts, as it can only be had from the small and apparently
insignificant item falling into place and thereby completing a complex pattern
of historical understanding. Thus one reads with a poignant sense for past
actuality Zeitblom's opening passage to one of his last chapters: "My tale is
hastening to its end—like all else today," side by side with Thomas Mann's
entry in *Genesis* for mid-February 1945: "*The Kölnische Zeitung*, evidently
no longer hampered by censorship, frankly reported that panic had seized
the Reich from one end of the country to the other . . . While I was writing
the passage in the lecture about German romanticism, I read Friedrich Heb-
bel's diaries and found in them the great sentence (noted down in Paris):

'Previous history has only grasped the idea of eternal justice; the future will have to apply it.'"

The historical perspective is more than a double or even triple perspective of the frame in which the events are reported to take place, the frame in which they are told, and the overlapping of these two forming a third. Inside the novel, historical perspectives and historical parallels are broken up or constructed in abundance and with exuberant craftsmanship and mastery of detailed merging of fact and fiction. There is also, noticeably and disconcertingly, the historical approach as a deliberate parody of itself. In the historical perspective of the tortuous and meticulously accurate narrator, we have the attempt to get back to "the beginning of it all," and Zeitblom often gets involved in Tristram Shandy's difficulty. This return to the beginning of the story told is mirrored by a parallel and equally involved attempt to return to the beginning of the time in which the story is told, the time leading up to the last war. The wish to find out what contributed to the disastrous development, how it all began, and what went wrong, underlies many of Zeitblom's ponderings and speculations. Here again the turn to the past is used ironically to emphasize that the more one tries to escape into a search for an explanation, the more one is apt to delude oneself about the significance of cause and effect, and the implications of the present. So that Zeitblom can write with deep conviction towards the end of his narrative: "What word did not shake, as only too often the hand that wrote it, with the vibrations not alone of the catastrophe towards which my story strives but simultaneously of the cataclysm in whose sign the world—at least the bourgeois, the human world—stands today?" The completely honest searching of heart—the heart of an individual and the heart of a nation—which can so easily turn into subtle self-justification by translation to the cosmic scale, is parodied in the most skilful manner, often only barely distinguishable from the real pathos which, of course, pervades much of the telling of contemporary disastrous events.

The archaism of Zeitblom's deliberations functions in this context as a device to highlight the escape aspect of the historical approach. The same can be said of the frequent drawing on the sixteenth century, either in manner of speech or in magical-Faustian content. An ironical parallelism emerges between two end periods, and two periods of passionately felt doom. Like the time in which Zeitblom speaks, the sixteenth century was a century of cataclysms, when worn-out forms were breaking and crumbling with the eventual waning of the Middle Ages and their conception of *ordo* at the cost of the individual. But the parallel reveals also an ironical contrast. For the sixteenth century was in upheaval by reason of the painful birth of individ-

ualism; now *Doctor Faustus* is in protest against its death-struggle, in which
the precarious achievements of centuries of civilization are in mortal danger
of being swept away and swallowed up by the rising tide of evil. The return
upon history, however praiseworthy in itself, can be sought as a reassurance,
almost as a deliverance from absolute individual freedom, a subtly disguised
return to the fold of the collective. Thomas Mann, with his acute and invincible moral sense, here recognizes one of the most dangerous traps in twentieth-century civilization, the outcome of, and reaction to the excess of
Romantic individualism. Tired of too much individual liberty, exhausted by
rootlessness and disconnection, twentieth-century apathy often played
straight into the hands of its lowest animal elements. This treason of the
intellect, this weakening of moral resistance under pressure from below, is a
constant theme of Thomas Mann's work. He recognizes with unclouded eyes
the comfort which reassuring collectivism can provide for the weary, the
tired, and leave-me-out-of-it-all mentality. The slogans of *Volksgeist* and
Volksseele, Blut und Boden, Rasse, and all the rest of it, had their attraction
by no means for the debased and crude alone.

In an important respect *Doctor Faustus* openly proclaims itself a novel
about the fate of Germany. Thomas Mann, though understandably obsessed
with the German problem, involved from his Californian distance almost to
distraction in the catastrophe he had seen being deliberately brought about
by the country of his birth, his love, and his basic loyalty, here again managed
the near-impossible. He gives Zeitblom the freedom to construct his narrative
as an obvious parallel, symbolically interrelated, between Adrian Leverkühn's
disastrous but glorious life, and the guilt and disaster of Germany; nevertheless, while letting this parallel be proclaimed with deadly seriousness by
a narrator whom the reader has come to respect, he conveys with superb
irony where the parallel breaks down. For the apparent equation of the life
and road to utter damnation (from which yet the immortal work survives
and rises like a phoenix from the ashes) of Adrian Leverkühn with the rise
and fall of Germany and the realization of undreamt depths of evil does not
quite work. Adrian's story of how he went to the devil is almost, but not
quite, the story of the German road to ruin. Not quite, for that would be a
typically "German" solution, an explanation of evil through creative excess
and agony of the spirit, such as the biographer unwittingly implies—with
the devastating, but surely intended result of arousing our moral protest. We
feel that this will not do. The attempt has been made only too often to
identify the German break-through of evil with some tragic inevitable happening for which the germs lie deeply embedded in the very structure of our
age. No glory attaches to "the German fate"—the very phrase spells the

hybris of the insane. Zeitblom's innocent and pathetic use of it, as of other equally loaded phrases such as "the German soul," "the tragic hour of the German people" and even "our beloved Homeland," sometimes has an ominous and slightly monstrous ring. He speaks of his sons as "serving their Führer," despite his own complete dissociation from the regime, and in a telling passage confesses unconsciously the basic moral weakness of so many upright Germans who were "against it all," but in it:

> I cannot but cherish a deep and strong resentment against the men who have reduced so good a people to a state of mind *which I believe bears far harder on it than it would on any other*, estranging it beyond healing from itself. I have only to imagine that my own sons, through some unlucky chance, became acquainted with the contents of these pages and in Spartan denial of every gentler feeling denounced me to the secret police—to be able to measure, yes, *actually with a sort of patriotic pride, the abysmal nature of this conflict* [my italics].

Fiction or no fiction, we feel that we must protest. And this, I take it, was Thomas Mann's intention. He achieved this effect with grim irony as another display of the pathos of the *inadaequatio rei*. Letting the narrator get away with "the German fate," embroidered innocently by the regime's innocuous terminology ("Fortress Europe," "Final Solution," etc.) makes the dramatic fallacy painfully, though ironically obvious. And yet—this ironical twist to the historical perspective on Germany in which the story is told, miraculously allows the real pathos of the narrator's last line to rise above the suspicion of unconscious conceit: "A lonely man folds his hands and speaks: 'God be merciful to thy poor soul, my friend, my Fatherland!'"

DOCTOR FAUSTUS AS A NOVEL ABOUT THE ARTIST IN A MODERN AGE

The German scene in which the story is set and told elicits the Faustian theme, the theme of the devil's pact, of damnation and salvation. What links the novel as a German document and the novel as a Faustian confession is the important aspect in which it is a novel about art and the artist, a *Künstlerroman* in the German tradition, and not only in the German tradition. For the European mind has for two hundred and more years (and more recently also the American mind) found the problem of the artistic personality of the utmost fascination. This could be illustrated from Cervantes's *Don Quixote* to Kierkegaard's artist of the broken spirit, from Wordsworth's *Prelude* to Henry James's probing into the intricacies of creative freedom and creative blockage, from Goethe's *Wilhelm Meister* to James Joyce's portrait of that part of himself to which he could gain enough fictional distance, from E. T. A. Hoffmann's and Dostoievski's haunted artists to Kafka's artistic nightmares and Hugo von Hofmannsthal's lucid despair—not to mention even more recent writers with whom the artistic predicament has become not only an obsession, but representative of the human condition in a late age. Hugo von Hofmannsthal, in his letter of an imaginary nobleman, Lord Chandos, has given the classical formulation of this modern predicament as the crisis of confidence in the very powers of expression. It seems that after being able to go to the full extent of creative freedom in ever subtler exploitations of the written and spoken word as token of the inner complexity and receptivity for outer events, we have reached the point where we seem to be saying less and less, where words are inadequate and degenerate into stale clichés, having been overburdened with meaning for too long. The modern artist has come to dread the words that don't quite make it, the words which are preoccupied with the adequacy of expression and fail in the last desperate attempt to be at the heart of the matter. Things fall apart in this crisis of expression, a crisis in which so many artists have lost confidence in the elucidatory and interpretative power of language. Rilke, in the first *Elegy,* has the telling lines,

> And the sensitive animals know already
> That we are no longer at home in an interpreted world.

Rilke could still give voice to this particular suffering, this painful homelessness of the artist in a world of his own making. Later and not always lesser minds have faltered before the inarticulate and inarticulable. Thomas Mann's artist-heroes are still of the expressive variety. They suffer the crisis which develops into creative paralysis, and they speak about their inability to say what they suffer. From Hanno Buddenbrook and Tonio Kröger, from Gustav Aschenbach to Adrian Leverkühn, Thomas Mann's artists are damaged spirits and lost souls, who show a brave face to a world of which they represent the highest achievement and the most sensitive awareness.

Doctor Faustus more than any other of Thomas Mann's novels is preoccupied with the agony of the often unproductive genius, with the tortured mentality of the artist who for long periods cannot force his creative insight into externalization. But here we have not simply the suffering of an artist in the crisis of expression and the well-known dread of going stale, of having nothing more to say. The novel puts even this artistic predicament into an ironical key. This happens by means of the intricate narrative framework, which allows the narrator to reproduce at length the agonized speculations of Leverkühn, adding his own, interweaving both with sometimes comical effect: for Adrian is nothing if not slightly cynical about the artistic dilemma, Zeitblom nothing if not pathetically earnest, compassionate, kindly. Adrian's often bitter, always brilliant ruminating on the intricacies of creativity and the easy dangers of the bogus, and his incessantly sparkling and frequently bewildering conversations on musical topics prompt Zeitblom to the remark: "Obviously he did not feel comfortable so long as any of his audience knew what they were to think." But he, Zeitblom, nevertheless believes that by faithful and searching recollection he can represent what was really said, felt and meant. The ironical result is that he achieves this end so often, though not through what he says, but through the incongruity of his calm manner of reporting and the monstrous difficulty of that which he wishes to convey. Of him can be said what Thomas Mann makes another—this time a definitely failed artist—say of himself in *Tristan*:

> because it is my inevitable task on this earth to call things by their right names, to make them speak, to illuminate the unconscious. The world is full of what I call the unconscious type, and I cannot endure it; I cannot endure all these unconscious types! I cannot bear all this dull, uncomprehending, unperceiving living and behaving, this world of maddening *naïveté* about me! It tortures me until I am driven irresistibly to set it all in relief, in the round, to explain, express and make self-conscious everything in the world.

This, in a way, is Zeitblom all over, and the glory of Thomas Mann's irony is perhaps never more obvious than when Zeitblom turns his full honesty to the task of saying what the artist suffers, be it in words or sounds. The creative paralysis itself becoming the object of repeated and massively serious discussion, in highly articulate terms dissecting the phenomenon of musical and general creative inarticulateness, cannot but lead to comic results. The double perspective of narrator and hero here again helps, together with the skilfully maintained fiction that this is not fiction, but biography, written down by someone totally unqualified for creativeness at first hand, and therefore alone in a position to turn Rilke's homelessness in an interpreted world into something which cannot only be endured, but parodied. The irony is that it is the ostensibly unsuccessful artist, the apparent failure, or he who claims not to be an artist at all, who is the only one who can and may still attempt to do the job from which many genuine artists have tended to abdicate.

Thomas Mann's heroes, like many artist figures in modern fiction, all somehow have a bad conscience because of the artist's position as privileged awareness, as seismograph of the intelligence of the age. The artist has become a voluntary exile within society, and he is uneasily aware of it. Thomas Mann realized the irony in this final stage of the process of emancipation of the artist, the ironical conclusion of the long drawn-out emergence of the individual from his Renaissance conception, which superseded that of the anonymous humble craftsman of the Middle Ages. The modern artist, having reached the point of total emancipation, and having developed a bad conscience about it, only too often seeks to get back into the fold of some communal reassurance.

In our century, religious and social commitments are passionately attempted, folk art and the arts of strictly codified rules appear of magical attractiveness. Art in the service of something else, and art as purely for its own sake strangely occur hand in hand, one the dialectical counterpart of the other, with the pendulum swing from one extreme of unfettered freedom to the other of voluntary commitment, often enacted within one artistic temperament, one artistic career. All this is gently parodied in *Doctor Faustus,* thrown into relief by the ironical handling of a narrative in which the creative temperament of the twentieth century is scrupulously measured by the non-involvement of the innocent and uncreative observer. The homely, non-artistic artistry of Zeitblom's telling not only of Adrian's story, but the stories of many other artists as well, brings out how many traps there are for the modern artist who finds the complete, hard-won freedom and accompanying loneliness and desolation hard to sustain. The sober and pedantic Serenus Zeitblom, so often contributing the ironical perspective by his own ignorance of the significance of the observations he puts forward, startles the reader by the acuteness with which he is aware of a flaw in one of Adrian's most impassioned speeches on art, a speech full of nostalgia for wholeness, ending in a prophecy of the art of the future. Thus Adrian: "We can only with difficulty imagine such a thing; and yet it will be, and be the natural thing: an art without anguish, psychologically healthy, not solemn, unsadly confiding, an art *per du* with humanity." Zeitblom is deeply affected, and one should have thought that this statement of the beloved friend would only too adequately put into words the good narrator's own ideal vision. Yet he is able to comment, putting his finger unerringly on the moral flabbiness of this attitude:

> With all my emotions I was yet in my deepest soul unsatisfied with his utterance, directly dissatisfied with him. What he had said did not fit with him, his pride, his arrogance if you like,

which I loved, and to which art has a right. Art is mind, and mind does not at all need to feel itself obligated to the community, to society—it may not, in my view, for the sake of its freedom, its nobility. An art that "gives in unto" the folk, which makes her own the needs of the crowd, of the little man, of small minds, arrives at wretchedness, and to make it her duty *is* the worst small-mindedness and the murder of mind and spirit. And it is my conviction that mind, in its most audacious, unrestrained advance and researches, can, however unsuited to the masses, be certain in some indirect way to serve man—in the long run men.

This is superb irony. The prosaic philistine, from which the artist of the Romantic emancipated creed, the outsider, was trying to dissociate himself, not merely is now the only one who is still moderately successful in telling the extraordinary tale, but also the only one who can detect the subtle lure of retreat from an uncomfortable outpost. This arrogant pride of the modern artist, to which Zeitblom here resentfully demands Adrian's unwavering allegiance, is the pride of the intellect, the worst hybris of man, and yet the foundation of every valid artistic gesture. This is the point where the theme of Faust and the devil's pact becomes inseparable from that of the modern artist. . . .

DOCTOR FAUSTUS AS A FAUSTIAN NOVEL

The title proclaims this novel as a member of the genre which has for its hero the ever striving, the never content, the irredeemably haunted mind, who cannot stop short with anything partial. Our considerations so far give us reason to suspect that here too the theme is played out in the ironical key.

The charge has often been levelled at this novel—as it has at other novels by Thomas Mann—that it contains too much material in the form of treatises on as many disciplines of knowledge as it is possible to incorporate on often only slender pretexts. Excursions into politics, sociology, music, musicology, philosophy, and aesthetics certainly abound. Yet there is no padding here, no showing off the richness of Thomas Mann's information. It is done with full deliberation. Moreover, the emphasis on the achievements of the intellect is implied in Thomas Mann's attitude to the problem of the poetic, artistic and generally creative situation. He regarded the intellectual weighting of his fictional writing as a completely legitimate procedure, inevitable in our age and at the present stage of civilisation, where there simply *is* such a vast amount to know about that any attempt to shun the discursive, and even the academic and scholastic, would lead to lopsided effects. The Romantic dichotomy of feeling and intellect is decisively repudiated by the novelist Thomas Mann, whose unflagging energy was devoted to an ever more explicit and classical mastery of emotional confusion.

In *Doctor Faustus*, however, the intellectualization of art has become, in an important respect, the subject matter of the novel, its own critique, and an ironical monument to this particular trend in modern fiction which counterbalances, and goes to the other extreme of, the "back to the soil of feeling" movement. *Doctor Faustus* presents the subject of modern knowledge, the achievement of a civilization which is tottering under the onslaught of destructive forces from within. An extraordinary fusion of scholarship, musicology, philosophy, speculation, theology, playfulness, sheer joy in elaborate storytelling, and a complex moralizing attitude contribute to the extravagant richness of the fictional content. At the same time the intellectual fireworks and brilliance are given an ironical distance in the manner of reporting, which constantly doubles back upon itself, and is always suspicious of blurring vital distinctions to the extent of deliberately extinguishing any spark of unleashed enthusiasm. The full range of intellectual modes of the last fifty years is nevertheless at issue. They all come in for their share in this novel about knowledge, about the striving after knowledge, and about the risk and even the curse of its achievement. The exuberant trust in unaided human reason, its development to higher power and greater freedom, from the Renaissance and Cartesian conception through the European Enlightenment, is shown as having reached the peak of civilized refinement; and the irony is clearly that at the time of this sophistication of the intellect, the forces of the irrational, so little tamed and daunted, can sweep away what has carefully been constructed. Thus the devil who came in at the beginning of the movement towards unfettered knowledge with the promise of fulfilment in the Faustian pacts of the sixteenth century, waits for man, the artist, again at its height. Adrian Leverkühn is the latest of a long line of Faust figures, of men desiring to know. He is the modern Hamlet, whom too much knowledge makes sick to death. Thus we have knowledge gained with the devilish and sinful connotation, reached in a surfeit of creative freedom, and knowledge gained at the cost of wholeness and health—the unholy alliance of knowledge and illness, another modern theme which Thomas Mann made his own in constantly fresh variations, in *The Magic Mountain, Tristan, Death in Venice,* and finally and superbly in *Doctor Faustus.* The twofold

relation of knowledge and guilt and knowledge and sickness emerges into
the full ironical light as the rediscovery of original sin, voluntarily repeated,
and the rediscovery of a Nietzschean Romantic heresy: that the knowing
artist is akin to the madman rather than to the scholar. Undoubtedly there
is irony in the modern situation, in which we no longer yearn for knowledge
and demand from the devil the freedom to know; on the contrary, our danger
is to refuse knowledge and to withdraw with the devil's help from the knowledge which will bring us face to face with the absurd, which exposes us to
the risk of insanity and death. And yet, only by facing it can the creative
effort be sustained. The sixteenth-century situation is inverted. Not knowledge is the temptation, but not to know. Yet there is still a price to be paid
for lost innocence of harmless ignorance: sickness to death and mental atro-
phy. The alternative, however, deliberate blindness, contains the worse guilt.
What is here ironically presented is an apparently unavoidable dilemma: that
we can either be seeing, sick, and damned, or ignorant, blind, and damned
just as well. The novel, through the whole momentum towards doom on the
personal, the national, and the generally human scale, seems to state these
alternatives in unambiguous terms. Adrian Leverkühn, the artist, is doomed,
and the world around him contains murder, suicide, and violence on the one
hand, apathy and criminal folly on the other. It seems impossible nowadays
to be an artist *and* to be healthy and sane. And yet, it is the whole and
healthy we have to beware of. For though the artist in the end goes mad, the
really frightening madness comes from the wholesome, the good, the people
who did not know what was happening. To the latter the devil gives peace
of mind, to the former the promise of creativity followed by peace in oblivion.
This dichotomy is handled with a threefold irony. First, as apparently inescapable alternatives which are yet put in doubt by the preferable achievement
of artistic vision at whatever price; secondly, as told by Serenus Zeitblom
who, himself one of the good and innocent, takes on a somewhat sinister
shape; and lastly, in the way the dilemma—that whatever path is taken, it
leads towards doom—emerges in the novel as a comment on the claustro-
phobic situation of damnation. For it is here that we rebel, and are thus by
an ironical sweep taken out of the novel in order to reflect on this fateful
inevitability. It leads to the insight that here we are offered, despite the tragic
quality of the deeply moving story, what is in the last resort a facile solution,
making it deceptively easy, in the face of all roads leading to ruin, to avoid
taking a moral stand. The irony is here directed against an overstatement of
the tragic implications, against the dangers of accepting them gladly in order
to be absolved.

In this modern Faust book we encounter the strange inversion of the original Faust theme, the original theme of hot, warm-blooded, striving man, desiring and, at the cost of his immortal soul, receiving the fruit of knowledge from him whose infernal insight ruthlessly exploits the fatal lure of self-realization, the lure of fulfilment in the dominion over the present moment. But Adrian Leverkühn no longer demands from the devil the power to know—he knows already, and the terrifying coldness of severance from grace was his from the beginning. The price he can promise is not his immortal soul to be delivered to the devil; a soul is what he prays for from Satan himself. And he pays for it by the infinite richness of his mind, the light of his intellect—by that which the devil in earlier pacts promised his victims. The reversal of gifts and grants is as complete as the cycle from sixteenth-century Faustian man reaching for the power of the gods, to twentieth-century Faustian intellect longing for the deliverance from man's newly found inhumanity in knowledge, be it by the only remaining means of the evil one himself. For the devil, who cynically confesses to being now the only guardian of religious orthodoxy and theological fundamentalism, is also the last resort for those who know enough to know also that they possess no soul. The artist whose intellect tells him that the only real end and absolute fulfilment of his art is the completely authentic expression, knows that his knowledge must merge again with the living spring of his inner capacity to suffer and to endure for the sake of his humanity. Only when his soul, long killed by his mental and monstrous growth, is restored to him can he hope to achieve what alone matters: the "breakthrough," the work, the musical incarnation of fully understood expression which issues in lament beyond sorrow.

Adrian is granted this consummation, though, profanely speaking, his illness to eventual mental night is the simple outcome of a sickness contracted in his early manhood by a point-by-point repetition of Nietzsche's disastrous visit to a brothel. The strand of this illness—the devil's gift—weaves through the novel its scarlet thread, as it weaves through Adrian's music the *Leitmotiv* of the *hetaera esmeralda,* the bewitching butterfly, in which poison and beauty combine in the magic of ambiguity. The illness which Adrian carries with him and which shapes his life into the solitary, possessed pattern of the dedicated artist, is recognised with lucid irony not by the biographer, but by the hero himself as he comes to life in his biographer's revealing camouflage. What is more, it is recognised for what it is: the mainspring of his extraordinary creativity and musical capacity, up to the consummation in which the illness is cured by restoration to full humanity, at the ironical price of ceasing from thence to be ever again fully human. From the devil the artist, who is representative of the age of exhaustion of free creative invention, receives the last gift of warmth of the human heart, which alone is the heart of the matter. As in Goethe's *Faust* the irony lies also in the defeat of the devil nevertheless: he has to grant what secures him his price, and the price now is nothing but the shell, the trappings, the hybris of the mind, the glory of a shaking civilization. What remains is the music, and the defeat of a genius whose futility is heightened by the reader's constant awareness that Adrian never lived but in the land of our own imaginings, implanted there by the supreme gift of Thomas Mann's ironical gesture. We need believe in the devil no more than we believe in the real life of Adrian Leverkühn; yet we cannot believe in Him through whose hands we all fall into the net of His grace any less than in the truth of this modern Faust's adventure of regaining his soul to deliver him from himself.

Thomas Mann's irony never fails to reflect even on this transposition to the cosmic scale. To the end the ironist is a protagonist with a critic built in. The perspective is constantly shifting between the two, not allowing the reader for a moment the satisfied rest with a comfortable conclusion or a reassuring attitude. Even an unambiguous moral stand is rarely sustained for any length of time. Thus the novelist achieves, through the impurity of irony, a moral awareness of the tensed equilibrium, in which the wavering of the scales indicate that they are filled—for empty scales too could be balanced: this would be the kind of morality Thomas Mann deeply detested and rejected in a life-time of creative effort to come to terms with the most important moral issues of our age. He came to terms with them ironically.

PETER HELLER

The Ambivalent Leitmotif

In one of his essays Thomas Mann refers almost reverently to a classic of nineteenth-century literature as a work composed in four movements like a symphony, a book "resting in itself," entirely convinced of itself and permeated by its own essence. He finds that it confirms itself "by being and doing what it says and teaches: wherever you open it, it is present in its entirety." True, "in order to reveal itself in time and space," it requires the multifarious universe that emerges "from more than thirteen hundred printed pages" or "twenty-five thousand lines of print." But actually it is "a *nunc stans,* [an] abiding presence of [a] central idea," and hence the perfect illustration of Goethe's verse:

> Thy song rolls round as doth the starry sphere
> End and beginning one for evermore,
> And when the turning middle doth appear,
> 'tis still what end and what beginning are.

Mann is discussing Schopenhauer's *The World as Will and Idea,* which he connects with another guide and mythical model, Goethe's *Diwan,* the cycle of poetry which contains the stanza quoted above. In the *Diwan* Goethe turned toward the East, as Mann himself was to do in his own most ambitious undertaking. Implicitly the passage refers to the *Joseph Novels,* Mann's attempt to write in four movements a symphony or symphonic poem of man.

From *Dialectics and Nihilism.* © 1966 by the University of Massachusetts Press.

How, then, does Mann's Joseph tetralogy succeed in doing and being what it says and teaches? A partial answer to this comprehensive question would be: by way of the leitmotif or perhaps by way of the principle of the leitmotif. On first sight, this answer seems simple enough. Always concerned with his own work and with himself, Mann is most obliging in offering up the keys to the interpretation of his fiction. To quote Mann on Lessing and thus to quote Mann on Mann, it was he who always said "the best things about himself." It was he who taught the critics to recognize the leitmotif as "the crystallization of an all-pervasive element in [his] literary mind." Yet the reader should be forewarned. The nature and function of Mann's leitmotif are as ambiguous and elusive as the author's conceptions of the human condition. Mann moves in spheres of elaborate ambiguity.

What is Mann's leitmotif? At first, in *Buddenbrooks,* in the guise of an "unchanging attribute of a person's appearance, character, or manner of speech, or of identical words to describe significantly similar situations," it appeared to be only a slight extension of an ancient device, a variation of the Homeric epithet. The repetition of descriptive terms or turns of speech apparently served the purpose of concretization. It helped the reader to form an exact, if stereotyped, impression of a person, situation, or mentality. For the imagination is so constituted that a single detail is often sufficient to suggest a vivid impression or illusion of presence. The leitmotif gave life even to an abstraction such as decadence, which the reader learned to associate with the "bluish shadows" under the eyes of Gerda and Hanno Buddenbrook. And even where it conveyed a mood or atmosphere, the descriptive leitmotif appeared to be a device in the service of literary realism.

The characteristic verbal tags were used by Mann to pin down the objects to which he attached them. Situations, whatever their apparent variety, were stamped once and for all and reduced to one recurrent configuration. The figures thereby marked were in a sense done for as soon as they had received their unchanging imprint. Mann himself had expressed this clearly enough when he spoke of "die erledigende Wirkung des Wortes," of the cold and pitiless accuracy of the writer, the winged arrow of the word piercing its mark. The early Mann was prone to generalize on the basis of such sentiments, to assert that the word or indeed the Spirit killed the object of perception, that Spirit and consequently literature represented a force hostile to life. The later Mann substituted for the simple hostility of the Spirit an ambivalent passion: the Spirit tortured and delighted with love *and* hate or love in hate or loving contempt or contemptuous love, or denial *and* affirmation, of life. Mann was always aware that words can be used to kill. In his experience as a writer, the palpable connection between intellect or consciousness and a sublimated aggression was by no means restricted to the scientific impulse to dissect nature. But if the verbal motifs did transfix their objects, if, by identifying them once and for all, they seemed to translate them into a realm beyond change and consequently beyond "life" in the realist's sense of the term, the leitmotifs appeared to be subservient not to Mann's realism or naturalism but, on the contrary, to his intellectualism or to his symbolism and metaphysics.

Other approaches to the description of Mann's leitmotif revealed a similar ambiguity. The leitmotifs established a sense of familiarity. They created an illusion of thorough acquaintance, affording the pleasure of repeated recognition of the seemingly ever-recurrent sentence, speech-habit, figure, character, situation, emotion, mood, or concept. "Dem Menschen ist am Wiedererkennen gelegen"—the leitmotifs achieved these effects through an increase in the vividness of perception. For unlike the fact or state of familiarity, the experience of a sense of familiarity requires some quickening of awareness. This occurs, for instance, on a grand scale when the Egyptian Joseph, after decades of separation and estrangement from his youngest brother Benjamin, confronts him once again. As yet unrecognized by the "little one" (who is now an elderly man), Joseph takes his hand and waves it in the air like a fan, just as he used to do when, as boys, they played together in the olive grove. The recurrent verbal motifs produce similar effects of recognition on a minor and minute scale. While the mere mention of a name might barely remind the reader of the presence of a man, the allusion to one of his characteristic habits conjures up not only his image but the memory of one's entire relationship with him. Even in producing familiarity, the leitmotif, specifically the *Erinnerungsmotiv,* seemed to increase one's sense of the impact of a specific and realistic experience. And yet this interpretation remained open to doubt. For though there was perhaps no specific point of dialectical change, the experience and re-experience of the familiar reached a stage where, by dint of repetition, it no longer heightened one's sense for the claims of specific concretions of fictitious realities. Instead it persuaded the reader that the new was in essence identical with the old or, to put this with some degree of exaggeration, that nothing changed. To use Mann's favorite image of the sea: one wave is much like the other. Upon seeing a new wave approach the shore line, we have a sense of the familiar. And yet such familiarity scarcely increases our interest in the specific wave about to break on the sand. The effect is rather soporific, of a perennial sameness, a static identity which underlies all apparent variety and motion.

Basic data have a wonderful way of escaping final definition. All elementary verbal devices are perhaps multifunctional; perhaps they will admit only a purely formal and somewhat sterile definition. A formal definition of rhyme does not suggest the variety of ways in which rhyme can be used. And yet a linguistic device, presumably designed for a human purpose, can hardly be described adequately without regard to the use to which it is put. Erich Heller observed that a novella such as *Tonio Kröger* was, in a sense, rhymed. Particularly as a bracketing device, Mann's verbal leitmotifs served a rhythmic function. But while these recurrent motifs were distantly related to the major linguistic phenomena of rhythmic recurrence, they were certainly not so basic as rhyme or even refrain. Their derivative quality and their specialized use in the works of a single author encourage attempts at close delimitation. However, if the term leitmotif is restricted to the repeated and significant recurrence of identical phrases, it fails to do justice to the fact that a sufficient similarity in wording or, for that matter, in the recurrence of situations, mentalities, moods and ideas, often achieves essentially the same effect as the precise repetition. If, on the other hand, we start with the identity of effect, we tend to lose sight of the very device we set out to describe. For different devices may work toward the same end. And evidently the leitmotif or, to use a larger term, the principle of the significant recurring (and varied) pattern is applied by Mann in various ways to produce a great variety of effects.

Some of these effects are placed sufficiently far apart to suggest a framework of interdependent opposites, others suggest the possibilities of intermediary positions. The attempt to trace the manifestations of Mann's device requires this elaborate structure. Yet the very inclusiveness of such a system exposes it to the charge of absurdity. It is all very well to claim that Mann's leitmotifs are vehicles both of his realism and of his symbolism, that they stimulate awareness of the concrete or specific and suggest simultaneously the universal, that they serve to put a stress on ceaseless change and on static permanence, that they emphasize—as *Erinnerungsmotiv*—the passage in time, and yet manage to intimate that the present contains the past and the future, or rather that, despite the illusions of time and place, everything always *is*. But the reader begins to suspect that to have suffered such increase in knowledge is tantamount to a recurrence of initial ignorance. Even if the interpreter claims that he can place his leitmotif-experiences on a continuum between the polarities, the reader will be wary of this all too perfect arrangement.

The apparent paradox that opposite effects can be attributed to Mann's leitmotifs corresponds to the paradox that is at the heart of Mann's universe. Those bluish shadows under the eyes of the later Buddenbrooks stress a particular; but since they are treated as symptom and symbol of decadence, they also recall to the reader's mind the universal concept of a novel telling of the decay and decadence of a family. Conversely, the generalized motto of Joseph's Pharaoh—that a man may be on the right way but not be the right man for that way—establishes a perennial type. However, within the limited world of the novel it recalls the particular image of the pale and well-intentioned Amenhotep whenever it is repeated. The facetious leitmotif-lingo in which Pharaoh is called "the false right one," suggests that he is the decadent counterpart to the Jacob-Joseph tradition of "right false ones," a tradition of beneficiaries of cheatings in blessings, of ambiguous men blessed not only from above but equally from the depths—treacherous, vital, and false—that lie below. And beyond that, there is a kind of dizziness created in the reader's mind: for who can be quite sure to keep "the false right ones who are *on* the right way though not the right ones *for* the way" securely apart from "the right false ones who are so often on the false way though they are certainly the right ones for the right way"? Presumably this dizziness should lead the reader to an ironical sense of a higher unity between the contrasts, to a sense of the ineffable identity that is beyond all opposites, even though the author's own juggling of motifs serves at the same time as a parody of his intimations of such ultimate unity.

We are concerned with the simultaneity of seemingly opposite effects. To return to an example: the motif of the "little one" attached to Jacob's youngest son, Benjamin, reminds us vividly of the passage of time when, toward the end of the Biblical tale, it is used as an ironical leitmotif to refer to a sturdy old man. Notwithstanding the apparent contradiction, the verbal tag tells us at the same time that Benjamin always has been and always will be the little brother, even if he lives to be one hundred years old.

The ocean of scholarship surrounding the works of Mann seems at one in stressing the static effects of the leitmotif. The unity of form and content is most readily apparent when the interpretation is restricted to these static aspects. The recurring phrases reveal or suggest the omnipresence of basic unchanging patterns. Mann himself had established the principles for this interpretation. In *Buddenbrooks,* he observed in his autobiographical sketch of 1930, the leitmotif had served a physiognomic or naturalistic purpose. In *Tonio Kröger,* however, it had attained an emotional and intellectual transparency transcending the sphere of a mechanical device and approaching the condition of music. For the first time, epic prose composition had been conceived as the weaving of a spiritual tissue, as a musical complex of significantly interrelated themes—a conception subsequently to be realized on a larger scale in *The Magic Mountain.* And later, in discussing Schopenhauer and Plato, Mann added that through the "conception of the world as colorful and moving phantasmagoria of images which are transparent for the spiritual, the artist, as it were, first comes into his own."

Applied to Mann's artistic practice, this suggested that the physiognomic leitmotif, although it established an element of stability, could not approximate the ultimate truth of the Spirit. Cognition, according to Schopenhauer and his occasional disciple, led ultimately to the suspension of time and space and individuation. If the magic of art was to penetrate the veil of Maya, to render the phantasmagoria of images transparent for the spiritual and ultimately to suggest the metaphysical state of eternal unity, the *nunc stans,* this miracle could be approximated only through a true vehicle of cognition (*Erkenntnis, Geist*), or, to speak in terms of technique, through the symbolic leitmotif. Peacock developed these implications. He found that the leitmotifs express not an event but a permanent condition, that the art of the leitmotif means to Mann suspension of individuation, suspension of the sense of time.

The approximation to this staggering and transcendent unity would have been impossible without the formation of what Mann had called a spiritual tissue or complex of themes (*ein geistiges Themengewebe*). Even the single motif displays powers of condensation and unification. Humming with overtones, fraught with associations of contexts to which it has been applied, it can be made to clarify and to summarize a far-reaching development. It unifies a work by conveying the impression that the configuration it evokes is present in its entirety at any point in the story. Peacock spoke of the effect peculiar to the leitmotif of "represent[ing] continually and everywhere the entire configuration of forces which underlie the human events and the action of a novel." However, the allusive potential of a single motif would soon be overworked, or by sheer monotony, exhaust the reader, if it did not have the support of kins and clans. Without loss of identity, Mann's leitmotifs enter into alliances, groups and hierarchies. Motifs merge with one another to form a complex of themes. Equations are then introduced to suggest the affinity of one complex to another, to establish identities on a higher level, to persuade us that "ultimately" the two, the three, the many are but one.

Peacock showed how the perennial bluish shadows leading from Gerda to Hanno Buddenbrook were not only transparent for Mann's universal law and theme of decadence but formed a cluster with other symbols of decadence as they led on and into the motifs surrounding Hanno, music, and death. To give another example: the introduction to the *Joseph Novels,* entitled *Höllenfahrt,* purports to be a descent into the well or underworld of the past and, incidentally, into the nether regions of man's archaic and collective unconscious. The first chapter of the first novel ("Am Brunnen") reveals Joseph, the son of Rahel, at a well reminiscent of (or from the reader's point of view, anticipating) the well at which Jacob first met Joseph's mother. The symbolic implications of the motif of the well are developed in the novel when his furious brothers throw young Joseph, a male Rahel to his father Jacob, into the well. For like the stars that set and rise, like the seedcorn buried in the darkness of the soil to be reborn in the spring, like the gods who were killed and buried and mourned only to ascend again, young Joseph will be reborn from this well and pit, to become an Egyptian, and, finally, attain some maturity. The well is the pit, the pit is the grave, the grave the womb. When Joseph, the steward in the house of Pharaoh's eunuch Petepre (the Biblical Potiphar) and the victim of Muth's passionate fury, is sent down again into the pit and well and underworld of a rather enlightened and cheerful prison, the relativity of upper and lower sphere is made explicit. Egypt itself is a nether region of sorts, a pit of abomination, a well, a (rather sunny) underworld of the cult of death. But the world as a whole is a realm of darkness, a pit, well, grave, womb (at least to the angels and to the aboriginal Soul and Spirit, the two metaphysical protagonists of Mann's tetralogy). Evidently the "fall" of the Soul, and the "descent" of the Spirit provide the archetype for the author's own *Höllenfahrt*. And yet there is some doubt as to the final validity of the invidious distinction between above and below. To recall another leitmotif: the double blessing of Jacob and Joseph, and so of man, descends *and* rises. It comes from the heavens above and from the depths below. Similarly, Joseph's descent into Egypt will make him rise so high that in the end his brothers will bow before him as the stars bow before the moon. The narrator's own "descent" into the hell of the past is strangely akin to an escape from the pit and underworld of his own time and thus is a movement upward into the happier region of myth. Ultimately the relativity of upper and lower realm, of pit and elevation, points to the "mystery" of the "revolving sphere," the most comprehensive symbol and concept of the tetralogy and the master key to its interpretation.

The abundant mergers and fusions displayed in Mann's later works are only another manifestation of the tendency displayed in the formation of individual leitmotifs. The individual leitmotif identifies, appropriates or as-similates the new and different as the recurrence of the old and familiar. It sets up equations. It creates analogues. The same holds true for the mergers between motifs and motif-complexes. In all of this there is something akin to the art of metaphor, to the faculty considered unteachable by Aristotle, essential to poetry, and a mark of genius, namely the capacity to recognize similarity in dissimilars. But the opposite faculty, though perhaps more akin to criticism than to poetry, the faculty of recognizing dissimilarity in similars,

is no less a requirement of intelligent perception. If indulged somewhat un-
critically, the tendency to equate and to analogize leads to "moon grammar."
It is akin to a "dreamy inexactitude" frequently designated as poetic, to a
sense of interfusion, eternal recurrence, timeless identity and all-pervasive
unity. It corresponds to the mentality of people who "did not quite know
who they were or who knew it in a more deeply exact way" than we do.
This ambiguous phrase is Mann's definition of life "in the myth" of a state
of mind, a mode of thought, a way of living which provides not merely the
atmosphere but the central theme of his Biblical tetralogy.

MOON GRAMMAR

Moon grammar. The phrase suggests Mann's own tendency to analogize
and equate, as well as his ambivalence toward this tendency. A method of
analogical interpretation may hope to do justice to the far-flung networks of
correspondencies and dreamy equations which are inherent in Mann's use
of the leitmotif. And yet the interpreter should be aware of the pitfalls of
moon grammar. In the hope of gaining clarity, we shall therefore re-examine
some authoritative works on Mann. Perhaps their answers concerning the
nature and functions of Mann's leitmotifs will elucidate a device that seems
to display as many aspects as the works in which it occurs.

What of the leitmotifs in *The Magic Mountain*? What of Settembrini's
checked trousers, the rabbit's teeth bared by garrulous Mrs. Stöhr, the poised
head, the blue cheeks, the bloodshot eyes of Hofrat Behrens? As Weigand
points out, such motifs, used in abundant measure, are a means of giving
"full-bodied sensuous presence" to the characters in the novel. Mann himself, disparaging mere action and somewhat contemptuous of the storyteller's
gift of inventing new tales, had often expressed his envy and admiration of
the luminous presence achieved by works of plastic art which were "unrelated to time, save as all bodies are" while, as Lessing had shown, narration
and music were bound to succession. But if this is so, even *Buddenbrooks*
and certainly *Tonio Kröger* suggest that Mann's use of the leitmotif, and
perhaps not only of its physiognomic variant, conveyed the author's productive resistance to a condition of his art. The leitmotif was "a strategy of the
storyteller to make his medium Time yield a little to his vain desire to establish the whole story like a picture or a sculpture, at every moment of its
duration."

The leitmotif enabled Mann to give enduring shape to a world of bewildering experience. It was a triumph of form. To Tonio the artist, conceived
as representative of the Spirit, the existence of the burgher seemed normal,

real, sustained by affectionate warmth, but so utterly alien to the aspirations of the Spirit, so impermeable to art, that he felt the "loss of real existence—'dying to life'—to be the condition of artistic creativeness." *Künstler* and *Bürger,* Art and Life, Spirit and Nature—whatever the polar terms preferred for a statement of his dilemma—Tonio's world and (as Erich Heller pointed out) the world of his author were faced by a double threat. Tonio, it seems, was unable to choose between the loss of meaning (cognition, significance, Spirit and Art being one) and the loss of reality. For Life was to him the life of the blond, blue-eyed and dumb bourgeoisie. And yet this exile between two worlds managed in the end to secure a tenuous balance between Art and Life by his mediatory, gently contemptuous and ambivalent "burgher-love," a leitmotif, Heller observed, that might "still save the problematic literary existence of the hero." And similarly, through the art of the leitmotif the author Mann established *his* precarious victory. For the leitmotif, the "tidy symbol of a significantly ordered life," was the "seal of possession," the proof "of having mastered reality through knowing the secret of its organization. . . . To make sure that the world makes sense despite all insinuations to the contrary, indeed to make it yield sense if it is unwilling to do so on its own, wholly to possess it on the strength of the created order of the work of art—it is this kind of creativeness, both possessive and melancholy, which Thomas Mann's style suggests." Hence, Heller concluded, in *Tonio Kröger* the leitmotif conveyed "more effectively than any explicit utterance, the foremost problem of the hero: how to defend his work, and indeed himself, against the encroachment of nonentity." For "entity consists in meaningful organization, visibly vindicated by the leitmotif."

Seizing upon a clause in *The Magic Mountain,* Weigand asked himself how a novel of some thousand pages could possibly have the unique artistic aim "to be all there all the time." Mann's invocation of the sea offered a metaphorical answer: "Just as the eternal rhythm of the sea, the vastest sensuous symbol of the pulse of time has played with uninterrupted beat upon the author's inner ear, so the philosophic experience of time, merging into the experience of eternity, pervades every page of the 'Zauberberg.'" And what indeed is *there* all the time if not eternity? The image of the sea led Weigand to the "concrete and tangible" device. The repeated verbal motif, "while coined originally to express specific situations [had] an inherent tendency to expand the radius of its meaning." It was "surrounded by an aura of suggestion. It [was] a focal point" from which lines extended in a complex network of relations. In fact, to quote Mann, the leitmotif was a "regular magic word with vaguely ramified associations." Structurally, Weigand observed, *The Magic Mountain* was an accumulation of such magic formulas or "code-words" which carried increasing loads at every successive point of the narrative, so that our experience in reading the novel was "more like a cumulative addition than a mere succession of elements." In life, as in a tale, Mann reminded us, "we can never see the whole picture at once—unless we propose to throw overboard all the God-conditioned forms of human knowledge." But according to Weigand, the web of interpenetrating themes was so close that this truism assumed an air of ironical ambiguity. The very rebellion against the God-given conditions of temporal knowledge was, perhaps, the secret ambition of Mann's work.

Erich Heller's conclusions on *The Magic Mountain* pointed the same way. What "brings forth Time?" "Change," is the Mountain's answer. But "as the changing motion by which we describe time is circular, 'it is a motion which we might just as well describe as rest; for the There constantly recurs in the Here, the Then in the Now.'" Every day is to Hans Castorp like the other, all days are "literally the same,—one and the same day." The paradox suggested by Mann as the nature of Time, the dialectic of change and rest, of temporal and eternal aspects, of *Maya* and *nunc stans* are mirrored in the effects ascribed to Mann's chief device. In *The Magic Mountain* time is not only the subject of reflection but almost the protagonist; its circular motion determines the form of the work: "the omnipresence of the *leitmotif* as a means of realizing the idea of the ever-present."

There is a parallel between Mann's experience of the ocean and the leitmotif. (For both, we learned, were intimations of the ever-present.) Mann himself tells us that *Meer* [ocean] and *Epik* [epic] were forever associated in his mind. What, then, is the ocean to Mann, and what can his conception of the ocean tell us about the nature and function of the epic leitmotif? The sea, according to Mann, is "cosmic emptiness," it is elemental (*"elementar im Sinne letzter und wüster, außermenschlicher Großartigkeit"*), horribly indifferent in its hostility (*gräßlich gleichgültige Feindseligkeit*). Like the desert and the icy mountains, it is a region of blind gigantic powers which man should resist with scorn and irony and defiance, even if, in their over-whelming stupidity, they annihilate him. But perhaps this is not quite what we want to hear. We want Mann to love the sea as we know he does, and as Tonio Kröger loves it: "Oh thou wild friend of my youth / Once more we are united." It is an experience of "eternity" and of an "immense dream," the "experience of death." (And death, we know, has for Mann supreme dignity, superlative form and formality, though it also has its aspects of shameful dissolution. Mann's ocean inspires "fear," "veneration," "religious awe" though mingled with "physical" and "metaphysical" horror. It is an experience of "eternity" and of an "immense simplicity." Good enough—if only Mann did not go on to tell us that his oceanic sentiment for the eternal, his "heavy lazy hankering after the form of formlessness (*Form oder Unform*) of perfection which is called nirvana or nothingness" is "very inartistic" and deeply immoral. What are we to do? Reading on, we find that "sin" and "morality" are really "one," that—to abbreviate at this point—only the morality of morality and the morality of immorality are truly moral, just as we may be sure that the truly artistic is to be found in the conjunction of the very artistic revulsion from the ocean and the inartistic craving for it. Thomas Mann's sea, we are told [by Heller], is the "element of infinite fluidity,—symbol . . . of life blissfully halted at the stage of boundless potentiality and not yet subject to the rigorous restriction of forms, intimation of the inarticulate, immeasurable, infinite, and closest approximation within the material world to the eternal void and nothingness."

It is truly an ocean, this symbol of life, death, void, and incidentally of "nonsense" (*Unfug*), of grandeur, stupidity, eternity, time. But what will it tell us about the leitmotif? The everpresent, it will be recalled, was the common denominator. The leitmotif "signifies timelessness, the a-historical." But what is the timeless to Mann? Where there is no transcience, there is no beginning, no end, no birth, no death, no time—and timelessness is stagnant nothingness. . . . Timelessness is absolutely uninteresting.

Is the leitmotif then an intimation of "*das absolut Uninteressante*" or of the nihil's traditional next of kin, the "full" chaos of mere matter or of the eternally structured Will,—of *das stehende Nichts* or *das stehende Jetzt,* of the "form" or "formlessness" of perfection? Or is it an intimation of death as excess of form and of the crystal's dead duration, or of death as formlessness, of the blissful and boundless potentiality of life, or of temporal and shaped life? Is it an intimation of form as *Mitte,* as happy mediation between *Überform* and *Unform*? We recall that a definition of life as the preservation of form in a changing substance (*daß im Wechsel der Materie die Form erhalten bleibt*) was applied by Weigand to the leitmotif. Evidently we have both, or rather we have everything. The leitmotif is [according to Erich Heller] a symbol of the timeless and boring void and of the "everpresent." It is a vindication of form, of "life everlasting through the indestructible type," and of life blissfully, oceanically free from the rigor of finite forms. And it is the "tidy symbol of a significantly ordered life," as well as a symbol of the "depressing" eternal recurrence which is a soup or "gloom everlasting" and of the cheerful recurrence that might suggest the serenity of faith.

Moon grammar. Over the years, within single works and often within single sentences, Mann's major themes run the gamut between polar extremes. They are defined by the simultaneity of apparent or true incompatibles. The artist is a weakling, a monster, the most inhuman man, the most human man, both and neither and the middle—a mediator. Art is *Allbejahung* and *Allverneinung* (total affirmation and total negation); art is mediation. Top is bottom, bottom is top, and both are the middle.

CORROSIVE DOUBT

Let us proceed from this point of despair by a strategy which is, perhaps, too radical for the delicate task of literary criticism. Let us assume that to understand Mann is merely to understand his ambivalence and the perennial irony of his oscillations, that to understand Mann is to understand that his is a world rife with contradictions and abysmal uncertainties, a world in which almost nothing is sure to mean anything and almost anything may mean almost anything else. For meanings abound and run amok where a central meaning is about to vanish.

What dizzy effort is this which manages to keep from disintegration a world that is forever on the verge of falling apart? Rich and sparkling, summa and melting pot of all too available traditions and countertraditions, Mann's world is united after a fashion by that Western inheritance of meaning which the author has assimilated both to affirm and to corrode. It is a world on the verge of meaninglessness, conscientiously arranged by a stupendous artistic intelligence. It is kept in shape by a conscious restraint from intellectual consistency, by moon grammar, a vast and naive curiosity, impassioned juggling and solemn charlatanry, a sensuous infatuation with beauty, by good will and immense vanity. The ego is well-nigh the only point of support for all the positively negative and negatively positive games of reference. Or is this honest impostor Mann saved by his habitual trust in the reality of the commonplace, by his "burgher-love," by an addiction to work, by a solid ambition, a willingness to behave "as if," to be representative even where there is little to represent, to turn out the goods, to put up a show? Mann's works report elaborate experiments with faith, but what is the faith sustaining these experiments?

Mann's humanism is built on paradox, since top and bottom, upper and lower sphere are in constant rotation and ironically interchangeable. How are we to conceive man's position as the intermediary between angel and animal if the angels, at least, seem to be but man-created fictions, if in fact the only reality, the futile, endearing farce of man's perennial task of mediation, may be nothing but an illusion? Mann's habit of setting up the extremes provides him with occasions to do his mediatory stunts. However, the humanistic syntheses break up in turn into new polarities, in order that the performance may go on. To speak of Mann's humanism is perhaps to be euphemistic about the overripe condition of his eclectic universe. Mann's faith in man is supererogatory, sheer benevolence, in no way due to a belief in the surpassing merit of the object of the faith. Rather, the merit is all on the part of the believer who feels, more often than not, that it is very good of him to condescend to be worshipful despite all the negative evidence. And indeed who is man to believe in man! One understands all too well why Mann should have praised Lessing, as artist, for not having left the battlefield with a burst of mocking laughter. And yet Mann's last major work, the confessions of his sensitive, versatile, faithless, aimless and superlatively conscientious crook and darling Krull, is in fact pure mockery. Nevertheless, Mann's work is not lacking in love, however questionable its shape and mode and object may be. Nor can one deny this author a penetrating concern and a profound understanding of the human condition.

Mann never failed to let his readers know that he shared their doubts about himself. He spoke quite seriously of his basic and playful lack of seriousness, a condition which he attributed to all artists and which he identified in turn with the artist's seriousness in playing. He spoke of the artist's intellectual consciousness: a subject "to ponder . . . and perhaps to shudder at." "What to do?" As the mere ghost of a leitmotif, this unanswerable question flits through the pages of one of Mann's last essays in which he identifies himself with Chekhov's art and despair. "Am I not cheating the reader," Mann quotes, "since I have really no answer to the most important questions?" What to do? "Upon my honor and conscience . . . I don't know." Doubt is the theme, self-doubt reaching beyond self and art and ever recurrent until man's universe is reduced to a timid circle of impossibilities. Shall we depend upon science and its truth? No, man needs a religion, a central idea. But "every feeling and every thought has an isolated existence in my mind . . . and the most experienced analyst will not find in [my views] what one would call a central idea, or the God of the living man. And if that is lacking there is nothing at all." Ideas, ideals are but illusions. The truth is in art but art is nihilistic, believes in nothing and makes one believe in nothing. And yet one goes on working. What for? "The main thing" is to reform and change man's life; everything else is of no use. But that is impossible. Man, with spirit and nature forever at loggerheads, is creation's failure ([ein] verfehltes Wesen). And yet one expects something of Russia, of the future? But these are minor euphorias induced perhaps by the proximity of death.

As things are, the life of the artist is meaningless, and the more

gifted he is the stranger and more incomprehensible his role, because it is a proven fact that he works for the entertainment of
an unclean beast of prey.

And yet you work, tell stories, [and delight with them a needy
world] in the dark hope, in the confidence almost, that truth and
serene form can have a liberating effect upon the soul and prepare
the world for a better and more beautiful life that will be more
adequate to the demands of the Spirit.

There is in this essay, as in *Doctor Faustus,* the faint glimmer of a hope
beyond hope. But although Mann always considered himself to be one of the
artists experimenting tentatively with the possibilities of overcoming nihilism, he never crossed the zero line nor ever seriously thought he had. For
almost everything that came close to his heart and that really mattered to
him became subject to ambivalence, doubt and ironical oscillation. It is futile
to extract from such persistent ambiguity a simple statement, for such a
statement would be nothing but a counterstatement or a statement calling
for the counterstatement. And this applies also to a statement of despair
which calls for an assertion of hope, as hope does for despair.

Mann found occasion to equate doubt and faith. But Mann notwithstanding, the distinction must be maintained. The claim that faith must pass
through the inferno of doubt is compatible with faith, for it maintains the
difference. If a man does his utmost and yet comprehends that all is in jest,
this may be seriousness, indeed, and more than compatible with faith. For
what does the work of a man amount to in the face of the absolute? Irony
and skepticism may be entirely compatible with faith provided an unironical
and unskeptical attitude is maintained toward the absolute. It is all very well
to suggest connections between Mann and Kierkegaard, but Kierkegaard's
dialectic is compatible with faith precisely because he does not subject the
object of his faith, God, to dialectical doubt. Nor is the irony of Socrates
directed at the absolute but, on the contrary, at the relative and imperfect
in the name of the absolute, because the relative and imperfect fall short of
the absolute.

But what if Mann's faith was "doubt and irony"? What if he made these
his absolutes? The truth in this matter seems to be simpler than some would
grant. The faith in doubt and irony is still not faith but doubt and irony, for
there are impossibles for faith, just as the absurd faith-in-nothing which has
"nothing" as its impossible absolute is not in truth a faith but the opposite
of it, namely nihilism. There are addictions and heresies, self-contradictory

as all heresies ought to be, but the distinction is nonetheless to be maintained between nihilistic negation, doubt, and faith. And Mann's works, less radical than the works of some authors who attempted to portray a world not on the brink of falling apart and on the verge of meaninglessness, but fallen apart and essentially meaningless, hover between negation and faith in the sphere of doubt.

To turn to the *Joseph Novels*: what is their living God? The myth has been humanized and with it religion. Are myth and religion illusion, jest, a projection of the psyche? Yes and no. For is not the reduction of myth and religion to psychological truth equally an illusion, the distorted reflection of an upper sphere? No and yes. For both the reduction of myth and religion to socio-psychoanalytical flatlands and the raising and sublimation and translation of the flatlands to the heights of religion and myth make up the truth. Or do they? Yes and no. For all this is mere hypothesis, a joke and jest; the pseudo-science *and* the pseudo-religion are sheer irony. But are they? No and yes. For it is all a poem of man and of man's progress. Towards what? Towards the synthesis between Nature and Spirit, or Soul and Spirit? Yes and no. For that synthesis is of course beyond time, a metaphysical utopia, forever relegated to a never-never-land, and possibly only another, though perhaps a beneficial, illusion. Is it not true that, in the *Joseph Novels,* the tangible aspects of man's gradual self-realization seem to point rather to the emergence of a welfare state? Yes and no. For though Mann does not disbelieve in metaphysical and/or social progress, he does not quite believe in them either.

It will be objected that art need not raise, let alone answer such questions. However, Mann's novels do raise and answer, and do not answer, such questions. For to a large extent his works are made of the stuff of such questions and answers, and they play on the answers and failures of answers surrounding the question concerning a central meaning, a question which is quite properly the central issue in an age of spiritual disorientation. The attentive reader will find, in Mann's works, the insistent, unrequited yearning for deliverance and redemption from the compulsion and curse of doubt, from the necessity of thinking and feeling forever within the unbreakable and charmed circle of the yes-and-no.

It has become customary to claim that the author of *Buddenbrooks* neatly combined Schopenhauer and Nietzsche. However, in the context of this early novel this means the combination of the radical denial *and* the enthusiastic affirmation of the Will, thus building the work on a contradiction. A lifetime later, in *Faustus,* Mann is still suspended in creative indecision. Ironically, complacently and desperately, he hovers between psychosomatic pathology and theology. Did the spirochetes of syphilis create Adrian's devil and liberate his genius? Or are the spirochetes the devil's symbol, are they in fact the emissaries of the devil's power and pact? Literary sophistication may obscure the alternative but will not remove it. And while the combination of myth and psychology is not per se objectionable, analogous considerations apply to their conjunction in the *Joseph Novels*. For either God created man and then there are both God and man, or man created God, in which case there is no God except as an illusion. The dialectics of doubt encroach on absolute and contingent alike. But then all is contingent, and instead of a theology of irony there are but the pretensions of a hybrid, vain and ultimately helpless relativism. For there can be no theology without God. There is indeed more faith in forthright atheism than in the subterfuges of a sophistication that would like to have it both ways and claim a smiling wisdom founded, in truth, on nothing but the vacuum of vacillating doubt.

But perhaps there is another and more accurate way of stating the alternative, if we assume that man will never do without an analogue of God. If there must be a god even for the dialectics of doubt, that god will be a hybrid of love-and-hate, good-and-evil, truth-and-falsehood, of Supreme Being and abstraction; he will be a sum of contradictions, a god ironically subject to evolution, a god in process. And one name of this idol will be History, though it should be granted that the god of dialectical materialism has more positive substance than the god of mere historicism and that History was not the only idol conceived when the Judaic and Classical and Christian traditions became increasingly subject to their emancipated offspring, Dialectic.

The tradition continues to sustain even those who must work its destruction. The danger inherent in the tendency which seeks to merge the unmergeable and to equate the unequatable is nonetheless apparent. It is a threat to man's self-awareness as a rational animal. In the sphere of the psyche the name of this tendency is ambivalence, a term which connotes the constant and explicit conjunction of positive and negative affective investment. As it grows in intensity, this conjunction of opposites becomes sadistically and masochistically destructive of feeling. It breaks down the structures of affection and corrodes them, ultimately to devour itself in indifference. In the sphere of morals its name is duplicity. In the intellectual sphere this tendency may find expression in a rebellion against the "God-given" forms of cognition, as attack on the principle of identity. In its conceptual form—the form of Mann's concepts—it may assume that *A* equals

A and *not-A,* that a thing is itself and its opposite, that God is God and the devil or, to misquote God's own statement, "I am that I am and am not."

THE MARGINAL BALANCE

Mann's ambivalence is, however, not unlimited, and it is balanced. He affirms and doubts the affirmation, and doubts the doubt in the affirmation, and proceeds to subject the affirmation regained to some doubt. He never quite breaks the circle of doubt. He never resolves the "yes-and-no." But there is yet something left beyond the circle of doubt, and above all, there is a universe of vivid shapes, of deeply felt emotion, of fully conceived ideas and ideals drawn into the circle to delight, to move, to enlighten, and to confuse us. Just as a medieval dance of death requires for its realization the pageant of life, Mann's dance of doubt requires for its performance the many-colored spectrum of life's positive assertions, manifestations, and incontrovertible realities. One should recall that Mann assimilated as large a part of the German and European literary heritage as any novelist of this century. There are two sides to the paradox of Mann, for he did accept and affirm a heritage which he proceeded to question and to corrode. Nor will it do to neglect the obvious: Mann's art commands considerable learning, it is highly civilized and, what is more, humane. These were advantages, particularly in an age given to the excessive worship of the tough and sterile mannerisms of semi-literate journalists and would-be bullfighters with pen in hand. The question which led us to neglect the obvious was merely whether the world beyond the cycle of doubt was more than the prerequisite for this cycle, and whether the world within the cycle yielded more than the occasion for a desperate game. There must be a stage. There must be players. But isn't the cycle the play?

However, even if the answer implied in this rhetorical question were granted, it would hold only on a level that is below the surface and the surface effects which constitute half the secret and relevance of art. Even if it were perfectly correct to regard the cycle of doubt as the *structure* or—to strain a metaphor—as the dynamic skeleton, the reader might be justified in considering the fully conceived and finely drawn figures and gestures the essential, or at least an essential, manifestation of Mann's art.

And if a rich and lively universe is drawn into this cycle, who does the drawing if not eros, a love not unmingled with resentment, and even thriving on ambivalence, but nonetheless a prodigious power of yearning and attraction, a zest for the embrace, particularly astonishing in an author such as

Mann. Nor are we here guilty of the biographical fallacy. For it is the work which is proof of this eros, and it is the literary personality made manifest in the work which emanates and communicates this power. This eros is not restricted to a few happy inventions but makes itself felt as tension in all of Mann's writing; it is the energy which he disciplined in his craft of prose, which sustains his effort and animates his power of observation and description. To achieve such closeness of vision, to draw a world of shapes so completely and fully into one's circle, requires a primary desire and delight which is the very opposite of hostile indifference, and thus a great erotic attachment beneath and beyond all modifications. And perhaps it is nothing but the spiritualization of such an endowment which makes the artist.

Perhaps. But even if all works of art might be founded in some remote or initial sense upon a labor of love, one should not forfeit the right to distinguish. Mann possessed the capacity and wielded the power of the artistic eros. And yet this power is subject to varied use and abuse. Merely to recognize qualifying merit is not enough. A critic must judge not only the adequacy of aesthetic texture but the spirit that pervades a work.

The very complexities of Mann's marginally balanced universe of doubt seems to require the constant reassurance of formal organization. Since *The Magic Mountain* is a work of art, Erich Heller remarks, "it will be in some sense symbolic." If symbolic, "it can be only symbolic of meaning" even though it may say: "The world is meaningless." And hence: "The worst is not, so long as we can say, 'This is the worst.' There is reason for rejoicing as long as tragedies can be written." For "the preserved form of a piece of literature gives the marginal lie to the expressed conviction that everything is in a state of dissolution." This "exceedingly ironical situation . . . has found in *The Magic Mountain* its appropriately ironical literary shape."

This aperçu seems to suggest a form-content relation other than the analogical nexus. The claim that the form of a work gives the marginal lie to what it "says and teaches" would seem to conflict with the claim that it "is and does" what it "says and teaches." In one respect at least the relation would be antithetical rather than analogical. However, while the analogical connections may represent only one type or species in a subtler manifold of interconnections, the apparent opposites can easily coexist, as they do, to use a simile, when a tree is reflected in a pond. The reflection will be upside down and left will be right. To give an example, parody and even satire frequently imitate in diction, plot and structure their very objects, but only in order to expose and annihilate them. Yet in a wider sense, it is also true to say that even in their antithetical relation, parody and satire proceed by an analogical process. For properly they conceive their objects as negations (of fitness, beauty, goodness, truth, and the like), and they proceed by negating the negations.

But even though one should grant in principle the existence of antithetical relationships and the possibility of their coexistence with the analogical nexus, the question remains whether Heller's particular statement should be accepted. Is it true that *The Magic Mountain* says that "the world is meaningless"? Once more one recalls that there are works more radical in the denial of meaning than *The Magic Mountain*, e.g., Kafka's *Trial*. Do not such works find a form which is itself more marginal, to give a still more marginal lie to an experience no longer of doubt but of despair?

The Magic Mountain shows the world not to be meaningless but to be in an extremely dubious state. It suggests that the world is almost in a state of dissolution, but it suggests at the same time that this very element of dissolution may be a prerequisite for the attainment of a higher form of integration. For the dialectics of disease and health, of passing through disease to greater awareness, of pervasive doubt as condition for dubious realization, determine the education and development of Hans Castorp and are thus of the novel's essence. And even if it were true that "the falling apart of all things [had] never before [been] treated with so intensely conscious an artistic determination to hold them together," the question remains whether this very effort of holding everything together does not suggest and dramatize the fact that everything is on the verge of falling apart. Considering the clashes of determined ideologies, the elaborate and ironical treatment of conventions and counterconventions, of well-regulated routine and of time which is not yet suspended into meaningless timelessness but maintained as dubious yet reassuring clock time, and the ironical maintenance of an atmosphere of bourgeois normalcy, one might claim, not that everything has fallen apart but only that it is marginally preserved.

This marginal condition is not unlike that of a group of people caught in a fog up in the mountains. Their leader constantly shouts, "Are you all there?" and receives the choral response he hopes for, though he is never quite sure from how many of his party. The group would seem to be integrated. And yet the insistence on reconfirmation, the constant reassertion of such integration would indicate simultaneously the imminent danger and doubt. Applied to Mann's novel: a work that is "all there all the time" suggests an excess rather than a lack of formal integration. It suggests formal integration with a vengeance. Yet the reader of Mann is too well acquainted with the author's speculations on the ominous significance of the excess of form (*Überform*) and its proximity to lack of form (*Unform*) to need a critic to suggest the possibility of a rather negative interpretation, though, as is fitting in the universe of Mann, it would be again a dubious interpretation.

The interpretation of Mann's works is at once an easy and a hopelessly complicated task. The labor is almost too rewarding, in view of the readiness of the work to promote its own interpretation. For as soon as one cares to look more closely, he finds that the author himself has drawn the lines along which to cut—and in several directions at that. But the work also frustrates one's effort, much as a cabinet of mirrors, none of which may be touched, so that one is unlikely ever to find out its dimensions.

ERICH KAHLER

The Elect: The Holy Sinner *and* Felix Krull

Thomas Mann followed up *Doctor Faustus,* the densest synthesis and most intimate statement of his central concerns, with two works of a lighter character—to all appearances satyr plays coming after the great tragedy. The first was the parable of Gregorius, the Holy Sinner; the second the confessions of Felix Krull, confidence man and fate's darling. After the supreme concentration of all his forces Mann craved relaxation; and in fact the relaxation in these two books goes very far. They are the most rollicking and high-spirited of his works.

Certainly Thomas Mann in these two works let himself go, gave free rein to his playfulness, indulged in all the intellectual games, linguistic tricks, erotic speculations, the private jokes both on himself and others which he always had in abundant store and which constituted a great temptation to him. Yet even when he lets himself go, an artist of such innate and highly developed powers of symbol-making, so disciplined a virtuoso, cannot help turning everything into form. With him, the most entertaining levity ends up as profundity.

The result is that these two books conceal extremely serious questions under that ebullient storytelling which partly delights and partly shocks the reader. The Gregorius story is in fact far more than a parody of the typical saint's legend, and *Krull* is far more than a modern picaresque novel. These

From *The Orbit of Thomas Mann.* © 1969 by Princeton University Press, 1986 by Alice L. Kahler. Translated from the German by Krishna Winston and Richard Winston. Originally entitled "The Elect."

tales are rich in reverberations. This essay is an attempt to register some of them and consider their meanings and interrelationships.

Both works, *The Holy Sinner* as well as *Felix Krull* in its expanded form, are offshoots of the central concerns of *Doctor Faustus*. For both of them again center on the problems of sin and grace, of what constitutes election. The German title of *The Holy Sinner, Der Erwählte,* means "The Elect or Chosen One." Gregorius and Krull, like Joseph and Adrian, are presented to us as a pair of opposites: Gregorius is led to grace through sinfulness; Felix Krull is seduced into refined roguery by inner talents and outer good fortune. The core of these two books—as indeed of Mann's entire work—is the sense that all life on earth is deeply paradoxical, that good and evil infect one another. Mann's feeling, the consequence of contemporary upheavals, is that this mongrel creature, man, is not so simple a matter, that the moral issues are not so clear-cut as earlier ages like to think. As Sartre has put it in *Le diable et le bon dieu,* his communistic *Faust*: "Sur cette terre et dans ces temps le Bien et le Mauvais sont inséperables."

This fundamental paradoxicality glints through the surface of both stories in a thousand different guises. It is implicit in the use of a mediating narrator, almost a standard practice with Mann since *The Beloved Returns.* The face of the narrator is reflected in his own descriptions; his ambivalent emotions and comments provide an ironic frame for the story. In *The Holy Sinner* "the spirit of storytelling"—an earthly mirror of almighty Providence—is personified in a life-craving little monk who relishes all the highly indecent happenings which in the end are fully legitimized. He is a humorous counterpart to Serenus Zeitblom: "Very oft is the telling only a substitute for enjoyment which we, or the heavens, deny ourselves." In *Krull* the mediator is the protagonist himself who looks back on himself and his adventures from the vantage point of age, and enjoys them more consciously in retrospect.

In *The Holy Sinner* the mighty ringing of the bells sounds the (Russian, Dostoevskian) theme on the very first page: "*Beati quorum tecta sunt peccata.*" "Blessed are they who are covered with [protected by] sins." He who would be raised to the highest sanctity must pass through deepest sinfulness. How else is the saint to acquire his knowledge of human nature? How else is the power of penance to propel man into heaven to be tested? How else, finally, is the overwhelming mightiness of Grace to be tested, if not against an overwhelming magnitude of sin? If Grace had only original virtue to contend with, it would have nothing to do. Accordingly, we are told that the kindly abbot who had taken the foundling into his care acted thus "because he knew that he was born in great sin, for that touches a Christian very near and moves his heart to a sort of reverence. . . . God has made our sin His own agony, sin and cross, they were one in Him, and above all He was the God of sinners." Grace springs from the abyss of sin, from the "hope beyond hopelessness," the "transcendence of despair."

But whence springs sin? In Christian dogma all sin derives from the cardinal sin of pride, man's original presumption, and in the case of Gregorius from that fundamentally anti-Christian pride of race and nobility, the arrogance of a perfectly pure lineage. The mischief begins with the simple animal pleasure of complete compatibility, with erotically charged delight in blood relationship, which offers total familiarity and the precious sense of finding oneself in the other person—for "the other" is no real other, but only a narcissistically idolized "other self." Incest is seen as a paroxysm of propinquity, of consuming propinquity which almost abolishes the polarity of love.

The Almighty wishes to demonstrate a point. There is "long hesitation" about doing this, for only after twenty years of marriage is the Flemish duchess Baduhenna doubly blessed with children. And a curse is present from the beginning, for the birth of the twins cost the mother's life. Thus the children, a boy and a girl, not only share the same birth, the same biological mystery, but they are also "death's dearest scions." Both are marked by chicken pox with identical sickle-shaped stigmata on the forehead, the brand of death stamped upon their exquisitely noble beauty. All the factors of their lives prepare them for a well-nigh inseparable intimacy, a unity in duality impervious to all outside influences. "For of us two no one is worthy," the boy Wiligis tells his sister Sibylla, "neither of you nor of me, worthy is only one of the other, since we are wholly exceptional children, high of birth . . . and born together out of death. . . ." The incest is, moreover, stimulated by the somewhat erotic partiality the widowed duke feels for his daughter. For in his "sinful nicety" he begrudges her even the most highly born suitor and sometimes takes such delight in her that he comes between her and her brother, thus arousing the boy's jealousy. Kept in bounds by the father, the adolescents' passion bursts forth on the very night of the duke's death, springing directly from his death, as it were. And as if that were not enough, the siblings' union takes place over the dead body of the faithful dog, whose howls uttered direst warning until Wiligis, in the wildness of his aroused instincts, cuts the dog's throat. A terrifying brutal deed— the chronicler calls it with full justification "the worst that happened this night . . . a spewing of love, murder and passion of the flesh, that may God pity."

From this bloody amour springs an unnamed child, burdened with the hereditary taint of incest. It must be committed to the hands of God, set sail on the sea inside a stout cask, well supplied with gold, costly fabrics, and an ivory tablet on which is written a cautious description of his noble origins, while the brother-father goes off to die on a Crusade and the sister-mother stays at home and devotes her life to penance, "a princess-nun whose heart is dead." But Providence, constantly at war with itself, pursues its cruelly paradoxical plan for the child's salvation. Providence rescues and preserves the child for further calamities. In utter ignorance, indeed through the very atoning for its existential guilt, it is driven still deeper into sinfulness, into the greater guilt of Oedipus.

Fishermen from the Island of St. Dunstan save the infant from the waves. The friendly abbot Gregorius stands godfather to the child and takes him under his wing. The boy Grigorss is reared in a fisherman's hut and then in the monastery. His physique and disposition reveal his noble origins. Despite his more delicate constitution he comes off better than the robust fishermen's boys in competitive games because of his intense discipline. "He understood better than they did how to pull himself together." Yet nobility has a flaw, the flaw of alienation, which dogged all of Thomas Mann's heroes since Tonio Kröger. The fishermen's children see this mysteriously superior and scholarly boy, this "thief of strength," as an outcast who does not belong among them. The feeling culminates in a decisive challenge from his milk-brother Flann, who feels a surge of rage at finding Grigorss reading a Latin book on the beach. Every phase of the ensuing fist fight is described in language charged with significance. Making a defensive movement, Grigorss involuntarily lands a blow on his opponent's nose. Flann is disadvantaged by his own brute strength and hatred, and Grigorss breaks his nose with a signet ring he is wearing. The ring is incised with an emblem of the lamb with the cross—the gentle one vanquishes the strong. This crisis leads to a further crisis in Grigorss's knowledge of himself. The fisherman's wife, distraught by her son's injury, cries out that Grigorss is a foundling and not her real child. What he had long unconsciously sensed, uncomprehendingly and with strange sorrow, is now confirmed. Like Tonio Kröger he had longed to overcome the qualities in himself that separated him from the harmless, normal people; now he knows that he does not belong among them. The abbot feels compelled to complete the revelation and let him read the description of his sinful origins. Grigorss is thereby launched upon his "quest for himself" and his origins, on his crusade to atone for his parents' guilt "by turning through all my life to other blood and as knight striving for its need." If nobility carries a flaw, the flaw of alienation, the Christian inversion now comes into force: "Where there is flaw, there is nobility."

Again, with hypocritical resistance to its own intentions, Providence opposes itself when the abbot begs Grigorss to remain and atone for inherited guilt as his pious and beloved successor within the cloister's peaceful walls. But Providence must know what it really intends to do with the young man, and cannot be unaware that it has introduced into his blood that knightly character which for the time being wins out over religious vocation.

Providence has also arranged the other side of the matter: Duchess Sibylla's bitter self-chastisement has kept her from taking a second husband. One aspect of this radical penance is only another expression of her old arrogant repudiation of "the other"; forbidden to love her brother, she will have none of love and marriage altogether. She thereby embroils her country in the "wooing war," when the affronted Roger of Arelat, determined to force the duchess to accept his suit, falls upon Sibylla's land and overruns it with fire and sword. Thus on both sides the constellation is prepared for the second abominable sin.

Young Grigorss is outfitted as a knight and adopts the fish for his crest— the symbol of both St. Peter and the sea. In his fine ship he sets out across the Channel, over the same waters that he drifted in as a baby, rocked by the seemingly errant waves. Now he drifts once more toward the mainland through a dense fog, projection of his own uncertainty. Once ashore, he immediately finds what he has wished for: innocence in distress in the form of a lady "wonder-strange" and "wonder-near" who must be delivered from dire peril. He delivers her and in turn receives an unlikely deliverance in combat with his far more experienced opponent. It is he who now overcomes the lady's vow of chastity. For alas, without quite knowing why, she experiences maternal and erotic feelings for one who looks so much like her first and only beloved, her brother. She is not only grateful to him, she is proud of him. She ought to be taken aback by this fact, but she pays no attention to it. She has even been on the verge of recognizing the brocade of his garments as the very same material she sent along with the baby, but the connection eludes her conscious mind. And so the original sin is repeated, is raised to a higher power; the same mad pride of consanguinity emerges once again. For somewhere, in the depths of her body, in her animal instinct, she knew in spite of all her ignorance; nature within her does not resist, but insists. She herself later admits it; it rises into clarity: "But underneath, where truth abides in quietness, the identity had been known at first glance, and conscious-unconscious she had taken her own child for husband, because again he had been the only one equal in birth." And it was just the same with Gregorius, as he admits to her in the end, from the pinnacle of his holiness:

The measure of the sinfulness is controvertible before God, the more so that thy child, in that place where the soul makes no pretence, likewise very well knew that it was his mother whom he loved. . . . A youth who sets out to find his mother and wins by conquest a wife who, however beautiful, could be his mother, must reckon with it that she might be his mother whom he marries. . . . But to his blood the identity of wife and mother was familiar long before he learned the truth.

This is the point where his personal sin begins, for he was born with the previous one. But should this sin really be called personal, since it takes place in the lower depths, over which man does not have full power? It is original sin, Christian original sin at any rate, and Adam's sin here merges with the specifically genealogical sin. In the same way Biblical man had to become man so that he must fall away from God—it is one and the same thing—and be redeemed by God's Grace, so it is here in the special case of Gregorius. He must be driven into an even deeper chasm of sin by marrying his mother and begetting two children who are his sisters. When he continues to brood over his unknown origins and the meddling of an inquisitive maidservant brings the truth to light, what we have is a repetition to a still higher degree of what had happened before. The sinful son does not merely go on a knightly crusade like his father. Rather, he inflicts upon himself the ultimate and truly Christian penance: in beggar's robes, without even bread or bowl, with only the ominous ivory tablet inscribed with his story, he sets forth into the wilds where "only the heavens could be his roof-tree," into the moors, the trackless forest, and stubble fields that bruise his bare feet, with nothing to eat but leftovers given him by charcoal burners. And once more he comes to fisherfolk, and this time the rude jeering and hearty insults of the man of the house are balm to him, although the wife, moved by some premonition, intercedes on his behalf. He is allowed to sleep in the shed. And then once more he is cast on an island, though not this time an island with a guardian cloister, but a barren reef in the lake, totally unpeopled. What is more, he eagerly accepts the fisherman's sadistic suggestion that his feet should be chained by a leg-iron. But wasteland, ignominy, exposure, the life of an anchorite, are not yet penance enough. He must be driven to the utmost extreme, beyond human limits; he shrivels to an unrecognizable spiny creature not much bigger than a hedgehog, barely kept alive by a few drops of "earth milk" that ooze from the rock. This minimum of nourishment is the sign of Grace. Henceforth, even as he contracts physically, he grows spiritually. Two Roman dignitaries are instructed by visions to summon Gregorious to the newly vacant papal throne, and he is fetched back into human life through a series of events explicable only by his miraculous elevation into saintliness.

The penitent Sibylla makes a pilgrimage to the celebrated pope in the hope that in his holy wisdom he can set her mind at rest concerning the souls of her loved ones. There is a scene similar to the audience of old Jacob and the band of brothers with the exalted Joseph: a scene of recognition and reconciliation. The sinful child has become the Holy Father; child, husband, and father form a trinity. In the end, the two, "in love and grief, in repentance and grace," cannot be anything to each other but brother and sister in Christ—brother and sister in the spiritually purified sense that implies chastity. Events have come full circle. Providence has drawn its paradigm and completed its demonstration.

To be sure, this parable presents the element of the miraculous in its most exaggerated form. Here is the saintly legend at its most basic, in which utmost sin is transformed by utmost penance into utmost salvation. The circle of meaning, however humanized by the colorful, humorous "spirit of narrative," is traced with such precision, with such indomitable logic, that the story and its moral inevitably become caricature. And Thomas Mann would not be himself if he had foregone the opportunity to develop a situation to its limit, even a situation bordering on the burlesque. Nevertheless, at a deeper level the story wonderfully illuminates the spirit of Christian doctrine: incest represents the summit of human presumption, of racial pride and self-idolization, and as such can be equated with Adam's primal original sin against God and his fellow-men. It is original sin insofar as it is buried deep within the animal part of man and is not quite accessible to the personal will. It is, however, also personal sin because even in ignorance there is germinal knowledge and underneath naked instinct there lies a spark of will. No one can claim pure innocence, and yet no one is so completely guilty that Grace cannot bring salvation. Indeed, Grace actually longs for the mighty sinner with his shattering repentance.

If *The Holy Sinner* shows an extreme of genealogical narcissism, exaltation of selfhood, *Felix Krull* exemplifies an excessive passion for otherness. The hero is endowed with a hypertrophic imagination whose locus is his own body. Therefore it is readily capable of assuming tangible forms. Imagination originating in the body gives rise to rapid impersonation.

Krull is drawn into delinquency by his lack of specific gravity, his lack of an inhibiting selfhood, his "receptivity to the subtlest stimuli," combined with a talent for all too easily assuming other roles. He is certainly a swindler, but of a very special sort. And can he really be considered a criminal? Only in a very limited sense.

From beginning to end this "Felix" appears as a darling of the gods, a "favorite child of heaven," someone convinced of his own charm. Despite the prison term he alludes to, the old man who is penning the confessions still preserves his sense of happiness and faith in his good fortune. From the outset he is favored, or rather blessed, not only with physical attractions and charm, but also with the dangerous talent for self-transformation. He has a knack for imitation, simulation, disguise. He can mimic people's voices and ways of speaking as facilely as he can forge their handwritings. Underlying these accomplishments is a gift for observation, "perceiving," "extension of feeling," and thus a faculty for love-making, for intensifying and enlarging his being by taking in the broadest and most variegated possibilities. Moreover, he has the remarkable ability to control and shape those qualities on which the success, happiness, and good fortune of his life depend. Because he feels himself composed of "finer flesh and blood," he musters all his talents and virtuosity to provide real proof of his "election." For his active imagination would do him little good were it not for the instinct and good taste whereby he guides it, were it not for the generosity, aristocratic feeling, and occasionally the modesty with which he selects his opportunities. He brings to bear a good deal of disciplined effort—so much so that one might almost speak of responsibility. All these things are what distinguish him from a "common criminal."

To be sure, he commits thefts, he lies, impersonates. But aside from the childish forays into the *pays de Cocaigne* of the delicatessen—and "it was not alone their high quality [of the sweetmeats] that enchanted me; even more it was the carrying over of my dream treasures into my waking life that made up the sum of my delight"—except for this incident, no one is ever a whit the worse off as a result of Krull's transgressions. Madame Houpflé's jewel case slips into Krull's suitcase by itself in the course of the customs inspection. Whatever profit he makes from its contents, as well as from the subsequent commanded robbery in her hotel room, is actually a gift from this half-motherly, masochistic lady novelist who has a passion for young men. All this comes about because Felix, boyishly shy and chivalrous on "grounds of taste," has refused to whip her as she requests. And the grandiose fraud of the aristocratic world tour which he later embarks on is not an affair of his own seeking, but is done as a favor to the young Marquis, whose role Krull casually agrees to assume. Felix even exchanges his own bank account for the Marquis' letter of credit. In concluding the agreement, he specifically forbids anyone to "presuppose something like cunning in me. Where cunning is concerned, I am quite useless. Cunning is not gentlemanly." Were it not that he really has gentlemanly qualities, he would be quite incapable of playing his role. He has already unhesitatingly rejected various tempting proposals made to him while he was still a waiter—by an infatuated English girl and a wealthy Scottish lord. Yet he declined these advantageous offers with the utmost consideration for the feelings of those concerned:

> The main thing was that a confident instinct within me rebelled against a form of reality that was simply handed to me and was in addition sloppy—rebelled in favor of free play and dreams, self-created and self-sufficient, dependent, that is, only on the imagination. When as a child I had waked up determined to be an eighteen-year-old prince named Karl, and had then freely maintained this pure and enchanting conceit for as long as I wished—that had been the right thing for me.

The point is that he cherishes freedom, and such freedom entails discipline.

Anyone who senses a great talent in himself longs to develop that talent creatively. Thus the boy Felix consciously practices the art of dissimulation, which stands him in good stead at his examination for military service; thus he delights in "dressing up," perfects his manners and accomplishments. Hailing cabs outside the theater is good training for the roles of elevator boy and waiter by which he will later mount into the upper reaches of society. All along, outside assistance flows toward him as if by magic, as always happens when any strong characterological trait manifests itself. He receives valuable education from his godfather Schimmelpreester, the carnival-loving painter who plays games of masquerade with Felix, as well as from the coarse prostitute Rosza, who puts him through a rigorous course in love. Krull feels keen enjoyment in practicing such arts and performing such roles. He enjoys playing on himself like an instrument. He enjoys the gentle transition from dream to reality, the haziness, the interchangeability of two conditions, the "delicate hovering quality of his existence." He enjoys disguises even when they are humbling; but even more pleasurable is an ambiguous role, such as that of being a liftboy with a bank account.

> And so, possessor of a checkbook though I was, I remained a liftboy. . . . There was a certain charm in playing this role against a background of secret wealth, thanks to which my becoming livery took on the quality of a costume. . . . My secret wealth

transformed my uniform and my job into a role, a simple extension of my talent for "dressing-up." Although later on I achieved
dazzling success in passing myself off for more than I was, I now
passed myself off for less, and it is an open question which deception gave me the greater inner amusement, the greater delight
in this fairytale magic.

If he is distinguished from the real criminal by these higher demands of
the imagination, by his pleasure not only in life's crude material satisfactions
but in airy, fastidious freedom, he is also distinguished from the professional
impersonator, the actor, by the seriousness he brings to his metamorphoses:
"It's not my custom to take life as a joke," he tells the Marquis whose identity
he is to assume. "Frivolity is not my style, especially in the matter of jokes;
for certain jokes are pointless if they are not taken seriously. A good joke
does not come off unless one approaches it with complete seriousness." This
is why acting, for which his gifts might have destined him, does not meet
his needs: in acting, the sphere of illusion is too sharply divided from reality.
The actor uses his art of impersonation on alien, distant material—the greater
the distance, the finer the art. Krull is his own material; his own reality is
his material. He does not merely dissimulate, he does not merely counterfeit
another role: he identifies with that other person, body and soul. His aim is
not imposture but identity, confusingly free, dreamlike, and protean identity.

As a child Krull came face to face with the crass reality of the actor
when his godfather took him to the theater and later dropped in on the
dressing rooms. The boy was captivated by the splendor and sovereignty of
the figure on the stage; he was all the more repelled by the real man behind
the illusion. The opposite principle is exemplified by the circus performers
whom he sees in Paris; as trapeze artists or clowns they commit their whole
being to the act, to the point where they no longer have lives of their own.
Felix Krull himself hovers between the two forms of existence, living "as a
likeness" and yet really living. In serious-minded freedom he juggles with his
lived life.

It is natural that a person as obsessed with transformation as Krull
should be attracted and excited by the cosmic aspects of the question, as
unfolded to him (while Krull is just setting out on his new aristocratic existence) by his table companion in the dining car, Professor Kuckuck. Kuckuck outlines the course of the world's evolutionary transformations and the
ascent of one form into another, from existence to life to man. Krull learns
that all forms are provisional, that life itself is but an episode. All this accords
with his own "praise of the transitory" and "universal sympathy," his sense

of the way things flow into one another and exert attraction on each other. The "vast expansiveness" of feeling which he acquires, thanks to this broad perspective, is closely akin to the erotic-sexual feeling which as a child he had named "The Great Joy." The strong impact of Kuckuck's lecture is reflected in the charming sermons Felix reads to Kuckuck's daughter, Zouzou, in Lisbon. Felix wants to convert the mocking, saucy girl to love. Hemmed in by the strict Latin conventions, the girl scorns and assails what repression denies her; she scoffs at love as "disgusting small-boy nastiness." And what Krull tells her, in fact almost sings to her—for he deliberately poeticizes love to counter the girl's foolish "crudeness"—is a theoretical glorification of love as that miracle of nature which succeeds "in wiping out the division between one person and the other." This miracle begins in the human eye and the intimacy of its gaze. This is a recurrent theme in the *Confessions,* and one which inspires some passages of moving beauty. (One is reminded of Werfel's poem *Blicke,* which similarly celebrates the power of the eye.) The eye is that "precious jelly made up of just such ordinary elements as the rest of creation, affirming like a precious stone that the elements count for nothing, but that imaginative and fortunate combination counts for everything . . . as long as the spark of life remains alert there, to throw such beautiful, airy bridges across all the chasms of strangeness that lie between man and man." The miracle leads to the embrace and the kiss, which "is after all, pledge of that marvelous release from separateness and from the fastidious refusal to be interested in anything that is not oneself." "Only at the opposite poles of human contact, where there are no words or at least words no more, in the glance and the embrace, is happiness really to be found, for there also are unconditional freedom, secrecy, and profound ruthlessness." And the book might indeed end on this little hymnic speech which celebrates the "denial of the aversion of stranger for the stranger, a secret sign of omnipresent love." It is the metaphoric apotheosis of Felix Krull's passion for the *other.*

However, the *Confessions* do not end here; in fact they do not end with the episode or this one volume alone, but promise events to come. Events lead up to a real kiss, a triumphant test case, whereby the girl's inhibitions are put to flight. But that marks the end of the adventure with the nubile girl. The tender embrace is interrupted by the appearance of the mother, an imposing beauty who, with her majestic sensuality, commandeers and devours the young "Marquis'" love. This makes good sense and is totally welcome to Krull, for actually he had fallen in love with both together, the pretty daughter and the beautiful mother; what attracted him was the scintillating doubleness, the "combination"—in this case the mother and daughter, as back in his Frankfurt days he had been unforgettably struck by the sight of a brother and sister who briefly stepped out on the balcony of their hotel: a reference, we might point out, to a remote but related sphere, the world of Gregorius.

In *The Holy Sinner* and in *Doctor Faustus,* even in *Joseph and His Brothers,* a particular paradox has been established: that grace proceeds to sin and sin to grace. In secular terms this means the blurring of the frontier between the impersonal and the person, between, on the one hand, inherited dispositions and circumstances, and, on the other, the will and accomplishments of the individual. In *Gregorius* the hand of Providence fulfills the same function that in *Faustus* is assumed by biological demonism—for the devil of *Faustus* was, after all, only an atavistic, theological projection of the inescapable law that evil is inextricably involved with the power of creation. Felix Krull gives much thought to the paradoxes of this problem:

> Education is not won in dull toil and labor; rather it is the fruit of freedom and apparent idleness; one does not achieve it by exertion, one breathes it in; some secret machinery is at work to that end; a hidden industry of the senses and the spirit . . . is hourly active to promote it, and you could go so far as to say that one who is chosen learns even in his sleep. For one must after all be of educable stuff in order to be educated. No one grasps what he has not possessed from birth . . . and here again it is very hard to draw a just and clear distinction between personal desert and what are called favorable circumstances.

But there are times when Felix considers the question from the opposite angle: "Was it not very difficult to make a sharp distinction between natural deserts and moral? . . . Was it true that I had had so little to do, in an inner sense, with those assets? Had I not instead the unmistakable assurance that they were my own work to a significant degree, and that my voice might easily have turned out common, my eyes dull, my legs crooked, had my soul been less watchful." Here the natural graces are represented as a product of moral qualities.

The same paradox is present in the relationship between freedom and discipline: freedom is preserved only through discipline, but initial freedom is required to make discipline possible. Though Felix Krull is so talented and trained for love's pleasures, "the extraordinary demands" imposed on his energies forbid him to squander himself "in enervating passion." And yet he holds that it is "the enervating that benerves us—if vital prerequisites are met—and makes us capable of performances and enjoyments in the world that are beyond the compass of the un-benerved."

These intricate and varied paradoxes are the motive force of Krull's whole existence; in fact, they are the very substance of this improbable existence, in which dream and reality, truth and deception, all but merge. Here the very truth is elusive mutability, transformation of identity, olympian manipulation of identity. In this graceful, deceptively easy book Thomas Mann has once more given us a picture of the artist, this time of an artist who works with his own flesh and blood.

LARRY DAVID NACHMAN AND
ALBERT S. BRAVERMAN

Thomas Mann's Buddenbrooks:
Bourgeois Society and the Inner Life

In his essay on Schopenhauer, written in 1933, Thomas Mann, describing his early and momentous encounter with the philosopher, remarks: "one can think in the *sense* of a philosopher without in the least thinking according to his sense; I mean that one can avail oneself of his thoughts and thus can think as he would by no means have thought."

He thus suggests that his youthful relation to this beloved and admired system was, like his attitude to his middle-class background, equivocal and complex.

Equivocal and complex, indeed, is the whole body of Mann's early work and weighty with implications for the unique and extraordinary achievements of his later years. It is, nevertheless, our contention that the early works of Thomas Mann are entirely intelligible, provided only that one grasps two points. First, from the very beginning of his career, his relation to the presumed antipodes of his thought—bourgeois society and the late German Romanticism of Schopenhauer, Nietzsche, and Wagner—was critical and dialectical and never involved merely an unconscious influence or naïve acceptance. Secondly, Mann's art was a direct and conscious encounter with the specific structure and problems of his own age and place.

Erich Heller's approach is of interest in this context. After considering briefly the possibility that *Buddenbrooks* might be regarded as a "sociological novel," Heller rejects the idea and then goes on to analyze *Buddenbrooks*

From *The Germanic Review* 45, no. 3 (May 1970). © 1970 by Columbia University Press.

entirely in terms of abstract categories drawn from Schopenhauer's metaphysics. We believe that *Buddenbrooks* is unintelligible in such terms. The problem involved in Heller's analysis, and, as we shall see, in other important critics, is a failure to understand the fundamental ground that underlies the whole opus of the young Thomas Mann. For this deep and hidden entity, this metaphysical substratum, is not the will, not Nirvana, not the realm of the Dionysian and Apollonian, nor even the overwhelming power of Wagner's music.

What Mann begins with, what he is sundered from, what he longs for, and what he continually returns to, is the world of an active and effective life, amidst other men, and in intimate contact with them. The note of joy, rare for Mann's works in this period, in *Royal Highness* is, after all, based upon the fact that its hero, though *like* an artist, is, at least potentially, a ruler of men. Mann's relation to bourgeois society was certainly equivocal because, as *Buddenbrooks* demonstrates, its specific character had the effect of alienating one's humanity. But the world, society in its most general sense, remained Mann's deepest love and deepest need.

At the time he wrote *Buddenbrooks*, Mann was certainly apolitical in the sense that he believed that society, as he knew it, was immutable. German upper-middle-class life, or middle-class life in general, was for him, the world itself. Therefore, if bourgeois society was insufferable, his only conclusion was that somehow the world must be abandoned. The source of the poignancy of Mann's early period was that he could neither abandon his deep commitment to the human community nor live as a member of the only community he knew.

It has often been noted that society was for Mann a problem and that the antithesis between the artist and the burgher was the dominant theme of his early works. But for this child of the city and scion of an old and powerful merchant family, society was more than a problem: it was the sphere of action of his fathers. What we see, then, in Mann's early works is, first of all, a serious effort to depict the reality, bourgeois society, in precise and concrete terms.

Buddenbrooks provides us with the strongest possible evidence for this assertion. For, after all, the graphic detail of Mann's description of the specific social structure is a far more striking and pervasive feature of the work than those direct allusions to Schopenhauer's philosophy which have received so much critical attention. The social structure portrayed in *Buddenbrooks* has, in general, not been taken seriously, as if to do so were to belittle the book. But the condition of life at a certain moment in time, in a certain place and in a certain class, is at least as much Mann's concern in *Buddenbrooks* as is Schopenhauer's system.

We hope to show that the ultimate reality of *Buddenbrooks* is a human society; that the development of the book is a demonstration of the exact manner in which this specific human society destroyed self-conscious human personality or alienated it from the world; and, finally that the function of Schopenhauer's philosophy in *Buddenbrooks* is to provide a key to the psychology of this alienated soul.

A word about the method which will be employed in this study. Because we are concerned with demonstrating the concreteness with which Mann describes his society, it will be necessary to consider his novel in considerable detail. Moreover, a novel in the tradition of realism insists that we accept a whole unseen world by implication. Above all, we cannot get beyond its characters; they may never have had flesh, but if we think of them only as characterizations we are lost. Whatever Thomas Mann had to say must emerge from a serious and thorough consideration of the personalities of his characters. And we will consider them from any point of view that seems helpful, including psychoanalysis.

Buddenbrooks is concerned with the history of a family. To speak of the history of a family implies a certain peculiar status for that family, as distinct from the usual, almost biological connotation of the term. A family which, in any real sense, has a history, is one whose forbears wrested significant reserves of power and property from the world. It is a family thereby freed from that necessity which reduces the great majority of men to laboring for the simplest needs of life. The history of such a family is the way in which it used its freedom.

We encounter the earliest Buddenbrook of the book, Johann the elder, in the midst of a vigorous and productive old age. Here, at the beginning of the novel, is a successful and, at times, ruthless businessman who is, nevertheless, cultured, liberal, receptive to new ideas, and, in contrast to his son, a freethinker and mocker of piety. Johann's breadth and complexity is most concretely revealed by the varied society that appears at his housewarming: nouveau riche, patrician bourgeoisie, clergymen, physician and poet. Probably never before, and certainly never again, will a Buddenbrook move at ease in such a company and be at home in so many worlds.

What is noteworthy about Johann is not so much a concern with culture (as a retired merchant might take up art), but a free and natural intercourse with ideas. There is no strain or tension in his culture because it had never been severed from his life. Both his worldly activities and his culture were expressions of his strikingly independent personality.

At this point we might consider Erich Heller's view of old Johann as somehow a manifestation of will unsullied by the idea. He bases his position on the old man's strength of character, self-confidence and "naïveté." It is this last attribute which suggests the problems with Heller's position. For Johann is hardly naïve. He seems to have been a fairly sophisticated man of the enlightenment. His breadth of culture, insistence on arranging his garden in a civilized manner, his objections to "practical education" and generally explicit rationalism are hardly comprehensible in terms of pure and brutal will to live.

Heller's analysis seems to us to be posited on a fundamental over-extension of Schopenhauer's categories. They are appropriate to an age and a human type which embody an ineluctable contradiction between thought and action. Now Johann Buddenbrook was not forced to suppress his self-consciousness—the spontaneous and refined activities of his mind—in order to play an effective role in the world. Moreover, this was not merely his good fortune; his confidence was a reflection of an age in which the new mercantile elite rejoiced to find its deepest values articulated in the thought of a Voltaire and a Diderot. Of this age he was a very late representative—perhaps the last.

Mann clearly recognized that this extraordinary form of human fulfillment was associated with a specific historical moment. He grasped the fragile and perishable nature of such integration and his portrayal of Johann can be understood as a nostalgia for the classical.

What emerges directly from the novel, then, is a sense of association between spontaneous, healthy personality, fulfilled in the world, rationality, and culture. By implication, Johann Buddenbrook represents the claim of bourgeois society that it alone provides a completely fulfilled and materially self-sufficient life. *Buddenbrooks,* from this point on, can be considered an examination and criticism of the ultimate validity of this claim.

Johann Buddenbrook was in a position to be the source of an enlargement of freedom. Instead, because of his peculiar emotional relation to his sons, in the context of the nature of the family business, freedom was ultimately stifled. For after all, there was a sense in which Johann was naïve; he expected his son to be naturally disposed to obey him. He could not handle his elder son's independence, but dealt with Gotthold with Spartan severity for marrying out of his class. But this reaction was related to the old man's arbitrary dislike for his elder son, whose birth had caused the death of his first and beloved wife. The unreasonable actions which arose from these passions was, perhaps, a result of a certain bogus rationality, which led to clumsy dealing with the inner life. This self-certainty, unconscious rage posing as reason, is the perversion of enlightenment.

Thus, Johann was ultimately left with an obedient son, Jean, who had the most profound respect for his father's ethical and commercial principles and practices. But what was the real content of this respect? Johann Buddenbrook, the elder, determined his world: the patterns of his active and contemplative lives emerged from an interplay between his personality and experience. For him, self-consciousness did not involve conflict with the world, because his life was an expression of his individuality. His son, Consul Buddenbrook, resolved such potential conflicts, not through active integration, but by passive acceptance of his role in the world.

In an early encounter we find Consul Buddenbrook alone writing long prayers into his diary and reverently reviewing the family history (his father, he notes, was far too "rooted in the present" to be very much concerned with the historical past). He is, in fact, the very embodiment of traditionalism and piety, in rather curious contrast to his enlightened father. There is, of course, little psychological ground for expecting close affinities between sons and fathers. In this case, however, the basis of the difference is not merely personal or reactive, but has, in fact, the broadest social implications. The elements of Jean's character are figured in the whole aftermath of the European enlightenment.

A period of radical social change is one in which there is a relatively abrupt adaptation of institutions to demands or claims of sections of the population whose interests can no longer be ignored. Yet, even when we applaud such progress, we can still recognize that it may profoundly undermine the inner security of people—even those benefited by the change—who had once, naturally, accepted the social order as something given, constant, and fundamental to their lives and who now see that order vanish, so to speak, before their eyes. This social change is, of course, the purposive reform, or destruction, of institutions by conscious act of human will. Prior to such an act, the members of the immemorial world will inevitably come to think of the social structure as part of the natural order of things—of nature itself, as it were. The institutions involved thus find their sanctification in something external to man—in custom, in nature or in God. But such a sanction is lost once it becomes clear that institutions can be manipulated by human will. Then, the whole structure of society is clearly demonstrated to be a work of man. The age and personality which generated the change will rejoice in this knowledge, because of their inevitable and deep-rooted confidence in their own reason and will, and in that of man in general. The enlightened mind thus pays the highest tribute to the human personality, for it attributes to that personality, and to it alone, the capacity to create a moral order in a universe whose essence is brute, indifferent nature.

It is hardly surprising that such ages of confidence are uncommon. For the offspring of the representatives of such an age, lacking, as well may be, the self-certainty of their fathers, may tremble in horror before a social order whose ultimate basis is supposed to lie in their own modest personalities. They are, as they see themselves, mere men and desire above all a fixed and stable order in the world.

In the scenes in which the older and the younger Buddenbrooks appear together, the differences in their epochs, their personalities, and their styles of life are thoroughly developed. The tone of their conversation is itself revealing. It is the old man who, even when speaking from deep conviction, adopts a light and jocular tone; the form of his speech suggests a tolerance, not merely of opposing positions, but of the men who express them. Johann's tolerance of diverse ideas was based on a philosophical detachment. There is, however, another form of detachment which makes a later appearance in the Buddenbrook family.

The moral earnestness of Jean is contrasted with his father's cool and subtle comments on Napoleon. The old man unashamedly admired the strength and brilliance of the conqueror of his native city and the plunderer of his house. He is clearly edified by the heroism and historic grandeur of the Great Man's actions, and the completeness with which his personality impressed itself on the world.

Jean, however, is evidently far more sensitive to Napoleon's crimes than his father, and it is in attacking them that we first observe the enthusiasm which draws "mocking smiles" from his father and Pastor Wunderlich. Before our eyes, enlightenment confronts Romantic sentimentality. The Consul's sentiments are certainly unexceptionable, as is his praise of Louis Philippe and "practical idealism." But as is often the case in unregulated and personal arguments (particularly between relatives) the reply Jean receives from his father appears, as we shall see, at best, obliquely related to what he says.

The second form of detachment from principle may be described as the practical. It is the attitude of the plain businessman for whom ideas are mere games—trifling play of the mind—and the supreme reality is that necessity by which he lives. The practical detachment from thought is thus the detachment of contempt.

Now it is, curiously enough, this philistinism that old Johann discerns in his son's humane arguments and refusal to appreciate great and free personality. The old man's spontaneous association to the mention of practical ideals is the following:

> "Practical ideals—well, ye-s—" The elder Buddenbrook gave his
> jaws a moment's rest and played with his gold snuff-box. "Prac-

tical ideals—well—h'm—they don't appeal to me in the least."
He dropped into dialect, out of sheer vexation. "We have trade
schools and technical schools and commercial schools springing
up on every corner; the high schools and the classical education
suddenly turn out to be all foolishness, and the whole world
thinks of nothing but mines and factories and making money . . .
That's all very fine, of course. But in the long run, pretty stupid,
isn't it? . . . I don't know why, but it irritates me like the deuce."

The sanctification of necessity is somehow unbearable for the old man, and
ideals seemed to him to have quite adequate substance and life without being
justified by practicality.

It is not long before we have a clear demonstration of what old Johann
objected to in his son. In their passionate discussion about whether to satisfy
Gotthold's demand for a larger share of the family fortune, the Consul's
personal attitude toward the problem has a striking peculiarity—it is quite
indefinable. Initially, he manifests sincere anxiety about being held responsible by his brother for his father's hostility and he is concerned with division
in the family. He then undergoes a rather abrupt change of heart, when his
horror at discord is replaced by fear of possible damage to the firm from a
large expenditure. His personal attitude to his brother and his plight is never
expressed. His doubts seem entirely lost in his concern with such objective
institutions as the family and the firm.

The firm was, to a large degree, the creation of the old Johann. It was
the extension of his personality, the instrument of his power. For his son,
the firm and family were venerable and immutable institutions to which he
and his were to be ultimately subordinated. The different positions of father
and son were made most explicit as the Consul reverently examined the
family records and heard his father's voice in the next room.

> What a pity he had so little taste for those old records! He stood
> with both feet planted firmly in the present, and concerned him-
> self seldom with the past of the family. Yet, in times gone by he
> too had made a few entries in the gilt-edged book. The Consul
> turned to those pages, written in a florid hand on rather coarse
> paper that was already yellowing with age. They were chiefly
> about his first marriage. Ah, Johann Buddenbrook must have
> adored his first wife, the daughter of a Bremen merchant! The
> one brief year it had been granted him to live with her was the
> happiest of his life—"*l'année la plus heureuse de ma vie.*" The

words were underlined with a wavy line, for all the world, even
Marie Antoinette to see.

For Consul Buddenbrook, the book was a memorial of the family tradition,
a repository of the history of an institution. But his father clearly regarded
it as something else—a personal diary. And he came to it, not to record the
objective details of his own history, but to satisfy his need to express his
passionate and joyful love for his wife. He needed no *Sturm und Drang*
Romanticism to realize and sanctify his personality, and found no inconsis-
tency between this sanctification and rationality. In his son we see the mutation of enlightened rationality into submission of the personal to the
practical and institutional. The most intimate human relationships, such as
those between members of a family, take on rigid and externalized forms
and become part of a social order with needs and demands of its own over
and against the desires and claims of its individual members. The world,
then, the objective order in which men live and act, has become intractable
and unresponsive; it is no longer a domain in which personality can realize
itself because there is no place for the free play of spirit. The human personality has become an outcast from the world and can find a place for itself
only in worldless inwardness, i.e., in pure subjectivity.

If the center of Jean's worldly life, the family and the firm, were institutions which stood above and beyond his personality, in what did he find
his real self-expression? The answer lies in his worldless religiosity. Consider
again the attitude for which his father reproached him—the idealization of
the practical. The danger here is not that the practical is elevated but that
the ideal is degraded: the social is exhausted in the economic and every
human relationship must be understood in economic terms and controlled
by economic imperatives. Without an autonomous idea of the social and the
human, the cultural values to which the old man alluded in his attack on
practical ideals are simply inexplicable.

We must not think of Jean as a money-grubber or brutal man of affairs.
It is his negativity which is striking. He is given over to the economic because
he has deprived himself of any alternative. Now the Romantic movement, in
all its stages, has taught us this lesson: if the social is identified with the
economic, if human reality is reduced to mechanism, the personal, nevertheless, will insist on its self-expression. It will assert its own reality against all
odds, but the assertion may be strained, sickly, and worldless. This, then,
is the explanation of Jean's Christian humility. Jean, of course, was no Romantic, but a pietist—that is, a representative of another historical alternative
to this reduction of human personality. The time spent in such devotional

exercises as entering long prayers in his diary was time stolen from his worldly obligations. His Christianity was a manifestation of an urgent personal need to abandon the world—the inevitable consequence of a lifeless practicality.

The real dangers of Jean's position are revealed by the part he played in his daughter's marriage. That he should have desired, or actually forced, his daughter to marry a man of wealth and good prospects was hardly surprising and quite consistent with his position in the world. Toni herself, despite her dislike for Grünlich, was in some sense in sympathy with her father's view, insofar as her feeling for social and financial status was, at least, as strong as his.

Jean had no apparent difficulty in grasping the general implications of his bourgeois position; the disaster that ensued lay in the rigid and unintelligent manner in which he applied his principles to a specific situation. With the most limited sensitivity (and Jean was by no means a coarse man), he might have seen what his family saw so quickly: that Grünlich, his daughter's suitor, was a shameless toady and manifestly her inferior. With his perfectly adequate business abilities, he might well have investigated more searchingly the recommendations of those who could have had a personal stake in Grünlich's making a rich marriage. He might even have discovered that this exemplary young merchant was close to bankruptcy.

Jean's devotion to practical ideals seems to have been related to a curious inability to act intelligently on a human level. Like many conservatives, he did not know that the worthiest and most time-honored principles must be applied to reality with some imagination. The very desperation with which he insisted on Toni's marriage suggests that his ideals were not general rules to guide him in his active life, but blindly accepted imperatives upon which he was utterly dependent. The irony of his apparent worldliness and practicality lay in the fact that the marriage of interest these tendencies inflexibly ordained proved, in the end, to be a major financial disaster, while, incidentally, destroying his daughter's life.

If Consul Buddenbrook represented a certain stagnation of middle-class life, Thomas, his eldest son, appeared to be the instrument of revitalization for the principles of that life and of his family's position in the world. For he was not merely a competent and industrious young businessman; he was an individual of unusual refinement, sensitivity, and demonstrably superior talents. He was, furthermore, ambitious and energetic. And if his principles and way of life were similar to his father's, one, nevertheless, had the feeling that he accepted them less blindly.

In the first decade or so after Jean's death, we see the effects of his son's talents. Business advanced, the family was enriched, a new and greater house was built and, as a crown to this success, Thomas became a Senator of the municipality. Yet, unexpectedly and with apparent abruptness, Thomas lost his nerve and with it, his capacity to act. This loss was followed by worldly failure, an early death and the total dissolution of the Buddenbrook firm and family. To understand the real nature of Thomas's collapse is of overwhelming importance. For not merely does this event constitute the central action of the novel, it is also the epitome of those problems which were the primary concern of the young Thomas Mann.

There are three types of critical approach to the decline of Thomas Buddenbrook. The simplest is embodied in statements such as these:

> One feels that this failure . . . is due less to any tangible defect in Thomas than to that inner weariness which, Mann implies, must be taken as given and lies beyond explanation.

> Decay (in *Buddenbrooks*) is considered an inevitable spiritual and biological process.

The problem with such a view is its lack of content. It is difficult to entertain seriously so naïve and antiquated an idea as "biological decay" as an explanatory principle for the events of human life. It recalls the naïve concept of atavism in late nineteenth-century psychiatry. It is our contention that Mann makes Thomas's life completely and extensively intelligible in *Buddenbrooks*. Thomas can be understood, but only through that combination of refined psychology and social awareness which was uniquely Thomas Mann's.

Erich Heller comes more closely to grips with the text and presents the two other ways of elucidating the problem of *Buddenbrooks*. He notes the significance of the Hagenstroms as a new type of decidedly non-patrician bourgeoisie with which Thomas could not compete. This is true as far as it goes, but we must not confuse Toni's view of the Hagenstroms with Mann's. They did not represent a merely new and crude class (their crudeness is questionable in the context of the novel). The fact is that the Hagenstroms' worldly position rested on the same basis as the Buddenbrooks': successful economic enterprise. The ostensible superiority of the Buddenbrooks was based only on the fact that they got there first.

Heller's second approach involves working out the events of the novel in terms of Schopenhauer's philosophy. Reference to Schopenhauer is never irrelevant when one is discussing Mann. However, there are various ways in which one can use a tool. Heller suggests that Thomas's decline was based on an increasing reflectiveness which must, inevitably, enervate the will and weaken the character. The idea of the necessary conflict between *Geist* and *Leben* is pervasive in Mann and surely related to Schopenhauer's metaphysics. Unfortunately, the bare concept has not much more content than "biological decay." It was Mann's enterprise in *Buddenbrooks* to elucidate the origins and substance of this very significant conflict. It is through his exploration of the interaction of consciousness and the world that the phenomenon of decadence is to be understood; to see it as the product of entirely autonomous psychological, biological or social phenomena is to ignore the substance of the novel and the reality it represents.

To understand the tragedy of Thomas Buddenbrook it is necessary to examine the lives of his two oldest siblings, Toni and Christian. They shared with him a common experience and their lives were ultimately as frustrated as his. But if we consider them in their youth, we find no real mental or physical evidence of that "biological and spiritual decay" which is supposed to account for their ultimate tragedies. It was only as they were confronted with the established patterns of Buddenbrook life that they found, long before Thomas, that conformity was impossible without the annihilation of their personalities.

The rigid, and rigidly enforced, patterns of the bourgeois life of Jean were for his haughty, vivacious, and attractive daughter, Toni, fairy tales set off against an ever more painful reality. The attack on her personality was most direct and devastating; she was forced to marry a man she loathed. Her submission to this requirement was based not only on the strength of the demand, but on her naïve conviction that this type of marriage was, after all, the right kind. For her, too, the family's position came first. Only in the short period of revolt prior to her marriage did she develop the one relationship that was suitable to her in human and personal terms. She might have actually attempted to marry the medical student whose character she was strong enough to appreciate despite the "social gap" between them. But she did not. This infatuation was the last expression of her individuality. For, when her marriage failed in its own terms and her husband was bankrupt, she was no longer capable of insight or action. She had become totally committed to the principles which were the source of her suffering and humiliation. She became, more than any member of the family, the most rigidly devoted to the Buddenbrook name and the Buddenbrook position. Her pride became more and more pathetic as the family dissolved, but she remained to the end without knowledge.

Christian was the black sheep of the third generation of the Buddenbrooks. He was undignified, irresponsible, lazy, and dissipated. He was the living contradiction of every quality necessary for success in bourgeois life. Throughout his life he remained a constant source of humiliation and exasperation to his family.

But we, as critics, would repeat the injustice done to Christian by his own, if we judge him solely by bourgeois standards. For after all, he had his good points; he was affable, clever, and genuinely sympathetic. And, in his demand to marry the humble woman he had loved so long, he showed that he was quite capable of recognizing certain responsibilities in the world.

What, then, was the basis of Christian's failure? What transformed him into a clown, a hypochondriac, and, ultimately, a madman, disdained and abandoned by his family? Christian, when all is said, had only one great defect—he could not work. He was not an economic man. He was hardly stupid or untalented and, perhaps, if he had not borne the burden of the Buddenbrook name he might have been a successful impressario. We would not deny that Christian's ability either to accommodate himself to or reject the world in which he was raised was limited; he was no Tonio Kröger. But the spontaneous development of his natural talents was suppressed in a very substantial way. And for what? Christian was destroyed in the name of an ethos which denies the status of human being to a man who does not work and produce in the most basic and economic sense of those terms. His name was, perhaps, not without significance. "Consider the lilies of the field, how they grow; they toil not, neither do they spin. And yet I say unto you that even Solomon in all his glory was not arrayed like one of these" [St. Matthew 6:28].

Christian embodied those qualities of man which cannot fulfill themselves in work. But such attributes—the aesthetic and the moral—may be more specifically and uniquely human than those which do not find their fulfillment in work.

What, then, was Christian? He stands for free, simple and unreflective self-consciousness; he was personality which loves itself, seeks to realize itself and is thereby ever sympathetic to other human beings. Yet Thomas disliked his brother: "Christian busies himself too much with himself, with what goes on in his own insides. Sometimes he has a regular mania for bringing out the deepest and the pettiest of these experiences—things a reasonable man does not trouble himself about, for the simple reason that he would not like to tell them to anyone else. There is such a lack of modesty in so much communicativeness."

Yet the willingness and capacity to talk about one's feelings is, in the first place, a recognition of their importance and, in the second place, the assertion that these feelings are universally experienced and thus can evoke that common sympathy which is a basis for morality. Thomas's reserve, on the other hand, was a wall erected around the personality and limited human communication to the purely necessary and practical. The exclusion of the private, the personal, and the intimate from one's consciousness stands for both lack of sympathy with mankind and for a certain callousness towards oneself.

Toni and Christian Buddenbrook were certainly failures in bourgeois terms. They had not been productive nor had they lived up to the demands of their station. We have argued that there was nothing about their characters which made their frustration inevitable and that they were weak only in the context of their environment. Nevertheless, it is in this context that they must be judged and somehow their personalities had to do with their inability to function. One may dismiss them with a shrug of the shoulders as two unfortunates who just did not have what it takes to succeed in the world. But it is impossible to attempt to explain the sudden and awful deterioration of Thomas Buddenbrook in terms of such arbitrary factors of personality. For at the time of his crisis, Thomas was not merely a successful man but one of the most substantial and influential citizens of his city. He had utterly mastered the world in which Toni and Christian floundered throughout their lives.

As we return to the question of Thomas's decline, we are alerted to the possibility that the ultimate explanation for it may well lie at least as much in a problem in the social structure in which he lived as in any weakness in his character. Now the work of Thomas's grandfather was the spontaneous expression of his personality; Jean, on the other hand, submerged his personality in his work. Thomas, however, implicitly asserted that his much wider ranging activities were, like his grandfather's, the result of free and enthusiastic personal commitment. His devotion and enthusiasm indicated that he desired to fulfill himself in his work, rather than merely to do his duty as his father had done.

Yet the very "violence" with which he performed his tasks and his peculiar inability to relax hardly suggest a state of mind comparable to Johann's. Thomas had a problem and by no means a simple one. The almost desperate intensity of his work was a clear indication that he had something to repress and forget which lay as deep as his nervous system. In this sense, the problem resembles the weakening of the will which Heller describes but its nature can be stated more precisely.

It is characteristic of the burgher to take his work and position seriously and Thomas was, indeed, a serious man. Yet it is clear that the consummation of his worldly ambitions did not fulfill his personality. His accomplishments were, to borrow a phrase, ego alien. But did the problem lie in his personality or in the nature of his ambition? From the beginning Thomas was aware that there were elements of his personality which would have to be suppressed in order for him to be able to function. He told his sister that,

> I have thought a great deal about this curious and useless self-preoccupation, because I once had an inclination to it myself. But I observed that it made me unsteady, hare-brained, and incapable—and control, equilibrium, is, at least for me, the important thing. There will always be men who are justified in this interest in themselves, this detailed observation of their own emotions; poets, who can express with clarity and beauty their privileged inner life, and thereby enrich the emotional world of other people. But the likes of us are simple merchants, my child; our self-observations are decidedly inconsiderable. We can sometimes go so far as to say that the sound of orchestra instruments give us unspeakable pleasure, and that we sometimes do not dare try to swallow—but it would be much better, deuce take it, if we sat down and accomplished something as our fathers did before us.

If Thomas's chosen mode of life was to become in some sense unsatisfactory, he was lost indeed. For so completely had he devoted himself to the pursuit of public and business achievement that he entirely lacked any escape or possible source of rejuvenation. It was part of Thomas's tragedy that he saw some of the richest elements in his personality as sources of moral weakness.

> Was he, Thomas Buddenbrook, a man of action, a business man,—or was he a finicking dreamer ... Ah, how many times had he asked himself that question? And how many times had he answered it: in strong, purposeful hours with one answer, in weak and discouraged ones with another! But he was too shrewd and honest not to admit, after all, that he was a mixture of both.

Thomas Buddenbrook would have agreed with Heller that any intrusion of self-consciousness is destructive to the will. But for Mann, this is not a metaphysical truth but a peculiar psychological and social phenomenon which must be understood. Thomas had so determined his life that there was for him no way out. But Mann, in one of the most remarkable transitions in the book, makes poignantly clear what might have been. He evokes this unrealized possibility in the person of the living representative of Thomas's unbusinesslike impulses—his wife.

During the celebration of the firm's centennial, Thomas received news of the failure of his inept and disgraceful attempt to revive the firm's fortunes—the usurious loan on a crop which was destroyed by hail. At this moment of overwhelming despair, as he saw his inner dissolution reflected as never before in his worldly activities, he was tormented by the cacophony of a third-rate band hired to celebrate the glory of the firm.

With a description of this music the chapter ends. But the next chapter opens with another music—the subtle, cultivated and deeply committed music-making and music-talk of Gerda Buddenbrook and Edmund Pfühl, the organist and learned musicologist of the local church. Here is the evocation of culture and, as such, the concrete symbol, the matchlessly eloquent expression of all that Thomas had long ago irretrievably lost.

Amidst Toni's vacuous and pathetic family pride, and Christian's increasing derangement, amidst Thomas's rapidly increasing deterioration and pitiful concentration on the forms of that life which he had ceased really to live, Gerda's quiet unworldly culture—the expression of her deepest personal need—stood forth as the only healthy, the only real and vital activity of the Buddenbrook house. Thomas could never share in this culture. His wife knew this and reproached him for the banality of his musical tastes for she had no doubt that he was capable of better things. She knew in fact, what was obvious from the beginning, that Thomas was not merely a more complex man than his father, but was a man of distinctly superior and (up to a point) developed personal gifts. *His* sacrifice did not merely mean the self-discipline necessary to play an active role in the world. It meant a total rejection of self-consciousness for life. But in this very act, for such a man as he, lay a contradiction. Too sensitive and able a man to live by predetermined forms, in order to suppress his "dreaming" he had vitiated what were precisely the well-springs of his life—creative personality and originality. In the end, he destroyed his ability to deal effectively with a changing and recalcitrant world. His self-consciousness did not weaken his will merely by its presence. It was rather that his denial and terror of his own impulses and aspirations poisoned his life and made willing futile.

The actual substance of Thomas's decline was a sudden loss of the ability to act effectively in commercial and public life. He became a failure.

> It is as though something had begun to slip—as though I hadn't the firm grip I had on events.—What is success? It is an inner, and indescribable force, resourcefulness, power of vision; a consciousness that I am, by mere existence, exerting pressure on the movement of life about me. It is my belief in the adaptability of life to my own ends. Fortune and success lie with ourselves. We

> must hold firmly—deep within us. For as soon as something
> begins to slip, to relax, to tire, *within us,* then everything without
> us will rebel and struggle to withdraw from our influence. One
> thing follows another, blow after blow—and the man is finished.

Clearly, Thomas's grip was weakened by the awareness of the nature of
striving and willing.

Fritz Kaufmann, one of Mann's most perceptive critics, argued that "At
the bottom of his heart man cannot rest content with a 'calling' which no
longer presses on toward any ultimate goal, but ensnares him in a network
of means." Kaufmann confronted Mann and the bourgeois society which
was his subject-matter from the perspective of a religious thinker. Kaufmann
took the position that work had been sanctified by the Protestant ethic which
looked to worldly success as the outward manifestation of inward grace.
Kaufmann believed that only with such a sanctification was it proper for the
human being to devote his energy and vitality to the pursuit of economic
goals. Now, with the religious sanction gone, work descended again to the
purely natural activity of providing for oneself the wherewithal to live. Kaufmann's
position was that not only a bourgeois but any naturalistic ethics is
inadequate. We need not follow Kaufmann in this broader attack on naturalism
to appreciate the real contribution he has made in elucidating the
limitations of the bourgeois imperatives of ceaseless work and unlimited
striving.

At the time we first encounter the Buddenbrook family, it had amassed
sufficient wealth to liberate itself from work for at least several generations.
We can understand why Johann continued to work into his old age: he
enjoyed it. But it becomes more difficult to understand why his descendants
felt it incumbent upon themselves to increase and enlarge the family fortune.
Jean did not question or analyze this obligation and, consequently, his life
as a burgher was exemplary. But his children, each in his own way, did
question this way of life and did seek to understand its justification. However,
the problem is that it cannot stand questioning and it cannot be justified.
Mann had learned from Schopenhauer that the fundamental metaphysical
principle of reality was futile striving. Mann then applied this metaphysical
conception to the world he knew most intimately, the commercial society of
his fathers. When Thomas says, "What is success? It is an inner, and indescribable
force, resourcefulness, power of vision; a consciousness that I am,
by my mere existence, exerting pressure on the movement of life around
me," he has completely cast aside the traditional values of the Buddenbrook
family. For it is characteristic of bourgeois society that it does establish

outward and visible standards of "fortune and success" and has absolutely no means for asserting that "fortune and success lie within ourselves."

Thomas Buddenbrook, who found in mid-career that he was dissatisfied with his life, discovered that he had an autonomous personality whose needs could not be met by the achievement of every goal to which he aspired. It is for this reason that the moment of greatest "outward and visible success" is often the moment of decline. For it is only when the consequences of a set of values have been actualized, that their implications for the self can really be understood.

> Often, in an hour of desperation, Thomas Buddenbrook asked himself what he was, or what there was about him to make him think even a little better of himself than he did of his honest, limited provincial fellow-burghers. The imaginative grasp, the brave idealism of his youth was gone. To work at his play, to play at his work, to bend an ambition that was half-earnest, half-whimsical, toward the accomplishment of aims that even to himself possessed but a symbolic value—for such blithe skepticism and such an enlightened spirit of compromise, a great deal of vitality is necessary, as well as a sense of humor. And Thomas Buddenbrook felt inexpressibly weary and disgusted. What there was in life for him to reach, he had reached. He was well aware that the high-water mark of his life—if that were a possible way to speak of such a commonplace, humdrum sort of existence—had long since passed.

It is important to emphasize the particular type of personality to which this experience of disillusionment is vouchsafed. Thomas Buddenbrook was consciously and strongly committed to the specific kind of life and system of values which he was eventually to reject. Without this initial commitment, and the superior individuality required to make it, the question of disappointment with success does not arise. Furthermore, the need for personal fulfillment in action arises in the historical context of bourgeois life. Only in this context can personality understand itself as thwarted.

Returning to the context of Thomas's life, we see the "symbolic" character of his aims exhibited in his subordination to economic imperatives, that is, to the problems associated with man's natural need to survive. But since the issue of survival, in practical terms, could never have been a problem to Thomas, and since he clearly had a developed sense of uniqueness, the futility of his life is clear on the most superficial level.

Mann, at the beginning of his career as a writer, was extremely sensitive to the bourgeois predilection for purposeless striving. This insight was not, at this stage in his career, explicit social criticism. Mann understood the mores of the middle class as being identical with life itself—with active and productive life. At the same time, he saw the immense and sombre human significance of such pure action:

> He (Thomas) recalled the catastrophe of the year 1866, and the inexpressibly painful emotions which had then overwhelmed him. He had lost a large sum of money in the affair—but that had not been the unbearable thing about it. For the first time in his career he had fully and personally experienced the ruthless brutality of business life and seen how all better, gentler, and kindlier sentiments creep away and hid themselves before the one, raw, naked dominating instinct of self-preservation. He had seen that when one suffers a misfortune in business, one is met by one's friends— and one's best friends—not with sympathy, not with compassion, but with suspicion—cold, cruel, hostile suspicion. But he had known all this before; why should he be surprised at it? And in stronger and hardier hours he had blushed for his own weakness, for his own distress and sleepless nights, for his revulsion and disgust at the hateful and shameless harshness of life.

Thomas was, therefore, right to fear the consummation of his ambitions; for this fulfillment gave him a clear insight into the real nature of his values and those of the world around him. The banality and destructiveness of bourgeois life were ruthlessly exposed.

What Thomas discovered, what was expressed in the meditations quoted above, was the impact of the values of commercial life on human personality. In an agonizing moment, Thomas grasped the psychology of bourgeois man and he drew back in horror at what he had seen. For the bourgeois man,

> the Felicity of this life, consisteth not in the repose of a mind satisfied. For there is no such *Finis ultimus,* (utmost ayme,) nor Summum Bonum, (greatest Good,) as is spoken of in the Books of the old Morall Philosophers. Nor can a man any more live, whose Desires are at an end, than he, whose Senses and Imaginations are at a stand. Felicity is a continuall progresse of the desire, from one object to another; the attaining of the former, being still but the way to the later . . . I put for a generall incli-

nation of all mankind, a prepetuall and restlesse desire of Power
after power, that ceaseth onely in Death.

Thomas Hobbes here gives us a positive expression of the approach to
that life which was so repellent to Thomas Buddenbrook. C. B. MacPherson
has demonstrated that Hobbes's idea of human psychology is peculiarly appropriate to life in a possessive market society. Thomas Buddenbrook, the
once committed bourgeois, has implicitly rejected this philosophy. To what
mode of thought, to what reality does he finally appeal for consolation? With
exquisite irony, Mann has him read Schopenhauer.

Schopenhauer's metaphysics of the will has, as its final significant content, the exploration of the realm of the unconscious. As such, it points to
the future and to a whole new realm of intelligibility. This aspect of the
philosophy had no meaning for Thomas Buddenbrook. But the world which
produced Schopenhauer's idea of the will as ultimate and total reality was
Hobbes's: it was that bourgeois society which crushed Thomas. The consolation Thomas finds in Schopenhauer is in the form of resignation. He
recognizes this intolerable world as being related to the very essence of reality, in fact, as being inevitable. Thus, he is caught in the toils of a system
which is derived from the very source of his own torment.

Of course, Schopenhauer's assertion of the will as ultimate reality—as
thing-in-itself—was pessimistic. Thomas's relation to Schopenhauer's
thought was, therefore, indirect. For it was Nietzsche, Schopenhauer's devoted pupil and opponent, who first extolled the will and made it the basis
of his ideal of spontaneous, strong personality. He was, in fact, the most
radical critic of the stultifying and destructive nature of nineteenth-century
middle class life. This assertion of personality moved Thomas, in a way which
no aspect of society had power to any longer.

At this point, it is proper to raise the question what are the differences
between the Hobbesian man who restlessly seeks "power after power" and
the Nietzschean man who asserts his own impulses in freedom from the
contamination of morality. Hannah Arendt has provided us with a very
useful insight into the consequences of Hobbes's psychological doctrines. She
has reminded us that the inevitable result of an endless striving for power is
the complete and absolute surrender of the individual to organized society
which alone can preserve him from the risks of such a perilous quest.

He (Hobbes) foresaw the necessary idolatry of power itself by
this new human type, that he would be flattered at being called
a power-thirsty animal, although actually society would force him
to surrender all his natural forces, his virtues and his vices, and

would make him the poor meek little fellow, who has not even the right to rise against tyranny, and who, far from striving for power, submits to any existing government and does not even stir even when his best friend falls an innocent victim to an incomprehensible raison d'état.

What makes this development not only possible but necessary is that, for Hobbes, the way in which men satisfy their desires is through domination of others. The Hobbesian man is quickly confronted by his fellow-man whom he must use or be used by. Competition is carried on for its own sake and, in the end, a man considers power, which is instrumental, more important than satisfaction of desires, which began as a goal.

It was against this inversion of human activity that Nietzsche protested when he demanded that men return to their own desires as the source of their action. Nietzsche was not repelled by the brutality of bourgeois society, but by its vulgarity. He opposed to the Hobbesian drive for power the autonomy of the inner life and made the aristocratic assertion that only a few had an inner life worth developing—artists and heroes, in particular. But behind this assertion lay the Romantic principles that only the individual *qua* individual is aristocratic and that only if uncorrupted by society and its morals can man develop a suitable humanity. Nietzsche thus asserted the human as over and against society, as against all civilization, in fact. But we can appreciate the motivation for this most radical attack on bourgeois society when we see its effects on the lives of the Buddenbrooks. Thomas was annihilated by his deliberate submission to the middle-class pattern of life. Yet we suspect that the child Thomas envisaged, who was to be completely at one with his will, would resemble his great-grandfather, Johann, far more than he would Zarathustra.

For Mann was exceedingly clever and in his hands Nietzsche's thought underwent a fascinating transmutation. Mann accepted Nietzsche's glorification of aristocratic individuality but rejected the idea that that individuality could ever be the achievement of the free-willing "blond beast." Mann knew the "blond beast" too well to have any illusions about his real identity: he was—irony of ironies—none other than the simple burgher, voracious for life and perpetually hostile to the whole realm of spirit. Mann, until much later in his career, identified nineteenth-century bourgeois society with life itself and saw no other worldly alternative. But because he, like Nietzsche, saw that in this world there was no opportunity for the higher, the aristocratic aspects of personality to develop, he became concerned with possible alternatives, such as the life of the artist. For as long as Mann could not conceive of the possibility of a reform or reconstruction of society, his writings would not be precisely social criticism and his solutions—if there were any—would have to lie in the direction of the development of pure "inwardness" in isolation from society.

Thomas Buddenbrook was even farther removed than his creator from critical social consciousness. The horror he experienced at the brutality of the life around him only convinced him of his own weakness and of his excessive sensibility. His reading of Schopenhauer served, as Mann himself later remarked, "to ripen him for death." "The human being stares hopelessly through the barred window of his personality at the high walls of outward circumstance, till Death comes and calls him home to freedom! Individuality?—All, all that one is, can, and has, seems poor, grey, inadequate, wearisome." Here Thomas *is* referring to Schopenhauer; in particular, to the philosopher's sense of the vanity of human life. Schopenhauer regarded the human being's sense of his own uniqueness and importance as a delusion. The world was, for him, absolutely inimical to human consciousness. The world, the only reality, was blind, brutal, purposeless will. We have seen, in *Buddenbrooks*, that the highly developed late nineteenth-century bourgeois society exhibited itself as just such a world. It was this truth, concealed behind the glories of an increasingly complex and powerful civilization, that horrified the thinkers of a whole epoch. Schopenhauer's system, when utilized as moral philosophy, or even a theology, is merely the statement of the absolute frustration of a sensitive individual who attempted to engage himself in this particular society.

We have the suspicion that Thomas Buddenbrook's life would have been much more successful, had he early been given the opportunity to develop his personal gifts. He himself complained of his lack of schooling and the opportunities he lost thereby. At the very least, liberal education might have given him the resources with which to refresh himself at the time of his depression, when his personality no longer seemed equal to his responsibilities.

This deprivation seems, however, to have been more or less inevitable. Consul Buddenbrook was not the man to consider something as original as educating his son for an unfamiliar role. That Thomas took the identical course with *his* son seems much less inevitable. In fact, Thomas's relationship with his son in general seems forced, cruel, and somehow inappropriate and obsolete. Thomas was far less completely and naïvely committed to the mercantile life than his father. Indeed, at the time of his greatest influence on

Hanno's development, he was hardly committed to that life at all. In the end, all he was able to give his son was a set of somewhat hollow standards without the self-confidence required for their realization.

Thomas's very considerable appreciation of those aspects of life which are not purely commercial did not enable him to sympathize with or encourage their manifestations in his son. He thwarted and discouraged Hanno's spontaneous cultural interests and thought of nothing better for him than the mercantile course at school. The result of this education in Hanno intensified his already committed worldlessness. His love of music, the most spontaneous expression of his personality, together with every humane impulse, existed as over and against almost any type of action or vitality.

In this context, we may refer again to Johann's indictment of practical education. What we must understand here is that Johann's comment has no relevance to contemporary questions such as the value of vocational schools. What he was talking about were the institutions which would train the sons of those who already held responsible positions in society. A commercial curriculum in this context implied an attitude on the part of both the school and the parents that the children must be educated to fulfill a precise, predetermined, and narrow role in society.

The classical education whose passing he lamented assumed a certain community of humane concerns: an identity between culture and the world. The very nature of this kind of education was to identify, for the child, the wide range of human potentials and responsibilities which would be his as a man. The practical curriculum meant the subordination of the cultural, the personal, and the human needs of the student to the external demands of commercial society. Johann's allusion was apt; the school was turned into a factory. And in the great-grandson Hanno's school experiences we see the operation of an institution whose mindless regimentation was a sign of its subjection to necessity. It was in this institution, above all, that Hanno's rich and vital personality was ruthlessly attacked and forced to turn ever more inward.

In Hanno, the last of the Buddenbrooks, uncompromising and unashamed personality appeared for the first time, and with tragic irony, for its vehicle was a child. Sensitive, imaginative, and refined, Hanno led, with his aristocratic friend, Kai, a rich and satisfying private life. He expressed his humanity by a complete rejection of the cruel and competitive standards of necessity he encountered at school. There was, therefore, a sense in which Hanno's short life was a triumph: a triumph of personal self-assertion, of free and rich imagination, unknown to his fathers. But this achievement, the work, after all, of a child, was as terribly fragile as his life. It involved an absolute retreat into his own childhood state and a rejection, not merely of the Buddenbrooks' world and its ethos, but all action. Hanno was neither a successful student nor a potentially competent pianist. He was not, in fact, capable of functioning at all. In order to meet the needs of his own personality, he had sacrificed the hope of all power to control the world and impress himself upon it.

The loss of power did not merely involve potential lack of success in the bourgeois world. It meant, in fact, impotence, deformity, and, ironically, the destruction of the personality. This weakness opened the way to destruction of a refined human soul by just those trifling and brutal forces which it had rejected so completely and had rejoiced to stand so far above. The saintly decision to retreat became, in the end, enforced seclusion and imprisonment in the self.

We are describing here what seems to have been Thomas Mann's earliest and deepest fear. Before beginning *Buddenbrooks,* he had already published *Little Herr Friedemann,* a story about a hunchback who, through immersion in culture and refined society, reconciled himself to a celibate and constricted life. He continually congratulated himself on the triumph of his most human parts over uncontrollable physical circumstances. But he fell in love and was at last driven to declare himself to the woman. She rejected him with scorn and he drowned himself. This deep and pathetic contradiction in the flesh is the metaphor, the physical symbol, for Hanno's tragic position. The irony of Hanno's life lay in this: that in seeking to free and develop his personality, he had, without the assistance of a bodily deformity, become a little Herr Friedemann.

Mann's almost somatic horror of the fate in store for such a character is illustrated in Hanno's early and gruesome death. We must view this event from two perspectives to grasp its significance. On the one hand, Hanno's death was the result of his weakness. He succumbed to his disease as he would, inevitably, have succumbed to any attack life might have made upon him. But from another point of view, this adolescent boy's dying was the strongest possible expression of Mann's terror at the condition of worldlessness. The death of one so young is especially painful because he has never lived—because he has never moved out into the world and developed a context for his life. There is simply no way of remembering what may have been a very gifted and attractive human being. But Hanno might well have become no more than this had he lived to maturity. The point of having Hanno die so young was perhaps to suggest that the years ahead were unlikely to have made much difference to him. He had only the horrible prospect of remaining pure potentiality. Such a man, who has retreated into himself and severed all vital connections with the world, has already made a pact with death. Decadence and self-absorption are most completely at the mercy of death.

Thus *Buddenbrooks* closes with unrelieved pathos: a totally unresolved conflict between personality and the world. It is appropriate that the last character is a child, who never reaches adult life. The necessarily sequestered and limited position of a child in the world suggests the burden of the latter part of the book—the extraordinarily limited opportunities for development that an ostensibly rich environment can provide for a human being.

The issue is, thus, clearly stated. Once self-consciousness, sensitive and gifted personality, makes its appearance as the not uncommon result of generations of worldly success and freedom from necessity, a problem exists. The personality may choose to submerge its unique gifts and consciousness in purely worldly activities, in which case it runs the risk of finding itself ultimately unfulfilled and lost. Or, on the other hand, it may, like Hanno, reject the world and action entirely, and concentrate on its own pure and uncorrupted enjoyment. In this fundamentally decadent state, personality must, eventually, find itself crushed by the world. At about the time he wrote *Buddenbrooks*, Mann wrote a short story, *The Dilettante*, which eloquently depicted the excruciating nature of such a state.

> It comes to the same thing: if you take care not to be a man of action, if you seek peace in solitude, you will find that life's vicissitudes fall upon you from within and it is upon that stage you must prove yourself a hero or a fool.

The setting of the story and the background of its hero are almost identical with that of *Buddenbrooks*, again indicating Mann's almost obsessive concern with the dangers of rejecting bourgeois life.

Yet it is clear, in *Buddenbrooks* and in later works, that Mann himself could not accept that life. Let us here reiterate that for Mann life is defined essentially as the commercial life of the bourgeoisie. What Mann had not grasped at this stage of his intellectual development was that this equation of the economy with the totality of social life was not a general and inevitable human condition but the historically conditioned result of the development of capitalism with its characteristic view of society as fundamentally an organization for the production and distribution of economic goods. Mann saw that, if society, life, and the commercial world were looked upon as completely congruent terms, the needs of the personality which could not be satisfied by a commercial career would appear to be somehow dissevered from life and the world, and would seem to represent an illegitimate and irresponsible desire to fly from reality. But Mann did not yet understand that such a conception and such a society were not the only ones possible. He had not yet arrived at the idea of society, which he would later term civilization, as the domain in which man, in all the richness and complexity of his life and personality, can find his fulfillment. And so, in this early period, he was faced with mutually exclusive alternatives neither of which he could bring himself to choose. He would not forsake the world and sacrifice vitality for the sake of an aesthete's dream paradise. On the other hand, he could not accept the world as it was. He could not substitute his sensibility, his refinement, and his critical self-consciousness for the grossness and hard-headedness of the typical man of affairs. Thus, the problem posed was how was the personality to find its unique development in a fundamentally inimical environment.

The initial solution, which Mann examined in his writings up to the First World War, was escape into the purely private and personal, yet active and creative, life of the artist. But the ultimate answer that Mann made to this problem of his youth was quite different. It involved a critique of that supposedly given and immutable society and the actual construction of alternatives.

OSKAR SEIDLIN

Mynheer Peeperkorn
and the Lofty Game of Numbers

No matter how assiduously the critics and interpreters of Thomas Mann's works have made them the conveyors of ideological, political, or sociological problems and questions, no matter how seriously Mann himself took the responsibility of speaking out against the crimes and outrages of an inhuman regime, in the last analysis he considered art—his art—not as a vehicle to carry time-bound messages, but as the great comforter man invented to assuage his sufferings. On the occasion of Hermann Hesse's seventy-fifth anniversary Mann wrote his old friend and literary companion a touching letter, which ends with the following words: "Auf Wiedersehen, lieber alter Weggenosse durches Tal der Tränen, worin uns beiden der Trost der Träume gegeben war, des Spiels und der Form [Good-bye, dear old traveling companion through the vale of tears, where to both of us was given the consolation of dreams, of play and of form]." The agony of life is not denied; this world is, indeed, a vale of tears. But the playfulness of art is the saving counterpoint to the heavy burden of our existence, just as the stringent form of art gives us a glimpse of order in the midst of the overwhelming chaos and disparateness of reality.

Music is the medium, for Hermann Hesse no less than for Thomas Mann, in which the essential ingredients, playfulness and form, reign supreme, because it carries no "meaning"; and as Hermann Hesse's wildest

From *PMLA* 86, no. 5 (1971). © 1971 by the Modern Language Association of America. Originally entitled "The Lofty Game of Numbers: The Mynheer Peeperkorn Episode in Thomas Mann's *Der Zauberberg*."

book, *Steppenwolf,* ends with the hopeful assurance "Mozart is waiting for me," so Thomas Mann's wildest book, *Doktor Faustus,* was bound to become a deep probing into the wellspring, beatific but also with a diabolic taint, of music. At the moment when Adrian Leverkühn irrevocably dedicates himself to the world of sound and composition, Serenus Zeitblom, the narrator of his friend's passion, tells us what music is and what Leverkühn finds and realizes in it: "Längst war er kein Anfänger mehr im Studium der Musik, ihres seltsam kabbalistichen, zugleich spielerischen und strengen, ingeniösen und tiefsinnigen Handwerks [He had long ceased to be a beginner in music, that curiously cabbalistic craft, at once playful and profound, artful and austere]" (*Doctor Faustus: The Life of the German Composer Adrian Leverkühn as Told by a Friend,* trans. H. T. Lowe-Porter. New York: Knopf, 1978). Zeitblom speaks of music, but the elements of playfulness and stringency are the same as the ones which, according to Thomas Mann's birthday letter, were given to him and Hesse as the essences of their artistic medium, the sources from which their art, all arts, spring.

We shall take Zeitblom's characterization of music as a point of departure when looking at a famous and important episode of *Der Zauberberg* [*The Magic Mountain*], frequently discussed although never before in terms in which I shall try to do it: the appearance, reign, and death of Mynheer Pieter Peeperkorn in the enchanted territory. The first attribute that Zeitblom ascribes to music is its strange cabalism; and cabalistic indeed is Thomas Mann's use of the number seven in his *Zauberberg*. There is no need to dwell here on the innumerable instances, since the fact has been pointed out frequently enough, although we shall add some of the most startling and revealing examples. But we must stress that seven is not like any other figure; it is, in Christian terms and throughout Christian tradition, a holy number, the union of the human and the divine, the phenomenal and the noumenal, the Incarnation. Before we turn to our subject proper, let us look at the almost obsessive urgency with which the number seven imposed itself upon Thomas Mann after he had discovered it in *Der Zauberberg*: and let us be mindful of the fact that such cabalistic number mysticism is indeed the fusion of playfulness and form: the number seven structures the entire work and determines its inner and outer design, but, at the same time, it offers, as we shall see, the delight of a hidden hide-and-seek, a teasing charade, whose unriddling is as amusing as it is satisfying.

After the *Zauberberg*, Thomas Mann's work was simply inundated by the figure seven. Each part of the biblical tetralogy, which was to follow the *Zauberberg, Joseph und seine Brüder* [*Joseph and His Brothers*], even the relatively short second part, *Der junge Joseph* [*Young Joseph*], is subdivided into "Sieben Hauptstücke [Seven Main Parts]." In the first part, *Die Geschichten Jaakobs* [*The Tales of Jacob*], sub-chapter forty-nine (seven times seven) is the one in which Joseph is being born. In the third part, *Joseph in Ägypten* [*Joseph in Egypt*], sub-chapter forty-nine leads us to the "Hochstunde unserer Geschichte [climax of our tale]" (*Joseph and His Brothers,* trans. H. T. Lowe-Porter. New York: Knopf, 1956), Joseph's seduction or attempted seduction by Potiphar's wife, which, at the end of the chapter, results in the frenzied accusations by the slighted woman, her furious outcry leading to Joseph's arrest, and eventually back into the "pit" from which he had risen at the beginning of the book to start out on the first phase of his fabulous Egyptian career. In the last part, *Joseph der Ernährer* [*Joseph the Provider*], the forty-ninth sub-chapter gives the cabalistic number secret away by being entitled "Ihrer Siebzig [Seventy of Them]," while one of the previous and most decisive sections, dealing with the seven fat and the seven lean years, had carried the heading "Sieben oder fünf [Seven or Five]." (This sub-chapter, by the way, is No. 17 of the book, seven plus ten, corresponding to the seven times ten, "Ihrer Siebzig [Seventy of Them]," of the forty-ninth sub-chapter.)

The number seven game is played again in Thomas Mann's next novel, *Lotte in Weimar* [*The Beloved Returns: Lotte in Weimar*]. It is divided into nine chapters, headed quite innocuously "Erstes Kapitel [First Chapter]," "Zweites Kapitel [Second Chapter]," "Drittes Kapitel [Third Chapter]," and so on—with one exception, the seventh, which is the only one in the book given a definite article: "Das Siebente Kapitel [The Seventh Chapter]." It is, of course, not only by far the longest of them all, but the one in which for the first time Goethe himself appears, all the preceding ones having been reflections and refractions of his personality as seen by the various visitors who had come to call on Lotte in her hotel.

But the game is played most subtly in *Doktor Faustus*—and how could it be otherwise since it is the novel dealing with that special art which is the paradigm of art itself: strangely cabalistic, playful and disciplined, ingenious and profound? We can expect the number magician to outdo himself, and we shall not be disappointed. The book is divided into sections, called neither "Kapitel [Chapter]," nor "Hauptstück [Main Part]," but simply counted through by numbers (plus an unnumbered "Nachschrift [Epilogue]," the postscript starting with the words: "Es ist getan [It is finished]," and thus indicating that we are beyond the *finis*). Having become wise to the magician's tricks, we are sure that the numbers will run to forty-nine. But we are wrong, or rather, something is wrong. The number at the head of the last section is 47. How embarrassing! The sorcerer has let us down. But has he? We leaf through the book and make a strange discovery. One section, and the only one in the whole novel, is subdivided into three parts, clearly indicated as such by the repetition of the number and the insertion of "Fortsetzung [continuation]" and "Schluß [conclusion]." So the same number appears actually three times (we are not going to give our game away by mentioning the number at this point); and this breaking up of the section is, at first glance, quite startling, because it deals with a unified theme (we are not going to give our game away by identifying the theme at this point). But one thing is certain: our disappointment has turned into gratification. *Doktor Faustus is* divided into forty-nine sections, yet so ingeniously and playfully that to the unsuspecting reader it looks as if it were not. But, then, we must not forget that cabala is a secretive science.

Since we have been right, after all, with regard to the playful form or formal playfulness of the novel as a whole, seeing through the sleight-of-hand by which 47 has been made into 49, we shall not be wrong in guessing which section it is that is broken up into three parts so that the same chapter number can appear three times in the book. It is bound to be number 34. The sum of the digits makes 7, and each of the two digits, 3 and 4, are indeed the reason why 7, as their sum, is the holy number: 3 is the Trinity, the divine and noumenal; 4 is the earth with its four corners, seen under this symbol all through the ages. In addition, 34 is the number imbedded in the magic square, the "cabalistic" arrangement of figures (from 1 to 16) that, no matter in which of the possible ten directions they are being read, horizontally, vertically, or diagonally, will always yield the sum 34. And if we are familiar with Leverkühn's compositions, we know what this tripartite thirty-four section must be dealing with. What else but the extended discussion of his startling oratorio, based on a series of Albrecht Dürer's woodcuts, "Apocalipsis cum figuris," which name might as well be the title of the novel as a whole? It is not; but in the diary which Thomas Mann kept while working on *Doktor Faustus* and which he incorporated into *Die Entstehung des Doktor Faustus* [*The Story of a Novel: The Genesis of Doctor Faustus*], he calls "Apocalipsis cum figuris" Leverkühn's "Hauptwerk [major work]," only to correct himself immediately by adding "sein erstes Hauptwerk [his first major work]," because the real "Hauptwerk [major work]," the final apocalypse (*sine figuris*), the heartrending lamentation and confession of the diabolically inspired composer, who with the piano arrangement in front of him "performs" his ultimate music, his ultimate doom—in Chapter 47 which, as we very well know, must be Chapter 49. By holding fast to this number, we come to realize that the book is indeed structured in a most ingenious way. If we work out the arithmetical middle of 49, we arrive at

25, twenty-four chapters preceding and twenty-four chapters following. Does anyone have any doubts as to what this section 25 is bound to contain? Of course, the pact-scene between Adrian and the Devil.

II

It may seem that we have lost our way, since we promised to deal with an episode of *Der Zauberberg,* where the magic of the number seven commenced. But there is sound justification for our detour. We have established this number as something much more than a "private joke." It is an essential element in Thomas Mann's later work, and as such it is fraught with "Tiefsinn [deep meaning]," that "Tiefsinn" which may be the key to the appearance of Mynheer Peeperkorn on the magic mountain. We have along the way also established the prime importance of the numbers three and four on which the holiness of their sum, the number seven, rests. Of course, we could have learned it from the *Zauberberg* itself, because the second sub-chapter of the first main chapter (the book has, of course, a total of seven main chapters) is simply entitled: "Nr. 34." It is at this point that Hans Castorp enters for the first time the Sanatorium Berghof, and the Nr. 34 at the head of this sub-chapter is the number of the room which he will occupy during his seven-year stay on the magic mountain.

If we now turn from this second subdivision of the first chapter to the corresponding place in the last, the seventh chapter, the heading reads: "Mynheer Peeperkorn." But this correspondence is only the first step; for if we count all the subdivisions of the seven main chapters throughout, we discover that Mynheer Peeperkorn is introduced in the novel in sub-chapter 43, the same digits 3 and 4 again, only in a reversed order. This reversal or transposition will give us the clue to the meaning of the entire Peeperkorn episode; but before we are ready to discuss it, we have to pursue a bit further the number game with which this part of the book is suffused.

To tell the story of Mynheer Peeperkorn within the framework of the total novel, Thomas Mann needs four sub-chapters. Of these four, three bear his name in their titles: "Mynheer Peeperkorn [Mynheer Peeperkorn]," "Mynheer Peeperkorn (des weiteren) [Mynheer Peeperkorn (continued)]," "Mynheer Peeperkorn (Schluß) [Mynheer Peeperkorn (conclusion)]," needless to say the only instance within the novel where such a splitting up of the sub-chapter titles occurs. The result is obvious: again we have the interplay of four and three. The life and death of Peeperkorn unfolds in four steps, three of which are specifically designated by the use of his name in the titles. This corresponds exactly to the tripartite division of section 34 in

Doktor Faustus. By dividing section 34 of the musician's novel into three parts, the total book needed only 47 numbers to run its course, since 47 was actually 49. But by dividing the single "unit" Peeperkorn into the three parts that bear his name, *Der Zauberberg* as a whole needs a total of fifty-one sub-chapters (and this is exactly the number of sub-chapters it has) in order to arrive "cabalistically" at the required 49. In one case, *Doktor Faustus,* we are being asked to count one as three; in the other, *Der Zauberberg,* to count the three united by their headings as one.

But since the whole Peeperkorn story unfolds in four subdivisions, there is one that bears a heading which does not carry the protagonist's name. Strangely enough, it is wedged within the sequence of "Peeperkorn" chapters, as number two of the four-step movement, between the one entitled "Mynheer Peeperkorn" and the one entitled "Mynheer Peeperkorn (des weiteren)": and, somewhat less strange, this chapter is headed by a number: "Vingt et un"—three times seven. [In the English translation, as in the original German, the sub-chapter is entitled "Vingt et un."] But even more important to us is the structural arrangement. The Peeperkorn story, as far as the chapter headings are concerned, is presented under the following titles: "Mynheer Peeperkorn"; (no Mynheer Peeperkorn but) "Vingt et un"; "Mynheer Peeperkorn (des weiteren)"; "Mynheer Peeperkorn (Schluß)." Thus the sequence uses the rule: 1 followed by 2; now, the chapter that is wedged in reverses this sequence: 2 followed by 1, "Vingt et un."

What does the sub-chapter "Vingt et un" contain? After Mynheer Peeperkorn, "die Persönlichkeit [the personality]" *kat' exochen,* as he will be referred to in the novel over and over again, has spent some weeks on the magic mountain—does it surprise us to hear that it was "wohl drei bis vier [some three or four (*The Magic Mountain,* trans. H. T. Lowe-Porter. New York: Knopf, 1967)]" weeks?—he assembles after dinner a few of his co-patients, and there begins a sumptuous feast presided over by the majestic figure of the Dutchman and lasting into the early morning hours. It is, so we are being told at a certain point, a veritable "Bacchanal," although it begins quite harmlessly as a game (naturally, a game!) of cards, to the course of which only a little over one page out of the total of twenty-five is accorded, and yet considered important enough to furnish the title for the whole chapter. What is it that makes it so important, considering the fact that it plays such a minuscule part in Mynheer Peeperkorn's long-drawn-out party? What else but its name, the figure twenty-one? When reading the description of the game, when witnessing the excitement it arouses among the players, we recognize it immediately as one of the most common, in Germany and elsewhere. However, in German it is known under a different name: *Siebzehn und vier* [seventeen and four] (Blackjack). Mann has rejected the German name and substituted the French, unfamiliar to German readers, and he has done so because the French designation offered him the number which he needed as a signal. Also he has transposed a German expression into its French equivalent, and as we have already noticed and shall note in our further discussion, the principle of transposition is, indeed, at the core of the episode dealing with Mynheer Peeperkorn.

Convinced of the compulsive validity of reversal and transposition, we look now in the sub-chapter called "Vingt et un" for the reversal of the digits, the number twelve (which, in addition, is three times four). Of course, we do not look in vain. There are, so we are being told, twelve people assembled around the table at this midnight banquet: Mynheer Peeperkorn in the middle of the group, Hans Castorp, his favorite, at his side—but we should now call him by his full first name, Johannes, the favorite disciple, because what we are witnessing here is as much a simile of the Last Supper as it is a "Bacchanal." There is no doubt that "die Persönlichkeit" which Thomas Mann introduces into his novel at the eleventh hour is a strange compound of Dionysos and Christ, clearly though shroudedly recognizable in the novel as such, and verified by some of its interpreters, even if so astute a critic as Hermann Weigand has to confess: "It is not easy to find a just formula for this weird synthesis of the reeling Dionysos and Jesus in Gethsemane." It is not a weird synthesis at all; but at this point we merely want to stress that not only every event involves Mynheer Peeperkorn, but that he himself stands under the law of transposition, a change of configuration which controls everything.

Holy Supper and Bacchanalia—yet this is not all. Because within the setting, in both its biblical and pagan aspects, a reversal occurs. As in the New Testament the Last Supper, Christ's sharing and feasting with his disciples, is followed by the night in the Garden of Gethsemane, the moment of utter loneliness, so suddenly Mr. Peeperkorn's gorgeous repast threatens to turn into desolation and the desertion of the master. At this moment the scene in the Sanatorium Berghof becomes translucent and lets us perceive in the background the biblical model, for Mynheer Peeperkorn now proves to be thoroughly conversant with the New Testament, and, interspersing it with his own exclamations, he quotes the whole passage verbatim:

> Gethsemane! "Und nahm zu sich Petrum und die zween Söhne Zebedei. Und sprach zu ihnen: Bleibet hie und wachet mit mir." Sie erinnern sich? "Und kam zu ihnen und fand sie schlafend und sprach zu Petro: Könnet ihr denn nicht eine Stunde mit mir wa-

chen?" Intensiv, meine Herrschaften! Durchdringend. Herzbe-
wegend. "Und kam und fand sie aber schlafend, und ihre Augen
waren voll Schlafs. Und sprach zu ihnen: Ach, wollt ihr nun schla-
fen und ruhen? Siehe, die Stunde ist hie—." Meine Herrschaften:
Durchbohrend, herzversehrend.

[Gethsemane. "And took with him Peter and the two sons of
Zebedee. . . . Then saith he unto them: . . . Tarry ye here and
watch with me." You remember? "And he cometh unto the disciples and findeth them asleep, and saith unto Peter: What, could
ye not watch with me one hour?" Immense, my friends. Heart
piercing. Moving to the last—very. "And came and found them
asleep again, for their eyes were heavy. And saith unto them:
Sleep on now, and take your rest, behold the hour is at hand."
Ladies and gentlemen, that pierces the heart, it sears.]

But Gethsemane is not the last word. The scene reverses itself again.
Mr. Peeperkorn repeats the words that announce the beginning of the Passion: "Die Stunde ist hie [the hour is at hand]," those words which he himself
just termed "durchbohrend, herzversehrend [heartrending, searing]," but
when he utters them now they are meant as a signal to the waitress to bring
to the table still more sumptuous supplies of food and drink so that the Last
Supper may continue.

It is not only the Last Supper and Gethsemane that are intertwined in
Mr. Peeperkorn's grandiose "Vint et un" entertainment. The same admix-
ture takes place on the classical, the pagan level, for the Bacchanalia is at
any moment ready to transform itself into its opposite. The intoxicating and
highly intoxicated exuberance is threatened at more than one point by the
majestic host's latent "Kollers [torrents of wrath]," these outbursts of divine
anger which hover over the assembled satyrs, sileni, and maenads and which
Mann quite fittingly and revealingly calls the flickerings of a "panischer
Schrecken [panic]." So Dionysos coincides with his closest participant in the
Bacchanalia, the great God Pan, who, when the hour comes ("Die Stunde
ist hie"), spreads the deadly stillness over the landscape when nature holds
its breath and is overcome by drowsiness.

The parallelism of the Christian and pagan models is apparent, as is the
transmutation that occurs within each. But now we turn to the master and
host of these ceremonies, in whom the images of Dionysos and Christ meet
in such a way that each can transform itself into the other, holy in both
aspects. It is not by chance that at a certain moment of the great carousing

Mynheer Peeperkorn can exclaim: "Meine Herrschaften—heilig! Heilig in jederlei Sinn, im christlichen wie im heidnischen [Holy, holy, my friends. In every sense. Christian and pagan]." Parenthetically, it should be noted that, in the direct discourse conducted during the Last Supper and Bacchanalia, the word "heilig [holy]" appears seven times, counting the repetition of the word in the just proffered quotation as one; this we are surely justified to do since this duplication is to be taken as a climactic emphasis when the word is being uttered for the last, the seventh time. Surely, this synthesis is not "weird" and, at least to the German reader, it is anything but blasphemous. It was at one of the proudest moments of German poetry when Dionysos and Christ were seen in close companionship, so close that Christ could be apostrophized as "du bist Bruder auch des Eviers [you are also the brother of Evier]" (= Dionysus). I am speaking of Hölderlin.

This brotherhood is no superficial connection, for Hölderlin as little as for Thomas Mann. The two divinities seem, at first glance, to stand at opposite poles: the one the embodiment of everything earthy, the bursting fertility of productive nature, boisterously displaying the most vital instincts and joys of carnal creativity; the other who declared his kingdom not of this world, pointing toward a home in a beyond where all matter falls away. And still, brothers they are, brothers in reversal, "heilig in jederlei Sinne, im christlichen wie im heidnischen [holy in every sense, Christian and pagan]." What unites them is the idea of the Incarnation: in Christ the word, the divine spirit becomes flesh, the heavenly descends upon the earth, light shineth in the darkness; in Dionysos the seemingly blind forces of nature are transfigured into the divine, the seeds imbedded in the black womb of the earth break through into the brightness above, in the festive appearance of the god the light of the torches illuminates the darkness of the night. The figure in which the earthy and the noumenal meet is Mynheer Peeperkorn, or, if we take "figure" in its mathematical sense, it is the number seven, which suffuses the *Zauberberg* from beginning to end.

There is, in spite of Hermann Weigand's hesitation, "a just formula" by which the Incarnation becomes reality, and this formula governs the whole Peeperkorn episode. It is, of necessity, the gift of nature, of the earth which, by an act of transformation, is changed into the spirit at the moment of "Vingt et un," Last Supper and Bacchanalia in one. It is the formula which Hölderlin chose as the title for one of his greatest elegies, in which again the brotherhood of Dionysus and Christ is celebrated: "Bread and Wine"— blessing from below and blessing from above, which will play such a decisive role in Thomas Mann's biblical work, and which enhances the dignity and true fulfillment of man, who is the meeting ground of both realities. Now we see how Last Supper and Bacchanalia can become one. The feasting of Christ and his disciples is, by the breaking of bread and imbibing of wine, the institution of the Eucharist ("This is my flesh, this is my blood"); the mysteries of Dionysos culminate in the outburst (in the word's literal meaning), by which the bacchanti in their highest spirits—spirit to be taken in both the meanings of *spiritus*—become one with the god. Only if we read the detailed description of the banquet in the Berghof sanatorium in this sense does its true importance become clear. We must listen carefully to the comments Hans Castorp makes in his "spirited" state, his paeans—we might, since they are addressed to "Dionysos," easily call them dithyrambs—on the "einfachen und natürlichen Gaben des Lebens, die so groß und heilig sind [great, simple, sacred gifts (of life)]" and again, on the "klassichen Lebensgaben ... des Einfachen und Heiligen [classic gifts of life: ... simple, sacred]," above all "der Wein also, ein göttliches Geschenk an die Menschen [wine, the gift of the gods to man]." In his dithyrambs Hans Castorp shows himself well versed in humanistic lore: it is the wine, he lectures his majestically divine neighbor, which brought culture to mankind, the liquid whose perfection was mainly responsible for the fact that "die Menschen aus dem Stande der Rohheit traten und Gesittung erlangten, und noch heute gelten die Völker, bei denen Wein wächst, für gesitteter ... als die weinlosen, die Kimerer, was sicher bemerkenswert ist [man emerged from his barbaric state, and achieved culture; even today, where the grape grows, those people are accounted ... possessed of a higher culture than the Cimmerians, a fact which is worthy of our attention]." Yes, it *is* eminently noteworthy. The ennoblement of man, in the Christian and pagan sense, his "Gesittung [culture]," his being raised from the state of barbarism to true life is the work of the God of the Wine no less than the God of the Eucharist.

Thomas Mann would not be in his best form if he did not play his ingenious and meaningful games with the formula of bread and wine. Into this formula he again builds his principle of reversal and transposition so that, from the very beginning, we are in no doubt that it is, indeed, the formula of transubstantiation. From the very beginning: for when we meet Mr. Peeperkorn for the first time—after the narrator has reported the fact of his arrival and Hans Castorp's reaction to this arrival—we see him, quite appropriately, in his seat at one of the seven tables in the dining room of the sanatorium, heartily enjoying his meal, for whose quality the health institute of Dr. Behrens is justly famous. It is surely not by chance that here, "three or four weeks" before the "real" meal, Hans and Mynheer Peeperkorn "saßen ... sozusagen nebeneinander [sat, in a way, as neighbours]," in an intricate arrangement admittedly, since they do not occupy the same table.

After having run through the opulent menu, Peeperkorn orders "ein wenig Brot . . . Gottesbrot, klares Brot [A little bread . . . Bread of God, bread of sunshine]." But since we are dealing with an episode at whose heart is the idea of transubstantiation, he does not really mean bread. What he means and what is served to him forthwith is fluid bread, "einen Genever [a geneva]," which, so we read, "er schluckte [he gulped]" (of course, he does not drink it since it is bread, although bread it is not), "nachdem er es kurz gekaut hatte [he appeared to chew . . . somewhat, then swallowed it down]." What a strange thing to do with a beverage! But the formula of bread and wine has to be fulfilled—by not being fulfilled; what the Dutchman consumes when ingesting "bread" and wine at his first meal is spirit and spirit. He calls it a "Schnaps," but Thomas Mann in the same line gives a much better designation: a "Korndestillat [distillate of corn]," and we must be grateful to the German language for offering one of its supreme masters a word, "Korn [corn]," which means the grain from which bread is made, and which is, at the same time, simply by changing its article, the name of a highly alcoholic beverage.

We are not indulging in marginal minutiae. We can now understand why the Dutchman is called what he is called: Peeper-korn. The key metaphor pointing to bread and wine is already inscribed in his name, which means nothing else but Spicy-grain. And the spice, the pepper, is of course not without significance, either. Pepper, spices in general, point to India, a geographical hint at the origin of the Dutchman, who is a "Kolonialholländer [colonial Dutchman]" from Java, i.e., the Netherlandic Indies, a significant "reversal" of our global orientation since the northwesternmost corner of Continental Europe thus becomes fused with southeasternmost Asia. But India evokes other associations as well: it is the country which Dionysos had conquered in order to teach its inhabitants the art of wine growing—a mythical story so vividly alive in Greek consciousness that it served Alexander the Great, who counted Dionysos among his ancestors, as the main inspiration for crossing the river Indus. Every slightest detail, including the constituent parts of his name, lead back to the formula: bread and wine. Even in certain idioms which Thomas Mann uses punningly (but only if we discover the heart of the matter can we relish the pun), the bread and wine, the grain-syndrome is revealingly hidden. When Hans Castorp conveys his first impressions of the Dutchman to Hofrat Behrens—he has not even made Peeperkorn's acquaintance yet—the doctor reports approvingly: "Ich sehe, Sie haben ihn *aufs Korn* [my italics] genommen . . . und sich den Mann gut angesehen in seiner Eigenart [I see that you've taken *a shot* at him . . . and see the man well for his particularity]."

It is comforting to know that at least Hans Castorp has taken a good
look at the Indo-Dutchman's individuality from the start, because later ob-
servers have, with very few exceptions, seen nothing in him but a "caricature," an overbearing tyrant, at best a silly old man expressing himself by
pompous gestures because he is incapable of uttering a coherent sentence,
just stammering expletives whose explosive emphasis has to make up for
their lack of meaning. The text does not justify such a misreading, Peeperkorn's linguistic fumblings notwithstanding. The attributes "so groß wie
königlich [as great as regality]" or "biblische Größe [biblical grandeur]" are
applied to him in innumerable variations. It is Settembrini, not a very reliable
witness, who calls him a "dummer alter Mann [a stupid old man]," and it
is Hans Castorp who restores the proper perspective with his deeply perceptive answer: "Ach Dummheit! Es gibt so viele verschiedene Arten von
Dummheit, und die Gescheitheit ist nicht die beste davon [Stupid—well,
there are so many kinds of stupidity, and cleverness is one of the worst]." It
is testimony to Hans Castorp's true humanity that he recognizes the Dutchman's greatness and regality for what they are, although he should be the
first one to resent the "stupid old man" who has taken Clawdia Chauchat
away from him. He senses who Peeperkorn is: image of Dionysus and Christ
in one, for which he finds the exactly fitting word, "ein Mysterium [a mys-
tery]." This word will be repeated many times in the novel with regard to
Peeperkorn, and Hans Castorp knows that this "Mysterium" goes beyond
all the cleverness which his dialectic mentors, Settembrini and Naphta, have
to offer. We could not possibly refute Settembrini's nasty remark more eloquently than he does:

> das Körperliche geht ins Geistige über und umgekehrt, und sind
> nicht zu unterscheiden, und Dummheit und Gescheitheit sind
> nicht zu unterscheiden, aber di Wirkung ist da, das Dynamische,
> und wir werden in die Tasche gesteckt. Und dafür ist uns nur ein
> Wort an die Hand gegeben, und das heißt "Persönlichkeit" . . .
> als ein Mysterium, das über Dummheit und Gescheitheit hinaus-
> liegt und um das man sich doch muß kümmern dürfen,—teils
> um ihm nach Möglichkeit auf den Grund zu kommen, und teils,
> soweit das nicht möglich ist, um sich daran zu erbauen. Und wenn
> Sie für Werte sind, so ist Persönlichkeit am Ende doch auch ein
> positiver Wert, sollte ich denken—positiver als Dummheit und
> Gescheitheit, im höchsten Grade positiv, *absolut* [Thomas
> Mann's emphasis] positiv, wie das Leben, kurzum: ein Lebens-
> wert und ganz danach angetan, sich angelegentlich darum zu
> kümmern.

[The mystical goes over into the spiritual, and the other way on, and you can't tell them apart, nor can you cleverness and stupidity. But the result is what we see, the dynamic effect—he puts us in his pocket. We've only one word for that—personality. . . . I am speaking of the mystery of personality, something above either cleverness or stupidity, and something we all have to take into account: partly to try to understand it; but partly, where that is not possible, to be edified by it. You are all for values; but isn't personality a value too? It seems so to me, more so than either cleverness or stupidity, it seems positive and *absolute*, like life— in short, something quite worth while, and calculated to make us trouble about it].

Thomas Mann is obviously very pleased with this perceptive insight of his "Sorgenkind des Lebens [problem child of life]," because at the end of Hans Castorp's long expostulation he attests to him that he has spoken "wie ein Mann [like a man]." No matter how much Settembrini and Naphta may giggle behind the stupid old Hollander's back, they know perfectly well that he cocks them in a hat, that all their verbal pyrotechnics and dialectic balancing acts fall flat on the ground, paling into nothingless in the presence of Peeperkorn, because he is "wie das Leben [like life]," he is Presence, *Da-Sein*, Incarnation, the number seven.

Being Incarnation, he is and must be subject to "the thousand natural shocks that flesh is heir to." He is, so we hear right at the beginning, both "robust und spärlich [lean and robust]," endowed with all the majesty of appearance, but his eyes are "nur klein und blaß, ohne Farbe geradezu, und es nützt nichts, daß er sie immer aufzureißen sucht [very small and pale, hardly any colour to them at all. He keeps trying to open them wide]." Above all, Mr. Peeperkorn is sick. It is fabulous to contemplate the diagnostic propriety of the sickness with which Thomas Mann has afflicted him: a "Wechselfieber [intermittent fever]," a fever that permanently reverses itself; and when we now hear its specific name, we are overwhelmed by so much appropriateness. Its name is "Quartanfieber [quartan fever]," and it runs the following cycle: for three days (and three is the noumenal number) Peeperkorn is perfectly hale (hale and holy are, of course, the same word), on the fourth day (and four is the number of the phenomenal and earthly) he is seized by a fit that runs the whole gamut of carnal disorders, from shaking chill to burning heat.

But this medical diagnosis is, of course, only a metaphor of something much more essential. Being-in-the-flesh, Incarnation, involves necessarily the

Passion, and it is, like bread and wine, again this formula that links Christ and Dionysos together. Surely, Peeperkorn's vivid evocations of Gethsemane are not accidental, much less blasphemy. Neither is the attribute "der Schmerzensmann [the man of sorrows]" reserved, in German, to the Savior alone, nor the heartrending description in which Peeperkorn's face assumes the expression of Grünewald's Christ on the Cross: "Er neigte das Haupt zur Schulter und Brust, die wehen Lippen taten sich voneinander, schlaff-klagend klaffte der Mund, die Nüstern spannten und verbreiterten sich wie in Schmerzen, die Falten der Stirne stiegen und weiteten die Augen zu blassem Leidensblick—ein Bild der Bitternis" [His head would sink upon his shoulder or chest, the calamitous lips part as the mouth relaxed into pathetic curves, the nostrils dilate as with pain, the folds on the forehead rose until the eyes were fixed in a wide, suffering gaze.—It was a picture of bitterness and woe]."

But Passion, whether written with a small or large initial, means suffering, in both the Christian and pagan sense. We now understand why the passage which we quoted above, Peeperkorn's "Meine Herrschaften—heilig! Heilig in jederlei Sinn, im christlichen wie im heidnischen [Holy, holy, my friends. In every sense. Christian and pagan]," stands at the place where we found it. It was Peeperkorn's reaction to the misery and uncontrolled weeping of the wretchedly unhappy Mr. Wehsal, one of the twelve "apostles" at the supper, who, in the midst of the feasting, was suddenly overcome by so profound a suffering ("Wehsal" is the German for suffering) that thick tears were running down his cheeks. Peeperkorn first turned to Mme Chauchat and asked her to wipe the poor man's tears off with her napkin. But then he thought better of it and stopped her, realizing that the response to such suffering can only be the exclamation: "heilig [holy]," repeated by him three times within the compass of three lines: "heilig . . . heilig . . . heilig," the chant with which we greet the divine. But it is not only the term "Passion" in its double meaning that unites again Christ and Dionysos. Thomas Mann was well aware that there is an aspect of the Dionysos myth in which the god undergoes the same suffering as Christ. This is the story of Dionysos Zagreus, which tells of Dionysos's being torn to pieces in his encounter with the Titans, and to make the parallel even more exact there is a tradition that Dionysos rode into this battle on a donkey.

We have not reached the deepest layer yet. With all the noumenal "Mysterium" and incarnation which we tried to elucidate, Peeperkorn is "only" a human being, and thus the task to embody the divine is bound to be unfulfillable. No matter how strong and enthusiastic the spirit, the flesh plays it a nasty trick. It cannot live up to the exuberance and overflow of life which

Peeperkorn feels to be his and whose emanation he considers his mission. In short, he is impotent, impotent in the crassest physical sense of the word: the flesh refuses to accept the challenge with which he knows himself entrusted. This explains the terror and anguish that overcome him; this is the deepest abyss of his Passion. He cannot be God, but at best God's deputy on earth—i.e., not Christ but Peter—and we are not surprised that this is his first name. We now understand, too, why the biblical passage relating to Christ's desolation in the Garden of Gethsemane is so firmly imbedded in Mynheer Peeperkorn's mind that he can recite it verbatim. It is his own story: Christ chiding Peter (and it is Peter whom Christ mainly addresses), who is no one else but he himself, the one who in shame and despair must recognize his insufficiency, because the flesh is weak no matter how willing the spirit.

The anguish of the Garden of Gethsemane has, of course, its pagan counterpart. It is the event that takes place on the last afternoon before Mynheer Peeperkorn's suicide, and is, in fact, the cause of his suicide: nothing more than an excursion to a waterfall near Davos, in which seven persons participate, driving out in two carriages, three in the one, four in the other. We notice, in passing, that the forest through which the seven travel on their way to their destination is sick: afflicted by a cancerous fungus, which overgrows the branches of the conifers and threatens to choke the trees. Upon Peeperkorn's insistence, the picnic (with plenty of bread and wine) is being held not only in full view of the waterfall, but actually so close to the roaring cataract that any conversation becomes impossible. After the collation something strange happens. Peeperkorn rises, faces the thundering waterfall (which bursts down from a height of approximately seven or eight meters), and starts talking to it as if trying to conjure the wild unleashed energy of nature, whose tumultuous uproar blots out every word the old man utters. Clearly he tries to measure himself against the riotously unchained force of the elemental, tries to transfix it, but in vain. His voice is drowned in the cosmic noise, and his companions can read from the motions of his lips only the two last words of the strange invocation "perfekt und erledigt [settled and finished]"—"erledigt," done with, finished. It is the last word that we hear Peeperkorn utter in the novel. On the way back to the sanatorium hardly a word is spoken in Peeperkorn's carriage. Shortly after two o'clock in the morning the night nurse, at Mme Chauchat's request, calls Hans Castorp to the Dutchman's room. He is dead. He has killed himself by injecting into his veins some of the violent, exotic poison, the "spice" that he brought with him from India.

Convinced that in the work of every great writer even the minutest detail is significant, we are, with the Dutchman's death, not yet at the end of the Peeperkorn episode. After Hofrat Behrens has diagnosed the suicide, he beckons Hans into a corner of the drawing room and demonstrates to him in a long technical explanation the workings of the instrument with which Peeperkorn ended his life. It is not a simple syringe, but a highly complicated outlandish mechanism, made up of teeth, honed to pinpoint sharpness, in which are imbedded hair-thin canulae leading to a "rubber-gland" that contains the poison. Upon pressure, the teeth, mounted on tiny springs, squeeze the rubber container which then squirts the deadly fluid through the tubulae outward. Teeth—gland: we would hardly need Dr. Behrens's explicit statement that this instrument is an exact mechanical replica of the "Beißzeugs der Brillenschlange [mechanism of the cobra's bite]." What caused Peeperkorn's death was the work of the snake. In the last analysis, he is not the new Adam, but Adam plain and simple, flesh in its weakness and sinfulness which is man, because this is what the Hebrew word Adam actually means.

Yet—and this is his greatness and dignity—he wanted to be and walked through the pages of the book as more than Adam. Just as Hans Castorp, immediately after Peeperkorn's appearance on the magic mountain, took a good look at the new guest and assessed his strange individuality, so now, standing at the old man's deathbed, he speaks the epitaph which compresses into a few words the Dutchman's substance and serves as a last verification of the argument we have presented: "er betrachtete sich als Gottes Hochzeitsorgan, müssen Sie wissen [For you must know, he regarded himself as the instrument of God's marriage]." Again the images of Dionysos and Christ appear united. The sexual implication, evoking the phallus, signal of carnal fertility and triumphant ruler over the Dionysian mysteries, is obvious. But equally obvious is Christ's role as the heavenly bridegroom, through whom man's soul is wedded to God. There could be no more fitting word than the one Thomas Mann has chosen. It points to the act of consummation, in its physical aspect by the anatomical part of the body, in its spiritual aspect by the *organon*, the medium through which the union of man and God is achieved. As we have tried to show, this was what Mynheer Peeperkorn wanted to live: the sum of three and four.

But Hans Castorp gives us more than just the pinpointing of the "Eigenart [particularity]" of the eleventh-hour visitor on the magic mountain. He pronounces judgment, and much confusion could have been avoided had the readers of the book taken the trouble to listen to him. This divine mission which Mynheer Peeperkorn considered his and which he could not fulfill because he was only Peter and not Christ, was, so we now hear, "eine königliche Narretei [a piece of majestic tomfoolery]." Foolishness it may have been, but all the detractors of Peeperkorn, inside and outside the book, should take notice that it was a regal foolishness. And Hans Castorp continues, making crystal clear that the word "foolishness" is not to be taken in a deprecatory sense, but as an expression of the deepest emotion and the most solemn respect: "Wenn man ergriffen ist, hat man den Mut zu Ausdrücken, die kraß und pietätlos klingen, aber feierlicher sind als konzessionierte Andachtsworte [when one is moved one can say things that sound crass and irreverent, but are after all more solemn than the conventional religious formulas]." Peeperkorn's is the rarest and noblest sort of foolishness—perhaps even the wisest—with which man can be afflicted: the self-identification with the living presence of the creatively divine.

III

We are at the end of the Peeperkorn episode. Yet there is still left an important question, perhaps the most important of all. What does this sequence mean within the framework of the novel, what does it mean and do to its hero, Hans Castorp, who, after all, had been taken by Thomas Mann to the magic mountain for a clear and specific purpose: to find, through death, the road into life? It has been argued "Peeperkorn ist kein Bildungserlebnis Hans Castorps, jedenfalls nicht mehr in irgendeinem positiven Sinn [Peeperkorn is no educational experience for Hans Castorp, at least not in any positive sense]." Apart from the fact that we would then have to ask what business he could possibly have in a novel which is conceived and carried out as an educational experiment, the text itself clearly demonstrates that Hans's encounter with the Dutchman is not only an "educational experience" but perhaps the most momentous that he undergoes on the magic mountain. Clearly, the revelation of the "Mysterium der Persönlichkeit [mystery of personality]" is not negligible in the formative process of a "Sorgenkind des Lebens [problem child of life]." This "Mysterium" is, as Hans Castorp himself stated in his refutation of Settembrini's stupidly clever remarks, his coming face to face with a "Lebenswert [life value]"; it is in fact in his own eyes the "absolutely positive" value. We must now see what happens to him as a result of his exposure to the exotic Dutchman, who is "wie das Leben [like life]."

We must return to previous stages of our novel, which are revitalized by the arrival of Mynheer Peeperkorn and the rearrival of his companion, Mme Chauchat. We see that the principle of reversal and transposition is fully at work again, a reversal and transposition which affect Hans Castorp most profoundly on his "educational journey." We have to recall the scene in which Hans Castorp, for the first time during his stay of seven years on the magic mountain, talked to Mme Chauchat, the passionately beloved (it is also the only time before her reappearance as Peeperkorn's mistress), and although Thomas Mann discreetly shrouds the event, did more than just talk to her. The momentous occurrence took place after Hans Castorp had been in the sanatorium for exactly seven months, on Mardi Gras, i.e., precisely forty days before Palm Sunday, Christ's entrance into the world, climaxing in the Resurrection, when the dead emerges as the living, and the flesh reveals itself as the God. This Tuesday before Ash Wednesday is but the Nordic counterpart of the chthonic, elemental instincts in man. But Thomas Mann did not entitle this subchapter Mardi Gras; he called it "Walpurgisnacht [Walpurgis Night]," thus underlining—apart from the conscious Goethe reminiscence—the specifically German variant of the wild Bacchanalia, proper to Hans Castorp. And here we find again a fabulous, cabalistically significant reversal: Walpurgisnacht is the night of the thirtieth of April, thirty preceding four, while Mardi Gras is forty (days) preceding three, the revelation of the noumenal.

Be that as it may, Dionysian mysteries, Mardi Gras or Walpurgisnacht, there is no question that all hell breaks loose in Hans Castorp. It is the nadir of his "educational journey," a complete abandon to the voluptuous desire of the flesh, to the nefarious irresponsible freedom that sickness and death grant, a wild indulgence in formlessness, and a dropping out of "civilization," a complete renunciation of any tie that binds him to his community—to the point that he loses the medium that makes him part of a specific human society, his own language, and conducts the whole conversation with Mme Chauchat in an alien tongue, in French, his passion exposed and over-riding all else. It is Mme Chauchat who formulates the "morality" of this complete abandon: "Il nous semble qu'il est plus morale de se perdre et même de se laisser dépérir que de se conserver [It seems to us that it is more moral to lose oneself and even allow oneself to perish than to conserve oneself]."It is the Gospel according to Lucifer, the anarchic embracing of dissolution, sickness, and death.

As far as I can see, nobody seems to have noticed that Mme Chauchat's confession of faith, faith in the deindividualization and deformation (in the word's literal meaning), is being repeated verbatim when the two meet and converse again for the first time after her return with Mr. Peeperkorn. Only the situation is reversed: it is now Hans Castorp who pronounces these frightfully meaningful words, and he transposes them into German: "Es ist übrigens moralischer, sich zu verlieren und selbst zu verderben als sich zu bewahren [But it is more moral to lose your life than to save it]." But realizing that the situation is now reversed, we may suspect that the meaning of the article of faith repeated by Hans Castorp in German has transformed itself, too. This we shall examine.

But before we do so there are at least two significant factors to be mentioned. This first conversation of Hans with Clawdia after her return to the magic mountain as Peeperkorn's mistress begins with the word "tot [dead]," and in order to make sure that we do not miss this point, Thomas Mann makes Hans Castorp note specifically "daß 'tot' das erste betonte Wort war, das wieder zwischen ihnen fiel [that this 'dead' was the first word to fall between them]." "Again," we are being told, so we must have heard it before. When was it uttered? Of course, during the "Walpurgisnacht," when Hans's febrile French fantasies circled from the beginning to the end around nothing but death: "le corps, l'amour, la mort, ces trois ne font qu'un [The body, love, death, these three are but one]." So this conversation is basically a continuation of the former one, only it may now end on an entirely opposite note. In order to stress the correspondence of the two chapters which are bound together by being the reverse of one another, the one, "Walpurgis-nacht," has a German title, but its language is French; the other, "Vingt et un," has a French title but the language is German.

We have to return to our key sentence, once uttered by Mme Chauchat in French, now repeated by Hans Castorp in German. It can be understood in two entirely different ways, completely reversing its meaning. In the French, in Mme Chauchat's version, it is a death-intoxicated credo, the complete loss and annihilation of self by letting go—dropping out of existence. In German, in Hans Castorp's version, it now means to forget self and one's own drives and desires, to master ego so that one becomes a humble servant of something higher and can merge and participate in a force which is holy and positive, "wie das Leben [like life]." Instead of being utterly free, lacking any ties with and responsibilities to a larger body (this is the way Mme Chauchat meant it originally), one can become a self-effacing link, capable of holding a world, of holding one's self together at the brink of dissolution.

This is exactly what happens to Hans, and what he is able to achieve thanks to Mynheer Peeperkorn's presence on the enchanted mountain. During the Dutchman's and Mme Chauchat's stay, Hans Castorp becomes engaged in two enterprises—and "engaged" is an intentionally chosen word—which are actually one and the same, or rather one enterprise and its reversed and transposed counterpart. The enterprises correspond exactly; the same language is employed in both cases. The event we talk about is the conclusion of a covenant.

In bondage to the woman whom he had possessed and in whom he had

lost himself to the point of perdition on that momentous Mardis Gras, waiting for her to return which is one of the reasons for his refusal to break out
of the deadly realm of the magic mountain, he now sees her return, belonging
to another man. We need not dwell upon the emotional turmoil which these
circumstances of her return must, of necessity, cause in him, nor even mention the partly gleeful, partly commiserating comments of the other guests
of the sanatorium, who well realize the deadly blow that has been dealt to
Hans Castorp. A deadly blow—and yet something unheard of happens. He,
possessed by his passion, truly in bondage, is now asked by the object of his
passion to enter into an alliance for the protection of the rival who has
deprived him of all his hopes and happiness. Here we have to use the German
word "Bündnis [alliance]." He, the possessed, is being offered the choice of
overcoming his possession and possessiveness, and entering, a free man, into
a bond to help the "God" who, as we know, is as "robust" as he is "lean."
What Clawdia expects him to do is, indeed, unbelievable: he is to lose himself
to the point of perdition—but not in the service of "le corps, l'amour, la
mort," but in the service of life, of helping another human being who, by
rights, should be his most hated enemy. This is what she proposes: "Wollen
wir Freundschaft halten, ein Bündnis schließen für ihn, wie man sonst gegen
jemand ein Bündnis schließt? Gibst du mir darauf die Hand? [Shall we be
friends, shall we make a league—not against but for him? Will you give me
your hand on it?]." And the inconceivable becomes reality. Hans Castorp
consents, consents proudly: "Das wäre im höchsten Grade linkisch, wenn
ich das Anerbieten deiner Freundschaft nicht zu schätzen wüßte, der Freundschaft mit dir für ihn [It would be very inept of me to refuse, not to know
how to value your friendship, friendship with me for his sake]."

Friendship with you for him—this is the formula that reverses the sick
addiction to "le corps, l'amour, la mort"—no longer bondage but a bond.
And in this renunciation there is victory. Because now we hear: "Da küßte
sie ihn auf den Mund [She kissed him on the mouth]," the first and only
time in our novel that we witness this "Liebesbesiegelung [seal of love]." A
sealing of love it is, and Thomas Mann now enters into a detailed analysis
of what this kiss means and what he wants us to understand by love. It is
eros, passion of the flesh, but it is at the same time "Charitas [charity]"—
and this word that we expect stands here exactly at the place where it
belongs. What happens between two lovers is the realization of the number
seven: the divine and noumenal which has become incarnate in this kiss on
the mouth. It is Hans Castorp's pledge to serve someone else, and by serving
to fulfill himself.

HILARY HELTAY

Virtuosity in Thomas Mann's Later Narrative Technique

It is a feature of the composition of the Joseph novels that certain chapters
and episodes emerge as focal points upon which diverse themes converge
and demonstrate their relevance to the central issue of Joseph's career. The
chapters "Der Adonishain" ["The Grave of Adonis"], "In der Höhle" ["In
the Pit"], and "Myrtenduft oder das Mahl mit den Brüdern" ["The Meal
With the Brothers: Fragrance of Myrtle"] variously provide examples of such
focal points, where themes reaching out into the vastly complex background
of history, myth, religion, phantasy, or into the earlier parts of the narrative
itself, are significantly assembled, regrouped or recapitulated. Unifying, integrating and clarifying, these thematic confluences are no mere decorative
arabesques. They open welcome enough vistas through the maze of material,
along which not only the author's current intentions become clearly discernible, but also the narrative means by which he has been consistently pursuing
them.

It may seem paradoxical to claim for the Man-on-the-Field episode a
similar integrating function in the novels. While the figure is memorable to
the casual reader for being intriguingly inconsequent (is he angel, god, Christ-
parallel, reincarnated spirit?), he seems to have escaped more penetrating
critical interest on the grounds of a more serious artistic incongruity. His
presence, for all its colorfulness, appears to represent a small flaw in the
fabric, a wilful self-indulgence of the creative imagination.

From *German Life and Letters,* n.s. 24, no. 2 (January 1971). © 1971 by Basil
Blackwell Ltd. Originally entitled "Der Mann auf dem Felde: Virtuosity in Thomas
Mann's Later Narrative Technique."

The analysis which follows attempts to find a justification for the Man-on-the-Field episode within Thomas Mann's artistic system, and to show that it can offer rewarding insight into the inner structures of the novels by providing a focal point where not only do principal themes converge into immediate relevance, but in which also aspects of the essential idea content, in artistic unity with the thematic form, unite to reaffirm a basic attitude of the author to the work upon which he is engaged.

To give a prompt and succinct reply to the question: "Who is the Man on the Field?," we would need to operate on the same level of mythic pre-analytical consciousness, of "Mondgrammatik [lunar syntax]" and "schönes Gespräch [fine language]," as the more gifted characters of the novels them-selves. The question presupposes for us an existing identity or integrity of identity such as is vital to all realistic, successfully three-dimensional char-acterization. Even in a novel where the basic idea content is carried by char-acters who fulfill precast roles and whose identities are constantly widening into mythical, astral, divine or heroic perspectives, the author views with satisfaction his achievement of a lively, realistic, unquestionably human three-dimensionality. In Mann's correspondence with René Schickele on this point, the figure of the Man on the Field does not escape remark as a dubious exception. A diary entry of Schickele's records the comment: "Fragwürdig nur der 'Mann auf dem Felde,' falls er eine Episode bleibt ["Only the 'Man-on-the-Field' episode dubious, if it remains (as it is)]." And Thomas Mann accepted his criticism with no more than a half-apologetic attempt to justify his creation of the "drollig-verdriessliche Figur [oddly annoying figure]."

Still, it would seem to do less than justice to Mann's well-known pre-dilection for the double perspective, for the interplay of his own particular categories of Myth and Pyschology, to accept his "Trotzdem . . . lassen wir's ja gut sein [All the same . . . let's leave well enough alone]" as the last word on the subject. If the function of the Man-on-the-Field episode is not identical with, or not entirely vindicated by the part he plays in the natural, story-plot progression of the narrative, then one must surely look elsewhere to discover the author's purpose. Scrutiny indeed reveals that the integral is consciously sacrificed in favor of the composite in the realization of the mysterious figure. Once he is absolved from the dictates of ordinary human dimensions, he is free to exist on a multi-dimensional level, uniting in a synthetic structure of themes and their corresponding associations countless threads of the novels' complex texture and obeying a law no less arbitrary than the omnipotent will of the narrator-creator himself.

To dispose first of all of the man's minimally realistic aspect, of the fact "dass er allenfalls doch ein etwas wunderliches Menschenkind sein kann [that in any case he could very well be a kind of supernatural human being]" we should describe what might well be called his "non-function" in terms of the natural, linear story. He is, as in the biblical source, the stranger who directs Joseph to his brothers in Dothan. Further, he is the stranger whom Reuben finds sitting by the well out of which he had hoped to rescue Joseph (identified as Joseph's traveling companion by the repetition of certain features of physique and dress, and of phrases of speech). Finally, he is the guide who offers his services to the Ishmaelites on their way down into Egypt. That Joseph would have reached Dothan without any interpretative elaboration of the biblical encounter goes without saying. Reuben's receipt at the well of the seed of expectation is no more functional: the seed remains buried and unfruitful in the depths of his mind. Joseph is gratified to hear of Reuben's good will, but it makes no difference to his subsequent career at any of its stages. As for guides through the desert, they were necessary to all travelers beyond a certain point and there were always plenty of them waiting to be hired.

Since the Man on the Field thus seems to be accorded no function which makes him indispensable to the natural, human-realistic level of the narrative, the next stage of inquiry would seem to open logically on to questions of form, structure or idea content. As a serial link in a progressive structural pattern, we shall find that the figure is entirely justifiable in the guise no less of Hermes Psychopompos. Even if there were not ample thematic indications of his assignment to this role throughout the narrative, an exchange between Thomas Mann and Karl Kerényi points reasonably enough to this conclusion:

> Es ist ganz ausgeschlossen, dass ich in der Jugend Gefallenn gefunden hätte an einer Szene, wie der von Ihnen erwähnten: dem Traum Jaakobs von Anup,—an einer Replik etwa wie der des Schakalköpfigen: "Ich werde meinen Kopf schon noch los." Es ist fast ein Privatspass, über den jedermann wegliest. Aber es handelt sich um die Carrière eines Gottes. Dieser Anup, jetzt noch halb tierisch und satyrhaft, ist ja der zukünftige Hermes-Psychopompos. Haben Sie bemerkt, dass ich ihn genau in der Pose des Hermes von Lysipp in Neapel auf seinen Stein gesetzt habe?

> [It is wholly out of the question that in my youth I could have found pleasure in a scene such as the one you mention—Jacob's dream about Anup—or in a reply such as the jackal-headed one's "I shall one day be rid of my head too." It's like a private joke, one which everyone passes by. But it has to do with the career of

a god. This Anup, as yet half animal, satyr-like, is actually the future Hermes-Psychopompos. Have you noticed that I have sat him exactly in the pose of the Hermes by Lysippos in Naples on his stone?]

(Thomas Mann-Karl Kerényi, *Gespräch in Briefen*
[Zurich, 1960])

The handling of the motif of the archetypal psychogogue is true to the basic pattern of recurrence and repetition which is one of the principal determinants of the form of the Joseph novels. Joseph's career is fashioned, at least in outline, after that of his father Jacob. Parallel ascents and descents are both commented by the narrator and piously recognized and celebrated by the actors. Accordingly, the early stages of the divine career in question are to be found in the dark and solemn depths of Jacob's past, where the god assumes a form suitable to the myth-bound atmosphere of the first novel: namely, the form of Anup or Anubis, the ancient Egyptian mortuary jackal-god. In this animal form, he appears to Jacob when, fleeing from the enmity of his brothers, he crosses the boundary into the desert, into the underworld of Laban's domain, or associatively speaking, when he crosses the boundary between life and death: "Jaakobs Wissen und Denken war viel zu beziehungsreich, als dass er ihn nicht erkannt hätte, den Öffner der ewigen Wege, den Führer ins Totenreich. Er hätte sich sehr gewundert, wenn er ihm nicht vorangelaufen wäre" [Jacob was far too well versed in such matters not to recognize in him the opening of the way, the everlasting guide into the kingdom of the dead. He would have been surprised not to see him] (*Joseph und seine Brüder* [*Joseph and His Brothers*, trans. H. T. Lowe-Porter. New York: Knopf, 1956. All further references will be to *Joseph*]).

Moving from myth to dream, it is at another such boundary point that Anup makes his second appearance, this time at the crossroads between celibacy and marriage. Ostensibly, his ugly jackal's head on an otherwise beautiful body, likewise his account of the accidental circumstances of his conception, are intended as an adumbration of Jacob's imminent false consummation of his love for Rachel with the "jackal-headed" Leah. (This adumbration provides a connection, however tenuous, between Anup and Reuben, which may be useful later on to the justification of the Man on the Field's appearance to Reuben at the well.) But at the same time his Psychopompos characteristic is given ample scope, patently in the form of the dream, which is a reconstruction of Jacob's original journey into the underworld, and more associatively and subtly in the narrator's almost celebrated discourse on the relationship between marriage and death, which has been the subject of Jacob's preoccupation just before his dream.

Without his jackal's head, which he predicted he would soon be rid of, Anup-Hermanubis makes his third appearance in a form dictated again by the stage reached in the narrative, namely, as Hermes Psychopompos in the human guise of the Man on the Field. Or, more accurately, as one part of the complex identity of the Man on the Field. In both epiphanies to Joseph, on the way to Dothan and on the way into the underworld of Egypt, he is the guide across the boundary from life into death.

The motif of the archetypal guide traditionally accompanying the descent into the underworld is played in a muted and subtle key, especially on the way to Dothan. Even so, at first sight it may appear out of character that Joseph, in spite of his talent for observation and adaptation, "Spiel" and "Anspielung," his feeling for repetition and *déja-vu*, comes to no immediate conclusions himself about the character-role of the man he meets. Paradoxically, however, what seems here an anomaly belongs in fact to the technical mastery apparent in this episode altogether. The situation is one of numerous perspectives. On its various levels the author manages simultaneously to keep faith with the biblical source; to recreate the encounter so that it fits the design he has imposed on the material as a whole; and to manipulate Joseph, in preparation for the climactic self-analysis in the pit, into a position which calls into question the level of consciousness on which he is actually operating (already sophisticated, pattern-liberated analytical, or still pattern-bound "gelebter Mythos"?). For at the deepest level of the situation, Joseph on the way to Dothan is playing out the final scenes of his first (self-assigned?) divine character-role. He is the willing sacrifice, "der Dulder und das Opfer," Tammuz-Osiris in the eternal present of his festival, accepting with ritual piety the knowledge that belongs to and is limited by each moment of the celebration in its order, irrespective of the theoretically possible knowledge that, as celebration and ritual recurrence, the successive stages can be recognized, the end predicted. As Mann presents it, the knowledge that Joseph's guide is a mythical Psychopompos and his goal the underworld of the dead is a communication from narrator to reader, an implicit understanding between those who know the outcome of events and merely observe the manner in which they are fulfilled. So, the narrator relies here upon the reader's own associative talents, leaving those of his main character temporarily out of play. The man says for instance: "Ich mache oft Botenwege an meinem Stabe. Aber ich bin auch ein Führer ... Ich führe die Reisenden und öffne ihnen die Wege, das ist mein Geschäft" [I often make journeys on foot with my staff. But also I am a guide ... I guide travellers and open the ways for them: that is my business]." Just in case, however, the reader fails to remember Anup-Hermes, or does not see in the messenger-guide's staff the caduceus of Hermes, Mann adds another clue. Without apparent rhyme or reason, the man steals. Joseph is prepared to view this aberration in the light of his profession as guide: "Auch war der Mann ja ein Führer und also dem Nabu geweiht, dem Herrn des Westpunktes im Kreislauf, der in die unterweltliche Welthälfte führt, ein Diener des Gottes der Diebe [Moreover, the man was a guide and thus dedicated to Nabû, the lord of the westernmost point in the cycle, leading down into the underworldly half of the world—a servant, that is, of the god of thieves]." But the scene is moving to its climax, Dothan is near and Joseph is soon to be brushed by a nameless anxiety whose source is certainly not just the loss of a few onions and some fruit. The change of atmosphere is introduced by this very attempt at rationalization. It is a characteristic example of a psychologically potent leitmotif, whereby the su-perficially principal idea (guide) brings with it and yet still overlays and subordinates more significant unconscious associations (underworld). More-over, instead of Nabû at this point we may read Hermes. This sentence is practically a quotation from Alfred Jeremias: *Handbuch der altorientalischen Geisteskultur* (Leipzig 1913), one of Thomas Mann's source books for the novels. Here we read: "Nabû offenbart sich unter den Gestirnen im Planeten Merkur, der als Morgenstern am Tag und als Glücks- und Neujahrsstern den Frühling verkündigt. Als Repräsentant des Westpunktes, der den Weg zur Unterwelt eröffnet, ist er zum Geleitsmanne der Toten geworden [Nabû man-ifests himself among the stars in the planet Mercury, that heralds the spring as the morning star in the daytime and as a lucky New Year's star. As the representative of the westernmost point, which opens the way to the underworld, he became the guide of the dead]." And a footnote to this paragraph then explains further: "Neben seiner Verwandtschaft mit Hermes-Merkur in verschiedenen Gestalten findet sich auch die Eigenschaft als 'Gott der Diebe,' die sich ebenfalls durch die Unterwelts-Stellung erklärt [Alongside his relationship with Hermes-Mercury in various forms, one finds him in the capacity of the 'god of thieves,' which likewise accounts for his placement in the underworld]." Could it be that the account of the guide's sale of the lame ass and its load, which parallels the theft in the first scene, was also inspired by Jeremias's description of "Nabû-Hermes als Gott der Kaufmän-nischen Geschäfte (im Sinne des Kaufens und Verkaufens) [Nabû-Hermes as the god of merchant's business (in the sense of buying and selling)]." Whether or not, we might safely presume, in view of the climax of the Hermes-career in the figure of Joseph the Provider, that Jeremias's characterization of Nabû in one of his astral positions as "Aufseher der Welt [overseer of the world]" could scarcely have left Thomas Mann unmoved.

On the way down into Egypt, by which time Joseph has had time to adapt himself to his symbolical death in the pit and even to find a name which expresses it: Osarsiph—Osiris Joseph—dead and deified Joseph—, the role of the archetypal guide, coinciding with the authentic requirements of the Ishmaelites, can be accorded the dominant aspect of the Man on the Field. An interesting point, though, deserves special note. He disappears, characteristically enough, at the entry-point into Egypt, the very gate of the underworld, without claiming his wages. This small point establishes a significant connection between Joseph's guide and the similarly conceived, multi-dimensional figure of death in *Der Tod in Venedig* [*Death in Venice*]. In the mythical double perspective of Charon, the gondolier who ferries Aschenbach to the Lido and who also disappears without payment is an early variation on the Psychopompos theme.

We are left with the encounter at the well with Reuben. Here again the realization of the scene draws upon numerous sources, but the Anup-Hermes theme sounds a dominant note. The man sits at the well, an apt position for Hermes in his character of god of boundaries, inasmuch as the well marks for Joseph, as it did for Jacob, the entrance to the underworld. His purpose here is to give Reuben a hint as to the outcome of the whole affair, to sink into the soil of Reuben's subconscious mind the seed of expectation, or, in hermetic or mercurial terms, the knowledge of life beyond death. For it is another attribute of Hermes that he is the god of mystic knowledge and of rebirth. That the stranger performs this service in the terms of reference of Joseph's particular Tammuz-Osiris- seed-corn death is yet another stroke of masterly narrative "Dichtung [poetry]."

There is, however, another, much more associative-complex connection between Anup-Hermes and Reuben here, which may further legitimize Mann's introduction of this encounter. We have already made, through Jacob's premarital dream, the connection between Anup and Reuben, a connection sealed by Jacob's dying words to his eldest son: "du bist meine früheste Macht und meiner Mannheit Erstling . . . Es war ein Versehen. Ein Abgott zeigte mir's an auf dem Felde im Traum, ein beizendes Tier der Wüste, ein Hundsknabe mit schönem Bein, auf dem Steine sitzend, gezeugt aus Versehen, gezeugt mit der Unrechten in blinder Nacht [You are the beginning of my strength, the firstling of my manhood . . . But it was all wrong. A heathen god showed it to me on the field in a dream, a biting beast, a dog-boy of the desert with beautiful legs, sitting on a stone. Begot by a mistake, begat with the wrong one in the blind night]." Waking from his dream, all Jacob had remembered of it was that after Osiris's death "Nebthot, die fälschlich Umarmte, mit Eset gesucht und geklagt und die Verfehlte vom irrtümlich Gezeugten sich hatte schützen und stützen lassen [Nephtys,

wrongfully embraced, had yet sought and mourned with Isis, and the be-
reaved one been cherished and supported by the wrongly begot]." Here at
the entrance to the underworld, the two "irrtümlich Gezeugte [wrongly be-
got]" meet as Reuben searches for Joseph *qua* murdered god. With a not
too strenuous leap of the imagination one can perceive a satisfying connection between Reuben-Anup, searching clamorously for dead Osiris-Joseph,
in support of, if not simultaneous with, the even more clamorous laments
of Jacob-Eset-Ishtar, whose grief for his son makes him temporarily deny his
God and identify himself with the Tammuz-Osiris ritual, as Joseph has done
in his symbolic death, and as Anup-Hermes has done in his veiled prophecy
of the resurrection of the dead.

Narrative virtuosity, technical expertise. There is a further, more prosaic
point to be made in reference to the encounter at the well. The biblical source
is almost excessively concise on the subject of Reuben's non-participation in
the sale of Joseph. All Thomas Mann had to go on was one verse: "Als nun
Ruben wieder zur Grube kam, und fand Joseph nicht darinnen, zerriss er
sein Kleid [And Reuben returned unto the pit; and, behold, Joseph was not
in the pit; and he rent his clothes (Genesis 37:29)]." A dramatic action
deserving of a dramatic scene. But how to create a drama with any intensity
if, through lack of a dialogue partner, the scene has merely to be narrated,
described? Hence the introduction of the only available actor for the part:
the mysterious Man on the Field. Already extraneous to the "plot" he is the
perfect solution to the technical problem, provided that his appearance on
the scene can be motivated within the homogeneous structure of the whole.

Once Anup has reached the height of his career in Hermes Psychopompos, there is no further for him to go, except towards sublimation in the
career of Joseph himself at Pharaoh's court. Yet, if one claims to justify the
Man-on-the-Field episode in terms of structural integrity and textual homogeneity, it obviously has to go beyond Joseph's first descent into the pit. In
searching further, we find evidence of the unity of form and content in this
work. The appearances of Anup-Hermes follow a progressive pattern according to the stages of the narrative, which in turn develop and change as
they reflect the separation and liberation of individual consciousness out of
the pattern-bound compound of the mythical collective. It would have been
a "Stilbruch [stylistic incongruity]" of the first order to have a jackal running
across Joseph's path into Egypt. Joseph's sophisticated consciousness requires the human form, however transparent a cloak this may be for the
divine perspective. The gap between primitive Egyptian Anup and sophisticated Olympian Hermes represents in itself a huge stride forward in man's
development towards enlightenment. But Joseph, at this particular stage of

his career, has still some considerable way to go. Accordingly, as the novels move on towards their more enlightened, later, spheres of consciousness, the patterns show a tendency to weaken. Myth as reality moves through the filter of human consciousness towards the psychological perception of myth as symbol. Epiphanies of gods give way to psychologically potent leitmotifs. Joseph has no death-dream before his marriage, though the guests at his wedding mime out for the sake of form the relationship between "Hochzeit und Tod, Brautgemach und Grab [death and marriage, a bridal chamber and a tomb]." Yet in Joseph's second descent into the pit, his three-year period in the underworld of Zawi-Rê, there are leitmotifs to be noted whose resonances echo back to the theme-tunes of the Man-on-the-Field episode. Cha'ma't, Joseph's "guide" into the grave, "quotes" from the words of the man himself, including a reference to the other major aspect of the man's identity which remains yet to be explored in this analysis: "Wir haben da die alte Frage, wer grösser und wichtiger ist: der zu Bewachende oder der Wächter. Ohne Zweifel ist es doch jener. Denn wird nicht auch ein König von seinen Knechten behütet, und heisst es nicht von dem Gerechten: 'Es ist Seinen Engeln befohlen, dich zu behüten auf deinen Wegen? [It is the old question: who is greater and more important, the watcher or the watched? But of course it is the latter. For is not even a king guarded by his servants, and is it not said of the just man: 'He shall give His angels charge over thee to keep thee in all thy ways'?]." More poignant than this, however, is the motif which resounds in Joseph's words to Mut on the subject of human beauty, spoken at a stage in his career when he knows, in the lower levels of his consciousness at least, that his path into the underworld is very definitely on the point of being opened again. The words he chooses are those of the Man on the Field with only the slightest variation:

> Man tut wirklich gut, sich daran zu erinnern—sich und auch den, der ihnen etwa lächelt—, was jeder ohnedies weiss, aber zu vergessen geneigt ist aus Schwachheit: aus wie minderem Stoffe das alles besteht, sofern es besteht, aber es ist ja unbeständig, dass Gott erbarm! Bedenke doch, dass diese Haare kläglich ausfallen werden über ein kleines und diese jetzt weissen Zähne auch. Diese Augen sind nur ein Gallert aus Blut und Wasser, sie sollen dahinrinnen, so, wie der ganze übrige Schein bestimmt ist, zu schrumpfen und schnöde zunichte zu werden.

> [One does well to remind oneself—and anyone who tends to smile upon them, for we know but in our weakness would forget of

what poor stuff it is, if indeed it may be said to be at all, so
pathetically perishable is it! Remember that in a little this hair
must fall out, and these teeth too, that now are white. The eyes
are but a jelly of water and blood, they will dissolve, as indeed
the whole outward show must shrivel and melt away to vileness
and nothing.

(Joseph)]

By this again characteristic employment of leitmotif, the author thus indicates
psychologically how Joseph's unconscious mind is dwelling on a previous
experience and projecting out of it a significant, if not yet consciously eval-
uated connection with the present situation. But he also shows here, through
the nature of the situations thus connected, the last stage in the development
of an image-pattern from external mythical reality towards assimilation into
the psychological apparatus of the individual consciousness. What Mann has
created here in his handling of this progressive image-pattern of symbolical
death, with the episode of the Man on the Field holding a central position
in its development, is a kind of narrative cipher which, not indispensable to
the explicit unfolding of the story, nevertheless parallels it faithfully at every
stage, restating and reaffirming in cryptographic form the basic idea content
of the whole.

The second, more readily apparent ingredient in the identity of the Man
on the Field, particularly in his first meeting with Joseph, is angelic. That
this feature does not stand in conflict with his hermetic nature, but rather
complements it, will become clear later on. Tongue in cheek, the author, on
the pretext of a slight dissension about whose turn it is to ride the ass,
amuses himself with remarks such as these: " 'Ich bin vorübergehend ge-
wisser Erleichterungen in meinem Fortkommen beraubt,' setzte er hinzu und
rückte die Schultern [I have been temporarily robbed of certain facilities for
travel,' he added, and shrugged his shoulders]"; or to a vexed and aggressive
Reuben: "Verschwinden könnte ich wohl und mit Leichtigkeit, aber es fehlte
nur, dass ich's auf dein Geheiss täte [Vanish of course I could and with ease,
but not at thy behest]." The fact that the man also says to Reuben "Rühre
mich nicht an! [Touch me not]" no more identifies the mysterious figure with
the risen Christ than Potiphar's walking in the garden in the cool of the day
identifies him with God. It is simply a quotation which is apt in this situation.
The novels are scattered with Old and New Testament quotations inspired
by narrative contingency and quite arbitrarily in or out of place as far as
religious-historical authenticity is concerned.

Apart from such playfully over-patent clues, it is the content of the man's

conversation with Joseph and, more expressly, the attitude that clearly inspires his point of view, which largely establishes his identity as an angel,
and in particular as a member of God's critical entourage in the Upper
Circles. Material and motivation for this conversation have already been
provided in the "Vorspiel: Höllenfahrt" ["Prelude: Descent into Hell"] and
"Himmelstraum" ["The Dream of Heaven"]. Now, at the stage in the narrative where the Man on the Field enters upon the scene, Thomas Mann sees
fit to parade the uneasy state of affairs in Heaven, albeit suitably enciphered,
in the temporal guise of a moderately urbane and admirably consequential
exchange between Joseph and his guide. Later, in the "Vorspiel in Oberen
Rängen" ["Prelude in the Upper Circles"], he will temporarily identify himself as narrator with the discontented angels in order to give a first-hand
account of the heavenly unrest, from which account a light falls retrospec-
tively on to Joseph's guide to Dothan which leaves no further doubt as to
the angelic component of his identity.

At issue among the angels is the question of God's creation of mankind.
His ambitious purposes for this new creation, His indulgence of its faults
and His jealous preference for it, expressed in terms of His covenant with
Abraham. The attitude of the angels to this new creative fantasy of God's is
compounded of envy of his fruitfulness, disdain for his moral constitution
and a certain amount of malicious expectation of disaster, based upon an
evidently incurable propensity of man for falling into sin. All these points
find their way into the conversation of the Man on the Field, woven around
a number of code-words (for example: "Klatsch [gossip]," "Angelegent-
lichkeit [urgency]," "Ein Geschlecht, das Unrecht trinkt wie Wasser [a breed,
that drinketh unrighteousness like water]") which link the episode with the
three others mentioned.

In addition to his personal and representative disposition towards mankind, the stranger's unnatural insight into Joseph's family circumstances and
personal history gives its own piquant flavor to this scene, heightened by the
latter's equally unnatural failure to react to it. Of course, such insight and
oversight can be ascribed to the man's supernatural origins. But omniscience
is also an attribute of the narrator, and one has the strong feeling here that
if the man's already eclectic personality were to borrow from yet another
source, it would be from the province of the narrator, that enviably omnipotent position which enables him to move in and out of his story as it pleases
him.

The narrator as extraneous interpreter is certainly discernible behind
the angel-messenger characteristic of the Man on the Field. Thomas Mann
wrote to René Shickele; "Die rabbinischen Kommentare fassen den 'Mann'

als Engel auf, und in meinem Buch spielt die pikierte Engelwelt ja auch von
Anfang an eine Rolle [The rabbinical commentaries conceive of the 'man' as
an angel, and in my book the piqued world of angels certainly also play a
role right from the beginning]." The text of the rabbinical commentaries is
most interesting: "R. Jannai said. He was met by three angels, for Scripture
says, 'And a certain man found him . . . and the man asked him . . . and the
man said: Let us go to Dothan.' For such are the designs of the Almighty"
(*Midrash Rabbah*, London 1939, Genesis II). A footnote to the last remark
then explains further: "This is obscure. Possibly there is a play on *dothaynah*
(to Dothan), which is read *dathe Jah*, 'the laws (here, the designs) of God'—
all these events led up to the fulfillment of God's designs, viz. Israel's ser-
vitude in Egypt."

Herein lies the motivation of the technically satisfying link between the
angel-messenger and Hermes Psychopompos. For the purposes of God involve Joseph's symbolical-mythical death, first in the pit at Dothan and subsequently in the Kingdom of the Dead, Egypt. On the two respective
journeys, the guide indicates in a single, repeated phrase that his mission
concerns Joseph exclusively: "wie nun auch ich dich Beutel voll Wind in die
Wege leiten muss, damit du zu deinem Ziele kommst [just as now, for instance, I must see that thou comest to thy right goal, thou bag of wind!]."
That this goal and the role played by the Man on the Field in helping him
to reach it are indeed God's purposes for him is an insight granted to Joseph
only after reflection in the pit, where he comes to the conclusion "dass Er
es weittragend vorhatte wie gewöhnlich und einen zukünftig-fernen Zweck
verfolgte, in dessen Diensten er, Joseph, die Brüder hatte zum Äussersten
treiben müssen [that He had far-reaching things in mind as usual and had
His eye upon some distant purpose, in the service of which he, Joseph, had
been made to drive his brethren to the uttermost]."

At this point it is vital for our insight into Mann's narrative technique
to note the distinction between the ordinary human dimension of the stranger
who shows Joseph the way to Dothan and the elaborately-conceived angel-
messenger whose function is to emphasize the working out of God's purposes
at this particular point. For instance, at the climax of the scene, when the
stranger reminds Joseph that he might need "einen Kopfschütz etwa gegen
die steigende Sonne [a head-cloth to shield thee from the sun]," we are
perfectly aware that this is a narrative gesture. Joseph would not have needed
the reminder about his "ketônet" had the narrator not decided to make him
forget it. On the other hand, this narrative gesture points suggestively beyond
the human-natural function of the stranger to his divine mission of seeing

that God's destructive purpose for Joseph is not foiled by the absence of a vital stage property.

The reason why it is desirable to be aware of God's purposes here is, it would seem, a technical and structural one. The author faces a technical problem inasmuch as he has to keep a constant watch on the credibility gap between a patently fallible human being and the success story of a fairy-tale hero. The more successfully he manages to realize a flesh-and-blood Joseph out of the mythical cocoon, the more determinedly he "de-mythizes" acts of God by interpreting them as achievements of the human intellect and personality, the more the gap threatens to widen. His solution is the handling of the theme of God's purposes. Each time he is hard put to it to convince his readers that fallibility in his hero does not *have* to end in permanent fall, he allows God and His entourage to take a hand in the narrative. Before Joseph's descent into the Egyptian prison of Zawi-Rê out of which he will rise to the heights of ministerial power, we have the "Vorspiel in Oberen Rängen [Prelude in the Upper Circles]." And as a parallel to this, but couched in a form suitable to the earlier stage of Joseph's career, where the ground is not yet quite prepared for the light-hearted, parodistic and emphatically extra-narrative tone of the "Vorspiel," we have the episode of the Man on the Field.

> Zwar habe ich die Hintertür halbwegs offen gelassen, dass er allenfalls doch ein etwas wunderliches Menschenkind sein kann; aber sie ist recht schmal, und man kommt fast nicht hindurch. Trotzdem! Ich möchte das Kapitel und die drollig-verdriessliche Figur nicht missen, auch di Szene nicht am leeren Brunnen mit Reuben.

> [To be sure I have left the back door half-way open, that in any case he could very well be a kind of supernatural human being; but it is quite small, and one can hardly get through. All the same, I wouldn't like to lose the chapter and the oddly annoying figure, nor the scene with Reuben at the empty well.
> (Unpublished letter from Mann to Schickele, July 3, 1934)]

It is interesting that Mann's defense of his creation to Schickele is not a serious attempt at justification but simply a statement of his unwillingness to sacrifice the episode to the demands of a consistently realistic interpretation. It is possible, as we have seen, to analyze the component parts of the Man on the Field's composite identity. The figure belongs, associatively and thematically, partly to the entourage of god in the Upper Circles; partly to the mythical pattern of death and resurrection, where the descent into the underworld is traditionally accompanied by an archetypal guide; and partly to the province of the author-interpreter, who has oversight of the whole and can manipulate those narrative devices which will bring order into the parts. But the sum of the analyses of the parts does not necessarily amount to an analysis of the whole. The figure emerges out of all investigation as a supernatural character in a natural story. Moreover, he is not supernatural according to the unavoidable dictates of the source, but consciously created so out of what might have been left as a simple human original.

This might look like a sudden about-face in an author whose claim was to humanize the myth through the medium of psychological enlightenment. The formula, however, was Myth *plus* Psychology; it was Mann's view that the reverence for myth as an elemental constituent of the human tradition should survive, and indeed be enhanced by new possibilities of knowledge. His "Umfunktionierung [functional change]" of myth is not so much an "Entmythisierung [demythicization]" as an attempt to find a mode of realization appropriate to a modern, analytical stage of consciousness. As Mann saw it, the great gain of analytical insight is not the power to destroy old mysteries, but rather the achievement of a dispassionate, objective appraisal of the old sources of fear. To illustrate from the novels, it is the advance made from the pathos, the grand gesture of Jacob wrestling to prevail over an angel by forcing him to give up the secret of his name, to Joseph's easy differentiation between "Sein [essence]" and "Bedeuten [meaning]" in his evaluation of the festival. The need to conquer and destroy the forces of the unknown, out of fear of reversion, belongs to an earlier stage of half-liberated enlightenment; it is only the objective distance of a later consciousness that allows the perception of a fruitful interrelation between the known and the unknowable. The attitude in which this enlightened tolerance ideally expresses itself, according to Mann, is that of "Bescheidenheit aus Bescheid wissen [not assuming too much]" "*Freud und die Zukunft*"—a formula which might well stand as motto for Joseph's life achievement. Joseph's exemplary lesson in this kind of "Bescheidenheit [unassumingness]" is administered in the well at Dothan as part of God's purposes for him. Here, in a tremendous effort of his apparently pattern-liberated consciousness, he wrestles with the problem of his own self-awareness. Reviewing his past actions and calculations he discovers that, for all his sophisticated play with the myth, he is still bound fast to a pattern designed by a more powerful hand than his. The extent of his knowledge of himself and his world is thus broadened by the ability to recognize and respect the boundaries of the unknown. From this point on he is content to fulfill himself in the knowledge that he can perceive only the *existence* of God's purposes, but that he cannot penetrate them, for they are that ultimate "other" of the myth which is beyond the periphery of his most acute calculation.

It is from the standpoint expressed in this aspect of the novels' content that we now draw the final perspective of the Man on the Field. Beyond the various functions, formal, structural, or technical, of the single facets of his composite identity, the ultimate namelessness of his integrity is a fitting expression of the author's attitude of reverence towards the myth. His "Na, lassen wir's ja gut sein [No, let's leave well enough alone]" is his claim to the right to play his own sophisticated game with his mythical subject matter. The configuration of the Man on the Field into which so many themes of the work resolve themselves is the virtuoso's cadenza, homage to the myth, paid in the form of lucid technical mastery.

WILLIAM M. HONSA, JR.

Parody and Narrator in Thomas
Mann's Doctor Faustus

Parody, in its broadest sense, imitates another piece of work; it need not simply ridicule it, for it may criticize and thus further define and clarify its object. [Again,] I find Blackmur's definition useful: "Parody is a means of treating reality so as to come short of it either on purpose or through necessity. . . . Because it involves, points at, and limits what it parodies, parody is a good name for a means of getting at material that—in our state of belief—does not submit to existing systems." A parodistic novel can cope with myth and legend because it does not attempt to come to grips with them; it can look at an ultimate state of being, at salvation, because it does not attempt to look at it directly.

In *The Holy Sinner* much of the beginning is devoted to setting up the conditions necessary for salvation. Mann's parody in these early parts is restricted to a recreation of the tone of the original legend. It would be misleading to say that the original was a deliberate parody, rather it was an unpremeditated result of "historical uninstructedness, pious Christian didacticism, and moral naïveté." Unable to partake of this mixture of qualities, Mann can induce the effect of them in his readers by his own deliberate parody of the original. But in his treatment of Grigorss's time on the rock Mann must go beyond his initial parodistic style. The legend can put it simply: Grigorss spends seventeen years chained on a rock doing penance,

From *Orbis Litterarum* 29, no. 1 (1974). © 1974 by Munksgaard, Copenhagen. Originally entitled "Parody and Narrator in Thomas Mann's *Doctor Faustus* and *The Holy Sinner*."

and the "existing system" of the time accepts this flat statement. But Mann's audience cannot, so rather than going beyond it, rather than demanding a suspension of disbelief, Mann turns to parody. Of course the parody is as impossible as the original statement, but the body of reason is disarmed when parody attacks it. Against the impossible one can stand firm; confronted with paradox there is no need to resist because it is clearly only parody, and thus the point comes through, though by the back door.

In *Doctor Faustus* the use of parody is quite different. In *The Holy Sinner* parody falls short of reality on purpose, in *Doctor Faustus* through necessity. Leverkühn's ability to work within the form of parody is the devil's gift, or rather, Leverkühn in his meeting with the devil confirms the grounds on which this ability has always been based. But on the other hand, it is only through parody that the breakthrough can ultimately come. In spite of what the devil says—"I know, I know. Parody. It might be fun, if it were not so melancholy in its aristocratic nihilism"—the gift of parody is a genuine step toward the breakthrough. This is the devil speaking, after all, and we cannot attribute certain truth to his words. Leverkühn's parodies lead to the writing of the *Apocalypse,* and this is the last of his parodies, for in this piece is "the devil's laughter all over again." Parody has brought Leverkühn as far as it is able to; in the devil's terms, this parody is as close as man can come to reality.

This crisis in Leverkühn's musical development is made clear in the novel by the narrator's switch following this point to the personal and social world. Immediately after the description of the *Apocalypse* Zeitblom turns to the death of Clarissa, next to the strange Mme de Tolna, then to the impressario Saul Fitelberg, and finally to the Marie Godeau, Rudi Schwerdtfeger, Inez Institoris complication and tragedy. The only music written by Leverkühn in this period is a violin concerto for Schwerdtfeger, a work which is outside the frame of Leverkühn's work as a whole, and corresponds only to the fact that he and Schwerdtfeger are *per du*—a relationship as meaningless as the concerto. For while it is his only work, it is merely partially human and in no sense a breakthrough.

The last work, *The Lamentation of Doctor Faustus,* is again in line with Leverkühn's development as a parodist, but here parody is so complete that instead of pointing from a distance, the form of parody is exactly superimposed on reality, and the breakthrough is achieved. It is accomplished through the devil, but it is no longer diabolic; as the devil is a parody of God and therefore points to God more clearly than theology, so the *Lamentation* points at salvation because it is the denial of it. The work permits "up to the very end no consolation, appeasement, transfiguration." But in the completeness of the negation lies the only possibility for hope to arise—not from the work itself, but from the silence that follows it, the tone that is no longer heard. It is the vibration that indicates the actuality of the breakthrough, not the work itself, for the work is only destruction and negation. The vibration stands outside and beyond it. Negation is not a creative act; the real creation is the intangible, unprovable hope which arises from the parody carried to completion.

In music, Leverkühn is a parodist of great technical ingenuity and virtuosity. In language, Thomas Mann may be said to be the same. "Parody," Blackmur writes in the essay from which I have already taken such useful formulations, "emphasizes mechanics, especially . . . in executive technique, and greedily fastens on the merest possibilities in the material." Both *Doctor Faustus* and *The Holy Sinner* display such an emphasis, especially in their deliberate play with archaic modes of expression.

By varying his language Mann makes necessary points obliquely. The letter written to Zeitblom by Leverkühn about his first meeting with Esmeralda is written in archaic language which is dropped when the episode with her is told. Zeitblom analyses this manner as "parody as pretext" and prepares for the whole subject of parody to arise again later. For it is true, even on this obvious level, that the parody by Leverkühn of the style associated with the religious Reformation enables him to say "pray for me." Already there is the suggestion that parody can do what sincerity cannot.

The next passage in which Mann, and again Leverkühn, chooses archaic German is the visit of the devil. The reader recalls the earlier passage, and Esmeralda and the devil are thus connected, though the devil makes the point even clearer in his "I, Esmeralda's friend and co-habitant." But the other person whose language has the same archaic quality is Nepomuk—surely he is not connected with the devil? The connection is made that it may be denied. When Leverkühn employs a language no longer current it is because only in that language can he express religious feelings unstateable in modern German. But Nepomuk has not yet lost his otherworld purity; his archaic language is as indicative of his state as his childish language is of his age. This coupling of diabolic and angelic archaisms suggests the interpretation of the *Lamentation*. The language of parody, the language given Leverkühn by the devil, is not restricted only to a use which will further the devil's purpose. Through a language previously connected with the diabolic the grace of Nepomuk shines, as after the destructive fire of the *Lamentation*, written with the devil's own tool, is burned out, a glow remains which can perhaps be hope.

But not assuredly hope. For in the last use of archaic language, Lever-

kühn's confession, it is no longer clear whether we witness the final manifestation of evil, or have returned to a world in which language has regained
its original purity. Is Leverkühn's stumbling over words—his inability to
choose between "pray" and "play"—an indication that words no longer are
significant? "My sin is greater than it can be forgiven me" can mean either
exactly that—in arrogance Leverkühn admits he is damned and is so—or it
can mean that, even adding the sin of speculation, the confession is indeed
complete and forgiveness is possible.

There is a third possibility. The speech itself may be meaningless, that
is, there may be no sure interpretation of its meaning possible. But this
interpretation is not fence-straddling; Mann is not posing a question without
an answer. The fence is apparently defined, not in terms of itself but in respect
to what is on each side of it. But actually the fence cannot exist, for in the
end the devil's side of it is not there. The devil has pointed too hard, he has
come too close to what he pointed at and has become God. His own parody,
the gift of parody Leverkühn always had and which was the means of his
breakthrough in music, also destroys the devil himself. Parody has dissolved.
Nothing can be decided on the basis of the speech, but the wail of Leverkühn
as he falls on the piano is the wail of the devil, and the devil it is who falls.
Beyond that it cannot be decided what happens to Leverkühn, for the question—saved or damned?—is not the question Mann asks. "Talked about
th'everlasting mercy, poor soul, I don't know if it goes's far's that, but human
understanding, believe me, that does!" Mann does not speculate, either, on
the extent of everlasting mercy, but remains at the furthest limits of human
understanding—at the point where the devil and God are one.

As parody becomes reality, so does the language of Mann in *Doctor
Faustus* approach "language"—which in *The Holy Sinner* Clemens defines
as language "in and for itself, language itself, which sets itself as absolute
and does not greatly care about idiom." Nevertheless, the language Clemens
employs is far from an absolute language; again, in so parodying the absolute
Mann is reaching toward it. The good life at Beaurepaire, described in terms
of silk cushions from Aleppo and Damascus, combats of Christian knights
in such lands as Ethnise, Gylstram, or Rankulat, shields from Toledo, Aza-
goger fineware, is both specifically and confusedly drawing everything into
itself. It is "no small thing, to align and keep in grammatical sequence such
encomiums as these," though it is all Clemens can do. Through Clemens's
inability to do more, through his parodistic style, Mann suggests that there
is an ultimate language which he parodies.

The power of events to determine the language in which they are told
is suggested most amusingly in the uncontrollable rhyming of M Poitevin as

he tells of Grigorss's first battle, and falls helplessly into the rhyming which is the common minnesinger form for such a tale. The real compulsion to rhyme comes from Grigorss's "blue blaze of the eyes in the pale face," from the idea behind the traditional action, which turns into jingles the usual shrewd reporting of M Poitevin. As he can only express the force of Grigorss's concentration in rhyme which differs from his customary dignified prose, so Mann in *The Holy Sinner* deliberately chooses a language removed from that of his time with which to look through the sinner Grigorss at Sin itself.

The lightness and effortlessness of the parody in *The Holy Sinner* is a result of the working out of the possibilities of parody in *Doctor Faustus*. In the latter novel parody is defined and its possibilities as a means of reaching reality are developed. *The Holy Sinner* demonstrates the way in which the problem—insoluble in any other terms—of making the unbelievable acceptable to the modern world, is worked out. Had *The Holy Sinner* been written before *Doctor Faustus*, it would not be so clear what Mann is doing; the book would not have the same effect because it might be seen as a simple burlesque of reality. The effect might be charming, as a fairy tale is charming, but as an escape from reality rather than as a clearer approach to it. In a sense *The Holy Sinner* is a greater achievement (though not a greater work) than *Doctor Faustus*, for in it a believable world is created rather than destroyed. We accept a set of conditions that we know are no longer true of the world we live in, and we see Pope Gregory reconcile humanity with itself. In *Doctor Faustus* humanity disintegrates in the person of Leverkühn and the German nation, but still the novel is no simple work of destruction— there is at least the possibility of a new creation. It is parody which makes this positive view possible in *Doctor Faustus*, and which makes it probable in *The Holy Sinner*. Parody is the only way in which we can, at the present time, catch a glimpse of an ultimate truth about good. *Doctor Faustus* illustrates the process through which parody becomes an effective tool of the modern artist, and *The Holy Sinner* is built with this tool.

II

Employed (like parody) with increasing skill and elaboration in Thomas Mann's later works, the device of the narrator is another means of getting at those realities of faith and feeling which are the source of artistic vitality. Mann agrees with Goethe's statement: "No one has a conscience except the onlooker," but would perhaps add that existing systems of belief cannot accept the reality of such an inner voice. He is convinced of the necessity for a conscience, however, for he feels the whole task of the artist is that of "keeping awake the conscience of life." Mann must bridge the gap between the need to recognize the validity of a conscience and the inability to do so. In a society which cannot accommodate a concept which it nevertheless must accept if it is to remain whole, the artist is the only person who is able to reunite man with his conscience. But the artist cannot do this with the power of his personal voice alone, which is only a kind of ultimately unconvincing rhetoric. To make his own view clear he must speak through someone else, someone who can take a stand that he, as the directing artist, cannot maintain.

Zeitblom is an onlooker; however much he would like to influence Leverkühn, he is resigned to the fact that he cannot. He is allowed only to look on, but this is still the most important function of his life. He has a conscience which at times leads him to become something more than an onlooker in respect to his country (he fights for Germany in the First World War, resigns from his profession in protest against Hitler). He is an onlooker, but not one without character or a position of his own. His Catholic humanism speaks through *Doctor Faustus*; Zeitblom does not hesitate to react against Leverkühn's demon when it reaches too far toward the powers of darkness, but neither does he ever utterly condemn Leverkühn. Human understanding in Zeitblom stretches far enough to suggest the possibility of everlasting mercy. "First and last . . . I loved him," and we do not question this statement.

But some of Zeitblom's remarks are not to be taken at face value, for he is not simply the mouthpiece for Thomas Mann—and in this lies his value in the novel. Zeitblom is the artist we see working out the form of the novel; he is the speaker in the epigraph from Dante on the title page. He will relate the war and the pity, but he will do it with the help of the Muse—the voice of Art—which is on one level significant but is reinforced and enlarged by a "high genius" beyond him.

If Mann's voice is the voice of the Muse, the Art, then is the artist Zeitblom or Leverkühn? We hear Leverkühn's music only through Zeitblom, and the novel itself is ostensibly Zeitblom's work, but in his struggles to write, the bourgeois rather than the demonic artist is revealed. Zeitblom is *per du* with humanity; he belongs to the human race; he marries an ordinary middle-class girl. But he is not completely ordinary, for the enchantment of the name Helene swings him strongly toward his choice, and his devotion to Leverkühn cannot be explained on the grounds of reciprocated friendship. All in all, however, the bourgeois predominates in him, as the artist does in Leverkühn. Similarly, Leverkühn is not wholly artist, for his impulse toward humanity allows him to love at least Nepomuk, and to be drawn to Schwerdt-feger and Marie Godeau. The types which are opposed in one man in *Tonio Kröger* are separated in *Doctor Faustus* into Zeitblom and Leverkühn, but the achievement of each belongs to the role of the other. It is Zeitblom who tells the story—his recurring concern with the manipulations of his material is annoyingly convincing—and the language of the bourgeois shapes the work of art. It is Leverkühn who stands for humanity, who breaks through as "a good and as a bad Christian," whose works cannot be played in the Germany of 1943, but whose life and death relate directly to the life, collapse, and rebirth of humanity. In remaining outside both the narrator and the protagonist, in separating and then confusing their roles and their accomplishments, Mann sees the artist and the bourgeois as unavoidably one.

Though Zeitblom is to some extent an artist, he is often the vehicle for Mann's irony. When Zeitblom says "that intellectual and wit [Spengler] . . . had most regretably succumbed to his heart trouble" he means exactly that, but Mann's intent is that we realize that the loss of a Spengler is not regrettable, and "heart trouble" is rather corruption which may have affected his heart, but more certainly his soul. Sometimes Zeitblom is the focus of an irony he does not himself see. Always a bit jealous of Rüdiger Schildknapp because Schildknapp's gallows humor often appeals to Leverkühn more than his own devoted earnestness, Zeitblom is able to recognize that the friendship is based on a profound indifference—a thought which consoles him rather than otherwise. But this recognition should be upsetting rather than consoling, for indifference simulating friendship should make Zeitblom look to the meaning of his own tie with Leverkühn, the *du* to which he clings. His being *per du* with Leverkühn is as meaningless as the other relationship, based as it is only on habit and indifference on the one side. It is a safe nothingness, however, for it cannot pull Leverkühn toward humanity, as does the *du* won by Schwerdtfeger. If pulled hard enough. Leverkühn appears to give in, but he is not in truth humanized. He makes it impossible for himself to win a humanizing Marie, and he kills the only other winner of his *du*. Zeitblom is saved from this fate because he does not reach Leverkühn, and the *du* he cherishes for the wrong reasons is without meaning except in his own mind. And yet, Zeitblom's *du* is a symbol of "human understanding," an understanding which is present from the beginning to the end of the relationship, whose very significance lies in its ability to love despite lack of reciprocation, and which points to possibility of "everlasting mercy."

Thus Zeitblom is more than narrator. He is the other protagonist of the novel, Leverkühn's alter ego, and to some degree also the voice of Mann, who cannot speak entirely as either Zeitblom or Leverkühn. Mann remains outside the work, pointing to the abyss which separates reality from its possible modes of expression. Zeitblom and Leverkühn are two modes of expression, each speaks partially for the author, but even taken together they do not make a whole, nor is the abyss bridged. Mann demonstrates the difficulty of making any kind of allegation, and the demonstration of this difficulty is his work, while the voices are those of Zeitblom and Leverkühn.

Zeitblom's "kindly view of the world" is mocked by Leverkühn's belief that the physical universe is dynamic and exploding. Zeitblom speaks for the "reverence of man for himself" as opposed to the ungraspable "data of the cosmic creation" as a means of understanding God. Leverkühn, on the other hand, finds in the very "monstrosity of a world set-up . . . the premise for the moral, without which it would have no soil, and perhaps one must call the good the flower of evil." Is Leverkühn suggesting here the justification for his death, and is Zeitblom too limited by the human to see beyond it? Is Leverkühn, for all his apparent withdrawal from humanity, actually the man of action, who takes on himself the responsibility for the breakthrough in human as well as in musical terms? And does not Zeitblom remain the onlooker, clutching his conscience but able to feel nothing but emptiness when the conscienceless Leverkühn is gone? Mann does not make it clear, but this juxtaposition of contradictions is not a negation, it is an approach to reality which is neither positive nor negative, which art alone can clothe with something approaching understanding. To draw a definite conclusion would be as inappropriate as to add a third movement to Beethoven's op. 111. The characteristic of the novel, as of the second movement of Beethoven's work "is the wide gap between the bass and the treble, between the right and the left hand," a gap that Beethoven can make less frightening by an added C sharp, but Mann only by the echo of the last high G of the *Lamentation*. The right and the left hand, Zeitblom and Leverkühn, remain unreconciled except as they are both part of Mann's work in which "coldness and heat, repose and ecstacy are one and the same."

BENJAMIN BENNETT

Structure, Parody, and Myth
in Tonio Kröger

One consequence of that leaning toward the autobiographical which
Thomas Mann so frequently indulges, is that when he speaks of his own
works he tends to concentrate more upon their spirit than upon their structure. The remarks about *Tonio Kröger* in the "Lebensabriß" ["A Sketch of
My Life"] of 1930, however, form somewhat of an exception to this rule:
"Die epische Prosakomposition war hier zum erstenmal als ein geistiges Themengewebe, als muskalischer Beziehungskomplex verstanden, wie es später,
in größerem Maßstabe, beim 'Zauberberg' geschah [Here for the first time
I grasped the idea of epic prose composition as a thought-texture woven of
different themes, as a musically related complex—and later, in *The Magic
Mountain*, I made use of it on an epic scale (trans. H. T. Lowe-Porter. New
York: Knopf, 1970)]." But although Mann's emphasis in this case has led
one or two critics at least to glance at the structure of *Tonio Kröger*, it does
not seem to me that the very simplest and most obvious points have yet been
made.

In particular, eight of the novella's nine chapters are arranged in pairs,
Chinese-box fashion (i.e. 1–9, 2–8, 3–7, 4–6), with Chapter 5 serving as
the pivot on which the whole is balanced. Or to express it differently, the
story represents first a descent and then an ascent through the same four
stages. Chapter 1 corresponds to Chapter 9 in that both deal generally with

From *Revue des langes vivantes* 42, no. 2 (1976). © 1976 by Société François Closset.
Originally entitled "Casting Out Nines: Structure, Parody and Myth in 'Tonio
Kröger.' "

Tonio's ambivalent, melancholy love for the bourgeois, which love is characterized at the end of both chapters in exactly the same words. Chapters 2 and 8 both treat the dance of life, from which the poet is excluded. Chapter 3 describes Tonio's extravagant existence with its violent oscillations between the sensual and the intellectual, which is then refigured by the storm in Chapter 7, along with the symbols of tiger and polar bear. Chapters 4 and 6 both focus directly upon the problem of self-consciousness and self-definition; in Chapter 4 Tonio is "erledigt [expressed]" by Lisaweta with the words "Sie sind ein Bürger [you are a bourgeois (trans. H. T. Lowe-Porter in *Death in Venice and Seven Other Stories*. New York: Vintage Books, 1954. All further references to *Tonio Kröger* are from this translation)]," and in Chapter 6, though he had experienced a certain superior satisfaction at the hotel manager's inability "ihn hierarchisch und bürgerlich unterzubringen [to assign him to his proper category, socially and hierarchically speaking]," still, at the end, by using his printer's proofs to legitimize himself, Tonio must admit in effect that his is a perfectly respectable bourgeois profession. Chapters 4 and 6 are the chapters where Tonio walks through a door and is confronted by a mirror to his true being, in Lisaweta's unfinished painting ("in meinem Kopf sieht es genau aus wie auf dieser Leinwand [inside my head it looks just the way it does on this canvass]") and in the spectacle of men writing against a background of nothing but books ("Literatur [literature]") in what had been the home of his childhood. The self-complicating emptiness of self-consciousness, which had been revealed discursively in Tonio's speeches to Lisaweta, now appears in visual form: "Das Geschoß war drei Stuben tief, deren Verbindungstüren offenstanden. Die Wände waren fast in ihrer ganzen Höhe mit gleichförmig gebundenen Büchern bedeckt, die auf dunklen Gestellen in langen Reihen standen. In jedem Zimmer saß hinter einer Art von Ladentisch ein dürftiger Mensch und schrieb [The storey was three rooms deep, and all the doors stood open. The walls were covered nearly all the way up with long rows of books in uniform bindings, standing in dark-colored bookcases. In each room a poor creature of a man sat writing behind a sort of counter]." These three men sitting one behind the other are clearly meant to remind us of the repeated image one sees when positioned between two mirrors, a phenomenon familiar to everyone who has ever sat in a barber-chair: hence the idea of Tonio's self-consciousness, as "ein dürftiger Mensch [a poor creature of a man]" among nothing but books, mirroring itself in endless hopelessness. And Chapter 5, finally, the central chapter, contains Tonio's decision to return to his "Ausgangspunkt [point of departure]," which he then in a sense does, by passing in reverse order through the stages represented by Chapters 1–4.

Not only is this structure clear in itself, but it also embodies an allusion to the completed first part of Novalis's *Heinrich von Ofterdingen,* which treats exactly the same theme, the development of a young poet, and is constructed on exactly the same pattern. Chapters 1 and 9 of *Ofterdingen* present the vision of universal salvation, first in the form of Heinrich's interrupted dream, then in the full development of Klingsohr's "Märchen [fairy tale]." Chapters 2 and 8 both center on discussions of the nature of poetry, first by way of the merchants' vague admiration for this art, then in the form of Klingsohr's clear, craftsmanlike advice. Chapter 3 is the story of the young man who wins his princess by singing, which prefigures the betrothal of Heinrich and Mathilde in Chapter 7. Chapters 4 and 6 are the two festivities, first that of the Crusaders, at which Heinrich feels somewhat out of place, then his grandfather's in which he can participate wholeheartedly, and Zulima of course corresponds to Mathilde. And Chapter 5 is the descent into the earth, symbolically into the self, the beginning of Heinrich's more explicit self-consciousness and awareness of his fate (which is depicted in the Provençal book), thus the nadir and turning-point at which a more fully realized reenactment of the novel's first four stages becomes possible.

But if *Tonio Kröger* and *Heinrich von Ofterdingen* are similar in structure and theme, the meaning of the two works is entirely different. Whereas self-consciousness is the very principle of Heinrich's development, equivalent in its increase to increasing self-realization—the better Heinrich *knows* himself, the more fully he *is* himself—self-consciousness for Tonio is a snare in which he becomes entangled (Chapters 1–4) and from which he must then extricate himself by a kind of half-deliberate regression (Chapters 6–9). Far from promoting self-development, self-consciousness in *Tonio Kröger,* especially as Tonio practices it in Chapter 4, is a mere aimless whirling upon itself of the intellect when it can seize no external object, and is thus symbolized later by the racing of the ship's propeller when it comes out of the water, which phenomenon, significantly, causes Tonio "arge Übelkeit [violent sickness]." This implied criticism of Novalis's idea of the artist's development is made still clearer by a specific parallel between the pivotal Chapters 5: like Heinrich, who here reads his actual destiny in a book, though he does not yet understand it, Tonio in this chapter *imagines* himself able to read his destiny in *Hamlet,* intends to enact that destiny on location in Elsinor—and turns out to be completely mistaken, for he is not a tragic figure after all. The references to *Hamlet,* incidentally, also remind us of Goethe's *Meister,* and this, together with the parody of Novalis, perhaps supplies a key to Tonio's apology in Chapter 1: "ich möchte, weiß Gott, lieber Heinrich oder Wilhelm heißen [Lord knows I'd rather be called Heinrich or Wilhelm]."

But Tonio is neither Wilhelm Meister, who renounces art, nor Heinrich von Ofterdingen, for whom artistic development is an unimpeded progress of self-discovery.

In its details the parody of Novalis is really quite bitter. There is a fairly clear relation in the Chapters 6 between Heinrich's arrival in Augsburg, where he is welcomed into a happy family, and Tonio's in Lübeck, where he is suspected of being a swindler; but the more specific object of parody here is the following passage from the introduction to Chapter 6 of *Ofterdingen*:

> Es sind die Dichter, diese seltenen Zugmenschen, die zuweilen durch unsere Wohnsitze wandeln, und überall den alten ehrwürdigen Dienst der Menschheit und ihrer ersten Götter, der Gestirne, des Frühlings, der Liebe, des Glücks, der Fruchtbarkeit, der Gesundheit, und des Frohsinns erneuern; sie, die schon hier im Besitz der himmlischen Ruhe sind, und von keinen törichten Begierden umhergetrieben, nur den Duft der irdischen Früchte einatmen, ohne sie zu verzehren und dann unwiderruflich an die Unterwelt gekettet zu sein. Freie Gäste sind sie, deren goldener Fuß nur leise auftritt, und deren Gegenwart in allen unwillkürlich die Flügel ausbreitet.

> [It is the poets, those rare wandering men, who at times stroll through our dwellings and everywhere renew the old and honorable office of mankind and its earliest gods,—the stars, the springtime, love, fortune, fruitfulness, health, and cheerfulness. They are already in possession of heavenly tranquility here on earth; they are not storm-tossed by foolish lusts but only breathe in the fragrance of earthly fruits without consuming them, thereby escaping the irrevocable chains of the underworld. They are untrammeled visitors, whose golden feet make no sound and whose presence involuntarily unfolds wings in everyone.
> (From Novalis, *Henry von Ofterdingen*, trans. Palmer Hitty.
> New York: Frederick Ungar, 1964.
> All further references will be to Novalis.)]

Tonio Kröger—especially in Chapter 6 where Tonio the wanderer delicately sniffs the atmosphere of Lübeck—includes a parody of practically every word here, but most particularly of the idea that our "inner wings" open instinctively in the poet's presence, which is burlesqued in the more or less aggressive suspiciousness of the librarian, the hotel manager and the policeman. There may even be a more specific reference to Novalis, suggested via the idea of "Nasenflügel [wing of the nose]," when we are told that the police-man, upon hearing Tonio's name, "reckte sich auf und öffnete plötzlich seine Nasenlöcher, so weit er konnte [suddenly erect, and expanding his nostrils as wide as he could]." This, in reality, is the way our "wings" open when the poet introduces himself to us.

And in Chapter 7 the parody becomes, if anything, even bitterer, in that Heinrich, who has himself had poetic thoughts about "Der Chor der Gestirne [choir of the stars]" at the end of Chapter 6, is now made to take the role of the freshly scrubbed merchant from Hamburg. In particular, Klingsohr's advice to an overenthusiastic Heinrich in Chapter 7—"Begeisterung ohne Verstand ist unnütz und gefährlich, und der Dichter wird wenig Wunder tun können, wenn er selbst über Wunder erstaunt [Enthusiasm without intelligence is useless and dangerous, and the poet will be capable of few miracles if he himself is astonished by miracles (Novalis)],"—reflects exactly that idea of poetry upon which Tonio bases his conclusion about the young Ham-burger: "Au . . . nein, der hat keine Literatur im Leibe! [Ah, no, he has no literature in his belly]." It is true that some of Klingsohr's advice can be applied to Tonio himself: for example, "Glaubt nicht . . . daß ich das letztere ['jenes überfließende Gefühl einer unbegreiflichen, überschwenglichen Herr-lichkeit'] tadle; aber es muß von selbst kommen, und nicht gesucht werden. Seine sparsame Erscheinung ist wohltätig; öfterer wird sie ermüdend und schwächend [Do not think . . . that I censure the latter ('that gushing feeling of an incomprehensible, exuberant glory'); but it must come of itself and not be sought after. Its infrequent occurrence is beneficent: occurring oftener it becomes fatiguing and enervating] (Novalis)." But in Chapter 7 of *Tonio Kröger*, Tonio, who in Lübeck had deliberately sought a rebirth of feeling, has already learned this lesson and is now about to experience an *unsought* enthusiasm ("es muß von selbst kommen [it must come of itself]") in the storm, whereas the position of the emotion-hunting amateur, Heinrich's po-sition in Chapter 7 of *Ofterdingen*, is occupied by the ridiculous young businessman.

II

We have not really accomplished anything, however, until we go further into the question of what this element of parody implies about the meaning of *Tonio Kröger*, and we can begin by noting that there is also a specific parallel between the Chapters 1 in Mann and Novalis. Heinrich's father, we recall, during his stay in Rome, had actually had a chance to achieve the blue flower but had failed to commit himself to that quest, and this idea is repeated in the figure of Tonio's father, a man "mit sinnenden blauen Augen [with thoughtful blue eyes]" who always wears "eine Feldblume [a wild-flower]" and who has imported his wife from even further south. The point of this parallel is to suggest, as is also suggested by Hans's flash of interest in *Don Carlos,* by the figure of the lieutenant reading his poetry, and by the Romantic merchant on shipboard, that even in normal bourgeois life there is an inherent poetic tendency, a desire for salvation through the intellect. Tonio and Heinrich are both the realization of a repressed or confused tendency in their own fathers. The poet merely realizes a power which is latent in all men, or as Klingsohr says, "Es ist recht übel . . . daß die Poesie einen besondern Namen hat, und die Dichter eine besondere Zunft ausma-chen. Es ist gar nichts Besonderes. Es ist die eigentümliche Handlungsweise des menschlichen Geistes. Dichtet und trachtet nicht jeder Mensch in jeder Minute? [It is too bad . . . that poetry has a special name and that poets make up a special guild. It is not anything special at all. It is the peculiar mode of activity of the human mind. Does not everybody use his mind and his imagination all the time? (Novalis)]."

In *Tonio Kröger,* in fact, despite Tonio's attempt to understand art as a kind of crime against bourgeois order, there is a suggestion of direct *kinship* between the blond, blue-eyed ones and precisely those artists who are most fully committed to their art. "Iwanowna" is of course the patronymic derived from the Russian equivalent of "Johann" or "Hans," so that it means essen-tially "Hansen," and Lisaweta is thus a kind of sister to Tonio's childhood friend; and when we hear of the "aggressive style" in which Tonio's colleague Adalbert exclaims "Gott verdamme den Frühling! [God damn the spring!]," we are inclined to recall Hans's "verwöhnte und selbstbewußte Art, seine Sympathien und Abneigungen kundzugeben [spoilt and arbitrary way of an-nouncing his likes and dislikes]." These touches, together with Tonio's use of his art as bourgeois self-legitimization in Lübeck, make clear that the basis for the parody of Novalis is a recognition that art, as practiced by those whom Tonio calls "ihr Anbeter der Schönheit [you adorers of the beautiful]," is nothing but bourgeois existence all over again. Tonio may be "ein verirrter Bürger [a bourgeois *manqué*]," but Lisaweta, Adalbert and Heinrich von Ofterdingen are "Bürger [bourgeois]" without even being "verirrt." They have all found a niche in society with which they are satisfied. The atmo-sphere in Lisaweta's studio may contain that "Konflikt und Gegensatz [con-flict and contradiction]" which torments Tonio, but Lisaweta herself is not at all bothered by it; she divides her life, like her room, into two distinct compartments, and does not let one interfere with the other. Her art is not a problem to her, and it is precisely the feeling of art as a *problem* that makes

Tonio consider himself unique in his "Künstlertum . . . so tief, so von An-
beginn und Schicksals wegen, daß keine Sehnsucht ihm süßer und empfin-
denswerter erscheint als die nach den Wonnen der Gewöhnlichkeit [way of
being an artist that goes so deep and is so much a matter of origins and
destinies that no longing seems to it sweeter and more worth knowing than
longing after the bliss of the commonplace]."

The idea of a close kinship between the fully committed artist and the
simple burgher is developed by yet another parody woven into the novella's
structure, the parody of yet another well-known nine-part work in German
literature, Goethe's *Hermann und Dorothea*. This poem as a whole of course
bears less relation to *Tonio Kröger* than *Ofterdingen* does, but the section-
by-section parallels are obvious enough to make the parody unmistakable. It
is not entirely clear why Canto II of *Hermann und Dorothea* should be entitled "Terpsichore," but it is perfectly clear that this muse presides over
Chapter 2 of *Tonio Kröger*, the dance-chapter, and Tonio's *faux pas* in dancing *moulinet des dames* corresponds to Hermann's at the neighbor's house
when he asks about "Pamina" and "Tamino." Then Tonio's going forth into
the world in Chapter 3 recalls the father's wish in Goethe's "es solle sich
Hermann auf Reisen / Bald begeben [that Hermann ought to travelling /
Soon betake himself]," and when we hear that "Die alte Familie der Kröger war
nach und nach in einen Zustand des Abbröckelns und der Zersetzung geraten
[the old Kröger family soon declined]," we think of the whole of the father's
long speech about degenerate modern youth and Hermann in particular. But
the most striking parody is Tonio's conversation with Lisaweta in Chapter 4,
which corresponds to Hermann's conversation with his mother in Canto IV;
both conversations arrive at exactly the same conclusion: that the young man
in question has been romanticizing his situation—Tonio in his self-image as
doomed artist, Hermann in his as a soldier—and really ought to be counted
as "ein Bürger [a bourgeois]." And then, finally, at the end of Chapter 8,
Tonio's assistance to the fallen Danish girl is a comic reenactment of Hermann's catching of Dorothea at the end of Canto VIII, when she stumbles.

The pattern of parody in *Tonio Kröger*, then, is the following: Chapter 1,
Ofterdingen; Chapters 2, 3, 4, *Hermann*; Chapter 5, 6, 7, *Ofterdingen*;
Chapter 8, *Hermann*. The parody of Novalis is thus interwoven with that of
Goethe, and the suggestion, clearly, is that the development of the quintessential artist, leading toward a metaphysical marriage by which the whole
world is redeemed, is not basically different from the development of the
quintessential bourgeois, which culminates in a thoroughly mundane marriage. In both cases the central character finds "the right way" to his destiny,
and from the perspective of *Tonio Kröger* this is a bit of an oversimplifica-

tion, "weil es für etliche einen richtigen Weg überhaupt nicht gibt [because for some people there is no such thing as a right way]." The parodies thus elaborate the idea of Tonio's position "zwischen zwei Welten [between two worlds]," but with the added suggestion that these "two worlds" are not really different from one another.

III

There is, however, more to be said about this suggestion. We have already pointed out that despite Tonio's references to the blue-eyed ones "die den Geist nicht nötig haben [who do not need minds]," a number of incidents in the story clearly reflect the existence of an ingrained intellectual tendency or desire in precisely these people. The main incidents we have in mind, moreover, are three in number and serve by their disposition to mark off yet another manifestation of the story's structure, a division into three phases of three chapters each. The first phase is introduced in Chapter 1 by Hans's interest in Tonio and in *Don Carlos*; the second in Chapter 4 by the story of the lieutenant with his poetry; and the third in Chapter 7 by the star-struck Hamburger. There is, moreover, a clear progression from phase to phase. At first, in the case of Hans, Tonio encourages this inchoate bourgeois intellectuality, hoping thereby to establish a bond between himself and society at large. In the second phase, Tonio specifically rejects the idea of such encouragement ("man sollte nicht Leute, die viel lieber in Pferdebüchern mit Momentaufnahmen lesen, zur Poesie verführen wollen! [one ought not to tempt to read poetry those who would much rather read books about the instantaneous photography of horses!]") and had been mortally embarrassed at the lieutenant's making a spectacle of himself, for it now somehow gratifies him to think of art as a kind of shameful offense against life. But by the time Tonio encounters the young man on shipboard, he has clearly passed beyond this stage, since he is not embarrassed at all; he simply discounts the notion that such forced cosmological humility has anything to do with literature ("nein, der hat keine Literatur im Leibe! [No, he has no literature in his belly]") and continuous listening to the man's chatter "mit einem heimlichen und freundschaftlichen Gefühl [and was privately drawn to it]."

By Chapter 7, therefore, Tonio has achieved a new equilibrium; he no longer reacts emotionally, as he had earlier, to signs of an intellectual stirring in the bourgeois. And what this at least ought to mean, as we have already suggested in connection with the structural similarity and philosophical contrast to *Ofterdingen*, is that Tonio is now somehow managing to extricate himself from the confusions of self-consciousness. We shall begin to understand more fully how this works if we note that each of at least the first two phases in the novella (Chapters 1–3 and 4–6) focuses upon a specific question.

The question Tonio finds himself asking in Chapter 1 is the fundamental question of self-consciousness, "What am I?"—"Was aber ist mit mir, und wie wird dies alles ablaufen? [But what is the matter with me, and what will be the end of it?]." In reality, however, even at this early point, Tonio has already begun writing and so already knows, or at least suspects, that his destiny has to do with "[die] Macht des Geistes und Wortes, die lächelnd über dem unbewußten und stummen Leben thront [the power of intellect, the power of the word, that lords it with a smile over the unconscious and inarticulate]." The attempt to draw Hans Hansen over to his side is merely an attempt to avoid, or at least postpone the uncomfortable consequences of this knowledge by establishing a direct link with human normality; and even as a child Tonio senses that this attempt is self-contradictory and futile, in the same way that later he knows there is no chance of Inge Holm's coming to him in the corridor. By Chapter 3, therefore, he at last seems to be facing the facts squarely, "Denn er war groß und klug geworden, hatte begriffen, was für eine Bewandtnis es mit ihm hatte [For he was grown up and sensible and had come to realize how things stood with him]."

But in the final analysis, even Tonio's commitment to literature is only another way of *avoiding* the question "What am I?"

> Er arbeitete nicht wie jemand, der arbeitet, um zu leben, sondern wie einer, der nichts will als arbeiten, weil er sich als lebendigen Menschen für nichts achtet, nur als Schaffender in Betracht zu kommen wünscht und im übrigen grau und unauffällig umhergeht, wie ein abgeschminkter Schauspieler, der nichts ist, solange er nichts darzustellen hat.

> [He worked, not like a man who works that he may live; but as one who is bent on doing nothing but work; having no regard for himself as a human being but only as a creator; moving about grey and unobtrusive among his fellows like an actor without his make-up, who counts for nothing as soon as he stops representing something else.]

Tonio thus attempts to resolve the question of the self by the simple expedient of *eliminating* the self, which cannot possibly work. The idea "daß man gestorben sein muß, um ganz ein Schaffender zu sein [that one must die to life in order to be utterly a creator]" contains an obvious logical contradiction, and Chapter 4, accordingly, opens with the question "Störe ich? [shall I disturb you?]." The answer to this question is of course yes; Tonio's "ich" is still there, as a "disturbing" element in his calculations.

In Chapter 4, then, at the beginning of the story's second phase, Tonio formulates his still unanswered question more generally, "Aber *was ist* der Künstler? [But what is it, to be an artist?]." And like the question in Chapter 1, this question is basically rhetorical, for Tonio thinks he already knows the answer. The artist, as opposed to the conventional, instinctive bourgeois, is that man who has committed himself wholly to the practice of intellectual consciousness and thus, by consequence, to a kind of self-destruction.

> Ist Ihnen das Herz zu voll, fühlen Sie sich von einem süßen oder erhabenen Erlebnis allzusehr ergriffen: nichts einfacher! Sie gehen zum Literaten, und alles wird in kürzester Frist geregelt sein. Er wird Ihnen Ihre Angelegenheit analysieren und formulieren, bei Namen nennen, aussprechen und zum Reden bringen, wird Ihnen das Ganze für alle Zeit erledigen und gleichgültig machen. . . . Was ausgesprochen ist, so lautet sein Glaubensbekenntnis, ist erledigt. Ist die ganze Welt ausgesprochen, so ist sie erledigt, erlöst, abgetan.

> [If your heart is too full, if you are overpowered with the emotions of some sweet or exalted moment—nothing simpler! Go to the literary man, he will put it all straight for you instanter. He will analyze and formulate your affair, label it and express it and polish it off and make you indifferent to it for time and eternity. . . . What is uttered, so runs this credo, is finished and done with. If the whole world could be expressed, it would be saved, finished and done.]

Explicit, articulable consciousness is the death of experience, and if we cease to experience, do we not cease to exist? Can the artist, therefore, even be said to exist in the first place? "Ist der Künstler überhaupt ein Mann? Man frage 'das Weib' danach! Mir scheint, wir Künstler teilen alle ein wenig das Schicksal jener präparierten päpstlichen Sänger [Is an artist a male, anyhow? Ask the females! It seems to me we artists are all of us something like those unsexed papal singers]." Not only is the artist not "ein Mann [a male]," he is not even "ein Mensch [a human being]": "Sie [you, the artist] werden kaum die Augen aufzuschlagen und ein Wort zu sprechen brauchen, und jedermann wird wissen, daß Sie kein Mensch sind, sondern irgend etwas

Fremdes, Befremdendes, anderes [you hardly need to give a glance or speak a word before everyone knows you are not a human being, but something else: something queer, different, inimical]."

This at least is what Tonio thinks, but it still does not answer his question because he himself after all still *does* exist. His own feeling refutes his definition of the artist as a mere intellectual, and it is for this reason that he decides to return to his native city, in the hope of penetrating beyond the domain of self-consciousness and rediscovering the true organic roots of his personal destiny. As we have already seen, however, he is unsuccessful in this. His search for his own origin is only a potentiation of self-consciousness, it is a self-consciousness now critically applied to self-consciousness itself, and this is revealed to Tonio when, on opening the door of his own house, he is confronted by that image of mirror-mirroring-mirror which we have discussed above. What Tonio learns here is that self-consciousness does in truth lead toward non-existence, that when developed to a sufficient degree it becomes not art but rather a useless, hopeless and above all unproductive vortex of self-preoccupation comparable to the racing of a ship's propeller when it leaves the water. This lesson, combined with the enforced recognition (when he legitimizes himself to the policeman) that his own art is not a daredevil teetering on the brink of nonentity so much as a perfectly acceptable bourgeois pursuit, implies for Tonio the very simple but very important conclusion that *there is no such thing as the quintessential artist*. There is no such thing as an artist *totally* committed to the conscious analysis and articulation of all reality, for such a man would be, even in relation to himself, *nothing* but a mirror, which is impossible, and even if he managed somehow to exist, he would certainly not produce.

As a corollary to this proposition, moreover, it follows that Tonio's distinction between those who live and those who sacrifice life to art is not in reality nearly so strict as he had wanted it to be, and his recognition of this now makes him receptive to a truth which is expressed throughout the story via the thematic appearance of intellectual tendencies in otherwise normal people: the truth that *there is no such thing as the quintessential bourgeois*. Hence Tonio's reaction, or lack of it, to the sentiments of the young man on deck. Earlier, he had felt the lieutenant's poetry as a kind of personal attack and had concluded his relation of the incident by saying, with perfect illogic but with a serious if strained tragic pride, "Da stand er und büßte in großer Verlegenheit den Irrtum, daß man ein Blättchen pflücken dürfe, ein einziges, vom Lorbeerbaume der Kunst, ohne mit seinem Leben dafür zu zahlen [There he stood, suffering embarrassment for the mistake of thinking that one may pluck a single leaf from the laurel tree of art without paying

for it with his life]." But now, confronted with the melancholy speculations
of his fellow-passenger, Tonio simply thinks, "nein, der hat keine Literatur
im Leibe [No, he has no literature in his belly]," and expresses thereby the
recognition that what he is being regaled with is a perfectly normal manifestation of bourgeois existence, having no special relation to his own profession or self-esteem. The pure bliss of a bourgeois existence wholly contained
within its narrow horizons simply never happens in reality, any more than
does the pure, horizonless universality of an artistic existence. Hence the two
interwoven parodies we have spoken of, for the works parodied represent
things and states that do not really exist. In reality there is not a world of
art opposed to a world of life. There is only one world, which includes all
men with their various degrees and modes of self-consciousness, the world
where Hans and Lisaweta are brother and sister, and although this is a world
in which Tonio can feel rather more at ease than he had before, it is also a
world in which the question of the nature and the role and the specific
necessity of art seems further than ever from being answered. . . .

But surely we cannot conclude with the idea that poetry is poetry, as
opposed to "literature," *only* by virtue of the poet's own subjective notion
of what he is doing. Surely true poetry must enter into a specifically poetic
relation with the *reader* as well. Or in particular, there must be a way for
the reader at least to sense that the work is the product of a poetic mentality;
otherwise the work is bound to affect him merely as "literature," as an
intellectually detached "Kaltstellen [putting on ice]" of human experience,
thus ultimately nihilistic, rather than a self-affirmative human activity by
which our existence is shaped and held fast.

And the key idea for understanding the relation of poetry to its reader
is an idea we have already introduced, the idea of *myth*, which we must now
go into a bit more deeply, especially in its Nietzschean sense. In the first
place, a myth is not something one *believes* in objectively:

> Denn dies ist die Art, wie Religionen abzusterben pflegen: wenn
> nämlich die mythischen Voraussetzungen einer Religion unter den
> strengen, verstandesmässigen Augen eines rechtgläubigen Dog-
> matismus als eine fertige Summe von historischen Ereignissen
> systematisirt werden und man anfängt, ängstlich di Glaubwür-
> digkeit der Mythen zu vertheidigen.

> [For this is the way in which religions are wont to die out: under
> the stern, intelligent eyes of an orthodox dogmatism, the mythical
> premises of a religion are systematized as a total sum of historical

events; one begins apprehensively to defend the credibility of the
myths.

> (Nietzsche, *The Birth of Tragedy and the Case of Wagner*,
> trans. Walter Kaufmann. New York: Vintage Books, 1967.
> All further references will be to Nietzsche.)]

The Greek did not believe in his gods, but rather he knew, in the very act
of worshipping, that those gods represented an illusion—"Es ist ein Traum!
Ich will ihn weiter träumen! [It is a dream! I will dream on! (Nietzsche)]"—
just as Tonio knows full well that his Danish vision of"das Leben [life]" is
illusory. A myth is not an object of belief but rather a continuing mental
activity, an artistic, illusion-creating activity, on the part of the celebrant.
The utter horror of existence on the brink of the nameless void, says
Nietzsche, that horror which the Greeks experienced more deeply than anyone else, "wurde von den Griechen durch jene künstlerische *Mittelwelt* der
Olympier fortwährend von Neuem überwunden, jedenfalls verhüllt und dem
Anblick entzogen [was again and again overcome by the Greeks with the aid
of the Olympian *middle world* of art; or at any rate it was veiled and withdrawn from sight]." Especially important here are the words "fortwährend
von Neuem"; a myth is not a fact that exists once and for all, but rather
exists only by virtue of the continuing creative activity that brings it forth.

The importance of these considerations becomes clear as soon as we
recognize that the myth with which *we* are presented as readers, in *Tonio
Kröger*, is not Tonio's own personal myth of the blond, blue-eyed ones. The
vision experienced by Tonio, after all, depends precisely upon his exclusion
from verbal intercourse, whereas we, as readers, are confronted with language and nothing but. Clearly, from the point of view of the reader, the
central myth of *Tonio Kröger* is *the myth of the poet*—again, as in Hölderlin—and that we are in fact meant to approach this idea as a myth is made
clear to us *by the analogy* with Tonio's vision of "das Leben." Just as Tonio
knows perfectly well that his Danish vision is illusory, so also we, for our
part, know that objectively speaking there is no difference whatever between
"poetry" and "literature." What we learn from Tonio's insistence upon his
"Bürgerliebe [bourgeois love]," however, is that we have an ethical duty to
insist upon the differentness of poetry, regardless of what we "know" objectively. There must be such a thing as poetry; otherwise mankind is utterly
abandoned to its intellectual penchant for nothingness. And to the extent,
then, that we do carry out that ethical duty, to the extent that we realize the
story as poetry by our insistence upon *taking* it as such, to precisely that
extent *Tonio Kröger is* poetry in its own definition.

The deepest intention of the story, therefore, is not to explain or demonstrate an objective difference between poetry and literature, but rather to maneuver the reader into a position of understanding the absolute need for poetry, a position in which he has no choice but to affirm the poetic as opposed to the literary, whereupon such affirmation, as a continuing creative attitude, becomes poetry's existence. The brilliance of *Tonio Kröger* is thus contained less in what it does say than in what it does *not* say. Tonio's concluding letter does not in any concrete particular reflect an advance beyond his position in Chapter 4; his mood is more reconciled but his position is still the same. And the decisive event in Chapter 8 ("Dann aber kam einer [ein Tag], an welchem etwas geschah [But then came one [day] on which something happened]" derives its eventfulness entirely from Tonio's imagination, from the way he insists on seeing it. Considered objectively, therefore, the story is unconvincing; it does not convince us that either Tonio or we ourselves have really learned anything about the nature of poetry. But again, precisely this is the intention. What we are meant to learn is that poetry exists, as distinct from literature, only by virtue of our continuing insistence upon it, not as a demonstrable quality of this or that text, and a more convincing demonstration of the nature of poetry would only have clouded this truth. Hölderlin's Great Night of the World does not pass over automatically; it requires of us, rather, that spirit of thanksgiving (at least "einiger Dank"), that poetically affirmative attitude which sees even in the most common and trivial things, like bread and wine or Hans and Inge, not their superficial objective nature but rather symbols of unchanging humanity, of that higher human state which was and will be and at the same time always *is,* by virtue of our own visionary energy.

ELAINE MURDAUGH

Joseph and His Brothers: *Myth, Historical Consciousness, and God Emerging*

In the beginning of his book *Myth and Reality* Mircea Eliade points out that the twentieth-century western scholars, in contrast to their predecessors, have once again taken the myth seriously and have come to view it as it was in the archaic societies, as something "sacred, exemplary, significant." Freud and Jung were, of course, among the first to make the myth "respectable" and more recently, Kerényi, Campbell, Graves, and Eliade himself have explored and illuminated the important role that myths have played in the development of culture.

Thomas Mann was very well read in (and sympathetic to) the works of Freud by the thirties, but we know from his own correspondence that he received a great deal, perhaps most, of his information on mythology from Karl Kerényi. What seems to have captured his imagination was the realization that myths do not belong to the far distant past but are operating in the present. Without the benefit of the later essays by Jung (who only began writing about the archetype and the collective consciousness in 1934), the theories of the structural anthropologists, or such insightful works as Eliade's *Myth of the Eternal Return*, Mann perceived himself the indestructable presence of the myth in everyday life and the ineluctability of its effect on even the most rational modes of thought and behavior.

In his essay, "Freud und die Zukunft" ["Freud and the Future"] (1936)

From *Salvation in the Secular: The Moral Law in Thomas Mann's "Joseph und seine Brüder"* (Stanford German Studies, vol. 10). © 1976 by Herbert Lang und Cie AG and Peter Lang GmbH. Originally entitled "Myth and the Emergence of Historical Consciousness" and "The Fallen God."

he concluded that life does not consist of an infinite number of unique occurrences but that it is, in fact, a mixture of elements, only part of which are individual. The rest are "formelhaft," that is, paradigmatic and prescribed and belong to a realm which both predates and transcends the individual occurrence. By "life" Mann meant more than just human behavior, although this is the locus of most of his interest, but rather all life, all natural phenomena and events. With dry humor he quipped:

> Tatsächlich wüsste (der Mensch) sich, wenn seine Realität im Einmalig-Gegenwärtigen läge, überhaupt nicht zu benehmen, wäre haltlos, ratlos, verlegen und verwirrt im Verhältnis zu sich selbst, wüsste nicht mit welchem Fusse antreten und was für ein Gesicht machen.

> [Actually if his existence consisted merely in the unique and the present, he would not know how to conduct himself at all; he would be confused, helpless, unstable in his own self-regard, would not know which foot to put foremost or what sort of face to put on.
> ("Freud and the Future," trans. H. T. Lowe-Porter.
> In *Freud, Goethe, Wagner.* New York: Knopf, 1937.
> Henceforth referred to as "Freud.")]

Both human dignity and the confidence of one's actions (Spielsicherheit) come from the fact that with each act a timeless pattern asserted itself once again in the individual, and the eternal once again clothed itself with the present. This he called "mythical dignity," dignified because it stemmed from the unconscious eternal. We can see then, that by the time he set to work on the Joseph novels, Mann had defined the whole of human experience as a theme in variations in which the individual life adheres, must adhere, and draws its dignity from the adherence to mythical formulae which are operating in the unconscious.

Although the above quotation appears in an essay on Freud, the "Formelhaft-Unpersönliche [formal and impersonal]" which directs human life, rather suggests the Jungian archetype, which [Jung] defined years later (1945) as "an autonomous primordial image which is universally present in the preconscious make-up of the human psyche." These archetypal images, according to Jung, are peculiar to the whole human species and probably originated with it, and the self-patterning after these images was the "human quality of the human being." Mann uses the Jungian term "mythical collective" both in the novel and in his discussions of it, and the archetype makes its appearance in such motifs as that of the "earth mother" (Isis-Ishtar-Mut) or the "demon brother" (Set-Cain-Ishmael). But in the Mannian concept of the "mythical-collective" both the myth, which is essentially verbal (i.e., Zeus murders Typhon), and the archetype, which is nominal (i.e., father murderer, demon brother, prankster, earth mother), are subsumed under the uniquely Mannian idea of the personal life-myth. The life-myth was given with the name (we will later see how coercive the name can be) so that Abraham obeys his name's obligation to be the "father of many." Isaak acts out the "spared sacrifice," Jaakob and Esau carry out their respective roles as the "Right wrong one" and the "Wrong right one," and all of Jaakob's sons, from the "tower of strength" to the "child of death" act out their name myths. But myth did not only prescribe life roles, it also dominated all facets of primitive life. As Lesser points out, even natural catastrophes lacked uniqueness. Both flood and drought were seen to follow the "Urvorgang und Muster aller Strafheimsuchung [archetypical pattern of divine visitation]," while both Babylonian Ark and Egyptian grain warehouses were manifestations of the "Beispiel und Urmuster aller Weisheit . . . aller wissenden Vorsorge [archetypical example of all wisdom . . . all-knowing precautions]."

Of greatest interest to us, however, is the force of the myth on human behavior, because this introduces the question of morality and responsibility, which by their nature tend to be predicated on an individualized decision-making process. The myth is extra-personal and stems from an experience common to all members of a given group, whether it be culture, sub-culture, or humanity in general. Whether the members of the group exist simultaneously (as in a class), or whether they arise consecutively over a period of generations (as in a lineage), does not greatly alter Jung's judgment that: "A group experience takes place on a lower level of consciousness than the experience of an individual." Certainly in Mann's treatment of the myth, it is axiomatic that the collective mentality belongs to a qualitatively different order than the individual mentality. The myth which the collective mind brings forth (and which appears to be the medium in which it exists) belongs to a "lower order" in the sense that it points to a more primitive level of psychic development, but at the same time it reflects the "higher" realm of the legendary heroes and gods. This ambiguous nature of the myth is clearly expressed in Kerényi's Prolegomena:

> The mythological "fundamentalist" (or "founder") who, by immersion in the self, dives down to his own foundations, founds his world. He builds it up for himself on a foundation where everything is an outflowing, a sprouting and springing up—"orig-

inal" (ursprünglich) in the fullest sense of the word, and consequently divine. *The divinity of everything mythological is as
obvious as the originality of everything divine* [emphasis mine].

The idea of the myth as "divine foundation," that is, as sub- and superhuman motivation, is present in the novel in the theme of the revolving
sphere, and in the fact that the myth is located both in the subconscious
(i.e., in Jaakob's and Joseph's dreams) and also "in the stars." This double
nature of myth, being both libidinal and at the same time, ideal, allows the
author to discredit the mythical existence as obsolete on the one hand and
to find it the source of human dignity on the other.

All the important characters in the first two books of the tetralogy lead
lives which are an enactment of their name-myth, but with the appearance
of Laban and the report of his filicide, the mythical life abruptly becomes
discredited. Indeed, it is this ritual of son-sacrifice, along with the variation
of son-castration, which reveals the demonic side of the myth, the side which
is not the source of human dignity, but potentially its anathema. Abraham
distinguishes himself morally from Laban and shows himself to be the servant
of the "new" precisely because he abandons the actual enactment of the
myth and substitutes the symbol instead, while Laban carries out literally
the sacrifice of the man-child. Yet while Abraham, by refraining from filicide,
lays aside the myth, Ishmael takes it up again by willingly acting the role of
Typhon, the father-castrator and murderer, who waits "in mörderischer An-
wärterschaft [in a state of murderous expectation]." To be sure, for lack of
opportunity he never literally carries it out, but he does attempt to "unman"
Abraham by toying ("Scherzen") homosexually with the manhood of his son
Isaak, and later he encourages Esau not only to commit patricide ("mit der
Sichel [with the sickle]") but also to consume the body—an obvious reference to Freud's account of original sin. By the time that Mut-em-enet whis-
pers to Joseph in the third volume that "das Weib ist die Mutter der Welt;
ihr Sohn ist der Mann, und jeder Mann zeugt in der Mutter [woman is the
mother of the world, her son is her husband, and every man begets upon his
mother]" the literal enactment of the myth has been well established as
morally dubious. Yet, offensive as these mythical roles of murder and incest
may be, they remain sanctioned, in a sense, by their sheer fundamentality.
That is, Freudian and Jungian psychology define them as fundamental components in the human psyche, and they therefore cannot simply be condemned and done away with. Indeed, the novel does not condemn these roles
themselves, but only the ignorance of those who carry them out literally
when the world spirit has moved on to a more abstract-symbolical relation-

ship to the myth, and son-circumcision has come to replace son-sacrifice. It is therefore the intention of this study to trace in detail the development of the conscious ego out of the mythical form of existence and the reintegration of the obsolete and morally questionable myth into the conscious and morally responsible life. While the narrator of the Joseph novel declares his intention to go back in time to the beginnings of human consciousness, we will proceed in the opposite direction and move from that earliest point forward, to determine when and under what circumstances God, the human ego, and the morally conscious self come into being.

THE ROLE OF TIME

The turning point in the reappraisal of the myth from the divine paradigm of human behavior to a morally questionable form of existence occurs simultaneously with the discovery of the self and its place in time. This does not occur at a specific point, but emerges gradually in the novel as historical consciousness begins to assert itself; until that time, the early Hebrews must be considered "primitives." Mircea Eliade points out that among primitives, all aspects of life, "every responsible activity in pursuit of a definite end is, for the archaic world, a ritual" (Cosmos, p. 28). Moreover, the primitive mentality is not only not able to act with novelty, but when confronted with the unique event, will not even recognize it as such. After two or three centuries the memory of historical events is modified to such an extent that these events lose their uniqueness and "enter into the mold of archaic mentality, which cannot accept what is individual and preserves only what is exemplary." "Interest in the 'irreversible' and the 'new' in history is a recent discovery in the life of humanity. On the contrary, archaic humanity ... defended itself, to the utmost of its powers against all the novelty and irreversibility which history entails." Eliade stresses the traumatic nature of a primitive people's discovery of history, and points out that among such peoples, the mythical mode keeps trying to reassert itself. He notes that the New Year "scenarios" in which the world is recreated, seem to be especially dramatic among such peoples as the Hebrews and Egyptians, and suggests that their discovery of history causes them to feel "a deeper need to regenerate themselves periodically by abolishing past time and reactualizing the cosmogony." We might recall that in the novel, Egypt has a New Year's celebration second to none, one which involves days of feasting on food provided by the state. The timelessness represented by the myth is seen by the author as an undesirable state because it amounted to "das stehende Nichts, so gut und schlecht wie dieses, das absolut Uninteressante [the per-

manent nothingness, as good and bad as this, the absolutely uninteresting],"
but the growth out of the mythical mode into historicity was fraught with
hazards. One of these hazards was the incursion of guilt. The narrator reminds us that the discovery of Jahwe brought with it the possibility of falling
away from Him and thereby sinning: "Durch Abraham und seinen Bund
war etwas in die Welt gekommen, was zuvor nicht darin gewesen war und
was die Völker nicht kannten: die verfluchte Möglichkeit des Bundesbruches,
des Abfalls von Gott [through Abraham and his bond something had come
into the world that had never been there before and which the peoples did
not know—the accursed possibility that the bond might be broken, that one
might fall away from God]." Eliade points out, however, that historical memory itself is a source of guilt and anxiety, and that the recollection of personal
events "that derive from no archetype" may well be felt as "sinful." We
recall that Joseph declares to Potiphar of his tribe "Wir wissen so gut wie
allein in der Welt, was die Sünde ist [We, almost alone in the world, know
what sin is]," and we detect an unmistakable note of boastfulness in this
remark. To be sure, Eliade has attached the element of guilt to the individual-
historical urge, while the children of Abraham are sinful precisely when they
revert to the obsolete myth, as when Ishmael suggests to Esau that he kill
and devour his father. But this seeming contradiction is accounted for by the
paradoxical nature of "sin," which is commanded and yet accursed, "was
gefordert ist und doch verwehrt, geboten aber verflucht [what is commanded
and yet forbidden, ordered but accursed]." And it is precisely this paradox
which makes up the rigorous progressive element among the Jahwe followers,
not only the punishing renunciation of the comforts of the mythical mode,
but also the precarious situation of the developing ego. The assertion of ego
was accursed because, in Freudian terms, it was in defiance of the parental
authority (i.e. God) yet among the children of the Covenant it was also
commanded. (See "Wie Abraham Gott entdeckte" ["How Abraham Found
God"]). This is illustrated most clearly in Jaakob's denial that Eliezer could
be the original servant to Abraham, a declaration that he himself regards as
sinful, but which, as we will later discuss, is actually a breakthrough of the
historical-individual element in the "god-concern" of the patriarchs.

But aside from the question of guilt, how is it that the perception of
historical time is considered to be simultaneous in occurrence with the appearance of ego, and what is it about the perception of a series of single,
irreversible events that presupposes a governing consciousness while the existence among repeated (i.e. timeless) events does not? Hans Meyerhof, in a
discussion of Kant, provides an answer to this question by exploring the
nature of the perception of time which, we might recall, Kant located in the

human mind and not in the 'thing in itself." Meyerhof explains, using Kant's ideas, that one must assume the presence of some synthesizing or organizing agent with the self whose function it is to make the experience of temporal flow intelligible. "The self, from this point of view, is not only a passive recipient of stimuli . . . but an active center, controlling, modifying, organizing, and integrating these stimuli. . . . In other words, time has the quality of duration because some functions of the self endure through time; or, conversely, we gain a primitive notion of an enduring, identical self in and through the experience of temporal duration." The experience of temporal flow and the recognition of change presupposes a fixed self-consciousness, an ego which identifies itself or part of itself as constant while witnessing or undergoing change. In the Schopenhauerean world view as well, time is one of the conditions brought (along with space and causality) to the world-as-will by the conscious subject, "even without the knowledge of the object itself, that is to say, in Kant's language, they reside a priori in our consciousness." We need only make a slight shift in perspective to suggest that time is not only a priori in consciousness, but also that the advent of consciousness (out of unconsciousness) brings with it the discovery of time, and with it, the discovery of the individual. The rather high degree of consciousness called for by the "Gottessorge [anxiety about God]" in *Joseph* has as its first stage and manifestation the consciousness of historical time, as we will see developing among the patriarchs. It is as if self-knowledge, or any degree of knowledge at all, must be bought at the cost of mortality. (This, as we might recall from Genesis, is precisely what occurs in the Garden of Eden when the punishment for the knowledge of good and evil is a lifetime of labor ending in death.) Schopenhauer specifically states: "Time is the form by means of which self-knowledge becomes possible to the individual will, which originally and in itself is without knowledge." In addition, time (with space) makes up the principle by which individuation takes place, "for it is only by means of time and space that something which is one and the same according to its nature . . . appears as different, as a plurality of coexistent and successive things. Consequently, time and space are the *principium individuationis*." Historicization, individualization, and consciousness are subsumed under the single idea of personal development, and Abraham's discovery of time, his ego, and the historical world (which we will discuss in the chapter on patriarchs) were not only simultaneous, but merely different facets of a single magnificent idea, the idea of the historically developing self. Thus the Covenant, Abraham's contract with himself, is born out of the awareness of individual becoming, out of "das Gefühl für den Weg, das Weiterschreiten, die Aenderung, die Entwicklung [the feeling for the way, for moving on, change, development]." Not only on the personal but also on the racial level, the advent of the awareness of time and history is equated with the advent of human rationality. Schopenhauer equates the historical consciousness of the human race to the faculty of reason in the individual, and we may clearly consider this a positive value judgment of the historical experience. Schopenhauer also suggests that the acquisition of history in the human race marks the point of transition from bestial life to humanity, for only through history does a people become conscious of itself. History is therefore "rational self-consciousness of the human race; it is to the race what the reflected and connected consciousness, conditioned by the faculty of reason, is to the individual." It is for lack of this historical awareness that the beasts remain imprisoned in momentary perception and the timeless mythical existence of the primitive, even while it is harmless, is prerational, immature, and not wholly worthy of the human being.

THE MEDIATION OF "GESCHICHTE [NARRATIVE HISTORY]"

The development from the unconscious-mythical to the conscious-historical is therefore vital to the spiritual maturation of the Hebrews, and the transition from the one state to the other reveals itself in the gradual changing of their (and the novel's) understanding of the meaning of "Geschichte," from "myth" or "festival" to "history." In the "Höllenfahrt" ["Descent into Hell"], the narrator initially establishes "Geschichte" as meaning myth when he says of the Romance of the Soul: "Die Geschichte des Menschen ist älter als die materielle Welt, die seines Willens Werk ist, älter als das Leben, das auf seinem Willen steht [the history of man is older than the material world which is the work of his will, older than life, which rests upon his will]." Shortly thereafter, however, the term "Geschichte" becomes tied up with the concept of time and the word begins to carry the additional meaning of a single narrated event:

> Geschichte ist das Geschehene und was fort und fort geschieht in der Zeit. Aber so ist sie auch das Geschichtete und das Geschicht, das unter dem Boden ist, auf dem wir wandeln, und je tiefer die Wurzeln unseres Seins hinabreichen ins unergründliche Geschichte dessen, was ausser- und unterhalb liegt der fleischlichen Grenzen unseres Ich, es aber doch bestimmt und ernährt, so dass wir in minder genauen Stunden in der ersten Person davon sprechen mögen und als gehöre es unserem Fleische zu,—desto sinnigschwerer ist unser Leben und desto würdiger unseres Fleisches Seele.

[History is that which has happened and that which goes on happening in time. But also it is the stratified record upon which we set our feet, the ground beneath us; and the deeper the roots of our being go down into the layers that lie below and beyond the fleshly confines of our ego, yet at the same time feed and condition it—so that in our moments of less precision we may speak of them in the first person and as though they were part of our flesh-and-blood experiences—the heavier is our life with thought, the weightier is the soul of our flesh.]

The narrator is playing here with the word's etymology and forcing it slightly to carry two meanings: that of a single event conditioned by time and that of myth, timeless by virtue of its eternal recurrence. There is no mention yet of history, and the word is meant primarily to suggest preconscious elements of motivation which originate outside and "below" the individual ego. By the time Eliezer appears with his talks of Abraham, the double nature of "Geschichte" is clearly established, so that it represents both the paradigmatic myth and its individual manifestation in the event. It is "die Gegenwart dessen, was umschwingt, die Einheit des Doppelten, das Standbild mit Namen zugleich [the present of the revolving sphere, the unity of the dual, the image that resolves the riddle of time]." "Geschichte" here amounts to an irrevocable law of life, and there is no value judgment associated with the awareness of one's story. However, in the fourth book of the tetralogy, when Joseph playfully chastises his brothers: "Schämt euch! Habt ihr keine Bildung und keine Geschichten? [Shame! Have you, then, no education, no history?]," the word "Geschichte" has taken on positive value as "tribal history," "fundament," and "culture." To have stories, in the judgment of Joseph and the narrator, was to have culture, fate, and weight in the world, as Jaakob did, while to be storyless, that is, to not be consciously aware of one's myth, was to live as savages and barbarians. By now, the consciousness of story as life progressing in rational linear fashion toward a goal has become a prerequisite to cultural maturity, and is the central idea around which the progeny of Abraham congeal to become a people. Furthermore, "Geschichte" has become coupled with "Bildung," education, or learned knowledge, implying not only that the individual life must be rich in experiences, but also that the individual must stand in a conscious relationship to them, i.e., be able to interpret them. In addition, Joseph's question is ironic because, while the brothers indeed have stories, they quite definitely have no "Bildung," and since the intellectual component is missing from their lives, they remain mere mythical characters, objects in Joseph's story. Not only is the individual life

viewed as a story, but the world itself is considered to be a narrated phenomenon, with a main plot and much secondary and peripheral activity:

> Wohlverstanden: in der Geschichte der Welt steht jeder. Man
> braucht nur in die Welt geboren zu sein, um so oder so und
> schlecht und recht durch sein bisschen Lebensgang zur Gänze des
> Weltprozesses sein Scherflein beizutragen. Die meisten aber wim-
> meln peripherisch weitabseitab, unkund des Hauptgeschehens
> und ohne Anteil in ihm, bescheiden und im Grunde froh, nicht
> zu seinem erlauchten Personal zu gehören.

> [Let me be clear: everybody has a place in the history of the
> world. Simply to be born into it one must, one way or the other,
> and roughly speaking, contribute by one's little span one's mite
> to the whole of the world span. Most of us, however, swarm in
> the periphery, far off to one side, unaware of the world-history,
> unsharing in it, modest and at bottom not displeased at not be-
> longing to its illustrious dramatis personae.]

The word "Geschichte" here clearly means "history," yet it is a world-history
which is a narration and "narrates itself":

> Die Stunde ... ist da,—eine Haupt-Feststunde und ein Wende-
> punkt der Geschichte, feststehend, seit sie in die Welt kam und
> zuerst sich selber erzählte.

> Hier schweigt di Geschichte. Das will sagen: sie schweigt in
> gegenwärtiger Fassung und Festaufführung, denn als sie im Orig-
> inal geschah und sich selbst erzählte, schwieg sie keineswegs.

> Ihre (die erste Nacherzählung der Geschichte) Beziehung zur ei-
> genen Urform, das ist: zu dem geschehenden Sich-selbst-Erzählen
> der Geschichte, deutet sich an in gewissen derben Wendungen
> von ausgesprochen komischer Prägung.

> [The hour ... is at hand, the climax of the story (*Geschichte*),
> the chief hour of the feast, which has been since it first came to
> pass and related itself.]

> [Here our story (*Geschichte*) loses its tongue. I mean our present
> version and repetition in the feast does so; for in the original, as
> it happened and told itself, it by no means lost its tongue.]

[The relation of our source, the original narrator of the story (*Geschichte*), to its own original—I mean the self-narrating events themselves—is betrayed by certain crude phrases of comic relief.]

A narrated world-story is not only subject to time, it also implies the presence of a narrating consciousness which can be variously interpreted as God or the human intellect. The fact that the world-story "narrates itself" points to the fact that this narrative consciousness is consequent and not antecedent to the narrated world, that is, is not independent of it. Ultimately it is this agile exploitation of the German word "Geschichte" which allows the narrator to equate the external (historical) world with his own fictional narrative and to treat them both as "double natured"—that is, as simultaneously mythical and historical, a timeless festival of reenactment and a "world process" with low beginnings and an urge to elevation.

THE MYTH OF CONSCIOUSNESS

As "Geschichte" the world is both mythical and historical, as is the novel itself. However, the world's history, according to the novel, exists within the framework of the myth and is explainable by it. That is, as an eternally recurring phenomenon, the world has as its model the Gnostic myth of the Romance of the Soul, the primordial story of the fall of light, and yet it is this same myth which accounts for the origin of the world of time. Both accounts of the myth, as the narrator reports them, tell of the infatuation of the soul—God's first creature of pure light—with base matter, and of God sending the spirit—his second creature, also of pure light—into the newly created world of forms to free the soul and dissolve the forms which captivated it. But, according to the second account of the myth, the effect of the spirit in the world was not to "liberate" the soul, but merely to make it aware of itself, to comprehend its heavenly origin as well as its earthly involvement, and to take on that constant troubled consciousness of the divine, which, eons later, would appear in a certain Semitic tribe as the "Gottessorge."

There are two interesting points to be gotten from the narrator's unique interpretation of this myth. First of all, the narrator's second account of the myth lets slip that God himself created the world of form for the infatuated soul, and strongly suggests that there is every possibility that the spirit too will succumb, at least in part, to that same love of life which held the soul. This being the case, there can hardly be talk of guilt or "Sündenfall [fall (of

man)]," and if the soul has, indeed, sinned, it is the "Felix Culpa" which is
very much in harmony with God's own intentions. The created world of
forms is "fallen," but it is the necessary fall from childhood to maturity and
from innocence to enlightenment. There is a wonderfully ironic section in
Zauberberg [*The Magic Mountain*] called "Forschungen [Research]" in
which Hans Castorp discovers that Creation itself was the Fall, that life in
its essence is sin, and that ever higher life forms are ever more fallen away
from the original purity of the empty universe. In a rather more optimistic
and less ironic voice, Mann later pointed out: "Zum Bewusstsein kommen
heisst: ein Gewissen bekommen, heisst wissen, was Gut und Böse ist,—die
untermenschliche Natur weiss es nicht. Sie ist unschuldig; im Menschen wird
sie schuldig. Der Mensch ist der Sündenfall der Natur, aber das ist kein Fall,
sondern gewiss eine Erhebung, wie das Gewissen höher ist als die Unschuld
[To attain consciousness means to become aware, to know what is good and
what is evil—nature does not know the distinction. It is innocent: in mankind
it becomes guilty. Mankind is nature's fall from grace, but it is no fall, but
to be sure an elevation, for awareness is higher than innocence]." It is for
this reason that the cultivation of the historically conscious ego among the
Hebrews was "required and yet forbidden, commanded but accursed."

The second fact that the Romance of the Soul reveals to us is that the
primordial myth is a myth about the overcoming of the Myth! Käte Ham-
burger interprets the myth in Freudian terms, as the "Bewusstmachen des
Unbewussten [Making conscious the unconscious]" and Erich Heller describes it as the "exact theological version of Schopenhauer's metaphysics"
and there is no contradiction, insofar as Freud's psychology of the Consciousness and Unconsciousness corresponds very closely to Schopenhauer's
duality of Will and Idea. In fact, Thomas Mann points this out himself in
his essay "Freud und die Zukunft"; "Freuds Beschreibung des 'Es' und
'Ich'—ist sie nicht aufs Haar die Beschreibung von Schopenhauers 'Wille'
und 'Intellekt,'—eine Übersetzung seiner Metaphysik ins Psychologische?
[But Freud's description of the Id and the Ego—is it not to a hair Schopenhauer's description of the Will and the Intellect, a translation of the latter's
metaphysics into psychology?]." All three of these observations reveal a connection between the Gnostic myth and the novel's interpretation of Abraham's discovery of God as being the discovery of the divine element within
the earthly and of the emergence of the ego out of the unconscious. The
myth of the entrance of the spirit into the world marks the advent of consciousness, and because the spirit brings death with it, it also marks the
beginning of time. We are confronted then with a myth, which by definition
is unconscious and ahistorical, whose very theme and subject is the advent

of consciousness and history! It appears then that the lesson of the novel, which is that the human being should liberate himself from the mythical existence, looks to the myth of myths for its pattern and example. The Proto-myth then at once provides the source and resolution for all the stories of the dualistic world. All the conflicts between matter and spirit, good and evil, 'Mutterdunkel' und 'Vaterlicht,' ['maternal darkness,' and 'paternal light'],'' between the "Red one" and the "Fair one," all stem from the original dualism of the first story and are resolved by the narrator's reinterpretation of it. The narrator himself explains that the soul's mythical fall was "die bedingte Grundlage für alles erzählbare Geschehen . . . Und war es der Höchste nicht, der ihr bei ihrem weit über ihre Kräfte gehenden Liebesringen zu Hilfe kam und die erzählbare Welt des Geschehens, die Welt der Formen und des Todes schuf? [the conditioned basis of everything that followed (*alles erzählbare Geschehen,* lit. "all narratable events"). . . . Surely it was the Highest who came to the rescue of the soul in that wrestling for love which was far beyond its power? He thereupon created the world, where things happen and can be told, the world of forms, the world of death]." The Romance of the Soul is "erzählbares Geschehen" and the source of all other narrative (i.e., temporal) events and we must therefore conclude that the myth itself, insofar as it is narratable, is itself an intermediary stage between bestiality and the conscious life. The myth is timeless, but through both its subject and the fact of its story, it carries the seed of its opposite, which is history, and the word "Geschichte," as we have pointed out, is the connecting link between these two.

In Schopenhauerean terms, the myth is a middle-thing between the world as will and the world as representation. As the pre-ego, unconscious motivating force behind human character and behavior, it is "the innermost essence, the kernel, of every particular thing and also of the whole. It appears in every blindly acting force of nature and also in the deliberate conduct of man." This is the definition of the will. However, this urge and force is structured into forms and roles, and clothed in story, and therefore implies the operation from without of an ordering consciousness. We may therefore designate the mythical urge as being of the will, but not the myth itself, which is the representation put upon it. In the novel, not only the myth but also the Schopenhauerean metaphysics is "umfunktioniert [transformed]" into an optimistic world-view. For if the myth not only motivates such base and "swamplike" acts as patricide, filicide, and incest, but also provides a model for the appearance of consciousness and conscience in nature, then it would seem that the primal element carries the seed of its own transcendence. Seen in these terms, the will is not only a will-to-live, but insofar as it moves up a scale of complexity, culminating in consciousness, it appears to be an almost Darwinian will-to-enlightenment as well. As a matter of fact, Schopenhauer himself describes his World-as-Will as undergoing degrees of objectification independently of the effect of the form-giving intellect. That is, there is a higher degree of "objectification" in the plant than in the forces of nature, a higher degree still in the animal, and the will passes thusly "into visibility" through gradations "as endless as those between the feeblest twilight and the brightest sunlight." And although he does not recognize a temporal or causal relationship between these degrees (time, space, and causality being supplied only in the representation), any system of gradations necessarily implies that the higher phase must pass through and include the lower phase. Not only does Schopenhauer refer to the will's "passage" into visibility, but he also must grant the will a certain urge to development toward ever higher degrees of objectification. Just as the myth contains the element of history, its antithesis, so the Schopenhauerean will contains the element of knowledge which is its own abolishment.

> The will cannot be abolished by anything except knowledge. Therefore the only path to salvation is that the will should appear freely and without hindrance, in order that it can recognize or know its own inner nature in this phenomenon. Only in consequence of this knowledge can the will abolish itself, and thus end the suffering that is inseparable from its phenomenon . . . *Nature leads the will to the light, just because only in the light can it find its salvation.* Therefore the purposes of nature are to be promoted in every way, as soon as the will-to-live, that is her inner being, has determined itself. [my emphasis]

Thus the advent of knowledge/light/consciousness is not to be viewed as the violent disruption of a primordial state of darkness and rest, but rather more as an organic occurrence, a natural metamorphosis to motion inherent in the initial inert state. Freud makes a similar observation in the succinct formulation: "Wo Es war, soll Ich werden [Where id was, shall be ego]," which Thomas Mann notes in his essay on Freud, and this forms the pattern by which the conscious ego emerges in the Abrahamitic lineage to Joseph.

The development of the ego out of the mythical collective is not a straightforward one from Abraham to Joseph. There are hindrances, delays, mythical "throwbacks," as it were, such as the massacre at Schekem in which Jaakob's sons reenacted the victory of Mardug over the dragon Tiamat. Furthermore, the ego itself is a rather problematic phenomenon and its unconditional assertion is a dubious goal. In his essay on Freud, Mann sees the ego as "besorgniserregend [alarming]," a fragile phenomenon engaged, by its nature, in a constant struggle for existence: "Eingeengt zwischen Unbewusstem, Aussenwelt, und dem, was Freud das 'Über-ich' nennt, dem Gewissen, führt es ein ziemlich nervöses und geängstigtes Dasein [Hemmed in between the unconscious, the outer world, and what Freud calls the Super-Ego, it leads a pretty nervous and anguished existence]." However, in the artistic personality, the ego is a far more aggressive phenomenon which, because it is a connecting link between the private consciousness and the outside world, has positive social implications. Of Tolstoy's boundless egotism, Mann wrote: "Ichliebe und Weltliebe sind gar nicht auseinander zu halten [Love of the self and love of the world are hardly to be kept apart]," and seems to mean by this that love for the "Thou" is predicated on the conscious existence of the loving "I." This same notion appears in the novel in Jaakob's "Verinnigung der Welt zur Geschichte des Ich und seines Heils [internalization of the world as the history of the self and its salvation]" which the narrator calls "pious," and in Mann's essayistic interpretation of Abraham's "Gottesentdeckung [discovery of God]" as being the discovery of his ego. However, just as the participation in the myth is both inescapable and necessary, yet archaic and questionable, so the bare assertion of the ego is sought and pious yet also dangerous and inhumane. Outside the novel, the author warns of the dangers of the "unbedingte Befangenheit im principium individuationis [bias in favor of the individual]," and considers the ego's awareness of its origins in the collective to be vital to the evolution of morality: "Die aufdämmernde Ahnung von der Unterschiedslosigkeit von Ich und Du: die Gefühlseinsicht, dass der Wille in allem und allen der eine und selbe ist: das ist der Beginn und das Wesen aller Ethik [The dawning awareness of the inseparability of 'I' and 'Thou': the intuitive feeling that the will is the same in one and all things: that is the beginning of all ethics]." We are reminded of Joseph's youthful arrogance before his brothers and his disregard for Mut-em-enet's emotions, both of which are punished by his "death." Each time, of course, Joseph is "reborn," and each rebirth brings a new level of removal and elevation until his detachment is from the novel itself and he steps out of and assumes control of his story. But at this point he returns to the collective, makes a career of "nourishing" his fellow men and, as a worldly and enlightened individual is reunited (albeit conditionally) with the people of his origins. In Joseph the ego finds its place in the mythical collective; it is not engulfed by it, but rather draws from it as the mythical giant Antaeus drew strength from the ground. In Joseph the conscious ego looks back and sheds light on the world of its origin, relating to that world in the deliberate way that the narrator does to his novel, and life itself becomes an "erzählerische Begegnung von Psychologie und Mythus [narrative encounter between psychology and myth]." "Psychology" refers to the post-Freudian analytical understanding of the ego which permits it to detect and "humanize" the myth which it is living. This analytical attitude, which is also the attitude of the novel's narrator, is unmythical insofar as it is conscious, but at the same time its vocabulary is mythical, and it therefore relocates the myth from the "Angeschauten [viewed]" to the "Anschauenden [viewing]." The myth remains binding, because it is universal and fundamental, but the ego asserts its autonomy by humanizing the myth and bending it to the unique requirements of the historical age. The fully mature individual therefore both celebrates the myth and "scherzt mit ihm [plays with it]" and identifies himself, as Joseph does, with the phrase: "Ich bin's," by which both the "Ich" and the "Es," the conscious ego and the unconscious id, assert themselves.

> Ich bin's—ich bin's und bin's nicht, eben weil Ich es bin, das will sagen: weil das Allgemeine und die Form eine Abwandlung erfahren, wenn sie sich im Besonderen erfüllen . . . das Musterhalt-Überlieferte kommt aus der Tiefe, die unten liegt, und ist, was uns bindet. Aber das Ich ist vom Gott und ist des Geistes, der ist frei.

> [I am I. For I am and am not just because I am I. I mean that the general and the typical vary when they fulfill themselves in the particular . . . for the pattern and the traditional come from the depths which lie beneath and are what bind us, whereas the I is from God and is of the spirit, which is free.]

This and this alone made the moral life (gesittetes Leben), that the compelling mythical urge of the depths fulfill itself in the divine freedom of the conscious self, "und ist keine Menschensittung ohne das eine und ohne das andere [and there is no human morality without one and without the other]."

THE IMPERATIVE OF CONSCIOUSNESS

This double blessing of achieving the "mythische Anschauungsweise [mythic way of perception]" while living the mythically-motivated life is not only the great achievement of the Hebrews, it is also the imperative of the novel. In his speech before the Library of Congress, the author stated:

> In Sünde leben heisst gegen den Geist leben, aus Unaufmerksamkeit . . . am Veralteten, Rückständigen festhalten und fortfahren,

darin zu leben. Und von der gerechten Furcht vor dieser Sünde und Narrheit ist jedesmal die Rede in dem Buch, wo von der "Gottessorge" die Rede ist. . . . Sie ist . . . die Sorge . . . um das, was die Glocke geschlagen hat, die Forderung des Aons, der Weltstunde . . . sie ist das fromme Feingefühl für das Verworfene, Veraltete, innerlich Überschrittene.

[To live in sin means to live against the spirit, unacknowledging . . . to cling to and persevere in what is outmoded and residual, to live in that. Proper fear of this sin and foolishness is always the topic in the book that treats of "anxiety about God" . . . It is . . . the anxiety . . . for that which the clock has struck, what the aeons require, the hour of the world . . . it is the gentle feeling for the depraved, the outmoded, that which has overstepped its bounds.]

In this description the ignorance of time and change is the real sin against the spirit—not the assertion of the ego—and historical consciousness has become a moral imperative. The myth itself is not invalidated, and there is still the urge to patricide, incest, filicide, etc., but the literal enactment of these rituals in the face of new historical demands had become obsolete and therefore reprehensible. Laban's interment of his son, although it was carried out with pious intent, was nonetheless "ein Greuel [an atrocity]" because in the new age symbolic substitutes had been introduced, and the literal sacrifice of the son had become murder. The "Gottessorge" was essentially the attention to the world story and the belief in progress. Its opposite was "Gottesdummheit [God-stupidity]," was in fact "Dummheit" in all its forms, because it was unconscious behavior. A stupid man could not serve God because God, as we will see, is defined and secularized to stand for the human spirit at its highest.

Günter Reiss's designation of *Joseph* as "der sich nicht mehr sichere Roman, der sich reflektiert [the novel that is no longer sure of itself, that reflects on itself]" is therefore misleading. Indeed, the novel's imperative of reflection and self-consciousness arises precisely out of its certainty that the unexamined life is not only not worth living, but also morally reprehensible. Hermsdorf sees the detachment of the protagonist from the purely mythical existence to be negative: "Die Krullsituation wiederholt sich: die reale Entfremdung des Menschen von sich selbst kann nur für den erwählten Einzelnen und auf Schelmenweg überwunden werden [The Krull situation repeats itself: the factual alienation of mankind from itself can be overcome only for the chosen individual and on the road of mischief]." But Hermsdorf too makes the mistake of equating detachment with alienation, and overlooks the fact that the major goal of the whole Abrahamitic lineage was to gain detachment (i.e., perspective) over the muddy "swamp" of the mythical life. The achievement of this detachment does bring with it a certain humor and lightheartedness, but I believe it would be a mistake to view the tribe's entire religious endeavor to be a gradual advancement from solemnity to "Schelmentum [mischievousness]." Seidlin most nearly defines the novel's moral message by identifying the Covenant as the key to achieving that sort of morality which the author's New Humanism demanded. Joseph's individual "covenants" of helpfulness for Potiphar and Pharaoh are a reflection in miniature of the Great Covenant between Abraham and his god, i.e. between Israel and its highest self. The Great Covenant stands for the novel's "message" as well, that the spiritual is already contained in the earthly, in the world's children and that it waits upon them for its fulfillment.

In this respect, Joseph may be seen as setting an example for the enlightened and psychologically cognizant new humanity which the author hoped, perhaps overly optimistically, that the future would bring. It was to be a late sort of humanity, one in which life had transcended itself by "turning its reason back on itself." To Karl Kerényi he wrote: "Diese Verbindung (myth and psychology) repräsentiert mir geradezu die Welt der Zukunft, ein Menschentum, das gesegnet ist oben vom Geiste herab und 'aus der Tiefe, die unten liegt' [This combination represents for me the world of the future, a humanity that is blessed from above by the spirit and 'from the depths that lie below']." Mann's utopian phantasy was of an intellectual and slightly decadent humanism, which, unlike the earlier Humanism, would stand in a rather more "cheerful, free, impudent, but also more artistic relationship to the powers of the underworld." The "powers of the underworld," in addition to referring to the Freudian "id," were also those forces which the author saw as dominating Nazi Germany. Mann declared himself a passionate friend of psychology because he believed that by psychologically intellectualizing the myth, he could "tear it out of the hands of the fascistic obscurantists and make it humane." This critical-ironic approach to the myth was traditionally an achievement of the artist, as the author himself pointed out: "im Künstler (spielt) jeden Augenblick das Unbewusste ins lächelnd Bewusste und kindlich-tief Aufmerksame hinüber [in the artist the unconscious is always slipping into laughing consciousness and a childlike depth of awareness]," but we are not therefore to view this state as a rare one bestowed, in the Calvinist manner, upon an "elect" few. If this were so, one could not condemn Laban's filicide or Huij and Tuij's castration of their son, and we would be faced with a world view which is hopelessly pessimistic. If we are to condemn these "well-meaning" acts of ignorance, and I believe that the novel intends for us to condemn them, then we must view the artist's enlightenment as being accessible to all. And indeed, in his speech to the Viennese workers, Thomas Mann declared: "In besonders pragmatischer Ausprägung wiederholt der Künstler die Situation des Menschen überhaupt: als Geist und Natur auf einmal, und man verfälscht die Kunst, wie man den Menschen verfälscht, wenn man sie nur als vernunftgeboren oder nur als Geschöpf des Triebes fasst [The artist repeats the situation of mankind in general in a pragmatic way and bears its special stamp: spirit and nature at once, and one falsifies art, as one falsifies mankind, if one conceives it only as rationally born or only as the creature of impulse]." Therefore, in spite of the elitism which constantly seeps through (as when Joseph is referred to as "chosen") the novel is addressed to a world which it views as democratic, and the moral obligation it imposes on this world is democratic. Not only the artist, but also the common person is obliged to come to terms with both the conscious and the unconscious elements in himself. This view bespoke an optimistic liberalism which was not only in defiance of the intellectual trends of fascist Germany, it was also an attack on the very fundaments of Western dualistic philosophy since Plato. The Platonic dualism, as Thomas Mann points out, had pervaded both science and morality and had degraded the world of perception to a second-rate reality. The earliest utterances of the Western intellect had rent the world in two, elevating the Ideal to the only true reality and degrading the world of experience to mere meaningless ephemera. Such a division cast aspersions upon experienced life as much as any form of Christian asceticism: "denn gewissermassen ist damit die sterbliche erscheinung und das sinnliche Haften an ihr in Sündenzustand versetzt—das Heil, die Wahrheit findet nur der, welcher sich zum Ewigen wendet [for the moral aspect and our sensual attachment to it are thereby transposed into a state of sin—salvation and truth are found only in turning toward the eternal]." Mann resolves this dichotomy and raises the empirical world from its humiliation before the ideal by asserting the priority of the human being as flesh and as individual as well as spirit and name-role. The human being takes his definition as human neither from spirit nor from nature, for being human has always contained both mind and body, and "Es hat nie eine Stufe gegeben, auf der der Mensch noch nicht Geist, sondern nur Natur war [There was never a stage at which man was not as yet spirit, but only nature]." The discovery of *The Magic Mountain* which became the central idea of *Joseph and His Brothers* is the revolutionary rejection of a dualism where "above" and "below" have of themselves any moral value. The lesson of the snow dream and of the life of Joseph is that the dichotomy can be resolved without being dissolved, that myth can coexist with history, that the spirit can transcend nature without throwing it away, and that the supreme being in which it is transcended is the human being: "Der Mensch ist Herr der Gegensätze, sie sind durch ihn, und also ist er vornehmer als sie. Vornehmer als der Tod, zu vornehm für diesen—das ist die Freiheit seines Kopfes. Vornehmer als das Leben, zu vornehm für dieses—das ist die Frömmigkeit in seinem Herzen [Man is the lord of antitheses, they exist through him, and thus he is nobler than they. Nobler than death, too noble for this—that is the freedom of his head. Nobler, than life, too noble for this—that is the piety in his heart]." . . .

Having established that the Divine Covenant was the starting point for the development of historical consciousness among the Jews, and that the Covenant can therefore be seen as a symbol for a purely secular psychological phenomenon, we must then deal with the figure in the novel called "God." One of the difficulties in discussing the role of the divinity in the spiritual-intellectual development of the Jews is that God is not a single figure in the novel, but appears rather in a number of images, from the benign and very anthropomorphic deity of the "Vorspiel" ["Prelude"] to the abstract principle of light in Ikhnaton's theosophy. We can, however, isolate two distinct ways in which the novel treats God. In the "Vorspiel in oberen Rängen" ["Prelude in the Upper Circles"] he is presented with all seriousness as the purely transcendent God-of-the-Fairy-tales, stroking his beard as he listens to Semael describe the liveliness of the world below. On the other hand, there is the immanent God, who in the sections of the novel taking place on earth (i.e., the vast majority of the text), appears as a non-miraculous psychological and philosophical phenomenon. It is as if the transcendent God, in heeding his defrocked angel and becoming historicized, had moved from the position of narrator to the place of the narrated, into the living world of "alles er-zählbaren Geschehens [all narratable events]." In the process of becoming historicized, he also becomes, if I may coin a word, "storycized," and thereby falls into the hands of the critics, so to speak, to become interpreted.

REALM OF SEVERITY

The only aspect of the transcendent God which remains unchanged, that is, wholly detached from all earthly contact and therefore wholly unsympathetic, is the unrelentingly absolute and severe "Riech der Strenge." The Realm of Severity is the place of total detachment, and its inhabitants are the disembodied and therefore sterile "Kämmerer des Lichts [courtiers of the light]." Although the Realm of Severity is clearly part of the divine environment, and therefore part of divinity, we must nonetheless see it as distinct from God the Creator in that it adopts a clearly anti-human stance, while God continues to be loving and even defensive toward his "Gott-tier [God-animal]." In them, the indifference which is part of the definition of the absolute verges on hostility, and the living God's creative policy actually runs the risk of opposition from the rest of the heavenly folk. If we bring the Freudian psychological schemata to this extraordinary division among the heavenly forces, it will seem less extraordinary, for Freud has already accounted for the phenomenon of the divided ego. That is, if we interpret the figure of God as representative of the emerging ego of the Jews—and the narrator's treatment of Abraham's discovery of God certainly suggests this—then the Realm of Severity is readily explained by the super-ego. The super-ego, as Freud describes it, is an agency which, although part of the ego, is frequently in conflict with it. As a sort of internalized authority, its function is to observe, criticize, and inhibit the rest of the personality, most especially the ego. And insofar as the super-ego is purely inhibitory and concerned primarily with holding the self back from what it views as excessive expressions of either ego or libido, it can be seen as essentially anti-life. Its constant demand is for the renunciation of instinct, i.e., life, and its weapon is guilt. "The tension between the harsh super-ego and the ego that is subjected to it, is called by us the sense of guilt; it expresses itself as a need for punishment." Freud also points out that there are two origins for the sense of guilt, one arising from the fear of external authority, and the other, far more subtle, from fear of the super-ego which is merely the internalization of authority. "The first insists upon a renunciation of instinctual satisfaction; the second, as well as doing this, presses for punishment. . . . The severity of the super-ego . . . is simply a continuation of the severity of the external authority."

The events in the novel which correspond to these psychological phenomena are the emergence of the aggressive ego in the lineage of Abraham, and the simultaneous appearance of the critical super-ego in the Realm of Severity. Even the name "severity" seems to have been borrowed by the author from the Freudian text. The prissy angels and the bearded father-God are, of course, difficult to take seriously and, indeed, the "Vorspiel in oberen Rängen" is probably one of the funniest parts of the novel. It seems apparent that both are intended to be mere caricatures of the psychological components emerging and struggling for existence among the Jews. However, these psychological components, the drive toward self-assertion and the accompanying sense of guilt, must indeed be taken seriously, because they are what distinguish the children of the Covenant from the peoples who surround them, peoples who, while not godless (they are overcrowded with gods and godlets) are conscienceless and guiltless. Now a contradiction appears to arise in the fact that on the one hand God must free himself from the influence of the Realm of Severity in order to enter into the Covenant with the animal (i.e., libidinous) part of his creation that was life, but that on the other hand, guilt, which is the weapon of the angels against the God-animal, and certainly the tool of the super-ego, is also one of the driving forces which distinguishes the children of the Covenant from the non-chosen. Indeed, Joseph announces with some pride to Potiphar, "wir wissen's so gut wie allein in der Welt, was die Sünde ist [we, almost alone in the world, know what sin is]." However, guilt is, in a sense, wrested from the hands of the angels and its retarding influence removed from it. That is, although the angels' demand for punishment occurred whenever the God-animal asserted itself either too egotistically (as it does with young Joseph) or too libidinously (as in Sodom and Gomorrah) God himself had an annoying way of making punishment a means to ever greater elevation of (human) life. The guilt by which the angelic super-ego usually inhibits the ego which is subjected to it, is reversed so that the children of Abraham feel guilty whenever they *fail* to uphold the Covenant, that is, whenever they *fail* to grow and assert themselves and become holy "wie ich es bin [As I am holy]." As a result, it is God's "*living* majesty" which becomes "Massstab des Lebens, zur Quelle des Schuldgefühls [the measure of life, the source of the sense of guilt]." and not the abhorrence of the instincts. A contract of this sort, which commands that the worshipper be as great as the God, is itself a highly ambiguous phenomenon, and a curious twist of the Freudian theory of God. Freud sees God as an extension of the authority figure, a deification of the murdered father, and thus, by implication, a suppressor of the ego, while in *Joseph,* the command to the worshipper is to grow in ego. We may conclude that the author, while fundamentally sympathetic with the Freudian psychology, is nonetheless subjecting the Freudian theory of God to the same "Umfunktionierung ins Humane [transformation into human terms]" to which he subjected Schopenhauer and the myth. More precisely, it is human guilt, which is "umfunktioniert [transformed]" into a productive rather than inhibiting force.

In view of the existence of the living world and God's sympathy toward it, the bickering of the angels reflects badly on the transcended aspect; indeed, in them transcendence is equated not only with emotionlessness (the angels have no apparatus for feeling), but also with a stance which is anti-life. In this respect, with the entrance of the human element into the world, pure transcendence becomes as discredited and "obsolete" as the blind adherence to the urges of nature. The separation of the functions of censorship and punishment into a distinct body is the prerequisite for God's entry into immanence, for in order to become "living," the Creator must divest himself of those features which are anathema to life. The angels abhor all that smacks of the creative erotic, and in the "eternal struggle between Eros and the instinct of destruction or death" in the human personality, the angels represent the death instinct. This becomes especially clear in the "Gekröse und Gestank [guts and stink]" speech of the angel before Joseph. In the mysterious form of the "Mann auf dem Felde [Man on the Field]," the angel reveals both a supernatural understanding of the situation and a conspicuous abhorrence of the life of the flesh:

> Solche Geschöpfe wie du sind nichts als ein flüchtig gleissender Betrug über den inneren Greuel alles Fleisches unter der Oberfläche. Ich sage nicht, dass auch nur diese Haut und Hülle vom Appetitlichsten wäre mit ihren dünstenden Poren und Schweisshaaren; aber ritze sie nur ein wenig, und die salzige Brühe geht frevelrot hervor, und weiter innen wird's immer greulicher und ist eitel Gekröse und Gestank. Das Hübsche und Schöne müsste durch und durch hübsch und schön sein, massiv und aus edlem Stoff, nicht ausgefüllt mit Leimen und Unrat.

> Such creatures as you are naught but a fleeting and dissembling gloss upon the horror of all flesh beneath the surface. I do not say that even this skin and husk is the most appetizing in the world, with its steaming pores and sweat-glands; but scratch it ever so little and the salt scarlet brew comes out, while the deeper one goes, the worse it gets; it is sheer guts and stink. The beautiful and well-favoured should be beautiful through and through, solid and fine-grained and not filled up with dirt and jelly.]

Such a position is so alien to life that, in spite of the fact that it comes from an "angel," it can only represent death. The scene also harkens back to the Romance of the Soul, in which the original task of the spirit was to terminate all material life and return the soul to disembodied purity. The tirade of the angel, however, viewed alongside the tale of God's acceptance of physical life, reflects the author's division of spirit into two categories: spirit alone, which is rejected, and spirit in conjunction with life, which is the point and goal of the Covenant. This division also occurs in the Hebrews' conception of God which is alternatingly ascetic and vital, although the ascetic aspect is ultimately rejected. By Joseph's time, the otherworldliness which once was coupled with omnipotence had been undermined to the point that transcendence suggested impotence, and this becomes particularly clear both in the figure of the young Pharaoh and his light-god, Aton.

Through the Covenant, God undertakes the long process of becoming incarnated in his chosen people, an act which arouses the endless disapproval of the heavenly court. It is a state which the angels look upon as "fallen," but from a less biased perspective, it is merely "secularized." That is, the entrance of God into the world is the beginning of the process in which vitalized spirit met spiritualized life in fulfillment of the command "Sei heilig, wie ich es bin [Be holy, as I am holy]," and "holy" became synonymous with "enlightened life."

THE COVENANT OF LIFE AND SPIRIT

To return to the developing God of the novel, there is some evidence that vitality is so important to the outer-worldly spirit that he will not tolerate its being diminished in any way. Abraham's discovery of God, we might remember, is simultaneous with his discovery that he is once again virile and that his wife is with child. Many generations later, Joseph discusses with Mut-em-enet the merits of castration to eliminate the temptation to adultery, but he then remarks that this would be a sin against his god: "nicht so darf ich's halten; die Sünde wäre ebenso gross als wenn ich unterläge . . . und *ich taugte dann auch für Gott nicht mehr.* Sondern er will, dass ich bestehe, heil und komplett [I may not; the sin were as great as though I yielded, and *I should be no use to God any more.* For he wills that I remain whole and sound (my emphasis)]." Because we are dealing with a strongly patriarchal society, the mandate for "vitality" takes on the meaning of potency and virility, and took the form of the command to go forth and bear sons. Even Joseph, in spite of the theme of androgyny which is woven about him, retains an air of youthful virility, and is compared by the Egyptians to the bull-god Chapi, "mit seinem Schmuck [with his phallus]." Furthermore, God is represented throughout the novel as the "Vaterlicht," which is both "light" and "father," which is to say, both rational-intellectual and potent. There is then no doubt but that the spirit of the Covenant is not only sympathetic to life, but insists upon it.

With life, a new element is introduced into the divine Being, and that is motion, not the static circular motion of eternal recurrence, but the movement through differences which is characteristic only of time. Through his creatures, the eternal Being experiences becoming, from the "schnaubender Kobold [snorting goblin]" Jahu to the sophisticated spirit of enlightenment of Joseph and Ikhnaton, and the entire theology of the novel consists in the revelation of this divine becoming in the earthly behavior of the Hebrews. God's maturation is not only reflected in his people, it *is* the spiritual, intellectual and moral development of his people and may not be distinguished from it. "Denn auch Gott unterliegt der Entwicklung, auch er verändert sich und schreitet fort; . . . und er kann es so wenig ohne die Hilfe des Menschengeistes, wie dieser es vermag ohne Gott [For even God undergoes development, even he changes and moves on; and he can as little do this without the help of humanity as the latter is able to without God]." God's story was the story of his people's development: their historicization was his storycization, a pun which the author, had he been writing in English, would certainly have made, for history is central to the theology of the novel. In an earlier chapter we discussed the role of history and historical consciousness in the development of the Hebrew tribal ego out of the mythical-collective mode of existence. Here, however, God himself becomes "historically conscious," and in the process of becoming historicized, he comes to have a story, as did all the other earthly gods. But God's story was wholly historical, that is, non-mythical and therefore not subject to eternally returning celebrations, as were the "festive" stories of Tammuz, Adonis, and Osiris. God's story was one of linear development; it changed as his people changed, and its climax lay in "endlichster Zukunft [remotest future]," when his chosen realized the total of the potential as "God-animals." Until that time, God suffered and "lay in the bondage" of their savagery. God could not fully come into being until mankind had matured spiritually, and until that time he would exist in fragmentary form. That is, the inviolable unity of the transcendent God became incomplete and imperfect as it came into the imperfect world. Just as human enlightenment progressed in splintered fashion, often broken by lapses into primitiveness and patched again by inspiration, so the presence of God in his creatures took the form of multiplicity, and Jaakob spoke for the human condition as well as for God's when he lamented: "Der Herr ist nicht deutlich [The Lord is not distinct]." As men and women were divided, so also was God; wherever and however they envisioned Him. He was called El eljon, the highest God, El ro'i, the God who sees me, El olam, God of the eons and, since Jaakob, El bêtêl, the God of Lus. Of course, as the narrator reminds us, these were merely different manifestations of the one Great God. The streams and the trees in which they whispered, the storms in which they raged, the fertile spring and the withering draught—He was all of these. "Er war dies alles, was jene im einzelnen waren, Ihm eignete es, der Allgott war Er allhiervon, denn aus Ihm kam es, in Sich fasst Er's Ich sagend zusammen, das Sein alles Seins, Elohim, die Vielheit als Einheit [He was all that they singly were, to Him it all belonged, He was the All-God of all of it, for from Him it came, in Himself He comprehended it, saying I, the Being of all being, Elohim, the many as one]."

This notion of the "fragmented" God is not a uniquely Mannian idea: there are philosophical antecedents of which the philosophy of Ludwig Feuerbach is the most strikingly similar. Feuerbach, like Mann, found the advent of human egoism a prerequisite for the worship (i.e., "discovery") of God. Egotistical man, according to Feuerbach, holds in himself the measure and criterion of divinity insofar as he draws certain characteristics out of himself—wisdom, strength, love, etc.—and projects them into their maximum potential (i.e., perfection) in God. By worshipping those qualities in God, man therefore worships them in himself. "How shall I make Minerva a goddess of wisdom, if wisdom in itself is not a divine being for me . . . and . . . how shall I deify the being on which my life depends unless I look upon life itself as divine?" The Judeo-Christian God was a composite of an enormous number of virtues, all in their perfect state, but nonetheless human in origin, and the word "God" was "a collective or generic term as, for example, the words fruit, grain, or people." Because of the multiplicity of his attributes, there were, in a sense, many Gods in the One God: the all-knowing God, the all-loving God, the all-powerful God, and so forth. And the most important factor is that these God-attributes were essentially human attributes, that is to say, they were not other-worldly but rather this-worldly attributes in their perfect state, and man's worship of them implied a worship of himself and his world:

> The early theologians . . . said that God encompassed everything in the world, but that what in the world is multiple, dispersed, disjoined, sensuous, distributed among different being, is in God simple, non-sensuous, united. Here we have a clear statement that in God man concentrates the essential attributes of the many different things and beings in One Being. One Name, that in God man did not originally or truly conceive a being different from the world, but merely represented the world in a mode differing from sense perception; what man conceived of in the world or in sensuous reality as extensive, temporal, and corporeal he conceived of in God as without extension, atemporal, and incorporeal. In eternity he merely sums up the infinite temporal series . . . and in omnipresence he merely sums up the infinity of space in an abbreviated generic term or concept; for sound subjective reasons he makes use of eternity as a means of breaking off end-

less series of numbers and the infinitely tedious reckoning it entails.

Both in the novel and in the iconoclasm of Feuerbach, God is "auf den Menschen angewiesen [ordered after man]," and draws his life from the ever-growing and changing human imagination, but Mann's God is subject to development, while Feuerbach's is not. Both divinities form part of a dynamic and earthly maturation process, but while the God of the novel grows with his people, Feuerbach's God is the unchanging projected goal of that development: "Is the infinite Mind not simply man's mind, which desires to be infinite and perfect? . . . Is then the Christian God, their inifinite mind, anything other than the model and prototype of what they wish to be some day, an image of the future unfolding of their own essence?" As a further proof of the worldliness of the Judaic God, Feuerbach reminds us that the only immortality promised Abraham by Jehovah was that of his own endless progeny, and this is demonstrated in the novel by God's promise to Abraham: "er solle zu einem Volke werden, zahlreich wie Sand und Sterne, und allen Völkern ein Segen sein [he should become a folk in numbers like the sands of the sea and belonging to all peoples]."

GOD AS TOTALITY

Although Mann is unwilling to state overtly, like Feuerbach, that God is the exclusive product of the human imagination, it is clear that the immanent God of the novel is the same collective of earthly things and attributes as the God defined by the philosopher. In the novel, however, he was not projected earthliness, but rather literal earthliness ("in allem wesend [being in everything]") and his multiplicity lay in the fact that the beings through whom he lived were themselves divided, immature, and not yet in harmony with themselves. God contained these imperfect beings in the totality of his being, and therefore was at one time both perfect and imperfect. Or rather, in the Feuerbachian sense, God became perfect by virtue of the fact that he contained the totality of the world's imperfection. And the most unorthodox concomitant to this sort of perfection-by-virtue-of-totality is that it lays no claim to absolute goodness, or rather being absolutely good. Goodness necessarily excludes evil and a God of totality may not exclude anything. God's abdication from absolute goodness begins in the novel with the creation of humanity and the subsequent period of strained relations with the Realm of Severity. While God's chosen people are still obliged by the letter of the law to restrain their instincts for blood and sex, God himself overlooks a great deal. He is so concerned with having and being life that he punishes Jaakob for dallying with the infertile Rahel, yet when Jaakob's sons engage in an orgy of murder and castration at Schekem, God is silent. Moreover, one of the mass murderers is Judah, who in spite of his brutality, is still privileged to enter into the lineage leading to Christ. This paradox comes about because as soon as God came to represent life, he could no longer represent goodness. Abraham himself is aware of the moral dilemma of totality, and he confronts God with it: "Höre Herr [Harken, O Lord]," Abraham says, "so oder so, das eine oder das andere! Willst du eine Welt haben, kannst du nicht Recht verlangen; ist es dir aber ums Recht zu tun, so ist es aus mit der Welt [it must be one way or the other, but not both. If thou wilt have a world, then thou canst not demand justice, but if thou settest store by justice, then it is all over with the world]." According to Freud, "goodness" in a religious context consists in some sort of institutional renunciation, but by entering into life, God had to "rub shoulders," as it were, with the instincts. As a result, the function of proscribing instinctual behavior had to fall into the hands of the angels, who were incorruptible because they were non-living. Already the God of Abraham is so wholly committed to life, that he affirms it even in chaos, his utter opposite. Like a warrior who has felled an enemy and, by virtue of the victory, has absorbed the qualities of the defeated, so God, by overcoming the Chaos-monster, had taken its essence into himself, "und war vielleicht erst dadurch ganz und vollkommen geworden, erst dadurch zur vollen Majestät seiner Lebendigkeit gewachsen [only thereby grew to the full height of His living majesty]." He was not the ultimate good, but the ultimate totality. And he was holy, not out of goodness but out of vitality and wholeness. Not only Joseph, but his God, as Henry Hatfield points out, is "tâm," containing both the "above" and the "below." Joseph himself affirms that the holiness of God cannot be separated from the lower elements which are contained in him. God's mystery lay in the fact that every sacrifice brought to the earthly world was brought to him, a doctrine which ought to ring familiar since it is the essence of Christ's famous admonition, "Inasmuch as ye have done it unto the least of these my brethren, yet have done it unto me" (Matthew 25:40).

God is not pure spirit, "Gott ist das Ganze [God is the whole]." Joseph says this to the young Pharaoh who, by virtue of his double crown, is supposed to represent "das Ganze" of Egypt. Yet, while Jahwe is seen by the angels to have "fallen" from spirit, one might view the god, the culture, and even the person of Ikhnaton to be, in a sense "fallen" from nature. Ikhnaton's culture is an old one, but it is also a decadent and dying one. The erotic element which in Israel is the source of vitality and tribal growth, appears in Egypt in forms which are rather more perverse than life-giving: in incest, in the "Todesstarre [deathly rigidity]" of the mummies, in the ritualized coupling of virgin and goat, in sexually aroused "moon-nuns," and in ithy-phallic dwarfs. Ikhnaton himself, the "luxuriöse Spätling und Gottesträumer [luxurious latecomer and dreamer of God]," is feeble, and lies inclined so far backward in his throne, that he can scarcely pull himself into a standing position. Pharaoh's god reflects his discoverer's abhorrence of the low and the earthly: "Goldener Geist ist das Licht, Vatergeist, und zu Ihm ringt die Kraft sich empor aus Muttertiefen, dass sie sich läutere in seiner Flamme und Geist werde im Vater. Unstofflich ist Gott, wie Sein Sonnenschein, Geist ist Er, und der Pharaoh lehrt euch, Ihn im Geiste und in der Wahrheit an-zubeten [Golden spirit is the light, father-spirit; out of the mother-depths below power strives upward to it, to be purified in its flame and become spirit in the Father. Immaterial is God, like His sunshine, spirit is he, and Pharaoh teaches you to worship him in spirit and truth]." While Aton dwells safely above the black earth of Egypt in the pure light "in the sky," the God of Israel lives quite literally in the flesh and blood of his people. . . .

GOD AND PSYCHE

In a humanistic world-view which rejects the idea of transcendence, the locus of the spirit, its only locus, is in the human psyche, and the concept of "God," if it is retained at all, comes to represent the fully developed and harmonious human personality. Expressed in the Freudian vocabulary, the God of the novel is the ideal of the psychologically "perfect" human being, whose ego is in full harmony with the id which is its pre-condition, and who has been liberated from the death wish of the super-ego. "Das Ich ist von Gott und ist des Geistes, der ist frei [The I is from God and is of the spirit, which is free]," but the "es [it]" is also from God, or, more precisely, God is from it. God had taken the first step toward perfection in detaching from himself the anti-life aspects of the spirit in the Realm of Severity, which we have identified as corresponding to the super-ego. Once freed from the ab-solute rigidity of the super-ego, the ego could make its way back to the id from whence it had sprung. This movement back to the id was a late journey, a future and ultimate journey not anticipated by Freud, and following the law of the "einst [once]," it repeated that original journey of the "Licht-menschen [men of light]" into matter with which the world began. It is the culmination of this journey in the harmonious union of nature and spirit, and not *spirituality alone* which is the goal and purpose of the Covenent. By beginning with the "Licht-Menschen," Mann goes on where Freud and Schopenhauer left off, with the element of consciousness (ego, intellect) in conflict with nature (id, will). The purpose of the Covenant was to "bind" together what Freud and Schopenhauer and twenty centuries of Christianity had put asunder.

"Holiness" therefore did not have its traditional meaning of "spiritual-ization" and therefore "isolation from the world," rather it was that state in which spirit and nature in man were bound, not only in contract, but also in essence. It did not, could not, exclude that which was traditionally held to be evil, and even Abraham knew "dass er, der lebendige Gott, nicht gut, oder nur unter anderem gut, ausserdem böse war, dass seine Lebendigkeit das Böse mit umschloss und dabei heilig, das Heilige selbst war und Heilig-keit forderte! [that He, the living God, was not good, or only good among other attributes, including evil, and that accordingly His essence included evil and was therewith sacrosanct; was sanctity itself and demanded sanc-tity]." Holiness was not the renunciation of the instincts for an other-worldly God, but rather the purely secular awareness of the direction the world-story was going and the readiness to be helpful ("behilflich") in carrying it out. Holiness was the opposite of indifference or ignorance; it was the larger view of the world, it was "acht geben, beachten, bedenken, Gewissenhaftigkeit, als ein behutsames Verhalten, ja als metus und schliesslich als sorgend acht-same Empfindlichkeit gegenüber den Regungen des Weltgeistes [to pay at-tention, to observe, to consider; it was conscientiousness, as a measure of precaution, even as metus and finally as careful attentive sensitivity in the face of the movings of the world-spirit]." (Brief an K.K., Oct. 7, 1936). Piousness was "metus"—fear of error, of negligence and of misinterpreta-tion. The pious soul feared making the sort of error that Laban made when he sought to appease the old gods with son-sacrifice, or the misinterpretation that Huij and Tuij were guilty of when they presumed the new world spirit to be pure asceticism and sacrificed their son's virility to it. The Covenant was the very opposite and rejection of any sort of absolutism, since its fun-damental principle was movement and sensitivity to change, a sort of spiritual agility and ever-readiness to adjust life to new information. The fear of offending God was one with the fear of misusing man. Obedience to the Covenant automatically brought with it a sensitivity to the value of human life, and this is shown both by Jaakob's distate for violence and by Joseph's advice to Mai-Sachme to use twice the usual number of slaves to haul quarry blocks, so that none might die. Man was God's instrument of self-recogni-tion, but the reverse was also true, for in the fulfillment of the Covenant, man became as God ("heilig, wie ich es bin [holy, as I am holy]"). The holy one had then not only to comprehend the world as a historical phenomenon, but he also had to take responsibility for those events which made up its historicity. That is to say, the care of the world falls to mankind, for God as a separate protective entity leaves the picture. The command was therefore for alertness, not to the dictates of an external will, but to the human condition, and sin was "nahezu eines Sinnes mit der versäumten Vorsicht [almost the same sense as want of foresight]." The person who, in the face of a changing world, went about his private business, was neglectful of both God and man, for indifference was "Narrheit und lachhaftes Ungeschick in der Behandlung Gottes [folly, clumsy dealing with God, something to laugh at]." Not only the artist, but also the moral person was commanded to a continuous sort of "engagement," not toward the political or social situation (although Joseph does become involved with this in Egypt), but toward the whole story of the world:

> Die "Gottessorge" ist die Besorgnis, das, was einmal das Rechte war, es aber nicht mehr ist, noch immer für das Rechte zu halten und ihm anachronistischerweise nachzuleben; sie ist das fromme Feingefühl für das Verworfene, Veraltete, innerlich Überschrittene, das unmöglich skandalös oder, in der Sprache Israels, "ein Greuel" geworden ist. Sie ist das intelligente Lauschen auf das, was der Weltgeist will, auf die neue Wahrheit und Notwendigkeit

> Anxiety about God is the worry that what was once right no longer is so, but still to hold it as right and anachronistically to live in accordance with it; it is the pious feeling for the depraved, the outmoded, that which has overstepped its bounds and become impossibly scandalous or, in the speech of Israel, "an abomination." It is the intelligent listening to what the world-spirit wants, to new truth and necessity

Sin was rigidity, immobility, and insensitivity, and it stemmed from a sort of psychological simplicity. In a sense, innocence itself was sinful whenever that innocence manifested itself as ignorance and lack of wit, and the advent of God in the world must ultimately be viewed as the beginning of a psychologically complex humanity. Thomas Mann's theology of ethics is therefore the reverse of traditional Christianity, insofar as innocence is reprehensible and knowledge, which is Christianity's original sin, is viewed as the only way to godliness. The Expulsion from the Garden has its equivalent in Abraham's removal from the complacent city of Ur, but while Adam's entry into the world of time and change is viewed as a curse, Abraham's wandering is an inspiration and a command, the fulfillment of which actually brings God into earthly being. The myth of "the wandering" is itself humanized from a myth of trial, isolation, homelessness and perdition to one of striving and growth.

Henry Hatfield points out the necessity of wit and intelligence for the realization of the Mannian moral life, and he quotes Aristotle's idea that a stupid person cannot be good. This implies a certain elitist morality in which goodness is an achievement of the perspicacious few and immorality the necessary fate of the dull-witted. Certainly the narrator shows no great admiration for the masses, and this can be seen in the public scenes in Egypt where the common people always appear as a mob. Furthermore, Joseph's enlightened and generous treatment of the hungry multitude is at its best an enlightened despotism based on the premise that the leader understands the needs of the masses more than the masses themselves do. Joseph himself is more the Nietzschean natural aristocrat than the democrat, and we need only to look at a paragraph out of the essay "Herren und Sklavenmoral" ["Master Morality and Slave Morality"] to find a very accurate description of Joseph's generous and God-pleasing egotism.

> Die vornehme Art Mensch fühlt sich als wertbestimmend, sie hat nicht nötig, sich gutheissen zu lassen . . . sie weiss sich als das, was überhaupt erst Ehre den Dingen verleiht, sie ist wertschaffend. Alles, was sie an sich kennt, ehrt sie: eine solche Moral ist Selbstverherrlichung. Im Vordergrunde steht das Gefühl der Fülle, der Macht, die überströmen will, das Glück der hohen Spannung, das Bewusstsein eines Reichtums, der schenken und abgeben möchte:—auch der vornehme Mensch hilft dem Unglücklichen, aber nicht oder fast nicht aus Mitleid, sondern mehr aus einem Drang, den der Ueberfluss von Macht erzeugt.

> [The noble type of man experiences *itself* as determining values; it does not need approval . . . it knows itself to be that which first accords honor to things; it is *value-creating*. Everything it knows as part of itself it honors: such a morality is self-glorification. In the foreground there is the feeling of fullness, of power that seeks to overflow, the happiness of high tension, the consciousness of wealth that would give and bestow: the noble human being, too, helps the unfortunate, but not, or almost not, from pity, but prompted more by an urge begotten by excess of power.

> (From Nietzsche, *Beyond Good and Evil*,
> trans. Walter Kaufmann
> New York: Vintage Books, 1966.)]

Joseph clearly belongs to the category of the "Herren [masters] and his help-fulness to Potiphar and Pharaoh is that generosity which derives from a sense of full autonomy, even while enthralled in slavery. To be sure, Joseph lacks the ruthlessness of the Superman, a feature which significantly distinguishes him from the Nietzschean ideal, but his rise to power as the Bringer of the New does suggest a certain "Wille zur Macht [will to power]," pleasantly divested, however, of its destructive component. This is not to say that Joseph is in any way patterned after the Nietzschean Superman, only that Mann has invested his character with "aristocratic" features which reveal unmistakable Nietzschean influence. We are therefore faced with the task of reconciling Joseph's individual rise to consciousness and power as divine favorite, and the moral imperatives which the novel makes to humanity in general. How-ever, the level of awareness demanded by the world-spirit was not so difficult in the achievement as in the sustaining, and was not necessarily a function of intelligence. God and the moral life are held by a chosen few in the novel, but it was a morality which was nearly synonymous with enlightenment and was therefore potentially available to all. The world-will is, ultimately, the human will tempered by enlightenment and unhardened by dogma, and this was a state attainable by all who were educable. In this respect, the novel may indeed be considered elitist, but it is a very generous elitism, which excluded only the most dull-witted and is therefore rather far removed from the elitism of Nietzsche. However, if we recall the period in which the novel was written (1933–1943), the growing spectre of German fascism during that time, and the subsequent voluntary exile of the author, it appears likely that the novel is more concerned with condemning the ungenerous and un-yielding stance of fascist dogma than it is with reviling the sluggishness of well-meaning ignorance. In this respect, the absolute rigidity of the angels and the obstinate xenophobia of Beknechons are as reprehensible as the stupidity of Laban. The enlightened God-person would reject any such dog-matic stance—even if it were under the banner of the good—because it would immobilize him while the living world moved on.

ALLAN J. McINTYRE

Determinism in Mario and the Magician

As a writer in the classical tradition, it was instinctive for Thomas Mann to look for causal connections in experience and to embody them in the formal patterns of his art. The more refined the sensibility and intellect of the artist the deeper and more encompassing will be his vision, so that within the narrow limits of a small work it sometimes happens that the intensity of insight may produce an effect of such utter inevitability in the whole and the parts that the guiding principle thereof may aptly be characterized as determinism. Such a work is *Mario and the Magician*.

By determinism, then, is meant here the perception that practically all phenomena in the story, including what are usually termed moral decisions, are the certain result of a network of prior causes. This is not to claim that Mann himself was a determinist, pure and simple, any more than that he was a believer in free will. Rather, we would say that, insofar as this novella represents a world in itself, the determinism we see operating so powerfully within it through aesthetic means testifies to the author's protean ability to absorb and transform life inwardly, under what, and varying from work to work, are in logic often contradictory forms. Certainly, determinism, whether logical or aesthetic, answers to a desire in the mind that effects should have causes, and that all phenomena should somehow be interrelated and therefore interdependent. The intention of the present study, by demonstrating the pervasive workings of determinism in the novella, and in particular in the

From *The Germanic Review* 52, no. 3 (May 1977). © 1977 by Columbia University Press.

central figure of Cipolla, the magician, is to present an essentially new as well as cogent interpretation of this work.

In the composition of *Mario and the Magician* (1929), Mann based himself on a personal experience of some years before while a tourist in Italy, which, although thoroughly unpleasant, did not in fact culminate in the fatal violence of the story. The reader of the work of art, however, is disposed to feel at once the inevitability of the fateful outcome by the message telegraphed ahead in the words of the subtitle, *ein tragisches Reiseerlebnis* [A Tragic Travel Experience], for Mann's use of "tragic" as a descriptive term must be thought to carry overtones of a classic, not merely colloquial or canting significance, as of a perfect necessity. The clear eye of the artist foresaw a bad end to the concatenation of evil pranks which had been played around him on his tour, and so, eliminating the fortuitous, he telescoped and streamlined life—in his personal experience of which the horrible sequel of the story had not occurred—creating an imaginative work whose vital principle is an intuitively grasped and aesthetically expressed determinism.

We may analyze the determinism in the work for convenience's sake under three aspects. First, and most obviously, forming the groundwork, there is what we may call the poetic aspect, in which the entire subject matter from beginning to end is literally bathed and enveloped as in an aura of clairvoyance, lending a virtually unlimited dimension to every appearance, utterance and action. Out of this immediate, omnipresent, poetic representation arise certain conceptual aspects which we will term metaphysical and psychological. It will be seen in the course of discussion that these three, the poetic, the metaphysical and the psychological, are reflections of a single overriding necessity, which, because it conditions everything, makes the frightful ending a certainty. In the very configuration of that end, moreover, is revealed again *in nuce* the entire determinism which has brought it to pass.

An air of predestination hangs over the story from the beginning, for not only is there the key word "tragic" in the subtitle, but there occurs in the introductory paragraph the significant phrase, explicating the end before anything at all has happened: "einem vorgezeichneten und im Wesen der Dinge liegenden Ende [the horrible end of the affair had been preordained and lay in the nature of things (trans. H. T. Lowe-Porter in *Death in Venice and Seven Other Stories.* New York: Vintage Books, 1954. All further references will be from this translation)]," which directs the reader's attention to an ineluctable pattern in the events about to unfold, further preparing him to see in them a kind of classical outline. But apart from such explicit statements, Mann is at pains from the beginning to create and sustain an overall impression of perfect necessity by a subtle poetic technique which blends physical and moral qualities indistinguishably together.

The opening note of this technique is sounded in the first sentence of the story: "Die Erinnerung an Torre di Venere ist atmosphärisch unangenehm [The atmosphere of Torre di Venere remains unpleasant in the memory]." It is the sultry month of August, and we discover that the moral barometer of human society at the beach and in the hotels reflects the oppressive, threatening atmosphere of the natural world. Scarcely descending to mere comparisons, Mann proceeds as though from an immanent source in truth to portray the two spheres, physical and moral, as one. By this means the author lays a sure foundation of correspondence over which he will eventually move to the ominous figure of Cipolla, whom he has already pictured briefly in his opening paragraph as the incarnation of an impending storm: "in dessen Person sich das eigentümlich Bösartige der Stimmung auf verhängnishafte ... Weise zu verkörpern und bedrohlich zusammenzudrängen schien [that dreadful being who seemed to incorporate, in so fateful ... a way, all the peculiar evilness of the situation as a whole]." The eventual transition is masterly: the mounting atmospheric pressure, having been made to correspond to a disequilibrium of moral energies in a susceptible populace, is then led to Cipolla, who, by the magnetism of his personality, marshals and monopolizes those energies, draining his interlocutors of will. The dynamics of what happens then are at bottom as impersonal as energy transfers, as sheer action and reaction, cause and effect, for by this time the performance of Cipolla itself is felt by the reader to be subject to the same laws that unchain the lightning. Imperceptibly, Mann has passed from an electric imbalance in the air men breathe, through an abnormal psychic state in society at large, to a crisis of will-power without ever having let go the thread of determinism that holds all together.

Previous studies of this work have not directed enough attention to Cipolla; rather, criticism has been more interested in the magician's effect on the audience. It is in the person of the magician, however, not in the audience, that the quintessence of evil and its results are concentrated, and therefore the chief object of our analysis must be the moral and physical anatomy of the magician, who draws out the whole sum of evil, and like an adaptor sets alight a train of events leading to the final flash. Cipolla is actually an extreme type of the artist, who is both demonic and driven, a link in a chain of cause and effect from which he has no escape. Much of the tragic irony of the story, hitherto overlooked, arises precisely from the utter helplessness of this consummate villain who is at the same time his own victim.

At the magician's first entrance onstage, the reader's disquiet sharpens when he sees that something is wrong with him, something camouflaged by his costume, but so fundamentally awry as to suggest that life has been twisted in the sockets. The very vagueness of the deformity, decently hid from the public gaze, heightens the sense of a calamity lurking just beneath appearances. In Cipolla's ensuing exchanges with members of the audience, in which the physical is linked to the moral, he reveals a boundless desire to impose his will, barely masking savage resentment of the normal, and a powerful, thwarted sexuality. These implications must be sorted out in detail, but for the moment it is important to realize that the author conceives of Cipolla as an end product of some crippling process, a man whose tormenting and tormented will is as much the result thereof in the moral realm as his twisted body is in the physical. Not being a theologian, the storyteller does not concern himself with the ultimate origin of the causal chain, or with the question of which first produces the other, body or mind. In Cipolla it is enough that the idea of mutual correspondence of the moral and the physical is represented aesthetically to the last degree of consequence.

Continuing with our description of the poetic aspect of determinism, it is clear that an initial concentration of electricity in the external atmosphere has been linked to a later engrossing of will by the magician, both processes oppressive and due to some imbalance in the flux of nature, which must accelerate to a violent yet relieving climax. Will-power, or moral dynamism, can be seen operating here as though in quantums of physical energy. The amorphous, passive, or negative will of the audience is expropriated in ever-increasing quantums by the positive will of the tyrant, who degrades individuals by turning them into puppets and automatons, emptying them of everything but readiness to his suggestion. But nature abhors a moral vacuum as much as a physical one, and when the magician/artist at last succeeds in making a perfect vacuum, as it were, in the extreme and climactic scene with Mario, there is a recoil, a sudden violent discharge, which redistributes will once more around the hall, minus the magician, who has been destroyed.

Each detail and each event shows forth the poetic aspect: the noticeable inner weariness of Cipolla is the consequence of his continual exertions; the cognac, the cigarettes, and the whip in his hand that shrinks the will of the audience are all needed to buoy up the crippled master puppeteer who is under great strain, for mass hypnotism, with repeated challenges to his control, is devilish work indeed; and so Cipolla's entire being, which epitomizes resentment, it literally wearing itself out. The magician is actually bent on suicide without knowing it; he only senses the growing burden of fatigue. When at last he succeeds in turning members of the audience into puppets, making them dance senselessly together on the stage as though controlled by invisible wires, he has intolerably heightened the cause and effect spiral of tension, and opened an abyss at his own feet.

At the end, when Mario whirls about and fires the shots at his tormentor, the poetic presentation reaches its apogee. Significantly, at first, the pistol is not mentioned; it is his arm which Mario flings up "schleuderte," says the author, whereupon there are two "flach schmetternde Detonationen [flat, shattering detonations]," with grotesque and fatal results. The relative insignificance of the pistol in the long chain of cause and effect is underscored by Mann's following description of it after the deed, as a "kleine, stumpf-metallne, kaum pistolenförmige Maschinerie . . . deren fast nicht vorhandenen Lauf das Schicksal in so unvorhergesehene und fremde Richtung gelenkt hatte [small, dull-metal, scarcely pistol-shaped tool with hardly any barrel—in how strange and unexpected a direction had fate levelled it]." These concluding words refer of course to the audience, which is unaware, but the reader sees at once that this innocuous, snub-nosed contrivance is the proximate and visible conductor of the vast forces which have produced the catastrophe. Mario, in the moral sphere, is nothing but the extension of the physical pistol, and vice versa; together they are inseparable in their commission of the deed. Mario is an ordinary, decent and unassuming fellow, the last man to commit a crime, yet he is the one who finishes the magician. It is Mario, to be sure, who does it, but at bottom the deed is not the product of moral courage or free choice; rather it is the necessary outcome of a natural, compensatory function, which, in moral terms, may be called retributive or karmic, and Mario is the simple instrument of a poetic justice. His arm is flung up and his finger tightens on the trigger in obedience to the same laws in himself that drive the clouds and flings a tree branch in the wind. It is quite impossible and unthinkable, after all the groundwork laid by the author, that either Mario or Cipolla can act otherwise than they do at the end.

Immediately after the shots, the determinism which has been moving through the story and has led to exactly this outcome and no other, is graphically summed up *in nuce* in the description of the mortally stricken magician:

> Cipolla war mit einem Satz vom Stuhle aufgesprungen. Er stand da mit abwehrend seitwärtsgestreckten Armen, als wollte er rufen: "Halt! Still! Alles weg von mir! Was ist das!", sackte im nächsten Augenblick mit auf die Brust kugelndem Kopf auf den Sitz zurück und fiel im übernächsten seitlich davon herunter, zu Boden, wo er liegen blieb, reglos, ein durcheinandergeworfenes Bündel Kleider und schiefer Knochen.

> [Cipolla bounded from his seat. He stood with his arms spread out, slanting as though to ward everybody off, as though next

moment he would cry out: 'Stop! Keep back! Silence! What was that?' Then, in that instant, he sank back in his seat, his head rolling on his chest; in the next he had fallen sideways, to the floor, where he lay motionless, a huddled heap of clothing, with limbs awry.]

In the use of language in this passage, with its unmistakable connotations of the puppet stage, lies the stark and final revelation of the puppet master, the demonic puller of invisible strings, as himself a mere puppet, lying now with his limbs askew in a heap on the stage where a moment before he had given the illusion of power, his own vital strings severed, with the real and greater power that had caused him to move suddenly gone out of him. The other puppets from the audience—Mann calls them *Zappler*—who have been flinging themselves orgiastically about the stage at the bidding of Cipolla, are released by his death and instantly stop dancing. They return to their rational selves, for their master, however powerful he was for having drawn on the irrational, was only human, whereas Cipolla's own demon manipulator was the impersonal Will itself.

This brings us to the metaphysical aspect under which the determinism of the story may be considered. The matter of will is crucial, for the onward impetus of events towards a climax results from the succession of victories by Cipolla over the wills of members of the audience. Obviously, Mann had Nietzsche in mind, along with the contemporary politico-cultural environment of Europe, when he wrote the story, and wanted to show the consequences of civilization when power as thing-in-itself is exalted. Nietzsche was important to Mann, yet it is generally agreed that Schopenhauer was the single most contributory influence on him, and in the present instance the phenomenon of Cipolla is in fact best understood by reference to Schopenhauer and his philosophy of the Will, although Nietzsche too must be taken into account. The Schopenhauerian Will may be shortly described as the universal, indiscriminate and mindless life-surge, which is objectified and differentiated in individual life-forms. In Cipolla, the intensity of Will, risen in him to the level of controlled mania, is reflected in his appearance. The distortion of his body is palpable evidence, an involuntary warning to the observer, of the maiming power of that urge, which is harnessed here to work the subjection and downfall of all opposition, all other wills. He is able figuratively to seize and violate others because his proper field of operation is the subterranean depth of Will common to all, where individuality is obliterated and mind is merely an instrument of suggestion. His personal will, whetted keen by ceaseless exertion, is a direct manifestation of universal

Will, the heavy burden of which on his own, limited person he voices to the effect that it is not his victims, but really he who suffers.

There is no doubt that Cipolla is the master of a demonic art, with a hypnotic personality of the first order. It must be clear, however, that because he is an incorporation, indeed, almost the caricature of Will, his actions must be completely determined thereby, and that therefore he is a slave, not a master. He rushes blindly on to personal catastrophe because his mind is nothing more than the obedient servant of the Power in him whose craving is limitless. Somewhere, sometime, in the economy of the natural order, Cipolla must go too far with somebody, and Mario is his logical nemesis. Why Mario? Because Will is at the moment also dominant in Mario himself. Beneath his cheerful, accommodating exterior, hidden fires are burning; he suffers the pangs of an unrequited love and hatred of a rival, and goes about secretly armed with a deadly weapon. The Will being differentiated in living forms, there must be conflict among the individuals who embody it, and so when Mario comes out of his trance and realizes that his lips have caressed that abominable flesh instead of the beloved object, he is profoundly wounded in the Will which is now his most vulnerable part. Outraged, he responds instinctively with the give-and-take of physical combat, and it is his blow which is mortal.

In Schopenhauer's scale of value, the mass of humanity are naturally at the bottom, dominated by the Will and enmeshed in the causal net; above them is the artist, still trapped, but now and then able selflessly to contemplate the vast network and so to rise above it; and at the highest stage, the saint, who has left means and ends permanently behind him. In the character of Cipolla we have what amounts to an addition, or a variation in the Schopenhauerian *scala*. Cipolla is the direct contrary of the saint, yet can hardly be classified with the mass. He represents, rather, a new category of the perverted or demonic artist. He is an artist because of the form and control he is able to impose on experience, perverted and demonic, however, because he cannot rise, even for a moment, above goals conditioned by means and ends, to pure, disinterested contemplation of the eternal. With all the power of his disciplined personal will, he remains the slave of the irrational world Will, with a predetermined end to his career when he shall have reached a certain degree of excess.

It is rather the storyteller, himself, who comes near the Schopenhauerian criteria of the artist. The narrator is in the middle position of the value scale, still held in the toils of Will, and to that degree tied to the scene by a certain morbid curiosity, or it may be by some slight intimidation, when reason and concern for his young children had urged him to leave, yet he is able to fathom the whole chain of events with a sovereign, impartial eye, and so transcend them. Besides, what could persuade a born storyteller to quit the scene before the last curtain? In fact, Mario's pistol shots signal the end as far as the narrator is concerned, and he gathers his family and hastily departs. His opposite, meanwhile, the perverted artist, Cipolla, has only found release in death from the Will he never transcended in life, even fleetingly.

As far as Nietzsche is concerned, Mann's evocation of Will in the person of Cipolla may be taken as an implied criticism of Nietzsche's belief in the ideal function of will as a liberation—as Nietzsche significantly put it, from "the obscurings of the intellect." For Nietzsche, the highest morality was natural action, in which the innermost laws of man's nature are in harmony with those of external and impersonal forces. This view implies that ordinary morality, supported by the dictates of reason, is inferior and contrary to the elemental and pure workings of nature. Such, in fact, is the moral milieu of Mann's story, where the limited, conventional and rational will of members of the audience is defeated by the master conjuror of instinctive, irrational forces. The implied criticism of Nietzsche, however, lies in the fact that this master is not good but evil, and that what lays him low in the end is not any limited reason or conventional morality but his own irrational weapon, the world Will, which in effect has made sport of him. The master of will has been shown to be a tool, now used up and cast aside.

We come now to the psychological aspect. As Thomas Mann saw it, the metaphysical Will of Schopenhauer had, in effect, been translated into a modern idiom by Freud in his psychology of the subconscious, that is, of the Id, with its roots in sexuality. In this context, Will being equivalent to the Id, the Schopenhauerian rational mind is likewise the equivalent to the Freudian ego, and it is readily apparent that in the terms of Mann's story, the transposition is perfectly feasible. Psychologically speaking, Cipolla is almost a caricature of the idea that the conscious ego is determined and controlled by the requirements of the subconscious Id. The key to Cipolla's craving to dominate, and the invisible counterpart of his misshapen body, is a thwarted and deformed sexual drive. His ego is its servant, and all other egos, or minds, must be inimical by the very reason of their existence. The total elimination of these minds and wills is his goal, and the orgiastic dance of the human automatons on the stage is the high water of his success. Thereafter he plunges straight to disaster in classical style.

That Cipolla's own master is in fact the thwarted Id is made abundantly clear by his frequent and otherwise unnecessary allusions to the sexual advantages supposedly enjoyed by members of the audience, as well as by his later "experiments" with the attractive Signora Angolieri and the enamored waiter, Mario. Whatever the final cause of his pathological state, about which the author is silent, the wellspring of Cipolla's conduct is envy of the sexually normal. His scarcely concealed envy and hate glance out of nearly every word and deed. He is an artist out of hate, a grotesque variant in the long Mann picture gallery of endangered species, man-as-artist, a distant cousin of Tonio Kröger and Gustav von Aschenbach, closer perhaps to his opposite, the dashing Felix Krull. Cipolla has to dominate all within his reach, and thus annihilate the distance which his deformity puts between himself and the rest of the world, which otherwise must spurn him. His self-pity, often noted disparagingly by critics, is a kind of narcissism, part of the morbid inversion which is a problem of the artist, a homoeroticism which takes the place of the normal relationships denied him. The fatal kiss, which Cipolla coaxes from the mesmerised Mario, is at once an expression of self-love and a supreme revenge on the normal world, a perversion which is the result of his complete alienation from it. In effect, Cipolla is driven to violate what he knows he cannot possess. The kiss represents the apotheosis of what for him is his sacred selfhood, which, however, is revealed in that moment as a pitiful, infantile thing.

The enormous power of the Id at work in the twisted frame of Cipolla puts him to death as surely as any executioner, and, moreover, in the dark, for he grasps nothing at all of what is happening to him. Because he hates reason, analysis, the mind in general—his antipathy is conveyed by his continual slighting references to it—he must hate it in himself, and as we have emphasized, his own mind is simply the instrument, however disciplined in its craft, of the Will, or the Id. Blindly, he has fashioned a weapon which works his own destruction, and it is his own death he seeks without being aware of it. Only when those two shots ring out does the true nature of the whole business start to penetrate the level of his conscious mind. Then he leaps to his feet, unable to utter a sound, but as though he would cry out: stop! everybody back! what is this? It looks very much as though he would now like to take everything back, to pretend that everything had been just a show, an illusionist performance, after all. He will not face the inevitable, for only when it is too late does he begin to see what it is. His voiceless cry is an attempt at evasion, a reproach to Mario, whom he has just graciously released from his clutch, and who is now taking the affair far too seriously. At this moment we have the complete revelation of the naïve, infantile personality behind the cynical mask of the magician, who was quite unaware that he was burning a candle at both ends. The master illusionist who was actually dealing in realities has been fatally disillusioned at the end.

There is a further, subtly ironic comment on Nietzsche's "will to power" in that Cipolla's psychology is delineated by Mann in terms that correspond to Nietzsche's description of the Christian power-pervert: Cipolla, like any Christian functionary, is a product of lack, of weakness, sickness and failure, who seeks in compensation a crude, vulgar power over others. It is wholly in accord with the picture developed of Cipolla that weakness, however variously it reveals itself, is seen by the reader to lurk behind the power facade, and it is this basic, determining weakness which, in an echo of Schopenhauer and Richard Wagner, is linked by Mann in Cipolla's deepest subconscious with the erotic, that final culmination of Will, which simultaneously with its expression, must incline towards individual extinction.

The greatest irony in the prolonged contest of wills between Cipolla and resisting members of his audience, including the passive resistance of the storyteller, lies in the fact, as we have seen, that the tug-of-war is basically an illusion, for its course and result are determined by causal factors external to, and independent of, any principle of final autonomy in individuals. The fate which overtakes the magician is conveyed by Mann with the overpowering sense that it is ultimately the result of an impersonal shifting of mighty weights, which yet serves justice, as in a great mill grinding small, or better, given its suddenness, like the slipping of a ship's cargo in a gale, a cargo critically poised from the start of the voyage, with the crumpled human form of the magician on the stage at the close, reduced to mere debris, as mute testimony to the fact that he was in the way.

This revelation of emptiness at the heart of power leads to a consideration of the author's attitude toward the creature whom he has portrayed without a single redeeming, let alone endearing, trait. On the level of determinism, apart from the grotesque and hateful manifestations of his personality, Cipolla is a pitiful character, and the reader senses that the large sympathy of a creator, who sees the problematical in everything, may not be entirely withheld even from him, although the strictures of the story may preclude an overt expression. After all, there can be nothing tragic about an archvillain and his just desserts, unless one can see him, too, somehow, as a victim. The last words of the storyteller provide a clue. Insisting on the liberating, cathartic effects of Cipolla's death he says: "ich konnte und kann nicht umhin, es so zu empfinden [I could not, and I cannot, but find it so]," by this comparative vehemence drawing the reader's attention once more to the enormity of the deterministic process which has caused it. Having grasped that process, we understand with the author that Cipolla simply had to be eliminated but the knowledge is a sobering one. This ending has brought us full circle to the fateful remark at the beginning of the story, only now a slightly different flavor is conveyed in these last expostulatory and somewhat agitated words of a man who has witnessed a terrible thing. A trace of pity seems to hang on the air. In this regard, it may be recalled that the humanist exile from his own land, Thomas Mann, was one who could write a probing essay on a subject he execrated, and entitle it, characteristically, "Bruder Hitler" ["Brother Hitler"].

In summation, the consequential determinism of *Mario and the Magician* is to be seen as an extreme expression of the traditional, classic, artistic vision, which sought patterns in experience, in breadth and depth, in the whole and in the parts, patterns which would omit nothing, even though they might not be finally reconcilable. Seen thus, the word, *magician,* signifies much more than skill in stage tricks or even in psychic expertise. Cipolla's powers were more impressive than that, and genuine enough, but ultimately the kingdom of the magician is shown to be an illusion, nevertheless, built in air, like the illusion of his aristocratic pedigree, a conceit often affected by people of the stage, a bubble of arrogance pricked in the mind of the reader even before the magician's performance by its being coupled with the common, earthy, plebeian name, *Cipolla,* i.e, onion. From the vantage of hindsight, i.e., from a reading of the novella, the title itself, *Mario and the Magician* is a statement of confrontation, of reality versus illusion, containing the implication that there is to be an explosion of pretence and presumption. The story is thus a kind of modern morality play, moral in that a bad man has been paid and the eternal balance righted, modern in the disturbing sense that we discover that he has not really been able to help himself. A deterministic process has made the man and then broken him. In a deeper sense, however, which reaches past the medical age, Mann continues here the classical inheritance from the ancient Greeks, the masters of tragedy, who conceived it in essentially the same terms.

Mario and the Magician, as interpreted here, is another of those supremely ironic works for which their author is renowned. It is poetic genius, however, which gives irony its bite. The reader of Mann is always convinced; he follows gladly on all of these winding ways because of the skill, the courage and the generosity of the guiding spirit.

MICHAEL MANN

Truth and Poetry
in Thomas Mann's Work

The book *A Tragic History of Literature* by the Swiss critic Walter Muschg
contains a sentence directed against Thomas Mann which, in quite a remarkable way, has become a part of world literature. The sentence reads:

> He [Mann] believed that with his ambiguities he had left all pre-
> vious notions of literature behind him. He amused a lost world
> which shared his belief, without bestowing upon that world the
> slightest trace of a saving idea.

Thomas Mann (on the whole astonishingly immune to Muschg's "beautiful
anger") commented on this attack in a letter of July 18, 1954:

> The poet Muschg is not so wrong with his contention about me
> that I "amuse a lost world, without bestowing upon it the slight-
> est trace of a saving truth."

Only why, so run Mann's objections, only why does he single out *me*? Many
a conscientious writer, Mann finds, was forced to ask himself: "Am I not
deluding readers with my talent since, after all, I have no answers for the
ultimate questions?" And as an example Mann thinks of Chekhov, whom
he was writing about at that time. Shortly afterwards, his "Essays on Chekhov" appeared; in the final section, we read:

From *Thomas Mann: Ein Kolloquium.* © 1978 by Bouvier Verlag Herbert Grundmann, Bonn.

> It is not otherwise: you "amuse a needy world with stories, with-
> out ever bestowing upon it the slightest trace of a saving truth."

The literary montage, here involved, becomes even more intriguing in what
follows:

> To poor Katja's question, "What am I to do?" there is only the
> answer, "On my honor and in all conscience, I don't know."

Katja is the name of the female protagonist in Chekhov's story "A Tedious
Tale," from which Thomas Mann is quoting more or less verbatim. But Katja
is also the name of his own wife!—If the unsuspecting reader tends to ascribe
the first quotation to Chekhov (in reality, it was Muschg's description of
Mann), then the second thought suggests that the author has left his subject,
Chekhov, to become immersed in autobiographical reflections.

"To paste on" objective facts and "blur the edges" between truth and
poetry—this is the way Thomas Mann once described the montage technique
which he used with the greatest consistency in his novel *Doctor Faustus*.
And there is no lack of blurred edges in the example at hand; we are struck
by several minor changes in the text which has been "pasted on" when Mann
quotes it in his letter; he simplifies by leaving out all subordinate clauses (in
other words, subordinate ideas) which in his view do not fit the topic, Chekhov. Also, there is a certain raising of the level of discourse, most significantly in Mann's "saving truth," in place of Muschg's "saving idea." In its
final form in the Chekhov essay, the Muschg excerpt had undergone another
decisive change: this time Muschg's "world lost" has become a "world in
need." A more human view! In harmony with the essay's conclusion:

> And yet one goes on working, telling stories, and giving form to
> truth . . . in the dim hope, indeed the confidence, that truth and
> serene form can have a liberating effect, preparing the world for
> a better, fairer, more dignified form of life.

That is perhaps not exactly a "saving" truth about life, but it is certainly an
attempt to save and vindicate art. Muschg has served his purpose. He was
simply a guru figure, a bit blurred around the edges, standing on Thomas
Mann's path to a *unio mystica* with Anton Chekhov.

The tendency toward autobiographical identification with his subject,
so characteristic of Mann's literary and cultural criticism, presumes a peculiar mix to exist between "self" and "world"—a problem which never
ceased to preoccupy the author, solved in different ways at different times.
Thus, in later years (in the lecture entitled "My Times") he confessed that,

in spite of his "distaste for autobiography" he couldn't keep "the autobiographical 'self' completely out of the picture when considering his times. This is a definite shift of accent in Mann's creative attitude from "self" to "world." Quite different from the attitude of the young author of *Buddenbrooks*. Indignantly he complained to his compatriots of Lübeck who felt compromised by being used as "models" for the novel:

> You are not the subject, never, you may rest assured; it is I, it is I. . . . But how can I reveal my whole self without at the same time revealing the world which is my Idea? *My* Idea, *my* experience, *my* dream, *my* suffering?
>
> (*Bilse and I*)

He revealed himself, sampled all the possibilities, anxieties and hopes of the inmost self so unreservedly that he could correctly describe a collection of his stories as "a sort of abbreviated, short chronicle of the author's life" (foreword to *Stories of Three Decades*). And he continued to reveal "his world." He worked from models, animate as well as inanimate, thereby letting himself in for a lot of unpleasantness. To the living models who had been wounded by Apollo's arrow he would then write apologetic letters, defending himself, from the time of *Buddenbrooks* until the last months of his life, against the use of erroneous biographical clues to his works. Occasionally, I believe, he also protested against the use of the right clues—a subject to which I shall return later. But he insisted that the world he depicted was only *his* "Idea," *his* "experience," *his* "dream," *his* "suffering." Until one day he discovered, eyebrows raised:

> One thinks that one is describing merely one's own person, and behold, out of a kind of unconscious communal identity, one has created something universal in which many recognize themselves.

This (the year 1925) is the period during which the accent shifted from "self" to "world": in other words, the period when he became conscious of his representative role. The poetic self is able to represent the world by means of a hidden synchronization, an "accidental" parallelism between the problems of the individual and those of society. This constellation has become obvious enough: in Mann's last story about an artist told before World War I, *Death in Venice*. Although the conscious accent here is still upon the self and its problems, and the "communal identity" is still "unconscious," the synchronization between the two is so apparent for the reader that the question could narrow down to this: is the ultimate concern here not rather the "world"—the dissolution of a society still maintaining itself by sheer dint of semblance and sham—than the very personal experience of that society's overburdened representative, the writer Gustav von Aschenbach? Once we have gained this perspective, a similar account can be found already in one of Thomas Mann's earliest stories, namely "Little Herr Friedemann," at least on its periphery. No doubt, this story is primarily the product of intensely private suffering, yet why is the fatal breakdown of the poor little protagonist and his carefully preserved world caused precisely by that woman whose arrival in town—like that of her husband, the new district commander—had "caused excitement in the whole community"? The departing old district commander is described as a

> portly, jovial gentleman who had held his post for many years, had been popular in social circles and his departure is seen with regret.

The "change" ("Heaven knows that circumstances brought it about!") suggests a historical turning point on a miniature scale much like the plague in Venice symbolizes the end of an epoch on a large scale. It may be said without oversimplification that in both cases the forces of a historical process, like the rays of the sun, are focused in a personal magnifying glass to cremate the individual chosen by the tragedy of history.

My quotation showing Mann's acknowledgment of the representative character of his art dates back to approximately the same time he is completing *The Magic Mountain*. This acknowledgment implies a joyful realization: he is surprised and greatly moved to find that his "devotion to an autobiographical, confessional type of literature whose aim is self-development has given birth to an ideal of social education" ("On the German Republic"). The classical model for this transformation is Goethe's *Wilhelm Meister*. In this novel "the idea of adventurous and personal self-development" merges, according to Thomas Mann, completely into "the social, even the political sphere" ("Goethe and Tolstoy"). The conscious raising of the "poetic self" to a representative position means a turn toward pedagogy; one might almost call it an activist tendency. A reciprocal relationship between self and world implies involvement, not only in articulating the burning issues of the day, but also in acting on them. This guarantees that the world can be transformed by individual effort, it means "the predominance of the individual and his destiny over the generally prevailing power of circumstance" (Letter, 10–7–1941). The words just quoted could have been written by Jean-Paul Sartre. And indeed, it is not such a long way to the Sartrean concept of existential freedom and responsibility from the new "concept of humanism" which has been the center of Thomas Mann's thoughts ever since the time of the First World War. For Mann, this concept meant the broadening of an obsolete and unpolitical German Romantic ideal of self-development into one which would embrace the democratic collectivity of Western Europe.

As late as *Death in Venice* he had been able to state apparently with an eye to his own work:

> Love of oneself . . . is . . . the beginning of all autobiography. For a person's impulse to celebrate his fate in literature and seek out the sympathies of his contemporaries and of posterity presupposes that rare and passionate egocentricity which . . . can make life seem like a novel, thus raising it into the sphere of objective interest and significance for everybody.

As proof of this, he pointed to those great documents of "a passionate or at any rate intense self-concern in sensuous and moral matters," the confessions of St. Augustine, Rousseau, and Goethe; these works meant much more to the world, so it seemed then to Mann, than "masterpieces of playfully inventive art." With a noticeable feeling of nostalgia Mann repeats the opening words of those reflections several years later, on the occasion of a public reading of a chapter from the *Felix Krull* fragment. "Love of oneself" as the main force in the creation of literature has become insufficient for Mann's morality, for the social sympathy inherent in his new humanism. Thus *The Confessions of Felix Krull, Confidence Man* became Mann's first swan song of the autobiographical novel, in which the main stylistic attraction lies precisely "in parodying the great autobiographies of the eighteenth century, including Goethe's *Poetry and Truth*." Similarly, and even "more clearly," Thomas Mann thought that with *The Magic Mountain* he was "bringing to a close the history of the German *bildungsroman* in a parodistic manner" (*On Myself*).

Despite his growing "distaste for autobiography" Mann confronts "his times"—as we already know—without keeping "the autobiographical 'self' . . . completely out of the picture." It remains present in the scheme of his fictional heroes' lives—a scheme which elsewhere I have attempted to define as variations on the theme of "*felix culpa*," that is to say: the old Christian idea of a "fortunate guilt," the elevation through guilt, that deeply felt experience to be elected for tragedy and grace alike. We may remember that the image of the guilty artist goes back to Greek antiquity and that Thomas Mann, as a schoolboy, immersed himself in Greek mythology, like other children would in Wild West stories. He surely was familiar at an early age with figures like Daedalus (Icarus's father), that ingenious artist–murderer

who after so many wicked wanderings was chosen to found a temple for the
god Apollo (not to speak of that greatest humanitarian rebel against the
gods, Prometheus, who became the patron saint for the artist from young
Goethe to the late Romantics). The classical image of the criminal artist finds
its direct reflection in Romantic literature. One may think particularly of
E. T. A. Hoffmann, his "Fräulein von Scudery" for instance, in which story
the ingenious goldsmith Cardillac, adored by the entire Court of Louis XV,
steals away at night to murder his customers. This literary tradition seems
in several cases fatally to have influenced the vision of artists of their own
real existence: thus the poet Jakob Lenz, one of the greatest talents among
the German Pre-Romantics, suffered from the hallucination that he had murdered his fiancée which finally drove him to complete insanity.

This side of the artist's potential guilt which, in theological terminology,
might be designated as *culpa commissionis* becomes thematic in Thomas
Mann's artist novel *Doctor Faustus* where the protagonist, Adrian Leverkühn, is actually responsible for the murder of his most beloved friend. It is
however another side of the artist's guilt which is more important for Thomas
Mann. It might be designated as *culpa omissionis*—the guilt of omission, of
not acting, against one's better knowledge, like Hamlet; the guilt of failing
to ask the timely question (like Parsival). Not without reason has Hans
Castorp in *The Magic Mountain* been associated with Parsival; and Tonio
Kröger (by the author) several times with Hamlet.

The redemption from the *culpa omissionis,* the social self-isolation, the
inhuman distance of the artist from his fellow-beings can logically be
achieved only by his social integration, his participation in the everyday
worries of the world. This is the course taken already by the protagonist of
one of Thomas Mann's earliest novels *Royal Highness*; it is the course probed
in *The Magic Mountain* and completed in the *Joseph* novels.

That the theme of *felix culpa* has for Thomas Mann a strongly autobiographical touch, that he looked at his own life as a rising from "guilt to
grace," he has made plain enough in some of his latest lectures, particularly
the one entitled "Der Künstler und die Gesellschaft" ("The Artist and Society"). So in this rather esoteric sense, the autobiographical element remained present in his novels even where one should not expect it.

To be sure, the discreet use of the subjective–autobiographical self did
not prevent him from making quite extensive use of "objective"–autobiographical materials. Especially in the shorter works from his middle period,
there is scarcely any occurrence which he freely invented. In several cases I
can say: "I am a witness." The little party given by my oldest brother and
sister which furnished the basis for the novella *Disorder and Early Sorrow*

is described in that work with a degree of realism hardly to be surpassed in accuracy. I remember the original event all too well. In *Mario and the Magician, nothing* was invented (children usually see more than adults suspect!)—with the exception of the shot at the end. It was not fired but certainly should have been.

Such external autobiographical elements fade in importance upon entering into the world of the *Joseph* novels. A work which tries, like all poetry based on myth, to describe what is typical and valid for all times has little use for specific "models." Here, it is neither the "I" nor is it the "you" which counts. Thomas Mann himself calls *Joseph* his "first work without human 'models.' " The characters in this novel, he claims, are "invented, without exception . . . in contrast to earlier dependence on observed reality" (Letter, 3–23–1940). And generally speaking, this is undoubtedly true.

Strange enough: also in reviewing his earlier works, he now cautions against overestimating even their "dependence" on "naturalistically observed material"; for, he says, his first concern has always been the "stylization and intellectual intensification" of his material. And, as an illustration, he uses *The Magic Mountain*: readers, he thinks, are correct in assuming that all the characters of this novel are something more than they appear to be:

> Exponents, representatives and messengers of intellectual realms, principles and worlds.

Although Thomas Mann hopes that for this reason his figures are not mere "shadows and walking allegories"; and he is "reassured by the reaction of his readers who experienced these persons—Joachim, Clawdia Chauchat, Peeperkorn, Settembrini, and the others—as real human beings," as, we may remember, the author himself had experienced them. Take Naphta as an example. As is known, the Hungarian critic Georg Lukács served as a model for him. In this portrait, though, the emphasis certainly is not on external resemblance but merely on intellectual trends. In contrast we may think of Peeperkorn whose model was Gerhart Hauptmann. Here however we are obviously dealing with a purely external resemblance—Hauptmann's gestures, his way of talking in broken sentences, incomplete phrases and obscure allusions.

What does Peeperkorn "represent"? I shall not attempt here fully to answer that question. To some degree, however, its answers will be found in the way in which Hauptmann's mask entered the picture. The narrator had arrived at a deadlock. Mme Chauchat was supposed to return to the sanatorium, but she should not return alone. The affair with Hans Castorp could not be prolonged. The lady was in need of an impressive escort, full of vitality yet not without a morbid touch. The author just did not envisage that kind of personage. It so happened that he spent a week at Bozen in Southern Tyrol together with the Hauptmanns. One evening, when engaged with Hauptmann in an absorbing conversation, it came to him like a flash: he had found his man. By taking out all artistic substance of Hauptmann, leaving him only the hollow shell of his imposing stature, he had transformed the great artist into Hans Castorp's guide who could turn him away from the sickly Mme Chauchat back into life ... not entirely successfully. Accordingly, the "principle" Peeperkorn is "representing" would be "life," the "spirit of health" in most "questionable shape."

From this it would follow that it is, first of all, the representative quality of the fictional characters and events—that *something beyond the work itself*—which makes up the intellectual intensification of reality in Mann's work, called also by him the "symbolic" intensification. And yet this reveals only one side of the artistic process of transformation. I should like to describe the other side as one which intensifies reality by means of symbolism *intrinsic to the work itself*. Thomas Mann likes to describe the system of references and allusions involved here in musical terminology. Thus, again in connection with *The Magic Mountain*, he speaks of "counterpoint" and a "thematic texture" in which "the ideas would play the role of musical motifs." In this case the fictional characters and events do not point beyond themselves to a world, perhaps, in need of "a saving truth"; rather, they point to one another as integral components of the literary composition.

We may assume that Thomas Mann is speaking of both types of literary symbolism, the representative as well as the intrinsic, when he answers the question, "What is a poet?" with the mystifying definition: to be a poet simply means "sich aus den Dingen etwas machen"—"to tease something out of things," to borrow from Shakespeare. To inspect these "things" a little closer, let us turn back once more to *Death in Venice*, Mann's last story to be based on the autobiographical "self"—as far as his conscious conception goes. As we know from the author himself, his point of departure was the experience or the anxiety-ridden imagination of "an elevated intellect" "to be degraded through passion" (*On Myself*). As an example Mann first thought, as we know, of the aged Goethe's passion for a young girl; however, the author chose to have his story take place in the present. On the one hand, the motif thereby gained in representative stature (the collapse of the aging artist stands for the collapse of an era, namely that of bourgeois individualism); on the other hand, placing the story in the present day permitted greater directness of autobiographical expression. It is only at this point that "the things" really come into play. The first "thing" to become part of the composition was a vacation-stay of several weeks at the Hotel des Bains on Venice's Lido and the presence there of a strikingly beautiful Polish boy. Apparently the poet is able to "tease" enough out of this encounter, and thereby to "intensify" his feelings for the boy, within the context of the novel, to such a point that Goethe's young girl could be replaced by the aristocratic Polish youth. Around this "significant" encounter, a number of Mann's other encounters and experiences—in themselves significant—begin to cluster: even before Thomas Mann's departure to Italy, his encounter with the unpleasant stranger at Munich's North Cemetery; and later on, the sight of the funny old man on board a steamer to Venice, or the cunning gondolier; rumors of a spreading sickness in the city, etc. etc.—all these everyday occurrences assumed sufficient significance to be integrated into the composition which imparted to the author a feeling of being carried along his creative path such as he "had never experienced before." Each episode became related to every other, thus producing a series of characters and events, mirroring and reflecting upon each other in their transparency. In this way, helped further by the mythological overtones, Mann arrived at that intrinsic symbolism of the novella which can no longer be unravelled.

Much later (in 1928), at a time when the autobiographical "self" had long since given up its claim to predominance, Thomas Mann described this creative process. When asked, "How do you preserve your initial inspiration for a work?" he replied:

> There is nothing to preserve. I don't keep a notebook in my pocket. But what I am going to write about becomes the center of all my attention, and I relate all my experiences to it, at least in an experimental way: not only present experiences but also what is already past and has become a part of me; whether the "work" is small or large, it becomes the focus of my entire perception of self and world.

We must admit: the "ambiguities" attributed to Thomas Mann by Muschg may be sensed here in a certain tendency toward an intellectual vicious circle. There is something "to be written about" which becomes "the focus of the entire perception of self and world" and yet there is no "initial inspiration" to be preserved. In other words, the "work" has no beginning. With its intrinsic symbolism the work turns in on itself.

Symbolism, the kind of symbolistic clairvoyance in the sense of Mann's gift to tease meaning out of "things," has something to do with *superstition*, to use a blunt word. No doubt, Thomas Mann (like so many artists) was superstitious. He firmly believed he would die at the age of seventy. True, at that very time he did contract an illness that could have been fatal. In an early story, called *Death,* the protagonist is convinced (for reasons not explained) that he will die on the twelfth of October. Instead, his daughter dies on that day. And it is true that Thomas Mann also died on the twelfth of a month, though it was not October but August.

In his earliest stories Mann indulges in superstitions with disarming naiveté. In "Herr Friedemann," for example, he paves the way for the catastrophe in none other than Box 13 at the opera. Later, as is well known, seven becomes the magic number for him.

The "evil omen," the superstitious belief in everyday life such as an encounter with an unpleasant stranger on a walk or the like, always refers to something finite; on the other hand, the same element in a literary context is raised to a symbolic level where its references within the work are *in*finite, that is to say, purely aesthetic.

What this amounts to is a raising of our fragmented, increasingly hollow reality, along with its "ultimate questions," into a self-contained and perfect totality; in this process, Thomas Mann found the "liberating" effect of art— of his art, of all "serene form."

His form became even more "serene" when the author immersed himself in myth. In the *Joseph* novels, each individual recognizes himself as part of an entity; so now this is not only *our* experience of the novels' characters, it is also their own experience of *themselves*: they all see themselves as transparent role-players in an infinite scheme of references and allusions. From that airy, serene world "where form confounded makes most form in mirth," Thomas Mann returned to the extremely somber and set scene in the novel *Doctor Faustus.* In this artist's novel Thomas Mann places the autobiographical "self" into its former central location; indeed, even more central than ever before, but this autobiographical self surveys "things" from that position with a vision remarkably broadened by mythic perspectives. The poet's eye has become so sensitive to the "transparency" of things that he scarcely needs to test them anymore for their aesthetic suitability. A certain lack of discrimination in the choice of factual material, a kind of greed for whatever material was available, is an essential aspect in the conception of this "reckless book of life." What could he not have conjured into the magic bottle of this poetically transformed autobiography? I can remember a dream, for example, which my mother recounted one morning at the breakfast table and which the Magician must have "incorporated" into the work that very morning or soon thereafter. All this resulted, as you may imagine, in the well-known personal unpleasantness of having to write apologetic letters. Some keen reader had detected a certain outer resemblance to Wiesengrund-

Adorno in the depiction of the devil as music–scholar. One might even find behind this a deeper meaning. But Thomas Mann turned full of dismay to Adorno: the charge, he thought, was absurd, and in all innocence he asks: "As a matter of fact, do you ever wear horn-rimmed glasses?" I, for one, couldn't imagine Adorno, whom I often saw in those days, without horn-rimmed glasses, not even in bed.

As in his earlier use of "naturalistically observed material" (only even more so now), Thomas Mann is apparently so interested in the compositional context that the outer resemblance to the "model" often seems to come about quite unconsciously, as the case mentioned above illustrates. In spite of all this, the author himself did sense a kind of *ruthlessness* in this inconsiderate way of incorporating his materials into the novel: long stretches of verbatim quotations, real names of real people transferred into the world of fiction, undisguised borrowing from philosophy, theology, musical theory.

How do we explain this ruthlessness, which the author called his "montage technique"? Mann himself tended to interpret the "breakthrough" to reality, to "life," brought about by this "montage," as the salvation of art insofar as art, as a separate world of "beauty and illusion," to him seemed no longer to have any right to exist. According to this interpretation, the "breakthrough" would merely be the ultimate consequence of that "social sympathy" the author had become aware of nearly half a century earlier. I don't doubt the validity of this self-interpretation. And yet, another aspect of the matter is still more important to me. Thomas Mann touches upon it in a note where he refers to his novel in progress and mentions somewhat laconically a certain "tendency of old age to view life as a culture-product, to see it through mythic clichés, which one prefers, in one's calcified dignity, to 'individual' creations" (Letter, 12–30–1945). This "calcified dignity" too seems to have caused a logical development, for here we find the connection between the symbolic clairvoyance which made *Death in Venice* possible, and the infinitely rich tapestry of allusions and references making up the structure of *Doctor Faustus*. So, it appears, the "breakthrough," contrary to the interpretation preferred by the author, does not so much lead from art to "life" but rather from "life" to art. Consequently, Arno Holz's famous dictum that all art has the tendency of becoming life again would have to be turned upside down for *Doctor Faustus*: here all life has the tendency of being transformed into art. If Mann's greed for material is any indication, then it would seem that reality today is in need of being raised into the aesthetic sphere even more than at the time of Schlegel's dream of a "progressive universal poetry."

I would like to conclude this lecture by referring to yet another consequence of Mann's inclination to see life as a "culture-product." This leads us beyond the confines of his works. They form such an integral part of his life that, more and more, they cast a perceptible reflection back onto his personal existence: *he lives the myth of his own works.* Thus, after finishing *The Holy Sinner,* the story of that great sinner Gregor who finally became the pope Gregorius, Thomas Mann visits the pope in Rome. He seems to have taken a completely new interest in that city, an interest revealed in his diary that unmistakably echoes the final pages of the novel. And that is an innocent game compared to the way the author "lived the myth" of his *Joseph* novels. I am not speaking of the similarity between the blue skies of California and Egypt (which the writer himself often called attention to) or the like. There are analogies of a much more comprehensive nature, and they seem to have "occurred" without the author's doing: first, the troubled beginnings of his emigration—the fall into the "pit" of Joseph—then the growth in the lands of exile—California and Egypt; finally, the conciliatory reunion with a starving homeland—all of which shows a remarkable parallelism between the writing of the novel and the life-scheme of the novel's hero.

"What is talent?" Thomas Mann once asked, and he answers his own question by musing that perhaps it "could simply be said that talent signifies nothing more than a readiness for fate," "Schicksalsfähigkeit"—a beautiful new word: the ability to face and interpret one's fate.

I think we may leave it at that. Truth and poetry in Thomas Mann's work—the problem comes down to his "readiness for fate."

DANIEL ALBRIGHT

Character in Thomas Mann's Early Work

One of the most remarkable aspects of Mann's narrative technique is his insistence that his characters understand that they amount to nothing but characters in a novel. A few indications of this can be found even in *Buddenbrooks*: when Toni Buddenbrook says that the traits of her character are determined and invariant, it has a certain disquieting feeling, as if she is a character who has a little too much insight into the tricks her author has employed in her construction; like the X-ray photographs in *The Magic Mountain,* there are certain kinds of insight into oneself that seem to be beyond what is good for us to know. In the short stories it sometimes happens that a minor character will look like "a figure out of Hoffmann," as in "The Wardrobe"; even in *Tonio [Kröger]* it happens that our hero sees "a comic figure stepped bodily out of a Danish novel," as everyone Tonio sees becomes assimilated into his novelist's eyes. But in the later novels more devastating kinds of awareness take place in the *dramatis personae.* In *Joseph and His Brothers,* for example, Joseph's brothers carry Toni Buddenbrook's self-complacence to almost undreamed-of extremes. Joseph's flaunting of the coat of many colors finally reaches such a point that the brothers take counsel on how to tear down this intolerable fop. Much of their conversation consists of their declarations of identity, as if Mann's epithets and similes for them were touchstones that they had to fondle often in order to remember who

---

From *Personality and Impersonality.* © 1978 by The University of Chicago. The University of Chicago Press, 1978. Excerpted from a chapter entitled "The Aesthetic."

they were. "It may be," says Dan, "that I am called snake and adder, for-sooth, because I am said to be somewhat malicious." This kind of utterance, in which the character does the narrator's work for him, should be taken as a joke; it is a smiling admission of technical artifice; it is a collection of the debt that the characters owe to the narrator for their definition. In the great rhetorical set pieces of *Joseph*—the enormous conversations of Joseph and Potiphar's wife, of Potiphar's wife and Potiphar, and of Joseph and Phar-aoh—the comprehension of the characters of their status as created fictions reaches its culmination. Here is a brief excerpt from the dialogue between Potiphar and his wife, Mut-em-enet, a sustained argument that extends for more than a score of pages; Potiphar, whose emotions about his wife are ambiguous and strong, is trying to conduct a decorous conversation, while his wife is trying slowly to bring around the conversation to the subject of Joseph, whose dismissal she wishes to demand:

> "I should be untruthful," he said at last with a little sigh, "were I to say that your share in our pleasant conversation is conducted with great tact. I made a skillful transition to the more worldly and material things of life, bringing the subject round to Pharaoh and the court. I expected you to return the ball by asking me some question, such as for instance whose ear-lobe Pharaoh tweaked in token of his favour when we went out of the hall of the canopy after the levee; but instead you turned aside into ob-servations about such irritating matters as mines and desert wells, about which, truly, my love, you must certainly understand even less than I."
>
> "You are right," she replied, shaking her head over her blunder. "Forgive me. My eagerness to know whose ear-lobe Pharaoh tweaked today was only too great. I dissembled it by small talk. Pray understand me: I thought to put off the question, feeling that a slow leading up to the important subject is the finest and most important feature of elegant conversation. Only the clumsy blunder in their approach by precipitation, betraying at once the whole content of their minds."

Husband and wife speak in rounded paragraphs, and it is within their rhe-torical rules to make analytical commentary upon the form of their conver-sation, as they struggle to impart elegance and suspense, all novelistic virtue, to the unwieldy material they must utter. They are trying to direct the flow of this rhetorical ceremony, to shape it satisfyingly; they let us in illicitly on Mann's troubles in organizing the chapter, whisper to us Mann's self-congratulation. The reader's ear can often discern how the voices of Mann's characters, especially in important or climatic utterance, betray the timbre of Mann's own voice; his major characters are all conceived fairly simply as self-extensions, masks that are easy to solve.

> I have always lived a very secluded life, and it was certainly not my way of handling people which has won me friends for my person and my work. I can hardly call myself a judge of human nature in the practical sense of the word, and I believe that this is true of many portrayers of humanity whose work shows much psychological insight. In my opinion, these insights spring from self-observation and self-criticism rather than from particular attention to others.

It is self-observation, the interior, that is the source of the whole multitude of Mann's characters; and when a character indicates, as Felix Krull does to Zouzou, exactly where the paragraph divisions fall in his speech, one is inclined to believe that Mann's description of his technique is accurate.

If the characters in Mann's novels like to pretend that they are characters in a novel, it is also true that some of Mann's characters pretend that they are authors. Tonio Kröger moves through society "grey and unobtrusive among his fellows like an actor without his make-up, who counts for nothing as soon as he stops representing something else"; and soon afterward Tonio tells his confidante Lisabeta the sad story of a great actor who, when he was not playing a role, always fell into a fit of insipidity, "an exaggerated consciousness of his ego." Tonio sees himself as a creator of characters, a man who, containing all roles within him, has therefore no role whatever in human society; he feels himself shapeless, inchoate, standing "between two worlds," "at home in neither." Yet this very lack of definition, this excess and overspilling of ego, that allows him to find order everywhere in the tale that is his life, compels him to understand that the luminous personages of his childhood are not haphazard characters, but the embodiment of a myth, the myth of Tonio Kröger; and by that route Hans and Inge lose their existence as distinct individuals, become projections of Tonio's fantasy. His amorousness toward the blue-eyed Nordic type becomes an emblem of the division in his being between the paternal and the maternal strain, the bourgeois and the aesthetic; he understands that Inge's personality is insignificant and commonplace, but the genetic myth demands that he should crave the ordinary. The progress of Hans and Inge through the story is in the direction of rarefaction and myth; Inge is first adored as a real girl, then as an undying image of love, then as the memory of an image of love, and finally as a racial

type, so easy and diffuse that an unknown Danish girl whom Tonio sees in
a resort can stand for Inge just as well as the original could. At every stage
Tonio's control over Inge becomes more acute; it is he who decides her
identity, her function, her recurrence in the story of Tonio Kröger; and the
satisfaction occurring in the fulfillment of the myth—that art loves nature
while nature cannot love art, a myth of tragically incomplete reciprocity—
is surely far greater than the satisfaction of Hans's awe, Inge's embrace. *Tonio
Kröger* ends in the "whirl of shadows of human figures who beckon to me
to weave spells to redeem them," Tonio's discovery of the plenitude of his
internal cosmos, the figures of his fantasy pressing forward to be converted
into literature. But what is Tonio about to write? Surely it is *Tonio Kröger,*
and those shadows are only Inge and Hans and the other characters. It is at
this moment that Mann's childhood is complete. He has converted the characters of his youth into art, and he has converted himself as a converter of
character into art, too.

   Tonio Kröger is distinguished from all of Mann's stories about artists
written in comparative youth by the successfulness of the aesthetic resolution
of the plot; in all the works even remotely contemporaneous with it the
aesthetic itch is disastrous. I have suggested that the mature artists of Mann's
later career, the prodigious builders, poets, composers, and confidence men
who occupy his fiction after 1930, are the sons of such rightminded and
thoughtful children as Hanno Buddenbrook and Tonio Kröger; but the literary paternity of Joseph, the Goethe of *Lotte in Weimar,* Adrian Leverkühn,
and Felix Krull is more complicated than that; for every marvelous child
there are a good many freaks, fools, overgrown embryos, and villains who
befoul the whole aesthetic mode, and who yet explore the same profound
problems as the great artists of Mann's maturity, prefigure their characters
with epic distortions. It is true of many artists that they must write a major
story in parody before they can write the sober version; T. S. Eliot had to
write *Sweeney Agonistes* with its music-hall tropical islands and missionaries
before he could tackle the serious plays of redemption and conversion, like
The Family Reunion and *The Cocktail Party*; similarly Mann could not
depict authentic greatness until he had given forth a number of rogues and
asses who claim talents they do not possess, who surround themselves with
the spurious trappings of creativity, or who employ their abilities to pervert,
slander, and mutilate.

   It is easy to commiserate with the frustration which is so prevalent in
Mann's early letters, his anger over the common verdict over his fiction that
it was icy, inhuman, lacking in feeling. Mann occasionally liked to terrify
his readers when he was young, but far more characteristic of his early work

is a certain overripeness that comes from the difficulty of controlling feeling grown nearly boundless. The author of "Tobias Mindernickel" could reasonably be described as icy: Tobias is described with great precision, a sharply defined puppet that contracts as the story proceeds into a still sharper, still punier configuration. But soft characters abound in these early stories; in "Disillusionment," the first story of Mann's which he wished to preserve, the central character is ageless, indescribable, so indefinite that he is no more than a literary phantom in pursuit of beauty and high sensation, as restless and vague as the hero of Shelley's *Alastor*:

> "Speech, it seems to me, is rich, is extravagantly rich compared with the poverty and limitations of life. Pain has its limits: physical pain in unconsciousness and mental in torpor; it is not different with joy. Our human need for communication has found itself a way to create sounds which lie beyond these limits.
>
> "Is the fault mine? Is it down my spine alone that certain words can run so as to awaken in me intuitions of sensations which do not exist?"

Here, at the beginning of Mann's canon, the aesthetic mode is the source of human depravity; the character of "Disillusionment" is bedeviled by the fantasies of poets into believing that there exist sensations in excess of what the spine can feel; the embodiment of beauty is too feeble and disfigured to compare with beauty itself. He rebels, beats his fists against the finitude of human emotion; yet he is overcome with a disillusionment so vast that it nearly refutes the principle that causes it. From him we learn the obsessiveness, the mania, that governs the relation between the sensitive man and the beautiful; and from him we learn that irony, critical detachment, self-remoteness is not sufficient to remove the pain of life, but instead is itself a source of pain; but the most important truth we learn here is that self-preoccupation is the first and most basic requisite for the artistic sensibility. Even this distended shadow of a sensitive man is ceaselessly attentive to the sensations of the spine, to the pleasures of his eye; he, who is almost the first character that Mann created, is the first connoisseur of his own body.

The theory of self-preoccupation haunts Mann's work, in "Disillusionment," "The Dilettante," and of course most of all in the character of Christian Buddenbrook, Tom's obnoxious brother and Hanno's dissolute uncle, a kind of artist of disease. It is in Christian that the narrowness of the boundary between artistic success and artistic failure is the most visible, because many of the traits of his childhood, and some of the traits of his maturity, closely resemble those of Felix Krull, who is perhaps the most successful

character Mann ever invented: Christian is an accomplished, even a virtuosic
mimic, fascinated by the theater to such an extent that at the age of fourteen
he is scandalously enamored of an actress—an experience similar to Felix's
encounter with Müller-Rosé; and at one point he does a delightful imitation
of a pianist, despite his inability to play the piano, an exact analogue to
Felix's famous violin trick. Mimicry is curiously precious to Mann, and his
writings are saturated with it: Christian, Felix, Ingrid in "Disorder and Early
Sorrow," Schildknapp in *Doctor Faustus*; Mann describes Chekhov's youthful powers of mimicry with detailed delight; his letters record again and
again how Artur Rubinstein captivated through mimicry, how he "laughed
till the tears came" for three hours at Charlie Chaplin's imitations and clown-
ing, as if the population of parties which Mann attended consisted principally
of mimics. This primacy can be explained as follows: the mimic is a low
analogue of the novelist, related to him as the body is to the mind. We have
seen how Tonio Kröger at the end of his story was preparing to project out
of himself the whole society which he had assimilated into his fantasy, thus
showing how self-preoccupation can exfoliate into social preoccupation, racial preoccupation. The case of the mimic is little different: he studies himself, measures his reflexes, experiments with the timbre of his voice, so
minutely that bodily gesture and facial expression can match another's. The
humor is not in the caricature but in the exactitude of reproduction; mimetic
accuracy, in the case of Felix Krull, is a secret sign of the indivisibility of all
that is human, a passage into glory, an authentication of the comic spirit
itself.

It is not so in Christian Buddenbrook; his mimicry is a symptom not
of the potency of his identity, not of suppleness under conscious control, but
of a will-lessness, a softness of being so great that it cannot help taking the
impress of any passing stamp. The self-preoccupation of the artist is a state
that is highly questionable even in the best of artists; Mann often perceives
it as a falling-off from spontaneous unity of being; and in Christian we see
how creaky and sputtering, inert, such self-preoccupation can become. Self-
preoccupation always requires a split in one's being between cognition and
affection; one's body, one's feelings, one's memories, all become objectified,
studied in the detached consciousness with an eye toward the useful potentiality of interior resources. Body and soul to the self-preoccupied man are
objects of speculation and play, even to the point of recklessness; both the
protagonist of "Disillusionment" and Christian Buddenbrook wonder what
would happen if they fell into a gorge, or jumped out the window. No act
is unthinkable, no crime too monstrous to the self-preoccupied man; that is
one reason why the artist is criminal. He is chiefly interested, whether novelist

or mimic, in uncovering possible selves, of demonstrating that what he perceives is not outside the range of his being; *nothing human is alien to me* is the explicit motto of some of Mann's artists, the implicit of all.

However, it is always dangerous to regard the self as raw material. The Dilettante, who originally regards himself as too fine for human intercourse, is eventually driven by his own incompetence to believe himself too base for any fate but isolation; in this case self-experimentation leads to a reversal of the desired fate, although to the self-preoccupied man his own dullness is just as interesting as his sensational refinement, and he can invest even the fact that he is a bat blinking in a cave with a kind of horrified glamor. Even Tonio Kröger does not emerge unscathed from such habits of mind. He feels that the emotional discipline of his artistry has become a mental mechanism from which he cannot escape; and in his compulsive rejection of simple human intimacy he feels sick, sick of himself:

> There is something I call being sick of knowledge, Lisabeta: when it is enough for you to see through a thing in order to be sick to death of it, and not in the least in a forgiving mood. Such was the case of Hamlet the Dane, that typical literary man. He knew what it meant to be called to knowledge without being born to it. To see things clear, if even through your tears, to recognize, notice, observe—and have to put it all down with a smile, at the very moment when hands are clinging, and lips meeting, and the human gaze is blinded with feeling—it is infamous, Lisabeta, it is indecent, outrageous—but what good does it do to be outraged?

Self-preoccupation almost always has a component of self-revulsion, which is made harder to bear by the fact that the existence of the self-revulsion is a kind of commentary upon itself. The self-preoccupied man does not feel an emotion, he says to himself "I am feeling an emotion"; then he starts to feel emotion—outrage, despair—about his lack of spontaneous emotion, but instead of feeling outrage and despair, he says to himself "I am feeling outrage and despair." We have seen this now in "The Dilettante" and *Tonio Kröger*; and it is through this kind of catch, this mirror-regression into the dim depths of self-devouring cognition, that the devil hopes to entrap Leverkühn in *Doctor Faustus*. Irony in Mann's work can rarely be the disinterested mode of balance and judgment to which it aspires; the ironic consciousness is usually tinged with self-contempt, because irony is thought an inadequate response to a world that requires our love as well as our accurate estimation; and tinged as well with contempt for the world, because the world, for all its clamoring and importunity, has not yet been quite potent enough to shake us into commitment and self-sacrifice.

In Christian Buddenbrook the ego is too weak to permit such disciplines as irony; the gifts of his self-preoccupation, which seemed so plentiful and promising in his boyhood, his quickness, his mimetic skill, his profound aesthetic emotion at the theater, come to nothing. The infant Felix Krull attains such mastery over his body that he can create fever; his eye is developed to such an extent that the muscles of the iris, usually so brutal and involuntary, obey the commands of his will, dilate and contract on demand. This unearthly control is far beyond Christian Buddenbrook's coarser clay; but even the minor aptitudes of his youth deteriorate as he grows up. Felix translates his body into a direct extension of his will, as swift and luminous as the mind itself; but in Christian's case the will atrophies, and his fascination with his body causes an unfortunate bloating and suppuration of the corporeal. The progress of Christian Buddenbrook is a steady growth of confusion, of falling out of touch, of self-abdication. One of his most telling anecdotes about himself is the story of a London operetta performance in which the curtain went up while he was accidentally on the stage, carrying on with one of the actresses; not only has the boundary between theatrical and real life become indistinct in his mind, but he shows a certain passivity that marks many of his tales. After telling this to Toni and Tom he says suddenly:

> "Strange—sometimes I can't swallow. Oh, it's no joke. I find it
> very serious. It enters my head that perhaps I can't swallow, and
> then all of a sudden I can't. The food is already swallowed, but
> the muscles—right here—they simply refuse. It isn't a question
> of willpower. Or rather, the thing is, I don't dare really will it."

His body has already begun—he is still fairly young—to take control of his existence, with the full compliance of his weakening will; by this deliberate self-relaxation and self-abandonment Christian discovers that his body has a thick, vegetable will of its own, and can thereby be induced to provide fascinating and unsuspected sensation. For hard characters discipline is no important matter, but for soft and potentially fine characters like Christian and Hanno discipline is all-important; in the absence of discipline Christian's body aches from infrared to ultraviolet, in a symphony of interesting pain, grows purulent, effloresces into rheumatism and stench, glorious decay. In Mann's corporeal myth, this seems to be the natural tendency of the human body; it is only through vigilance that we prevent disease. Christian, by surrendering himself to bodily insanity, shows the demonic aspect of the self-preoccupied man: the depths of the self must be disgorged; and it becomes only a measure of the boundlessness of one's own potentiality that such terrifying stuff can be found inside and manifested. As his brother Tom understands perfectly, his fascination with the unspeakable is a form of self-aggrandizement.

> Christian busies himself too much with himself, with what goes on in his own inside. Sometimes he has a regular mania for bringing out the deepest and the prettiest of these experiences—things a reasonable man does not trouble himself about or even want to know about, for the simple reason that he would not like to tell them to anyone else. There is such a lack of modesty in so much communicativeness. You see, Toni, anybody, except Christian, may say that he loves the theatre. But he would say it in a different tone, more *en passant*, more modestly, in short. Christian says it in a tone that says: "Is not my passion for the stage something very marvellous and interesting?" He struggles, he behaves as if he were really wrestling to express something supremely delicate and difficult.

Christian, like all artists, is all too prone to believe that his feelings are interesting to all men precisely because they are his; and this egotism declines quickly enough into a kind of solipsism. In his later days he has a hallucination of a man sitting on a sofa, when no one is there, a foreshadowing of the apparition of the devil that Leverkühn meets in *Doctor Faustus*; an odd badge of artistic kinship between such remote figures. At the death of his brother Tom he is alarmed, exactly in the manner of Tonio Kröger, that he cannot cry at the funeral: "His constant preoccupation with his own condition had used him up emotionally and made him insensitive." Neither Tonio nor Christian finds spontaneous emotion possible, but there is a difference: Tonio's self-preoccupation is a vehicle toward self-lability, and sympathy, and extension of his being; whereas Christian's methodical extraction of sensation from his body leads to breakdown of body and mind alike, until he sinks exhausted into a puddle, so yielding and inert that nothing can touch it and leave an imprint. He is soon sent off to an institution; but not before informing young Hanno, the nephew with whom he has a strong personal rapport, that he must never become too involved with puppets and the theater, a repudiation of the aesthetic which is in effect a repudiation of himself as well.

It is fair to say that Christian Buddenbrook is a child who never grows up, only withers into a senility that increasingly resembles a parody of childhood; and he is Hanno's true uncle in that neither of them can pass into the puberty of the spirit. There are in Mann's fiction a number of other characters whom Mann describes as elderly children: the cuckold Jacoby in "Little Lizzy," the good dwarf Bes in *Joseph in Egypt,* and, most of all, Detlev Spinell in *Tristan.* It is easy to fit the figure of the artist as elderly child into the general genetic myth by which Mann explains the origin of the artist. The bourgeois family, as its blood rarifies through its spasms of self-exhaustion, throws out progeny who are increasingly frail, nervous, incapable of practical endeavor, either beautiful themselves or masters of beauty. It matters little whether these effete children are artists or models of beauty for artists to employ: Spinell explains the glory of Frau Klöterjahn to her in exactly that same language that serves to account for Hanno Buddenbrook: "It not infrequently happens that a race with sober, practical bourgeois tradition will towards the end of its days flare up in some form of art." It may well happen that these "forms of art" may be too delicate to endure the rigors of human maturity; if they are beautiful women they marry at peril and are likely to be much weakened by childbirth; if they are male aesthetes they will be tempted to preserve the habits and furnishings of childhood, to build like Adrian Leverkühn a cloister or fortress that is a replica of the paternal house, in which the gratuitous play of childhood is maintained forever, its fertile loneliness, its questionable irresponsibility. Yet it may be that these elderly children, though their art is never very good, are nevertheless the purest examples of the artistic temperament. When Tonio Kröger tells Lisabeta that "we artists" are like "unsexed papal singers," he is stating a truth consistent with all of Mann's other pronouncements, yet the simile fits him badly; it is Spinell who is a *castrato,* not Tonio. Tonio, by contrast, participates in bouts of sexual excess, followed by bouts of revulsion against the senses; Tonio is in every way a mixed creature, a hybrid of the artistic and the bourgeois; and it is this plenitude of self which is the strength of his art. The internal cosmos of the great artist must include evil and good, ugliness and beauty, the dull and the exalted; while the artist who is oversensitive, intolerant, hyperesthetic, an axolotl, vitiates his art by excluding all matter that is not gorgeous, all emotion that cannot shiver away into ecstasy.

It is in *Tristan,* published in 1902, a year before *Tonio Kröger,* that Mann first masters the kind of narrative on which he almost holds the patent, in which a realistic story is informed in every detail by the phantasms of the central character's single mind. The plot is simple: the setting is a sanatorium for tuberculosis; an awkward and ludicrous aesthete, Detlev Spinell, a novelist of sorts, becomes infatuated with Frau Klöterjahn, an inconsequential young matron of great delicacy and beauty; Spinell undertakes what could be called an aesthetic seduction; he has no designs on her body, but wishes to convince her that her identity is equivalent to the identity he has invented for her in his fantasy, much derivative from Maeterlinck and the *symbolistes*. His power is irresistible; her thoughts become less and less occupied with the proper matters of a businessman's wife, and instead she is increasingly rapt, involuted in the contemplation of her own unearthly beauty, until she rejects Klöterjahn entirely, happily accepts the awesome and silvery identity of Hérodiade, where passion is quenched by its own excess, love by its own loveliness, or the identity of Mélisande, who with tremulous hope asks Spinell if he could actually see the golden crown he had imagined on her head. The difficulty of writing a story of hypnotism and alienation of affection should not be exaggerated; but *Tristan* is no tale of Svengali and Trilby, or even of artist and victim; Mann's preeminent keenness and subtlety lie in the overt complicity of Frau Klöterjahn in even the most initial phases of Spinell's wooing. Few relationships in fiction horrify by the same formula as that of Spinell and Frau Klöterjahn: the combination of thoughtless, almost off-handed murderousness and suicide with the most affable mutual gratification. It is hard to know which of them derives most pleasure from Frau Klöterjahn's consumption, her surrender into the refinement of death; indeed it is hard to know which of them is more the artist.

In this story the two major kinds of artists in Mann's early fiction come together, the novelist and the mimic; and it seems safe to say that Frau Klöterjahn is better at mimicry than Spinell is at novel writing. She accentuates all those traits of her character and body that Spinell esteems, the porcelain pallor, the emaciation, the contempt for the mundane, the yearning for the inanimate; her body is neatly responsive to her will, and she creates a fatal disease out of what was originally a light case. It is certain, however, that the impetus for this transformation is not entirely Spinell's. Frau Klöterjahn, one might say, is not banal enough to be identified strictly as a character of Spinell's imagination. He chose her gratuitously to enact a role in an allegory that is central to late nineteenth-century art as Mann understood it; but her alarming affinity for the role suggests that she was a character in search of an author. I have spoken before of the relish which the characters in Mann's fiction take in their status as creatures of literary artifice; and the ease with which Frau Klöterjahn lets herself fall into the character which Spinell ascribes to her, her matchless stageworthiness, is a mirror of this secret desire to take part in a fable, to utter resonant and literary words, which affects even the most ordinary personality in Mann's vision of human life. In the later books it is the homage that minor characters

pay to acknowledged greatness, this conformation of behavior to the unknown will of the protagonist; but so eager are Mann's characters to discover
their fable that even the most decrepit and carious novelist, if his desires are
traditional, will be obeyed. Whatever artistic talent Spinell lacks, Frau Klöterjahn is gladly willing to supply. During an early conversation between
them, Spinell inquires into her life before her marriage:

> "Yes, I have precious memories of all those years; and especially
> of the garden, our garden, back of the house. It was dreadfully
> wild and overgrown, and shut in by crumbling mossy walls. But
> it was just that gave it such charm. In the middle was a fountain
> with a wide border of sword-lilies. In summer I spent long hours
> there with my friends. We all sat round the fountain on little
> camp-stools—"

Here is a woman who needs no prompting to envision herself as a romantic
heroine; Spinell can but embroider that little narrative with his golden crown
and queenly songs. Her version of her mythic childhood and Spinell's coin-
cide essentially even before much of Spinell's imagination has begun; only
Klöterjahn hears the recipe for potato pancakes that was the actual content
of the fairy-tale court.

The actors must cast about for a long time before they find the right
myth. Maeterlinck and Villiers de l'Isle-Adam seemed a good start; but it is
the chance discovery of some sheet music from *Tristan und Isolde* that provides the mythic focus and template for which Spinell and Frau Klöterjahn
have been searching. It is just what they want; it is true that a story less
directly applicable to these lovers could hardly be devised, but the realm of
myth does not pertain to one's actual situation but to aspiration, desire,
fantasy. The wound that Melot gave to Tristan corresponds to nothing but
the cavities of Spinell's teeth—Hanno Buddenbrook's chief flaw consisted of
bad teeth also, a general sign of a softness, vulnerability, or incompetence
that persists to too great an age—and Isolde's rapture corresponds to little
more than Frau Klöterjahn's tubercular fever. It is all ironic reversal and
subversion of spirituality, but it is not pointless: the mystic union of Tristan
and Isolde, "Thou Isolde, Tristan I, yet no more Tristan, no more Isolde,"
is in a peculiar way validated by these gross beings trying to clothe themselves
in the finery of archetype, for Spinell and Frau Klöterjahn are in fact united
in the mystery of their interdependence, their need to constitute a theater,
their ability to impart an identity to each other that is no less comforting
because it is sham. In some of Mann's early stories about artists and myth,
one feels that the choice of myth is nearly arbitrary; but the arbitrariness of

the myth is itself a testimony to the potentiality and adaptability of the human species. We are all offered innumerable patterns through which we may seek to organize and give meaning to our lives; what does it matter that Isolde will be dispatched through hemorrhage of the lung as long as it is a modulation into ecstasy, what does it matter if Tristan be whirled away, tragically defeated by a brutal child with sunlight in his hair?

There is nothing wrong with living one's life aesthetically, in accordance with myth; indeed the point of the *Joseph* novels is that a life without myth is absurd if it is possible at all; if most of Mann's early characters get into trouble by fashioning their lives according to myth, it is either because the myth reveals the intolerable facts of their lives or because they wrongly decide to sacrifice everything for the sake of archetype. The attractiveness of even the most shabby and stupid story to these characters is astonishing. The major precursor of *Tristan* in Mann's canon is "Little Lizzie": a vile and beautiful woman, Amra Jacoby, married to a lawyer so fat, trusting, naïve, obsequious and flabby that he could give cuckolds a bad name, conspires with her lover, Alfred Läutner, a young composer, to humiliate her husband for no reason except pure malice. A party is planned for a great many guests in which the guests themselves design the musical entertainments; Läutner and Amra compose a little song and skit for Jacoby, in which he will dress up in an elephantine baby frock and sing the ditty that his wife's lover has written. Jacoby does so, and the shock of the assembled company at the spectacle of his degradation leads to his collapse and death. Just as in *Tristan* an artistic intelligence composes a scenario which has fatal consequences for a second party. It is easy to see the gratification of Frau Klöterjahn in following Spinell—but why does Jacoby agree to make a fool of himself on stage? He is certainly not enthusiastic when the idea is presented to him. Mann has established his passivity at some length, the ease with which Amra can convince him to obey; but one still wishes to inquire further about his reasons for accepting such remarkable humiliation. Again it is the appetite for a myth at work; when a script is put in front of a character, he cannot help reading the lines, no matter what the cost may be. It may seem improper to refer to Läutner's vicious little song, in which Jacoby must pretend he is a *soubrette* and tease called "Little Lizzie," as a myth, but it is in fact a role in which the hidden realities of Jacoby's life are manifested, his masculine incapacity, his infantile blindness, his epicene eagerness to please. The principle that governs Jacoby's conduct is the necessity for self-expression; a character may consciously try to suppress self-knowledge and public knowledge, but there are forces in the psyche that work toward manifestation and social display. Mann's characters fear few things more than public humiliation, but fear does not hinder them from committing public folly, if that folly is a true expression of their being.

There is a kind of healthiness about Jacoby's performance. Mann prided himself that he had developed certain of Freud's principles independently of Freud, and it is surely true that Mann felt from the beginning of his career that the repression of unpleasantness was a canker and a gnawing worm, and that the utterance of hidden horror was the first stage of cure. Thus, in a sense, Jacoby's grisly enactment may be called therapeutic, even though it is fatal; the "Little Lizzie" skit is the proper myth for Jacoby to enact, even if the script is sufficient evidence to damn its two authors. We may tentatively call mythic behavior healthy if it is a vehicle toward self-realization, or if, as in the case of all the major characters in *Joseph*, the myth imbues the man with a sense of his own awesome resonance and depth; it is unhealthy if the myth becomes prescriptive, limiting, confining. We distrust Frau Klöterjahn's identification of herself with Isolde because she is so much more than that; in repudiating her bourgeois husband she repudiates a great deal of her identity; her best solution would have been to embrace both Klöterjahn and Spinell, the gross and the oblique. What disturbs Mann about the unmixed aesthete is that the kind of life he wishes excludes so much of the human; and for Mann the rich is more valuable than the ideal.

LAWRENCE L. LANGER

Thomas Mann and Death on the Mountain

Historical time [in *The Magic Mountain*] begins to crack the mold of hermetic life on the mountain as rumbles of imminent war resound from the flatlands, finding a responsive echo from the inhabitants of the Berghof. The ensuing personal animosities, as anti-Semitism and nationalistic pride turn men against each other, anticipate the effect of this world catastrophe on our image of the human. Men's frantic desire to reclaim from mutability some vestige of permanence by embracing an absolute collapses not only because the appeal to violence now seems deeper than the impulse toward unity, but because all absolutes—at least as Mann dramatizes them in his novel—themselves contain the seeds of violence, briefly insulated by a veneer of form. As the health of both Settembrini and Naphta deteriorates, Naphta proves unequal to the challenge of accepting his fate with equanimity, despite his devotion to the idea of spirit. He responds to his illness not with sorrow or aversion, "but with a sort of jeering levity, an unnatural lust of combat, a mania of intellectual doubt, denial, and distraction, that was a sore irritant to [Settembrini's] melancholy, and daily embittered more the intellectual quarrel between them." Naphta's celebration of spirit reaches an absurd (and by implication a sinister) dead end when he declares that "matter was so bad a material that the spirit could not be realized within it ... nothing could come of it but distortion and fatuity." His physical self-disgust ill conceals a more general misanthropy, while the ludicrous illogic that rejects

From *The Age of Atrocity: Death in Modern Literature.* © 1978 by Lawrence L. Langer. Beacon Press, 1978.

matter while praising spirit ignores the obvious contradiction that, for man, spirit must be expressed *through* matter. Without reverence for the flesh the meaning of spirit disappears; this is the dismal secret behind Naphta's absolutism. Hence we are not surprised when he embraces history with the cry "War, war! For his part, he was for it."

Nor are we surprised when the interminable verbal disputes between Hans's two major mentors lead to literal combat, as the arsenal of words finally discharges more lethal weapons and Naphta challenges Settembrini to a duel. Neither is a lord of counter-positions, neither can reconcile in his imagination the blood sacrifice with a noble image of the human—neither cares to, since the premises of each forbid reconciliation and indeed thrive on controversy. As long as the discord remains intellectual, no one suffers; though Mann's canny point is that such discord never remains permanently intellectual, since intellectual dissension eventually crosses over into the personal, and "personal" disputes, especially between nations, are rarely settled with words. In trying to avert the duel between his friends, Hans reveals that he is still heir to a fundamental flaw of the late nineteenth- and early twentieth-century perception of reality. Hans distinguishes between an abstract affront and personal insult: "The whole affair was in the intellectual sphere, and has nothing to do with the personal. . . . The intellectual can never be personal." Do we need to be reminded how theories about a world made safe for democracy, or about the class struggle, or about a master race, led to the extermination of millions? Here Settembrini is far shrewder than Hans Castorp as he argues that the abstract, the ideal, or the absolute "contains within it more possibilities of deep and radical hatred, of unconditional and irreconcilable hostility, than any relation of social life can." Yet Settembrini does not recognize the full implications of his position, since behind its "logic" is a license to terror scarcely less destructive than Naphta's: the duel between the two seems lamentably inevitable.

The duel is a microcosmic prelude to the conflict about to erupt across the landscape of Europe, abdicating to death the destruction that intellect could not prevent and indeed, as we have seen, unconsciously encouraged. One is dazed by Settembrini's fusion of insight with rhetorical self-deception as he regales Hans with a version of reality that equates humanism with the violence of war:

> "The duel, my friend, is not an 'arrangement,' like another. It is the ultimate, the return to a state of nature, slightly mitigated by regulations which are chivalrous in character, but extremely superficial. The essential nature of the thing remains the primitive,

the physical struggle; and however civilized a man is, it is his duty to be ready for such a contingency, which may any day arise. Whoever is unable to offer his person, his arm, his blood, in the service of the ideal, is unworthy of it; however intellectualized, it is the duty of a man to remain a man."

Mouthing Hobbes while using the language of Rousseau, this champion of the human image blithely signs its death warrant with a flourish of the philosophical tongue. Like Naphta, Settembrini has become a tool of the prevailing temper, the war that echoes from the flatlands; unable to shape history, the mind of man adjusts to its least flattering features and twists language to justify the event when the event exceeds what the mind originally desired. Hans deplores the duel, but discovers "in affright" that he is powerless to stop it. The insight of man may make him lord of counter-positions, but when his literal sight is confronted by the spectacle of conflict, imagination defers to history:

> In [Hans] too the prevailing temper was strong, he was not the man to win free. There was an area of his brain where memory showed him Wiedemann and Sonnenschein [the anti-Semite and the Jew] grappled like animals; and with horror he understood that at the end of everything only the physical remained, only the teeth and the nails. Yes, they must fight.

In the duel, the intellectual becomes personal through necessity rather than choice when Naphta, baffled and exasperated by Settembrini's firing in the air—to the end, the Italian's instincts prove more humane than the logic of his arguments—turns his gun on himself and commits suicide. Lacking the courage to kill without provocation, he is driven to express his contempt for the human by taking his own life. By refusing to fire at him, Settembrini has eliminated the "regulations which are chivalrous in character, but extremely superficial," those "regulations" which gave soldiers license to kill, and left Naphta no alternative but the violence of self-destruction. In Dostoevsky, the atheism of Kirillov or the total absence of active love in the heart of Smerdyakov naturally joins the impulse to murder with the impulse to suicide. Naphta is more simply a victim of his own absolutism, of the viciously inhuman principle that "matter was so bad a material that spirit could not be realized within it." He returns us to Ernst Becker's conviction that the human dilemma in our time is to accept our "creatureliness" without losing reverence for the image of the human. Naphta pays for his failure to do so with his life; now that history through atrocity has confirmed his irreverence for the "matter" that is man by abusing the body in ways that Naphta himself only played with philosophically, the imagination must face an equally grotesque but entirely secular version of the *pietà*—without the hope of salvation that this image promised to men of more serene faith than Naphta.

Unlike Naphta, Hans Castorp goes through "the deep experience of sickness and death to arrive at a higher sanity and health." But the final unresolved problem of the novel (which ends with a question) is how to transfer the imaginative truth gained in the hermetic atmosphere of the mountain to the historical "actuality" of the flatlands, where we leave Hans Castorp slogging through the mud and splintering shells of World War I. Hans takes the risk of insight, "overcomes his inborn attraction to death and arrives at an understanding of a humanity that does not, indeed, rationalistically ignore death, nor scorn the dark, mysterious side of life, but takes account of it, without letting it get control over his mind." And no one can quarrel with Mann's summary of what his hero has endured or achieved. But Mann the artist is more complex than Mann the commentator, knowing as he does that history is no respecter of the imaginative vision. The human image in battle is reduced to "a body of troops calculated as sufficient, even after great losses, to attack and carry a position . . . there are so many of them, swarming on—they can survive a bloodletting and still come on in hosts."

One among that undifferentiated mass of potential victims is Hans Castorp, singing "half soundlessly" the words of Schubert's *Lindenbaum* that once had whispered to him with the consolation of aesthetic palliation its secret message of death. The shells shrieking over his head now echo a similar message, but with what consolation? The narrative voice introduces a dual viewpoint without attempting a synthesis—recalling the "human form divine" of Hans's timeless snow vision, and the war-doomed creature on the timebound battlefields of history:

> Ah, this young blood, with its knapsacks and bayonets, its mud-befouled boots and clothing! We look at it, our humanistic-aesthetic eye pictures it among scenes far other than these: We see these youths watering horses on a sunny arm of the sea; roving with the beloved along the strand, the lover's lips to the ear of the yielding bride; in happiest rivalry bending the bow. Alas, no, here they lie, their noses in fiery filth.

No mention of the blood-sacrifice here, or the relativism of counter-positions, which the "humanistic-aesthetic eye" once synthesized into imaginative truth. History is the last absolute man must contend with; in its abstract name inappropriate death is elevated into a principle of existence—and destruction. Our penultimate image of Hans Castorp reminds us of his origin in matter and the fate to which his physical form will return: "He lies with his face in the cool mire, legs sprawled out, feet twisted, heels turned down." He eludes death this time, but as we last see him "limping on his earth-bound feet," we hear that his prospects for survival are poor. His epitaph as he "vanished out of sight" are those ambiguous words from *Der Linden-baum*, drifting through the battle: "Its waving branches whispered / A message in my ear—." The word of that message is drowned in the whine of exploding shells, but also disappears beneath the ambiguous layers of Mann's art.

For once, in the sanctuary of the Berghof, Hans had convinced himself that "it was worth dying for, the enchanted *Lied*! But he who died for it, died indeed no longer for it; was a hero only because he died for the new, the new word of love and the future that whispered in his heart." Mann returns to this crucial moment in the closing lines of his novel, but with less certainty than Hans. Throughout *The Magic Mountain*, Mann has sought to dramatize a relationship between love and death, man's hope and man's fate, that would be more humanly valid than the spiritualized romanticism of Wagner and his predecessors in the tradition. A deficiency in imaginative vision had helped make possible the catastrophe of World War I, which could be justified only if "a new word of love and the future" emerged from its slaughter. Many atrocities later, we wonder whether that new word was "death" after all, the expectation of love only the last delusion to rescue man from the gloomy truth that one can take account of death "without letting it get control over his mind" in *art*, but not so easily in life. Indeed, *The Magic Mountain* is a prologue to the contemporary mind's failure to establish a balance between man in his physical embodiment as a victim of atrocity and man in his spiritual capacity as a vessel of love. The paradox is at the heart of the vision of reality revealed in the works of Camus, Solzhenitsyn, and Charlotte Delbo. They confront the question that ends Mann's novel with sober recognition of the fact that atrocity may have disfigured the human image beyond hope of an affirmative answer:

> Out of this universal feast of death, out of this extremity of fever, kindling the rain-washed evening sky to a fiery glow, may it be that Love one day shall mount?

But they unite in their belief that the language of art can still wash the eyes of history with a darkness to illuminate what atrocity has done to that image of man.

NORMAN RABKIN

The Holy Sinner *as Romance*

The double view of reality imposed on the audience of Shakespeare's romances has its analogues elsewhere in imaginative literature, and I propose
to illuminate it by going, not like Frye to other Shakespearean comedy or
like Kermode to Renaissance speculations on nature, but rather to the final
works of one of the great masters of the twentieth century, which in their
technique, their subject matter, their attitude toward that matter, and their
effect on an audience reveal an extraordinary affinity with Shakespeare's
final plays. Thomas Mann did not call *The Holy Sinner, The Confessions of
Felix Krull, Confidence Man,* and *The Black Swan* "romances"; but Shakespeare did not use the term either. What we are talking about is not a genre
but a kind of art produced by a certain kind of artist at the end of a life of
mastery. That Mann's novels differ from Shakespeare's plays in tone as much
as they do makes the essential similarities of the two bodies of work all the
more extraordinary. By looking at some points of correspondence between
Mann's late novels and Shakespeare's late plays I hope to suggest a new way
of bridging the useful but restrictive approaches of the critical schools represented by Frye and Kermode.

Written only four years before Mann's death in 1955, *The Holy Sinner*
is a redaction of Hartmann von Aue's *Gregorius vom Stein.* Nothing could
better illustrate its appropriateness to a consideration of Shakespeare's last

From *Shakespeare and the Problem of Meaning.* © 1981 by The University of Chicago. The University of Chicago Press, 1981. Excerpted from a chapter entitled
"Both/And: Nature and Illusion in the Romances."

plays than a brief summary of the plot. Wiligis and Sibylla, twin children of
the widowed Duke of Flaundres and Artoys, consummate a sudden access
of incestuous affection on the night of their father's death. Their affair produces its predictable fruit. Wiligis leaves Christian realms, entrusting his
pregnant sister to the Baron Eisengrein. When her boy is born, Sibylla and
the Baron's wife persuade Eisengrein to entrust him to the seas in a cask
laden with assorted medieval treasures. Wiligis dies; Sibylla copes with
courtship from men unacquainted with her secret; and the baby, found by
fishermen on the shores of the island of Saint Dunstan, is brought to the
saintly abbot Gregorius, who gives his name, abbreviated to Grigorss, to the
child and finds a foster home for him with the fisherman Wiglaf and his
wife Mahaute. Educated by the monk, Grigorss reaches a naturally aristocratic young manhood, instinctively chivalrous and mournful. When he is
seventeen, an unsolicited fight with another of Mahaute's children leads to
her angry revelation of Grigorss's mysterious arrival, and the young man
leaves to seek his fortunes in the world. Even those who know neither the
novel nor its source will scarcely be surprised to learn that the self-styled
Knight of the Fish promptly makes his unconscious way to a duel in which
he defeats one Roger the Invincible, who for years has sought the hand of
Sibylla, and that the upshot is Grigorss's marriage to his own mother. After
three years the couple learn the truth, and Grigorss, leaving his wife-mother-
aunt with two daughters and a sermon on atonement, dons rags and leg-
iron, persuades a fisherman to ferry him to a bare rock at sea, and spends
seventeen penitent years exposed to the elements, locked into the fetal position, nourished by a curious milk produced by the rock until he turns into
a tiny hedgehog-like creature. In the last sequence of the novel, a crisis occurs
in the papal succession, and inspired respectively by a vision and a miracle
two Romans set out to find the true successor: one Gregorius. Finding the
fisherman who took Grigorss to the rock, the Romans watch as he discovers
a key in the fish he is cleaning. The key, it turns out, is to the leg-iron locked
onto Grigorss by the fisherman seventeen years ago; at that time the fisherman had thrown the key into the waves, swearing he would believe his odd
passenger was genuinely a holy penitent only if he should see the key again.
The discovery leads rapidly to the restoration of Grigorss's human form, to
his investiture as Pope, and to a reunion with his penitent mother, now
promoted to Abbess, and with his daughters by her, who, as Clemens, the
narrator, points out, are the Pope's nieces; and the novel ends in a radiant
mood of reconciliation and praise of God.

Mann's romance is as rich and complex as the impulse that turned the
author of *Doctor Faustus* toward that novel's matter in his eighth decade,

and I can only hint now at those elements of *The Holy Sinner* that make it impossible when reading it not to think of Shakespeare's last phase. First of all there is the material: the outlandish saint's life, a fairy tale of familial separations, reunions, and sexual problems, baldly presented in all its absurdity, yet simultaneously in a lovingly realized ambiance of an authentic romance world replete with courts and tourneys, fishermen's huts and sparkling seas, hidden bedrooms, hunts, and anachronistic Toledo swords. It is a story hard for its own participants to believe without faith. Thus, when one of the churchmen who find Grigorss on the rock worries about how he will be received when he returns with a hedgehog in his bosom and crowns it with the papal tiara, Grigorss asks him to believe that the heaven that has nourished him on rock's milk will certainly restore him to man's estate; and with equal explicitness the narrator requests faith of the audience as the penitent is returned to his original condition by the sacramental function of the ordinary bread and wine he eats on the return trip. Demanding that we assent to a preposterous story so bewitchingly narrated as frequently to move us, Mann uses his tale to awaken us to the magical beauty of the ordinary: the fish with its belly cut open in the hut, the crowds in the streets of Rome, the love of man and woman. Grigorss's rebirth is absurd and tongue-in-cheek yet deeply affecting; parallel to his earlier "birth out of the wild waves," it reminds us as well of Joseph's rebirth from the well into which he had been cast, which almost two decades earlier Mann had detailed with a similar implication of the spiritual rebirth that is the central experience of all lives worth celebrating—those that William James called the "twice-born." As in Shakespeare's last plays, then, a self-consciously primitive narrative serves to provide an experience simultaneously entertaining and evocative of the self's inner life, and does so by making us regard its material all at once as mere storytelling and realer than life itself.

The virtuosity and charm of the narrative do not alone account for the excitement it arouses. At least as important is the sense Mann gives of the force that drives the events of the story. In the world of *The Holy Sinner* every event has three causes. To Wiligis, to Sibylla, to Grigorss, the action is a sequence of disasters apparently unmitigated until the end, but their medium is a plot in which each disaster proves to be part of a providential scheme. Life for the novel's characters has some of the qualities of a dream, in which circumstances move toward unforeseen but inevitable ends and the dreamer knows least the meaning of his own actions. Grigorss's sin is the foundation of his blessing; we shall learn later that at the crucial moment he knows deeply that he is committing an act of incest, yet watching him at that moment we see him so out of touch with the realities of his inner life that in a more important sense he does not know what he is doing. Such a welter of knowing and not knowing, sinfulness yet helplessness before impulses not of their own making, of suicidal steps toward their ultimate rebirth, touches the characterizations of Prospero, Pericles, and Leontes. Even the fisherman's angry toss of the key turns out to be a providential act which leads to the discovery of the penitent, who, it turns out, has grown small enough anyway to have slipped out of the leg-iron in which his antagonist had thought to imprison him. Thus two causes, one in the motions of the spirit and the other in the motions of the world, turn out to be identical.

But I said *three* causes. The third is the narrator, and here the analogy to Shakespeare is most striking. As God controls the world represented, so Clemens tells us he controls the story. At the beginning the bells of Rome are ringing wildly. At the end we will learn that the occasion of their ringing is the three-day coronation of Pope Gregory, from which point the garrulous narrator looks back to the story's beginning. Who rings the bells? he asks at the outset, and well he might: the bellringers have run into the street to see the new pope, the ropes hang slack. The ringing of the bells is a miracle, like the other miracles that have brought Grigorss to his final glory, additional proof of the operation of God's grace in the world. But Clemens has another answer to his question:

> Who is ringing the bells? . . . Shall one say that *nobody* rings them? No, only an ungrammatical head, without logic, would be capable of the utterance. "The bells are ringing": that means they are rung, and let the bell-chambers be never so empty.—So who is ringing the bells of Rome?—*It is the spirit of story-telling.* . . . He it is that says: "All the bells were ringing"; and, in consequence, it is he who rings them. So spiritual is this spirit, and so abstract that grammatically he can be talked of only in the third person and simply referred to as "It is he." And yet he can gather himself into a person, and be incarnate in somebody who speaks in him and says: "I am he. I am the spirit of story-telling, who, sitting in his time-place, namely in the library of the cloister of St. Gall in Allemannenland, . . . tells this story for entertainment and exceptional edification; in that I begin with its grace-abounding end and ring the bells of Rome; *id est*, report that on that day of processional entry they all together began to ring of themselves." (Italics Mann's)

Who rings the bells? Who chooses the "chosen" of Mann's German title, *Der Erwählte*? Providence does; the narrator does; there is no distinction.

Three years earlier Mann had focused *Doctor Faustus* on its narrator as well as its hero; in *The Holy Sinner* the split focus is even more important. As we respond to the events of the real world projected by the narrative, we repeatedly find the narrator calling attention to his role; God's manipulation of that world is identical to the storyteller's manipulation of the plot. Let me cite two characteristic moments. "Now behold how God brought it to pass, and with the utmost dexterity contrived against Himself, that the Lord Grimald's grandson, the child of the bad children, should come happily to shore in a cask." We need hardly have noticed that earlier Clemens had taken credit for imagining the loading of the cask himself—once again the multiple causes of narrated events—to see the implication that the life which is the subject of the plot is a work of art contrived by God, a comedy: even a joke, in which at the end the new pope can meet his ex-wife and call her "Mother" and she with equal accuracy can call him "Father." The second instance is an apotheosis. In that final scene, Grigorss and Sibylla confess what we have long suspected: when they broke the taboo, each of them was darkly aware of what he was doing: in pretending to be simply lovers, they "play-acted," Grigorss says,—ironically the interview occurs in a chapter entitled "The Audience"—and later: "We thought to offer God an entertainment."

Life as an entertainment for God! This, I propose, is the vision of the romances. It is a vision rather than a theme, a way of seeing, a mode of comprehension and response, and it explains the dual focus on the presentational and the representational with which we have been concerned here. It explains the otherwise inexplicable insistence in the plays that the life presented as a version of our lives is itself like art, the recurrent suggestion that as people who act we are like actors in a play, the haunting analogies between Prospero's mastery and Shakespeare's, the simultaneous presentation of irremediable evil in a context in which grace triumphs and the potency of evil becomes itself part of an enchanting landscape, a spectacle to amuse us as well as an image of our lives' reality.

> Go play, boy, play. Thy mother plays, and I
> Play too, but so disgrac'd a part, whose issue
> Will hiss me to my grave,

says Leontes, and later Hermione, defending herself against a grief that is "more / Than history can pattern, though devis'd / And play'd to take spectators," rightly guesses that because "pow'rs divine / Behold our human actions," her play must have a happy ending. "The dignity of this act was worth the audience [a pun identical to Mann's] of kings and princes, for by such was it acted."

> Good Paulina,
> Lead us from hence, where we may leisurely
> Each one demand, and answer to his part
> Perform'd in this wide gap of time since first
> We were dissever'd.

"We thought to offer God an entertainment."

MARTIN PRICE

Felix Krull *and the Comic Muse*

In contrast to the work of Joyce and Woolf, Thomas Mann's *The Confessions of Felix Krull, Confidence Man* takes pleasure in both time and appearance, finding the life of its hero and his art precisely in surface, costume, and illusion. Mann recognized the "comic kinship" of Krull's story with the Faust theme ("the motif of loneliness, in the one case mystic and tragic, in the other humorous and roguish"). Mann observes, of his use of Serenus Zeitblom in *Doctor Faustus,* that "to make the demonic strain pass through an undemonic medium, to entrust a harmless and simple soul, well-meaning and timid, with the recital of the story, was in itself a comic idea." In Felix Krull we have a different comic antithesis to Adrian Leverkühn, and in fact to the romantic artist-hero in general, or at least to the celebration of the artist-hero as a tragic figure. Krull is a criminal with great refinement of manner, much given to euphemism and to elegance of phrase, always writing of his career as if it were a series of performances in which he is both the instrument and the virtuoso. His "comic primness" couples criminal behavior with a sententious, sometimes even sanctimonious, tone; and, while we share the ironic pleasure Krull's tone provides, we know that we must expect him to sustain it with vigor. What we are to make of Krull is never quite clear, for, while he refers teasingly to later misadventures, including a term in prison, he scarcely shows a "later" consciousness with which to disown or even distance the exuberant younger self he presents.

From *Forms of Life: Character and Moral Imagination in the Novel.* © 1983 by Yale University. Yale University Press, 1983. Excerpted from a chapter entitled "Joyce, Woolf, Mann."

In the novel, Mann resumed a tale he had begun forty years earlier, and he completed only the first volume. It is "a fragment still," Mann remarked of it, "but fragment the strange book will surely remain, even if time and mood might permit me to continue. . . . the most characteristic description which I can make of it is that it will be broken off, stopped, but never finished." It is, like most exercises in the picaresque, a work which celebrates the onward movement of vitality. Felix can hardly be said to undergo an apprenticeship; we see him at the age of eight running a greased bow over a violin, imitating to perfection all the movements of a true musician while the orchestra performs, winning acclaim as a prodigy. "An aged Russian princess, wearing enormous white side curls and dressed from head to toe in violet silk, took my head between her beringed hands and kissed my brow, beaded as it was with perspiration." That sentence makes clear how differently Felix reveals himself from Joyce's or Woolf's characters; he records his experience from the outside as much as from within, with a syntactical elegance that is far from lyrical spontaneity, in an idiom that always exhibits refinement and artifice (often, in fact, parody of a higher style).

There is a distinctive mystery about Krull, for, while he is frank enough about what he feels and does, he is never so deeply involved in any experience that he shows any reluctance in dancing off, a typical picaresque hero, to the next episode. He is a man who loves the night and luxuriates in sleep, and he takes the narcissistic pleasure in himself that a child might show before the acknowledgment had been trained out of him. Krull, like Stephen Dedalus, moves toward myth—the figure of Hermes is his patron and model. He is a comprehensible enough confidence man, but he is full of fastidious pride in his artistry and benevolent condescension in supplying fantasies which others require but cannot create for themselves. Krull is too brilliant a performer, too arduously trained and dedicated an actor, to be understood merely as a confidence man. To see him as an artist is, of course, to gain remarkable insights into certain aspects of art.

The first of these is quite opposed to Virginia Woolf's emphasis upon the artistry of daily life which Mrs. Ramsay embodies. For Krull is first captivated by the matinée idol of musical comedy, Müller-Rosé. Müller-Rosé, his godfather's old friend, has an elegance that seems "not to belong to this world." His dress is perfect, his countenance debonaire, his movements marked with assurance and "fluid grace." He dispenses the "joy of life," allowing his audiences to participate for an evening in a life which is all that they would like their own to be. They watch him with a "precious and painful feeling, compounded of envy, yearning, hope, and love." He confers upon them the bliss of "self-forgetful absorption" in his art. But when Felix is taken backstage by his father, he is shocked to see of what materials such art is made. Müller-Rosé is seated at his dressing table, covered with sweat and grease-paint, his upper body spotted with clogged pores that have turned to pustules. The emphasis falls upon the remarkable transfiguration that Müller-Rosé has made himself undergo, as he has created an art of illusion, fantasy, and wish fulfillment for his middle-class audience.

Like Müller-Rosé, but in a body he preserves and cultivates with pride and affection, Felix Krull has a capacity to turn life into play. His joy in the gratuitous is illustrated by the deftness with which he serves as a painter's model, as a liftboy and waiter, and last as a spurious nobleman. Krull is in touch with nocturnal and subconcious powers that he can turn to conscious art; but we never know which needs of Felix's own nature his artistry fulfills, for we see little of his nature but the artistry. While Stephen Dedalus wrests his necessary freedom from family, church, and country, Felix Krull has no such bonds to throw off; nor does he have the high purpose with which Stephen undertakes his vocation. For all Felix's conservatism—an admiration of the splendid forms of power—there is also radical criminality in him, an indifference to conventional rules and limits, the energy of a self that does not live by the laws of the daylight world. His criminality is not the proud defiance of Stephen's "*non serviam*"; it is rather the adroitness of the confidence man, conjuror, acrobat—whose ultimate commitments have nothing to do with the beliefs of ordinary men.

Krull's devotion to the transitory is brought to a remarkable amplification late in the book. Professor Kuckuck first startles Krull, when they meet on the train, by referring casually to "this star and its present inhabitants." The words "star" and "present" open up sublime vistas of geological and astronomic time, much greater, as Kuckuck puts it, than that of "short-winded cultural history." Kuckuck summons up an almost unimaginable vision in which Being arises out of Nothingness, only "an interlude between Nothingness and Nothingness." In the brief interval of its duration Being celebrates a "tumultuous festival" whence comes the universe and its countless galactic systems, the Milky Way "one among billions"; and almost at the edge of that galaxy, thirty thousand light-years from its center, is our local solar system. Within the span of Being there emerges the much briefer span called Life. "For," Professor Kuckuck informs Krull, "Life has not always existed and will not always exist. Life is an episode, on the scale of the aeons a very fleeting one." And within that episode is the momentary appearance of Man. The episodic—the discontinuous, inexplicable emergence of a new quality—is in the form of all duration; and the form of the picaresque is thereby rooted in the nature of reality itself. Felix Krull welcomes the vision: "It was the knowledge of Beginning and End. I had pronounced what was most characteristically human when I had said that the fact of Life's being only an episode predisposed me in its favour. Transitoriness did not destroy value, far from it; it was exactly what lent all existence its worth, dignity, and charm. Only the episodic, only what possessed a beginning and an end, was interesting and worthy of sympathy because transitoriness had given it a soul."

Mann therefore turns cosmology into comedy, and this becomes more telling when Krull visits the natural history museum in Lisbon. Within the entrance hall stands a triumph of taxidermy, a splendid white stag. Felix sees only the evolutionary process. "If one examines the rump and hindquarters carefully and thinks about a horse—the horse is nervier, although one knows he is descended from the tapir—then the stag strikes one as a crowned cow." As often, Krull is obliviously, unconsciously witty. He feels that, like a visiting prince, he confers upon the display "the added charm of the contrast between my own fineness and elegance and the primitive crudity" of Nature's early works. "All this inspired in me," he writes, "the moving reflection that these first beginnings, however absurd and lacking in dignity and usefulness, were preliminary moves in the direction of me—that is, of Man." And so, "with probing eyes and beating heart," Felix sees "what had been striving toward me from the grey reaches of antiquity."

This amiable narcissism, which is only a parody of all anthropomorphic vision, sees a new and weak physical species emerging among the tusks, fangs, and iron jaws that rule the primeval world, a human species that senses, for all its lack of physical force, that it is made "of finer clay." A brilliant study follows of the emergence of consciousness. The primitive man paints in his cave images of game and hunters, or he shapes stones in the image of living forms. Stone pillars are raised as temples, and within the first roofless hall stands "a powerful-looking man . . . with upraised arms presenting a bouquet of flowers to the rising sun!" What makes him remarkable is that he is performing a gratuitous act, not one of utility or appeasement or "crude necessity." The temple and the gift of flowers mark the emergence of a new capacity, for celebration and worship. It is this gratuitousness, this aesthetic pleasure in his own actions, that characterizes Felix Krull from the first.

Among the finest passages on the vocation of the artist, more intense and exalted than the account of Müller-Rosé, is the treatment of the Stoudebecker Circus. There brilliant exploits "that lie at the extreme limits of human prowess" are achieved "with bright smiles and lightly thrown kisses";

it is the schooling in grace "at moments of utmost daring" that makes the performance so compelling. The clowns transcend their human limitations:

> Those basically alien beings . . . their handstands, their stumbling and falling over everything, their mindless running to and fro and unserviceable attempts to help, their hideously unsuccessful efforts to imitate their serious colleagues—in tightrope-walking, for instance . . . . With their chalk-white faces and utterly preposterous painted expressions—triangular eyebrows and deep perpendicular grooves in their cheeks under the reddened eyes, impossible noses, mouths twisted up at the corners with insane smiles. . . . [A]re they, I repeat, human beings, men that could conceivably find a place in everyday life? . . . [N]o, they are not, they are exceptions, side-splitting monsters of preposterousness, glittering, world-renouncing monks of unreason, cavorting hybrids, part human and part insane art.

Felix is fascinated by all transposition of human features into the materials of art. The supreme instance is the aerialist, Andromache. Felix watches her with awe: aloof, impassive, infallible. Was she, he wonders, really human?

> To imagine her as a wife and mother was simply stupid. . . . This was Andromache's way of consorting with a man; any other was unthinkable, for one recognizes too well that this disciplined body lavished upon the adventurous accomplishments of her art what others devote to love. She was not a woman; but she was not a man either and therefore not a human being. A solemn angel of daring with parted lips and dilated nostrils, that is what she was, an unapproachable Amazon of the realms of space beneath the canvas, high above the crowd, whose lust for her was transformed into awe.

Felix watches the performance with "passionate attention," with an "element of rebellion" that exerts a "counter-pressure against the overwhelming flood of impressions." He withdraws from the passive crowd, who revel in self-forgetfulness. He is himself "an entertainer and illusionist"; a passive enjoyment cannot satisfy one "who feels himself born to act and to achieve."

Andromache, that "solemn angel of daring," is as inhuman as the girl Stephen sees on the sands, a mythical as the Daedalus with whom Stephen identifies himself; and she is almost as abstract and purified a figure as the structure of volume and color that Lily Briscoe makes of Mrs. Ramsay. This emphasis upon the otherness of art, its necessary difference from the warmth and immediacy of life, finds various forms of statement. The role of artist requires of Stephen cruelty and ruthless self-protection, of Mrs. Ramsay a deep descent beneath personality, of Felix Krull a necessary isolation and loneliness.

While Felix takes pleasure in his skills and disciplines himself to wear each new costume or role with distinction, there is at least one splendid setback that his narcissism must suffer. That is the experience of being incorporated into another's shaping imagination, and a banal one at that. At the end of his train journey to Paris, in the Gare du Nord, Felix sees a wealthy middle-aged lady engaged in an altercation with a customs official; her luggage meanwhile lies unprotected and very close to Felix Krull's. A "very costly small morocco case" slips "unexpectedly" into Felix's bag. "This was an occurrence rather than an action," and Felix walks off with what he euphemistically calls his "accidental acquisition." It is a jewel case whose contents he sells to a fence in Paris. But he sees the former owner again when she arrives as a guest at the hotel where he runs the lift. She arouses not fear but a remarkable kind of gratification: "Without knowing me, without ever having seen me, without being aware of me, she had been carrying me, featureless, in her thoughts ever since the moment . . . when in unpacking her suitcase she had discovered that the jewel case was missing." (It is that sense of impingement which may be felt in a fainter form by the inscriber of graffiti.)

The former owner of the jewels, Mme Houpflé, is the wife of a manufacturer but she is also the author, under the name of Diane Philibert, of dubious novels "full of psychological insight" and volumes of passionate verse. She is a woman, by her own account, *"d'une intelligence extrême."* As she seduces, or thinks she seduces, Felix, she is really seeking someone base to love, as she copiously explains: "The intellect longs for the delights of the non-intellect, that which is alive and beautiful *dans sa stupidité,* in love with it to the point of idiocy, to the ultimate self-betrayal and self-denial, in love with the beautiful and the divinely stupid, it kneels before it, it prays to it in an ecstasy of self-abnegation, self-degradation, and finds it intoxicating to be degraded by it." This flood of egocentric masochism is too much for Felix: "You mustn't think me as stupid as all that, even if I haven't read your novels and poems—." But she is delighted when he restores his sense of himself by addressing her as "dear child": "A little naked liftboy lies beside me and calls me 'dear child,' me, Diane Philibert!" Her transports are only intensified when Felix reveals that he has never heard of Hermes,

the "suave god of thieves." For someone so narcissistic as Felix and so much
the master of the feelings of others, it is perturbing to be adored as an
ultimate debasement by the lyrical Diane Philibert. When she seeks more
brutal treatment, he refuses; but it occurs to him instead to reveal himself
as the thief who took her jewels at the customs barrier. This provides a
response of exquisite but rather patronizing delight: "*Mais ça c'est suprême!*
I am lying in bed with a thief! *C'est une humiliation merveilleuse, tout à
fait excitante, un rêve d'humiliation!* Not only a domestic—a common, ordinary thief!" And she demands that he conduct a new theft of her remaining
jewels in the dark. This done, she dismisses him, promising him immortality
in her writings. Felix is somewhat outraged by the assumptions that remain
unshaken, but he consoles himself with the experience of having been addressed in alexandrines.

In the course of the novel we see Felix Krull as forger, malingerer, model,
pimp, thief, actor. As a waiter he buys himself fine clothes and rents rooms
where he may change into them in order to live out another role as gentleman.
This in turn leads to his greatest impersonation. The Marquis de Venosta
has no wish to leave the young woman with whom he is happily living in
Paris, and he persuades Felix to adopt his identity and to take a world tour
in his place. This means not only playing the marquis with those who know
his family, but also corresponding regularly with his "parents." Felix is of
course a tremendous success; he pleases his "mother" with his charm and
consideration, and he delights her by his triumphant reception at court in
Portugal. All of these exploits demonstrate a mastery of style. When he agrees
to become the Marquis de Venosta, Felix shivers with joy "at the thought
of the equality of seeming and being which life was granting" him. And, in
fact, he finds a peculiar pleasure in a dual existence, "whose charm lay in
the ambiguity as to which figure was the real I and which the masquerade."
For he has "masqueraded in both capacities, and the undisguised reality
behind the two appearances, the real I, could not be identified because it
actually did not exist."

Here the artist has simply become his works. His life is a series of
performances, many of them improvisations. Mann has taken the artist to
the other side of art; beyond the austere discipline or the effort to achieve
an ordering vision. Those acts of difficult mastery we see in Joyce's or
Woolf's artists—and in Mann's version of Faustus—are here presented as
all but spontaneous; for while Felix Krull's self-discipline is intense, it is
achieved with such a pleasure in the exercise as to seem to cost very little.
The artist as comic hero creates a world where, himself his own creation,
he lives out his inventions, always eluding—as a masterful dancer seems to

defy gravity—the tug toward a reality he need not acknowledge. There is, of course, something preposterous and wishful about this ease. It catches what Susanne Langer calls a "comic rhythm," and Felix Krull is a superb refinement upon the figure she describes as the "buffoon":

> He is the personified *élan vital*; his chance adventures and mis-adventures, without much plot, though often with bizarre complications, his absurd expectations and disappointments, in fact his whole improvised existence has the rhythm of primitive, savage, if not animalistic life, coping with a world that is forever taking new uncalculated turns, frustrating, but exciting. He is neither a good man nor a bad one, but is genuinely amoral,— now triumphant, now worsted and rueful, but in his ruefulness and dismay he is funny, because his energy is really unimpaired and each failure prepares the situation for a fantastic new move.

Felix Krull embodies the "heightened vitality" of the comic hero, and he embodies it the better for his inclusiveness. He accepts in himself the regressive and narcissistic, the criminal and deceptive, the transitory and the superficial (at least as they are conventionally understood).

Felix Krull is open to a range of experience more characteristic of Stephen Dedalus than of the characters in *To the Lighthouse*. Felix can celebrate a theft not by its shopworn name but as the "primeval absolute deed." That is a young artist's creation. He does not seek permanence and stability as Virginia Woolf's artists do; nor does he seek some reality deep below the surface. It is the surface of life that is precisely its source of color and charm. Nor does Krull seek to transcend his limited nature in the power of spirit: Felix not only accepts his body; he glories in it. In his first encounter with the prostitute Rozsa, their conversation is "without introduction" and "without polite conventions of any sort; from the very beginning it had the free, exalted irresponsibility that is usually characteristic only of dreams."

It is in his defense of love against Zouzou, Professor Kuckuck's daughter, that Felix becomes the champion of the surfaces of life. Zouzou is embarrassed by a sexual energy she cannot control, and so she scorns lovemaking as both ugly and ludicrous. She cites the verse she once read in a book of spiritual instruction: "However smooth and fair the skin, / Stench and corruption lie within." Felix combats this bit of ugly asceticism with all the powers of his rhetoric: "Your spiritual verse is more blasphemous than the most sinful lust of the flesh, for it is a spoilsport, and to spoil the game of life is not only sinful, it is simply and entirely devilish. . . . If things went according to that altogether malicious verse, then the only thing really and not just apparently admirable would be, at most the inanimate world, inorganic Being." A mere "smart aleck," Felix protests, "might say that all Nature is nothing but mildew and corruption on the face of the earth, but that is simply the wisecrack of a smart aleck and never, to the end of time, will it succeed in killing love and joy—the joy in images. . . . Because at all times the earth has been full of fellows who paid not the slightest heed to your spiritual rhyme, but saw truth in form and appearance and surface." Krull is defending the beauty of mortal conditions.

The artist in Mann's novel is a counterpart in consciousness of the powers of the human eye as Felix celebrates them:

> What a wonderful phenomenon it is, carefully considered, when the human eye, that jewel of organic structures, concentrates its moist brilliance on another human creature! This precious jelly, made up of just such ordinary elements as the rest of creation, affirming, like a precious stone, that the elements count for nothing, but their imaginative and happy combination accounts for everything—this bit of slime embedded in a bony hole, destined some day to moulder lifeless in the grave, to dissolve back into watery refuse, is able, so long as the spark of life remains alert there, to throw such beautiful, airy bridges across all the chasms of strangeness that lie between man and man!

It is a macabre emblem but a brilliant one; the eye embodies as well as creates the beauty of mortal conditions. It represents for Krull the "unconditional freedom, secrecy, and profound ruthlessness" that he ascribes to the glance and to its opposite extreme, the embrace. Between them lies the realm of the word, "that cool, prosaic device, that begetter of tame, mediocre morality." In Felix Krull's world morality is an idiom to be cultivated in affectionate, straight-faced parody, what I have called comic primness. It is, for the most part, a delicious joke. Yet at another level we see in Krull a decent forbearance that, as it refuses the bypaths offered by Eleanor Twentyman or Lord Strathbogie, dismisses these suppliants charitably and tactfully. And while he rebukes Zouzou chiefly as a spoilsport in the game of life, he also speaks of her blasphemy. In the circus clowns, those "monks of unreason," Krull sees the asceticism of the artist that may account as well for the solitariness of Krull himself.

In these portraits of the artist—portraits created by writers we associate with modernism—much emphasis is given this solitariness, and not least in Virginia Woolf's characters. Even Mrs. Ramsay's dinner, that triumphant orchestration of feelings at times so ruthlessly elicited, provides only a momentary illusion of stability and unity—in contrast with the moments "when solidity suddenly vanished and . . . vast spaces lay between them." The force of Mrs. Ramsay's presence survives in the completion of the trip to the lighthouse and in the simultaneous completion of Lily's painting. The formal idiom of the painting allows Mrs. Ramsay the kind of survival a scrap of a personal letter might enjoy in a collage, and the reconciliation of her children with their father may belong to their journey more than to their later lives. The fragility of the eye is an emblem of these fusions, and its airy bridges require in turn "the chasms of strangeness between man and man."

Woolf's characters try hard to find a "coherence in things, a stability," a "wholeness not theirs in life." The refrain of William Cowper's castaway runs through the book, parodied by the histrionic self-pity with which Mr. Ramsay delivers it: "We perished each alone," But Mr. Ramsay's tyrannical self-indulgence is the obverse of his anxiety about change and supersession. His ultimate praise of James is perhaps a moral achievement; it relieves for the moment "that loneliness which was," for his children, "the truth about things." But these people are seen less in a moral vision than a metaphysical one. The "waters of annihilation" are as inclusive and as indifferent as are E. M. Forster's India and Conrad's Costaguana; but the eye is able, so long as the spark remains, to span the chasms of strangeness and provide the conditions of life. It is this fragile order, attenuated by the prose of the world, that is the novel's peculiar form and profound opportunity.

Chronology

1875   Paul Thomas Mann born on June 6 to Johann Thomas Heinrich Mann, merchant and senator of Lübeck, and Julia Da Silva Bruhns, daughter of a German planter and a Portuguese-Creole Brazilian.

1890   On the day of the centennial celebration of the Mann grain firm, Thomas resolves not to become a merchant, despite his father's wish. Shortly after his father's death the following year, the family firm is liquidated.

1893   With his friend Otto Grautoff, publishes the periodical *Frühlingssturm: Monatschrift für Kunst, Litteratur und Philosophie,* which fails after two issues.

1894   Works as unpaid apprentice at an insurance company in Munich, and writes his first commercially published story during working hours. Enrolls as auditor (and later as regular student) at the Munich Technische Hochschule, attending, from time to time, lecture courses on history, political economy, art, and literature.

1895   Writes "The Dilettante" and contributes book reviews and satirical pieces to the periodical *Das Zwanzigste Jahrhundert,* of which his elder brother Heinrich (1871–1950) is the editor. First visit to Italy, with Heinrich.

1896   Two-year stay in Italy, mostly in Rome and Palestrina with Heinrich, where he writes the stories later included in the collection *Little Herr Friedemann* (published in 1898).

1898–1900   Works as a reader for the periodical *Simplicissimus,* in Munich.

1900   Volunteers for the Royal Bavarian Infantry. Released after a few months because of an inflamed ankle tendon.

1901   *Buddenbrooks* published.

1902   Writes and publishes *Tonio Kröger.*

1903   The collection *Tristan* published.

1905   *Fiorenza,* a Renaissance drama, published; first performed in 1907. Marries Katja Pringsheim, the daughter of a well-to-do Jewish university professor. Daughter Erika Julia Hedwig born.

1906   "Blood of the Walsungs," printed for *Die Neue Rundschau,* is withdrawn before publication, not to appear until the private edition of 1921. Writes *Bilse und ich* to justify his portrayal of actual, living people in his fiction. Son Klaus Heinrich Thomas born.

1909   *Royal Highness* appears serially. Son Angelus Gottfried Thomas (Golo) born.

1910   Daughter Monika born.

1911   Travels to Brioni, off the Istrian coast, to recover from overwork, then to Venice. Mann's experiences on this trip are the germ of *Death in Venice,* published 1912.

1912   Three-week visit to his wife at a sanatorium in Davos, provides the original idea for *The Magic Mountain,* initially conceived of as a parodic counterpart to *Death in Venice.*

1914–18   Works mainly on the essays which make up the *Reflections of a Non-Political Man,* a reaction to the outbreak of World War I. He is again declared unfit for active service, this time on account of a weak stomach and general nervousness.

1918   Daughter Elisabeth Veronika born.

1919   Son Michael Thomas born. Publication of *A Man and His Dog.*

1920–24   Frequent lecture tours and readings from work in progress to sustain his family during the postwar economic crisis.

1924   *The Magic Mountain* is published.

1929   Awarded the Nobel Prize for literature.

1930   Publishes *Mario and the Magician* and *Sketch of My Life*.

1933   Following a trip to the Netherlands, he does not return to Germany, where his criticism of the National Socialists has made him unacceptable. Moves to Switzerland with his family. Publishes *The Tales of Jacob*, first volume of the Joseph tetralogy.

1934   Publishes *The Young Joseph*, second volume of the tetralogy.

1936   Publishes *Joseph in Egypt*, third volume of the Joseph tetralogy. Becomes a Czech citizen and consequently loses German citizenship.

1938   Accepts position at Princeton University.

1939   Publishes *The Beloved Returns: Lotte in Weimar*.

1940   Publishes *The Transposed Heads*.

1941   Moves to Pacific Palisades, California.

1943   Publishes *Joseph the Provider*.

1944   Receives American citizenship.

1945   Radio broadcasts to Germany.

1949   Publishes *Story of a Novel*. First visit to Germany since 1933. Son Klaus commits suicide in Cannes.

1951   Resumes work on *Felix Krull*, after having abandoned the project some forty years earlier. Publishes *The Holy Sinner*.

1952   Moves back to Switzerland.

1953   Publishes *The Black Swan* serially in the Frankfurter *Merkur*.

1954   Publishes *Confessions of Felix Krull, Confidence Man: The Early Years*.

1955   Dies in Zürich on August 12.

Contributors

HAROLD BLOOM, Sterling Professor of the Humanities at Yale University, is the author of *The Anxiety of Influence, Poetry and Repression,* and many other volumes of literary criticism. His forthcoming study, *Freud: Transference and Authority,* attempts a full-scale reading of all of Freud's major writings. A MacArthur Prize Fellow, he is general editor of five series of literary criticism published by Chelsea House.

HERMANN J. WEIGAND was Sterling Professor of German Literature at Yale University. He wrote *The Modern Ibsen, Surveys and Soundings in European Literature,* and *Wolfram's Parzival,* as well as many studies of the work of Thomas Mann.

VERNON VENABLE is the author of *Human Nature: The Marxian View.*

ERICH HELLER is Avalon Emeritus Professor of the Humanities at Northwestern University. His many books include *The Disinherited Mind, The Hazard of Modern Poetry, In the Age of Prose,* and *The Artist's Journey into the Interior,* as well as monographs on Franz Kafka and Friedrich Nietzsche. He is the editor, with Jürgen Born, of Kafka's *Briefe an Felice.*

GEORGE C. SCHOOLFIELD is Professor of Germanic Languages at Yale University. His books include *Edith Södergram: Modernist Poet in Finland, The Figure of the Musician in German Literature,* and *Rilke's Last Year.* He is the editor of *Studies in the German Drama* and has published a number of translations from the Finnish.

GUNILLA BERGSTEN is the author of *Thomas Mann's "Doctor Faustus."*

ISADORE TRASCHEN is the coeditor of *Short Fiction: A Critical Collection.*

EVA SCHAPER is the author of *Prelude to Aesthetics* and *Studies in Kant's*

Aesthetics, and has edited *Pleasure, Preference, and Value: Studies in Philosophical Aesthetics*.

PETER HELLER is Professor of German at the State University of New York at Buffalo. His work includes *Dialectics and Nihilism, Studies on Nietzsche, Von den ersten und letzten Dingen*, and *Probleme der Zivilisation*.

ERICH KAHLER was Professor of Humanities at Princeton University. His books include *The Germans, The Inward Turn of Narrative, Man the Measure, The Meaning of History*, and *The Tower and the Abyss*.

LARRY DAVID NACHMAN is a Professor in the Department of Political Science, Economy, and Philosophy at the City University of New York, College of Staten Island. He has written a number of articles with Albert S. Braverman on the work of Thomas Mann.

ALBERT S. BRAVERMAN teaches in the Department of Medicine at New York Medical College. He has written a number of articles with Larry David Nachman on the work of Thomas Mann.

OSKAR SEIDLIN is the author of *Essays in German and Comparative Literature* and numerous other articles on modern European literature.

HILARY HELTAY is the author of *The Articles and the Novelist: Reference Conventions and Reader Manipulation in Patrick White's Creation of Fictional Worlds*.

WILLIAM M. HONSA, JR., is Professor of English Literature at Humboldt State University.

BENJAMIN BENNETT teaches in the Germanic Languages Department of the University of Virginia. He has written *Modern Drama and German Classicism: Renaissance from Lessing to Brecht*.

ELAINE MURDAUGH is the author of *Salvation in the Secular*.

ALLAN J. McINTYRE teaches in the Department of Modern Languages at the University of Akron.

MICHAEL MANN was Thomas Mann's youngest son. He was a violinist.

DANIEL ALBRIGHT is Professor of English at the University of Virginia. His writings include *The Myth Against Myth: A Study of Yeats's Imagination in Old Age*, and *Representation and the Imagination: Beckett, Kafka, Nabokov, and Schoenberg*.

LAWRENCE L. LANGER is Professor of English at Simmons College. He is the author of *The Holocaust and the Literary Imagination, Versions of Survival: The Holocaust and the Human Spirit,* and *The Age of Atrocity: Death in Modern Literature.*

NORMAN RABKIN is Professor of English at the University of California at Berkeley. Among his writings are *Shakespeare and the Common Understanding,* and *Shakespeare and the Problem of Meaning.* He is the editor of several volumes of criticism on Elizabethan and Jacobean drama.

MARTIN PRICE is Sterling Professor of English at Yale University. Among his works are *Swift's Rhetorical Art: A Study in Structure and Meaning,* and *To the Palace of Wisdom: Studies in Order and Energy from Dryden to Blake.* He has also edited a number of volumes on seventeenth-, eighteenth-, and nineteenth-century literature.

Bibliography

Albright, Daniel. *Personality and Impersonality*. Chicago: The University of Chicago Press, 1978.

Apter, T. E. *Thomas Mann: The Devil's Advocate*. London: Macmillan, 1978.

Baron, Frank. "Sensuality and Morality in Thomas Mann's *Der Tod in Venedig*." *Germanic Review* 45, no. 2 (March 1970): 115–25.

Bauer, Arnold. *Thomas Mann*. New York: Ungar, 1971.

Berendsohn, H. *Thomas Mann: Artist and Partisan in Troubled Times*. University: University of Alabama Press, 1973.

Bergsten, Gunilla. *Thomas Mann's "Doctor Faustus."* Chicago: The University of Chicago Press, 1969.

Blackmur, R. P. *Eleven Essays in the European Novel*. New York: Harcourt, Brace & World, 1951.

Braverman, Albert S., and Larry David Nachman. "Nature and the Moral Order in *The Magic Mountain*." *Germanic Review* 53, no. 1 (1978): 1–12.

Brennan, J. G. *Thomas Mann's World*. New York: Columbia University Press, 1942.

Bürgin, Hans, and Hans-Otto Mayer. *Thomas Mann: A Chronicle of His Life*. University: University of Alabama Press, 1969.

Carnegy, Patrick. *Faust as Musician*. London: Chatto & Windus, 1973.

Gilliam, H. S. "Mann's Other Holy Sinner: Adrian Leverkühn as Faust and Christ." *Germanic Review* 52, no. 2 (March 1977): 122–47.

Gronicka, André von. *Thomas Mann: Profile and Perspectives*. New York: Random House, 1970.

Hatfield, Henry. *From "The Magic Mountain": Mann's Later Masterpieces*. Ithaca: Cornell University Press, 1979.

———. *Thomas Mann: A Collection of Critical Essays*. Englewood Cliffs, N.J.: Prentice-Hall, 1964.

Heller, Erich. *Thomas Mann: The Ironic German*. Mamaroneck, N.Y.: Appel, 1973.

Heller, Peter. *Dialectics and Nihilism*. Amherst: University of Massachusetts Press, 1966.

Hughes, Kenneth. "Theme and Structure in Thomas Mann's *Die Geschichten Jaakobs*." *Monatshefte* 62, no. 1 (Spring 1970): 24–36.

Kahler, Erich. *The Orbit of Thomas Mann*. Princeton: Princeton University Press, 1969.

Kaufmann, Fritz. *Thomas Mann: The World as Will and Representation*. Boston: Beacon Press, 1957.

Kenney, Joseph M. "Apotheosis and Incarnation Myths in Mann's *Joseph und seine Brüder*." *German Quarterly* 56, no. 1 (January 1983): 39–60.

King, J. Robin. "Thomas Mann's *Joseph and His Brothers*: Religious Themes and Modern Humanism." *Thought* 53 (December 1978): 416–32.

Koelb, Clayton. "The Use of Hebrew in the *Joseph* Novel." *Monatshefte* 70, no. 2 (1978): 138–50.

Langer, Lawrence L. *The Age of Atrocity: Death in Modern Literature*. Boston: Beacon Press, 1978.

Lehnert, Herbert. *Thomas Mann: Fiction, Mythos, Religion*. Stuttgart: Kohlhammer, 1965.

Lukács, Georg. *Essays on Thomas Mann*. New York: Grosset & Dunlap, 1964.

Mann, Erika. *The Last Year of Thomas Mann*. London: Secker and Warburg, 1958.

Mayer, Hans. *Thomas Mann*. Frankfurt am Main: Suhrkamp, 1980.

Murdaugh, Elaine. *Salvation in the Secular*. Frankfurt am Main: Lang Verlag, 1976.

———. "Thomas Mann and the Bitch Goddess: Rejection and Reconstruction of the Primal Mother in *Joseph and His Brothers*." *Revue des langues vivantes* 44, no. 5 (1978): 395–407.

Neider, Charles, ed. *The Stature of Thomas Mann*. New York: New Directions, 1947.

Nelson, Donald F. *Portrait of the Artist as Hermes*. Chapel Hill: University of North Carolina Press, 1971.

Nicholls, R. A. *Nietzsche in the Early Works of Thomas Mann*. Berkeley: University of California Press, 1955.

Oates, Joyce Carol. "Art at the Edge of Impossibility: Mann's *Dr. Faustus*." *Southern Review* 5 (Spring 1969): 375–97.

Rabkin, Norman. *Shakespeare and the Problem of Meaning*. Chicago: The University of Chicago Press, 1981.

Reed, T. J. *Thomas Mann: The Uses of Tradition*. Oxford: Clarendon Press, 1974.

Roth, Maria C. "Mynheer Peeperkorn in the Light of Schopenhauer's Philosophy." *Monatshefte* 58, no. 4 (1966): 335–44.

Weigand, Hermann J. *Thomas Mann's Novel "Der Zauberberg."* New York: Appleton-Century, 1933.

Winston, Richard. *Thomas Mann: The Making of an Artist, 1875–1911*. New York: Alfred A. Knopf, 1981.

Yourcenar, Marguerite. "Humanism in Thomas Mann." *Partisan Review* 23 (1956): 153–70.

Acknowledgments

"Thomas Mann's *Royal Highness* as Symbolic Autobiography" by Hermann J. Weigand, translated by Henry Hatfield, from *Thomas Mann: A Collection of Critical Essays,* edited by Henry Hatfield, © 1964 by Prentice-Hall, Inc. The German version of this essay appeared in *PMLA* 46 (1931), © 1931 by the Modern Language Association of America. Reprinted by permission of Prentice-Hall, Inc. and the Modern Language Association of America.

"Structural Elements in *Death in Venice*" (originally entitled "*Death in Venice*") by Vernon Venable from *The Structure of Thomas Mann,* edited by Charles Neider, © 1947 by New Directions Publishing Co. An earlier version of this essay appeared in *Virginia Quarterly Review* 14 (Winter 1938). Reprinted by permission of Charles Neider and *Virginia Quarterly Review.*

"Conversation on *The Magic Mountain*" by Erich Heller from *Thomas Mann: The Ironic German* by Erich Heller, © 1958 by Erich Heller. Reprinted by permission of the author.

"Thomas Mann's *The Black Swan*" (originally entitled "Thomas Mann's *Die Betrogene*") by George C. Schoolfield from *The Germanic Review* 30, no. 1 (January 1963), © 1963 by Columbia University Press. Reprinted by permission.

"*Doctor Faustus* as a 'Historical' Novel" by Gunilla Bergsten from *Thomas Mann's "Doctor Faustus"* by Gunilla Bergsten, translated by Krishna Winston, © 1969 by The University of Chicago. German version © 1963 by Gunilla Bergsten. Reprinted by permission of The University of Chicago Press.

"The Uses of Myth in *Death in Venice*" by Isadore Traschen from *Modern Fiction Studies* 11, no. 2 (Summer 1965), © 1965 by Purdue Research Foundation, West Lafayette, Indiana. Reprinted by permission.

"A Modern Faust: The Novel in the Ironical Key" by Eva Schaper from *Orbis Litterarum* 20, no. 3 (1965), © 1965 by Munksgaard International Publishers Ltd., Copenhagen, Denmark. Reprinted by permission of the publisher.

"The Ambivalent Leitmotif " (originally entitled "Thomas Mann and the Ambivalent Leitmotif ") by Peter Heller from *Dialectics and Nihilism* by Peter Heller, © 1966 by the University of Massachusetts Press. Reprinted by permission of the publisher.

"The Elect: *The Holy Sinner* and *Felix Krull*" (originally entitled "The Elect") by Erich Kahler, translated by Krishna Winston and Richard Winston, from *The Orbit of Thomas Mann* by Erich Kahler, © 1969 by Princeton University Press, 1986 by Alice L. Kahler. Reprinted by permission of Alice L. Kahler.

"Thomas Mann's *Buddenbrooks*: Bourgeois Society and the Inner Life" by Larry David Nachman and Albert S. Braverman from *The Germanic Review* 45, no. 3 (May 1970), © 1970 by Columbia University Press. Reprinted by permission.

"Mynheer Peeperkorn and the Lofty Game of Numbers" (originally entitled "The Lofty Game of Numbers: The Mynheer Peeperkorn Episode in Thomas Mann's *Der Zauberberg*") by Oskar Seidlin from *PMLA* 86, no. 5 (1971), © 1971 by the Modern Language Association of America. Reprinted by permission.

"Virtuosity in Thomas Mann's Later Narrative Technique" (originally entitled "Der Mann auf dem Felde: Virtuosity in Thomas Mann's Later Narrative Technique") by Hilary Heltay from *German Life and Letters,* n.s. 24, no. 2 (January 1971), © 1971 by Basil Blackwell Ltd. Reprinted by permission of the publisher.

"Parody and Narrator in Thomas Mann's *Doctor Faustus*" (originally entitled "Parody and Narrator in Thomas Mann's *Doctor Faustus* and *The Holy Sinner*") by William M. Honsa, Jr. from *Orbis Litterarum* 29, no. 1 (1974), © 1974 by Munksgaard International Publishers, Ltd., Copenhagen, Denmark. Reprinted by permission of the publisher.

"Structure, Parody, and Myth in *Tonio Kröger*" (originally entitled "Casting Out Nines: Structure, Parody and Myth in 'Tonio Kröger' ") by Benjamin Bennett from *Revue des langues vivantes* 42, no. 2 (1976), © 1976 by Société François Closset. Reprinted by permission of the publisher, Librarie M. Didier.

"*Joseph and His Brothers*: Myth, Historical Consciousness, and God Emerging" (originally entitled "Myth and the Emergence of Historical Consciousness" and "The Fallen God") by Elaine Murdaugh from *Salvation in the Secular: The Moral Law in Thomas Mann's "Joseph und seine Brüder"* (Stanford German Studies, vol. 10) by Elaine Murdaugh, © 1976 by Herbert Lang und Cie AG and Peter Lang GmbH. Reprinted by permission of Lang Druck AG, Bern.

"Determinism in *Mario and the Magician*" by Allan J. McIntyre from *The Germanic Review* 52, no. 3 (May 1977), © 1977 by Columbia University Press. Reprinted by permission of the publisher.

"Truth and Poetry in Thomas Mann's Work" by Michael Mann from *Thomas Mann: Ein Kolloquium,* edited by Hans H. Schulte and Gerald Chapple, © 1978 by Bouvier Verlag Herbert Grundmann, Bonn. Reprinted by permission of the publisher.

"Character in Thomas Mann's Early Work" (excerpted from a chapter entitled "The Aesthetic") by Daniel Albright from *Personality and Impersonality* by Daniel Albright, © 1978 by The University of Chicago. Reprinted by permission of The University of Chicago Press.

"Thomas Mann and Death on the Mountain" by Lawrence L. Langer from *The Age of Atrocity: Death in Modern Literature* by Lawrence L. Langer, © 1978 by Lawrence L. Langer. Reprinted by permission of the author.

"*The Holy Sinner* as Romance" (excerpted from a chapter entitled "Both/And: Nature and Illusion in the Romances") by Norman Rabkin from *Shakespeare and the Problem of Meaning,* © 1981 by The University of Chicago. Reprinted by permission of The University of Chicago Press.

"*Felix Krull* and the Comic Muse" (excerpted from a chapter entitled "Joyce, Woolf, Mann") by Martin Price from *Forms of Life: Character and Moral Imagination in the Novel,* © 1983 by Yale University. Reprinted by permission of Yale University Press.

Index